T0064850

63 DOCUMENTS THE GOVERNMENT DOESN'T WANT YOU TO READ

63 DOCUMENTS THE GOVERNMENT DOESN'T WANT YOU TO READ

JESSE VENTURA

WITH DICK RUSSELL

SKYHORSE PUBLISHING

Skyhorse Publishing books may be purchased in bulk at special discounts for sales promotion, corporate gifts, fund-raising, or educational purposes. Special editions can also be created to specifications. For details, contact the Special Sales Department, Skyhorse Publishing, 307 West 36th Street, 11th Floor, New York, NY 10018 or info@skyhorsepublishing.com.

Skyhorse® and Skyhorse Publishing® are registered trademarks of Skyhorse Publishing, Inc.®, a Delaware corporation.

www.skyhorsepublishing.com

10 9 8 7 6 5 4 3 2

2021 Edition ISBN: 978-1-5107-5958-9

Library of Congress Cataloging-in-Publication Data

Ventura, Jesse.
  63 documents the government doesn't want you to read / Jesse Ventura, with Dick Russell.
    p. cm.
  Includes bibliographical references.
  ISBN 978-1-61608-226-0 (alk. paper)
  1. Official secrets--United States. 2. Government information--United States. 3. Government information--Access control--United States. 4. Conspiracies--United States. I. Russell, Dick. II. Title. III. Title: Sixty three documents the government doesn't want you to read.
  JK468.S4V46 2011
  320.973--dc22
                                    2011006218

Printed in the United States of America

To Congressman Ron Paul, the only federal elected official who will stand up for America on the congressional floor.

CONTENTS

PART THREE
SHADY WHITE HOUSES

PART FOUR
9/11

PART FIVE
THE "WAR ON TERROR"

EPILOGUE

63 DOCUMENTS THE GOVERNMENT DOESN'T WANT YOU TO READ

INTRODUCTION TO THE
2021 EDITION

It has been a decade since this book first came out and became a *New York Times* bestseller. We've been through the Obama years and now we've got Donald Trump. I'm still out there calling for a third-party alternative, and I seriously thought about entering the 2020 race as an independent candidate. People are hungry for a straight shooter, and I like to think I qualify as one. We sure can't say that secrets and lies aren't the prevailing "wisdom" among our political leaders. Fake news wasn't even in our lexicon ten years ago, and now it's even harder to know what's real and what's a fabrication or straight-out lie. Walter Cronkite used to help us make an informed decision, and today we've got a thousand pundits competing for our attention on TV and social media. It's no longer about truth, but instead ratings and "clickbait" headlines.

So I've decided it's time for an updated edition of *63 Documents the Government Doesn't Want You to Read*. The historical perspective that the first edition of this book provided is more relevant than ever. But what I want to do here is bring you up to speed on some of the most important issues of our time as we enter the third decade of the twenty-first century.

You'll read about one of the companies involved in the race for a CO-VID-19 vaccine; about how the Russians used social media to influence the last election; about how climate change is considered a high-level national security threat *by our own military*; about how the Trump administration has covered up the truth about white supremacists, instigating the protests against racial injustice; and about what the Pentagon doesn't want us to know about UFO sightings and the projects in its Advanced Aerospace Threat and Identification Program (AATIP).

I hope these documents—kicking off this new edition—will help serve as a wake-up call to our citizenry in a world increasingly out of the pages of George Orwell. We can't afford to pretend any longer that "ignorance is strength."

THE VIRUS VACCINE

By the time this book comes out, there may already be a vaccine for the CO-VID-19 virus. One of the three companies in the race to make this happen is Moderna, based in Cambridge, Massachusetts. There are, however, some very strange things about this outfit. Firstly, they've never produced a vaccine. Secondly, they were on the verge of bankruptcy until Bill Gates and Anthony Fauci stepped in with funding.

We'll start with a shocking paragraph in Moderna's vaccine patent application in 2019, about the possibility of a "deliberate release" of coronavirus. This ties right into reports our intelligence agencies were looking into: that COVID-19 might have escaped from the lab in Wuhan, China, where it was created.

The main document about Moderna looks at the fact that the company never revealed any of the grant money it was receiving from the Pentagon's Defense Advanced Research Project Agency (DARPA), The RNA vaccine it's developing has never been made before. And guess what? It's designed to alter your genes.

US 10,543,269 B2

1

HMPV RNA VACCINES

RELATED APPLICATIONS

This application is a continuation of U.S. application Ser. No. 16/040,981, filed Jul. 20, 2018, which is a continuation of U.S. application Ser. No. 15/674,599, now U.S. Pat. No. 10,064,934, filed Aug. 11, 2017, which is a continuation of international application number PCT/US2016/058327, which claims the benefit under 35 U.S.C. § 119(e) of U.S. provisional application No. 62/244,802, filed Oct. 22, 2015, U.S. provisional application No. 62/247,297, filed Oct. 28, 2015, U.S. provisional application No. 62/244,946, filed Oct. 22, 2015, U.S. provisional application No. 62/247,362, filed Oct. 28, 2015, U.S. provisional application No. 62/244, 813, filed Oct. 22, 2015, U.S. provisional application No. 62/247,394, filed Oct. 28, 2015, U.S. provisional application No. 62/244,837, filed Oct. 22, 2015, U.S. provisional application No. 62/247,483, filed Oct. 28, 2015, and U.S. provisional application No. 62/245,031, filed Oct. 22, 2015, each of which is incorporated by reference herein in its entirety.

BACKGROUND

Respiratory disease is a medical term that encompasses pathological conditions affecting the organs and tissues that make gas exchange possible in higher organisms, and includes conditions of the upper respiratory tract, trachea, bronchi, bronchioles, alveoli, pleura and pleural cavity, and the nerves and muscles of breathing. Respiratory diseases range from mild and self-limiting, such as the common cold, to life-threatening entities like bacterial pneumonia, pulmonary embolism, acute asthma and lung cancer. Respiratory disease is a common and significant cause of illness and death around the world. In the US, approximately 1 billion "common colds" occur each year. Respiratory conditions are among the most frequent reasons for hospital stays among children.

The human metapneumovirus (hMPV) is a negative-sense, single-stranded RNA virus of the genus Pneumovirinae and of the family Paramyxoviridae and is closely related to the avian metapneumovirus (AMPV) subgroup C. It was isolated for the first time in 2001 in the Netherlands by using the RAP-PCR (RNA arbitrarily primed PCR) technique for identification of unknown viruses growing in cultured cells. hPMV is second only to RSV as an important cause of viral lower respiratory tract illness (LRI) in young children. The seasonal epidemiology of hMPV appears to be similar to that of RSV, but the incidence of infection and illness appears to be substantially lower.

Parainfluenza virus type 3 (PIV3), like hMPV, is also a negative-sense, single-stranded sense RNA virus of the genus Pneumovirinae and of the family Paramyxoviridae and is a major cause of ubiquitous acute respiratory infections of infancy and early childhood. Its incidence peaks around 4-12 months of age, and the virus is responsible for 3-10% of hospitalizations, mainly for bronchiolitis and pneumonia. PIV3 can be fatal, and in some instances is associated with neurologic diseases, such as febrile seizures. It can also result in airway remodeling, a significant cause of morbidity. In developing regions of the world, infants and young children are at the highest risk of mortality, either from primary PIV3 viral infection or a secondary consequences, such as bacterial infections. Human parainfluenza viruses (hPIV) types 1, 2 and 3 (hPIV1, hPIV2 and hPIV3, respectively), also like hMPV, are second only to RSV as important causes of viral LRI in young children.

2

RSV, too, is a negative-sense, single-stranded RNA virus of the genus Pneumovirinae and of the family Paramyxoviridae. Symptoms in adults typically resemble a sinus infection or the common cold, although the infection may be asymptomatic. In older adults (e.g., >60 years), RSV infection may progress to bronchiolitis or pneumonia. Symptoms in children are often more severe, including bronchiolitis and pneumonia. It is estimated that in the United States, most children are infected with RSV by the age of three. The RSV virion consists of an internal nucleocapsid comprised of the viral RNA bound to nucleoprotein (N), phosphoprotein (P), and large polymerase protein (L). The nucleocapsid is surrounded by matrix protein (M) and is encapsulated by a lipid bilayer into which the viral fusion (F) and attachment (G) proteins as well as the small hydrophobic protein (SH) are incorporated. The viral genome also encodes two nonstructural proteins (NS1 and NS2), which inhibit type I interferon activity as well as the M-2 protein.

The continuing health problems associated with hMPV, PIV3 and RSV are of concern internationally, reinforcing the importance of developing effective and safe vaccine candidates against these virus.

Despite decades of research, no vaccines currently exist (Sato and Wright, *Pediatr. Infect. Dis. J.* 2008; 27(10 Suppl): S123-5). Recombinant technology, however, has been used to target the formation of vaccines for hPIV-1, 2 and 3 serotypes, for example, and has taken the form of several live-attenuated intranasal vaccines. Two vaccines in particular were found to be immunogenic and well tolerated against hPIV-3 in phase I trials. hPIV1 and hPIV2 vaccine candidates remain less advanced (Durbin and Karron, Clinical infectious diseases: an official publication of the Infectious Diseases Society of America 2003; 37(12):1668-77).

Measles virus (MeV), like hMPV, PIV3 and RSV, is a negative-sense, single-stranded RNA virus that is the cause of measles, an infection of the respiratory system. MeV is of the genus Morbillivirus within the family Paramyxoviridae. Humans are the natural hosts of the virus; no animal reservoirs are known to exist. Symptoms of measles include fever, cough, runny nose, red eyes and a generalized, maculopapular, erythematous rash. The virus is highly contagious and is spread by coughing

In additional to hMPV, PIV, RSV and MeV, betacoronaviruses are known to cause respiratory illnesses. Betacoronaviruses (BetaCoVs) are one of four genera of coronaviruses of the subfamily Coronavirinae in the family Coronaviridae, of the order Nidovirales. They are enveloped, positive-sense, single-stranded RNA viruses of zoonotic origin. The coronavirus genera are each composed of varying viral lineages, with the betacoronavirus genus containing four such lineages. The BetaCoVs of the greatest clinical importance concerning humans are OC43 and HKU1 of the A lineage, SARS-CoV of the B lineage, and MERS-CoV of the C lineage. MERS-CoV is the first betacoronavirus belonging to lineage C that is known to infect humans.

The Middle East respiratory syndrome coronavirus (MERS-CoV), or EMC/2012 (HCoV-EMC/2012), initially referred to as novel coronavirus 2012 or simply novel coronavirus, was first reported in 2012 after genome sequencing of a virus isolated from sputum samples from a person who fell ill during a 2012 outbreak of a new flu. As of July 2015, MERS-CoV cases have been reported in over 21 countries. The outbreaks of MERS-CoV have raised serious concerns world-wide, reinforcing the importance of developing effective and safe vaccine candidates against MERS-CoV.

Severe acute respiratory syndrome (SARS) emerged in China in 2002 and spread to other countries before brought under control. Because of a concern for reemergence or a deliberate release of the SARS coronavirus, vaccine development was initiated.

Deoxyribonucleic acid (DNA) vaccination is one technique used to stimulate humoral and cellular immune responses to foreign antigens, such as hMPV antigens and/or PIV antigens and/or RSV antigens. The direct injection of genetically engineered DNA (e.g., naked plasmid DNA) into a living host results in a small number of its cells directly producing an antigen, resulting in a protective immunological response. With this technique, however, comes potential problems, including the possibility of insertional mutagenesis, which could lead to the activation of oncogenes or the inhibition of tumor suppressor genes.

SUMMARY

Provided herein are ribonucleic acid (RNA) vaccines that build on the knowledge that RNA (e.g., messenger RNA (mRNA)) can safely direct the body's cellular machinery to produce nearly any protein of interest, from native proteins to antibodies and other entirely novel protein constructs that can have therapeutic activity inside and outside of cells. The RNA (e.g., mRNA) vaccines of the present disclosure may be used to induce a balanced immune response against hMPV, PIV, RSV, MeV, and/or BetaCoV (e.g., MERS-CoV, SARS-CoV, HCoV-OC43, HCoV-229E, HCoV-NL63, HCoV-NL, HCoV-NH and/or HCoV-HKU1), or any combination of two or more of the foregoing viruses, comprising both cellular and humoral immunity, without risking the possibility of insertional mutagenesis, for example. hMPV, PIV, RSV, MeV, BetaCoV (e.g., MERS-CoV, SARS-CoV, HCoV-OC43, HCoV-229E, HCoV-NL63, HCoV-NL, HCoV-NH and HCoV-HKU1) and combinations thereof are referred to herein as "respiratory viruses." Thus, the term "respiratory virus RNA vaccines" encompasses hMPV RNA vaccines, PIV RNA vaccines, RSV RNA vaccines, MeV RNA vaccines, BetaCoV RNA vaccines, and any combination of two or more of hMPV RNA vaccines, PIV RNA vaccines, RSV RNA vaccines, MeV RNA vaccines, and BetaCoV RNA vaccines.

The RNA (e.g., mRNA) vaccines may be utilized in various settings depending on the prevalence of the infection or the degree or level of unmet medical need. The RNA (e.g. mRNA) vaccines may be utilized to treat and/or prevent a hMPV, PIV, RSV, MeV, a BetaCoV (e.g., MERS-CoV, SARS-CoV, HCoV-OC43, HCoV-229E, HCoV-NL63, HCoV-NL, HCoV-NH, HCoV-HKU1), or any combination of two or more of the foregoing viruses, of various genotypes, strains, and isolates. The RNA (e.g., mRNA) vaccines have superior properties in that they produce much larger antibody titers and produce responses earlier than commercially available anti-viral therapeutic treatments. While not wishing to be bound by theory, it is believed that the RNA (e.g., mRNA) vaccines, as mRNA polynucleotides, are better designed to produce the appropriate protein conformation upon translation as the RNA (e.g., mRNA) vaccines co-opt natural cellular machinery. Unlike traditional vaccines, which are manufactured ex vivo and may trigger unwanted cellular responses, RNA (e.g., mRNA) vaccines are presented to the cellular system in a more native fashion.

In some aspects the invention is a respiratory virus vaccine, comprising at least one RNA polynucleotide having an open reading frame encoding at least one respiratory virus antigenic polypeptide, formulated in a cationic lipid nanoparticle.

Surprisingly, in some aspects, it has also been shown that efficacy of mRNA vaccines can be significantly enhanced when combined with a flagellin adjuvant, in particular, when one or more antigen-encoding mRNAs is combined with an mRNA encoding flagellin.

RNA (e.g., mRNA) vaccines combined with the flagellin adjuvant (e.g., mRNA-encoded flagellin adjuvant) have superior properties in that they may produce much larger antibody titers and produce responses earlier than commercially available vaccine formulations. While not wishing to be bound by theory, it is believed that the RNA (e.g., mRNA) vaccines, for example, as mRNA polynucleotides, are better designed to produce the appropriate protein conformation upon translation, for both the antigen and the adjuvant, as the RNA (e.g., mRNA) vaccines co-opt natural cellular machinery. Unlike traditional vaccines, which are manufactured ex vivo and may trigger unwanted cellular responses, RNA (e.g., mRNA) vaccines are presented to the cellular system in a more native fashion.

Some embodiments of the present disclosure provide RNA (e.g., mRNA) vaccines that include at least one RNA (e.g., mRNA) polynucleotide having an open reading frame encoding at least one antigenic polypeptide or an immunogenic fragment thereof (e.g., an immunogenic fragment capable of inducing an immune response to the antigenic polypeptide) and at least one RNA (e.g., mRNA polynucleotide) having an open reading frame encoding a flagellin adjuvant.

In some embodiments, at least one flagellin polypeptide (e.g., encoded flagellin polypeptide) is a flagellin protein. In some embodiments, at least one flagellin polypeptide (e.g., encoded flagellin polypeptide) is an immunogenic flagellin fragment. In some embodiments, at least one flagellin polypeptide and at least one antigenic polypeptide are encoded by a single RNA (e.g., mRNA) polynucleotide. In other embodiments, at least one flagellin polypeptide and at least one antigenic polypeptide are each encoded by a different RNA polynucleotide.

In some embodiments at least one flagellin polypeptide has at least 80%, at least 85%, at least 90%, or at least 95% identity to a flagellin polypeptide having a sequence identified by any one of SEQ ID NO: 54-56.

Provided herein, in some embodiments, is a ribonucleic acid (RNA) (e.g., mRNA) vaccine, comprising at least one (e.g., at least 2, 3, 4 or 5) RNA (e.g., mRNA) polynucleotide having an open reading frame encoding at least one (e.g., at least 2, 3, 4 or 5) hMPV, PIV, RSV, MeV, or a BetaCoV (e.g., MERS-CoV, SARS-CoV, HCoV-OC43, HCoV-229E, HCoV-NL63, HCoV-NL, HCoV-NH, HCoV-HKU1) antigenic polypeptide, or any combination of two or more of the foregoing antigenic polypeptides. Herein, use of the term "antigenic polypeptide" encompasses immunogenic fragments of the antigenic polypeptide (an immunogenic fragment that is induces (or is capable of inducing) an immune response to hMPV, PIV, RSV, MeV, or a BetaCoV), unless otherwise stated.

Also provided herein, in some embodiments, is a RNA (e.g., mRNA) vaccine comprising at least one (e.g., at least 2, 3, 4 or 5) RNA polynucleotide having an open reading frame encoding at least one (e.g., at least 2, 3, 4 or 5) hMPV, PIV, RSV, MeV, and/or a BetaCoV (e.g., MERS-CoV, SARS-CoV, HCoV-OC43, HCoV-229E, HCoV-NL63,

1. Introduction

This research note examines apparent failures to disclose U.S. federal government funding of the inventions claimed in several patents assigned to Moderna Therapeutics ("Moderna"). It focuses on awards from the Defense Advanced Research Projects Agency (DARPA).

While similar issues can be raised regarding funding of Moderna from other agencies, including the Biomedical Advanced Research and Development Authority (BARDA) and the National Institutes of Health (NIH), this note focuses on the role of DARPA. KEI will publish a different research note examining the reporting of R&D funding by BARDA and the NIH.

The obligation to disclose U.S. federal government support in patent applications is a requirement of the Bayh-Dole Act and regulations issued by the U.S. Patent and Trademark Office.

Moderna was one of the awardees under the Autonomous Diagnostics to Enable Prevention and Therapeutics (ADEPT) program and performed research related to mRNA vaccines with funds granted by DARPA. Moderna used the ADEPT funding in their Chikungunya and Zika vaccines programs. It is likely that the DARPA awards more generally supported the establishment of their mRNA platform, which can be used against other viral infections, including COVID-19. This support is acknowledged by DARPA itself, for instance on the DARPA website It currently has a statement stating "[t]he first coronavirus vaccine to start human testing is from DARPA investment in the Moderna company."[1]

Several of the patents filed by Moderna since March 22, 2013 (when their first grant from DARPA was awarded), claim inventions related to methods and compositions for inducing an immune response by administering an mRNA vaccine. Some of these patents are specifically related to their Chikungunya and Zika vaccines programs, some are directed to vaccines

---

[1] https://www.darpa.mil/ddm_gallery/ModernaAntibodybasedVaccine.JPG

against other viral infections, and others are generally relevant to the mRNA platform Moderna has developed.

KEI examined the 126 patents assigned to "Moderna" or "ModernaTx" as well as 154 patent applications. Despite the evidence that multiple inventions were conceived in the course of research supported by the DARPA awards, not a single one of the patents or applications assigned to Moderna disclose U.S. federal government funding.

2. DARPA backed mRNA vaccines research early on

Messenger RNA (mRNA) is a ribonucleic acid (RNA) molecule complementary to one of the deoxyribonucleic acid (DNA) strands of a gene.[2] mRNA serves as an intermediary that carries the genetic information of a DNA molecule to the cell machinery responsible for protein synthesis.[3] Due to this role as an intermediary, mRNA has been considered for years as a candidate for prophylactic and therapeutic applications. One of the potential mRNA applications is in vaccine development. Conventional vaccines usually contain inactivated pathogens that mimic the infectious agent. When administered, they stimulate an immune response. In mRNA-based vaccines, however, no pathogens are introduced. Rather, the instructions on how to produce an immune response are encoded in mRNA and provided to a subject.
Some scientists have been advocating for the use of mRNA as a vaccine platform for years.[4] One of the key benefits of mRNA in vaccine development is flexibility. In principle, any protein can be encoded and expressed by mRNA; this, in theory, enables the development of a wide range of therapeutic and prophylactic applications. Another key feature is safety. Because mRNA is non-infectious, there is no potential risk of infection or insertional mutagenesis.[5]

Successful use of mRNA in vivo to elicit a physiological response has been reported since the early 1990s.[6] However, despite promising results, these findings did not lead to substantial private investment towards developing mRNA therapeutics largely due to concerns associated with mRNA instability, high innate immunogenicity and inefficient in vivo delivery.[7] It took decades before using mRNA as a vaccine platform became an attractive approach for private investors. Nevertheless, at a time when private investors were still skeptical about mRNA, DARPA made an early push in support of this approach to vaccine development. Starting in 2011, the agency allocated millions of dollars towards developing mRNA platform technologies.

DARPA initially pioneered the research into mRNA vaccines through their *Autonomous Diagnostics to Enable Prevention and Therapeutics: Prophylactic Options to Environmental and*

---

[2] https://www.genome.gov/genetics-glossary/messenger-rna
[3] http://sitn.hms.harvard.edu/flash/2015/rna-vaccines-a-novel-technology-to-prevent-and-treat-disease/
[4] https://www.ncbi.nlm.nih.gov/pmc/articles/PMC3597572/
[5] https://www.nature.com/articles/nrd.2017.243
[6] *See* https://pubmed.ncbi.nlm.nih.gov/1690918/ and https://pubmed.ncbi.nlm.nih.gov/1546298/
[7] https://www.nature.com/articles/nrd.2017.243

Contagious Threats (ADEPT-PROTECT) program.[8] One of the goals of this program was to "develop methods to transiently deliver nucleic acids for vaccines and therapeutics, and kinetically control the timing and levels of gene expression so that these drugs will be safe and effective for use in healthy subjects."[9] In 2017 the agency launched the Pandemic Prevention Platform (P3) to continue its work on "rapid discovery, characterization, production, testing, and delivery of efficacious DNA- and RNA-encoded medical countermeasures,"[10] such as the mRNA vaccines. All together, DARPA has awarded millions of dollars to de-risk early research in this field, including awards to pharmaceutical companies focused on the mRNA approach. Moderna is one of the beneficiaries of this funding, as the next section further explains.

3. DARPA was one of the first funders to support mRNA research at Moderna

Moderna was created in 2010 by Harvard University biologist Derrick Rossi and other academic co-founders.[11] Moderna launched their initial public offering (IPO) on December 6, 2018, selling approximately 26.3 million shares at $23 dollars each.[12] Since inception they have had several candidates in their pipeline, at different stages of development, but none have been approved or launched in the market. In January 2020 Moderna started their mRNA-1273 program, a potential COVID-19 vaccine that is based on the mRNA approach. Moderna has been awarded nearly a billion dollars by the Biomedical Advanced Research and Development Authority (BARDA), an agency of the U.S. federal government, to develop mRNA-1273.[13]

Long before the COVID-19 pandemic, however, Moderna had already received awards from federal agencies. DARPA, in particular, backed this company early on. On March 22, 2013, DARPA awarded Moderna "approximately $1.4 million" under the agreement *W31P4Q-13-1-0007*.[14] This award was titled "[m]odified RNA technology for production of antibodies for immune prophylaxis."[15] Next, on October 2, 2013, DARPA awarded Moderna "up to $25 million to research and develop its messenger RNA therapeutics platform as a rapid and reliable way to make antibody-producing drugs to protect against a wide range of known and unknown emerging infectious diseases and engineered biological threats."[16] The award was

---

[8] https://www.darpa.mil/attachments/ADEPTVignetteFINAL.pdf
[9] https://www.darpa.mil/attachments/DARPAFY19PresidentsBudgetRequest.pdf
[10] https://www.darpa.mil/program/pandemic-prevention-platform
[11] https://www.bostonmagazine.com/health/2013/02/26/moderna-therapeutics-new-medical-technology/
[12]
https://www.wsj.com/articles/highly-anticipated-moderna-listing-is-seen-as-test-of-new-ipos-1544092200
[13]
https://investors.modernatx.com/news-releases/news-release-details/moderna-announces-award-us-gove
rnment-agency-barda-483-million
[14] https://www.sec.gov/Archives/edgar/data/1682852/000119312518323562/d577473ds1.htm
[15] https://govtribe.com/award/federal-grant-award?searchId=5e60cd79448f914c9b10c15e
[16]
https://web.archive.org/web/20200727061854/https://investors.modernatx.com/news-releases/news-relea
se-details/darpa-awards-moderna-therapeutics-grant-25-million-develop/

identified under the number *W911NF-13-1-0417*, and was part of the ADEPT-PROTECT program. Moderna has stated in SEC disclosures that, as of December 31, 2019, $19.7 million of the amount committed under the *W911NF-13-1-0417* award had been funded.[17]

	W31P4Q-13-1-0007	W911NF-13-1-0417
Start date	March 22, 2013	October 2, 2013
Award amount	"approximately $1.4 million"	"up to $25 million", and as of December 31, 2019, $19.7 million had been funded
Summary of the research	"modified RNA technology for production of antibodies for immune prophylaxis."	"messenger RNA therapeutics platform as a rapid and reliable way to make antibody-producing drugs to protect against a wide range of known and unknown emerging infectious diseases and engineered biological threats."

At the time of the DARPA awards, Moderna was still a relatively small company. Although the company was created in 2010, the oldest press release currently in company archives dates back to December 6, 2012. On that day Moderna announced $40 million in venture funding from Flagship Pioneering.[18] The Flagship Pioneering venture capital appears to be one of the first significant investments in Moderna. The DARPA awards came shortly after, and it appears that they represented an important share of the total funding Moderna had raised at the time. As explained in the sections below, the DARPA awards in 2013 supported several aspects of their mRNA research and likely led to a number of patented inventions assigned to Moderna.

8. None of the Moderna patents or applications disclose the DARPA awards

On August 18, 2020, KEI searched the United States Patent and Trademark Office (USPTO) Patent Full-Text and Image Database (PatFT) database for patents assigned to "Moderna" or "ModernaTx." The search returned 126 patents.[45] There were also 154 applications located by searching the Patent Application Full-Text and Image Database (AppFT) with the same criteria.[46]

KEI then reviewed whether any of these patents or applications disclosed funding from the U.S. federal government as required by the Bayh-Dole Act. KEI examined the text of these patents and applications, including their certificates of corrections if any were present. Not a single one of these patents and applications disclosed grants or contracts from the U.S. federal government. Considering the history of DARPA support for this company, which likely led to at least some of their inventions, we believe that Moderna likely failed to meet their disclosure obligations.

This apparent failure to disclose U.S. government funding in patents contrasts with the disclosures Moderna has made to their investors. In several documents filed with the SEC Moderna has acknowledged that some of the research they have conducted has been funded by the U.S. federal government. The company has explained to their investors that, because of this, they "may not have the right to prohibit the U.S. government from using certain technologies developed by [them], and [they] may not be able to prohibit third-party companies, including [their] competitors, from using those technologies in providing products and services to the U.S. government."[47] Moderna has further told investors in several disclosures filed with the SEC that "[t]he U.S. government generally takes the position that it has the right to royalty-free use of technologies that are developed under U.S. government contracts."[48]

This apparent failure to disclose also contrasts with statements made by other DARPA awardees. In November 15, 2011, DARPA awarded $33.1 million to a consortium integrated by CureVac, Sanofi-Pasteur, and In-Cell-Art to develop mRNA vaccines.[49] This award was also part of the ADEPT program that supported the mRNA research performed by Moderna. In contrast with Moderna, however, CureVac has disclosed DARPA funding in several issued patents. For example, this is the case in U.S. patent 10,653,768 (the '768 patent) issued on May 19, 2020.

---

[45] Sixteen patents that appeared on this search were dropped because they were assigned to other companies that also had the term "Moderna" in their name.
[46] Seven patents applications that appeared on this search were dropped because they were assigned to other companies that also had the term "Moderna" in their name.
[47] https://www.sec.gov/Archives/edgar/data/1682852/000095012318009220/filename1.htm
[48] https://www.sec.gov/Archives/edgar/data/1682852/000095012318009220/filename1.htm
[49]
https://web.archive.org/web/20121207123349/http://www.curevac.com/pdf/CureVac_Sanofi%20Pasteur_DARPA_Collaboration_20111012_EN.pdf

KEI Series on inventors that fail to disclose U.S. government funding in patented inventions

---

9. KEI asks DARPA to investigate whether Moderna failed to disclose their awards

KEI asks DARPA to investigate the apparent failures to disclose government funding in patents and applications assigned to Moderna, and take remedial action.

An investigation on Moderna's failure to disclose should include but not limited to granted patents and pending applications broadly directed to (a) vaccines compositions and methods for inducing an immune response against the Chikungunya virus, (b) vaccines compositions and methods for inducing an immune response against the Zika virus, (c) vaccines compositions and methods for inducing an immune response against coronaviruses, including COVID-19, and (d) methods and compositions generally applicable to their mRNA platform, regardless of the indication for which they are useful. It should include all patents and applications claiming a priority benefit on or after March 22, 2013, the grant date of the first DARPA award. An investigation should also cover pending and unpublished applications, including any mRNA platform technologies that Moderna may be using in their COVID-19 vaccine mRNA-1273 program.

DARPA should conduct a comprehensive investigation of the patent portfolio Moderna has built since the first award supporting their research in 2013. Merely for illustration purposes, below KEI has provided a list of patents that, from our research, should be part of a DARPA investigation since they meet at least one of the three criteria explained above.

The '597, '342, and '731 patents

KEI urges DARPA to investigate failures to disclose government funding in U.S. patents 10,702,597 (the '597 patent), 10,675,342 (the '342 patents) and 10,238,731 (the '731 patent). These three patents all claim a priority date after the start of the DARPA awards in 2013. Most of their claims are directed to Chikungunya vaccine compositions, or methods of inducing an immune response in a subject by administering a Chikungunya vaccine. The inventions claimed in these patents are based on the mRNA vaccine approach. These patents name Sayda Elbashir, Giuseppe Ciaramella, and Sunny Himansu among the co-inventors, scientists that are also listed as co-authors in the *Science immunology* paper that reports research related to Chikungunya and acknowledges one of the DARPA awards.[50]

Since several of the above mentioned inventors have acknowledged performing work under the DARPA awards around the time when their inventions were likely conceived, there is strong evidence suggesting that they should have disclosed U.S. government funding in at least some of these patents. If that is the case, the U.S. government has certain rights over these patents. Despite this, none of these patents disclose contracts or awards from the U.S. government.

---

[50] Kose, Nurgun et al. "A lipid-encapsulated mRNA encoding a potently neutralizing human monoclonal antibody protects against chikungunya infection." Science immunology vol. 4,35 (2019): eaaw6647. doi:10.1126/sciimmunol.aaw6647

KEI Series on inventors that fail to disclose U.S. government funding in patented inventions

---

The '767, '940, '244, '269, and '055 patents

KEI urges DARPA to investigate failures to disclose government funding in U.S. patents 10,653,767 (the '767 patent), 10,517,940 (the '940 patent), 10,449,244 (the '244 patent), 10,273,269 (the '269 patent), and 10,124,055 (the '055 patent). These five patents all claim a priority date after the start of the DARPA awards in 2013. Most of their claims are directed to Zika vaccine compositions, or methods of inducing an immune response in a subject by administering a Zika vaccine. The inventions claimed in these patents are based on the mRNA vaccine approach. These patents name Giuseppe Ciaramella and Sunny Himansu among the co-inventors, scientists that are also listed as co-authors in the *Cell* paper describing research related to a mRNA Zika vaccine and acknowledges one of the DARPA awards.[51]

Since these two inventors have acknowledged performing work under the DARPA awards around the time when their inventions were likely conceived, there is strong evidence suggesting that they should have disclosed U.S. government funding in at least some of these patents. If that is the case, the U.S. government has certain rights over these patents. Despite this, none of these patents disclose contracts or awards from the U.S. government.

The '435 and '779 patents

KEI also urges DARPA to investigate apparent failures to disclose U.S. government funding in patents assigned to Moderna that are generally applicable to their mRNA platform. KEI believes this is reasonable considering that DARPA itself seems to believe that the mRNA platform Moderna used for their COVID-19 vaccine candidate was funded with their awards to the company. Of particular interest are the patents broadly directed to the mRNA platform that claimed priority benefits after March 22, 2013, and list as co-inventor any Moderna scientists that have acknowledged performing work under the DARPA awards, namely Sayda Elbashir, Matthew Theisen, Elisabeth Humphris-Narayanan, Giuseppe Ciaramella, or Sunny Himansu. U.S. patents 10,022,435 (the '435 patent) and 10,709,779 ('779 patent), which name Giuseppe Ciaramella as one of the co-inventors and are generally directed to methods of vaccinating a subject by administering an mRNA encoding an antigenic polypeptide, meet this criteria.

The '600 patent

KEI urges DARPA to investigate apparent failures to disclose U.S. government funding in patents assigned to Moderna that are directed to methods and compositions specifically against coronaviruses, including COVID-19. DARPA itself reports to shareholders that the mRNA-1273 program involves technology that they funded. Of particular interest is U.S. patent 10,702,600 (the '600 patent), which claimed "[a] composition, comprising: a messenger ribonucleic acid (mRNA) comprising an open reading frame encoding a betacoronavirus (BetaCoV) S protein or

---

[51] Richner, Justin M et al. "Vaccine Mediated Protection Against Zika Virus-Induced Congenital Disease." *Cell* vol. 170,2 (2017): 273-283.e12. doi:10.1016/j.cell.2017.06.040

KEI Series on inventors that fail to disclose U.S. government funding in patented inventions

S protein subunit formulated in a lipid nanoparticle." The '600 patent was disclosed in the conflict of interest section of an academic paper relating to COVID-19, published by the New England Journal of Medicine (NEJM) - which suggests that it is relevant to the mRNA-1273 program.[52] The patent names Giuseppe Ciaramella and Sunny Himansu as inventors, both of which acknowledged performing work under the DARPA awards in two academic papers.

Other patents

DARPA is also asked to investigate apparent failures to disclose U.S. government funding in patents assigned to Moderna that are generally applicable to their mRNA platform, even if none of the scientists that have acknowledged DARPA funding in academic papers are listed as co-inventors. Acknowledging funding from the U.S. government in an academic paper surely constitutes strong evidence indicating that the equivalent patents should have disclosed those grants or contracts. Nevertheless, the opposite is not necessarily true. Work supported under federal grants or contracts might have not yielded an academic paper making such disclosure, but this does not mean that the work was not funded by the U.S. government.

10. Remedies for Non-Disclosure

Failure to disclose subject inventions pursuant to 35 U.S.C. § 202(c)(1) permits the federal government to "receive title to any subject invention not disclosed to it within such time[.]"

> 35 U.S.C. 202   Disposition of rights.
> (c) Each funding agreement with a small business firm or nonprofit organization shall contain appropriate provisions to effectuate the following:
>
> (1) That the contractor disclose each subject invention to the Federal agency within a reasonable time after it becomes known to contractor personnel responsible for the administration of patent matters, and that the Federal Government may receive title to any subject invention not disclosed to it within such time.

The funding agencies should remedy a failure to disclose by at a minimum requiring a correction to the patent and more appropriately by taking title to the patents themselves, as the sanction for the failure to disclose.

---

[52] https://www.nejm.org/doi/suppl/10.1056/NEJMoa2024671/suppl_file/nejmoa2024671_disclosures.pdf

RUSSIAN INTERFERENCE IN THE 2016 PRESIDENTIAL ELECTION

We've been hearing for several years now about how the Russian government, under orders from Vladimir Putin, interfered in the 2016 presidential election. The Russians sought to undermine Hillary Clinton's campaign, boost the Trump candidacy, and increase political and social discord throughout the United States. The FBI's Crossfire Hurricane investigation homed in on links between Trump associates and Russian officials. In his Special Counsel Investigation, former FBI director Robert Mueller (in what is now "The Mueller Report") called Russian interference "sweeping and systematic." Meanwhile, President Trump called this a "hoax" perpetrated by Democrats upset that Hillary had lost the election.

When the Republican-led Senate Intelligence Committee released the final volume of its three-year investigation in August 2020, they concurred that the Russian government had mounted an "extensive campaign" to sabotage the election in Trump's favor, including their having received help from some of Trump's own campaign staff.

What we're reprinting here are excerpts from a National Security Agency (NSA) report on Russian hacking of the election, which should raise a few more eyebrows.

DIRNSA

⚠ National Security Agency

Russia/Cybersecurity: Main Intelligence Directorate Cyber Actors, ▮▮▮▮▮▮▮▮▮▮▮▮▮▮▮▮▮▮▮▮▮▮▮ Target U.S. Companies and Local U.S. Government Officials Using Voter Registration-Themed Emails, Spoof Election-Related Products and Services, Research Absentee Ballot Email Addresses; August to November 2016 (TS//SI//OC/REL TO USA, FVEY/FISA)

SUMMARY (U)

(TS//SI//OC//REL TO USA, FVEY/FISA) Russian General Staff Main Intelligence Directorate actors▮▮▮▮▮▮▮▮▮ ▮▮▮▮▮▮▮▮▮▮▮▮▮▮▮▮▮▮▮▮▮▮▮▮▮▮▮ executed cyber espionage operations against a named U.S. Company in August 2016, evidently to obtain information on elections-related software and hardware solutions, according to information that became available in April 2017. The actors likely used data obtained from that operation to create a new email account and launch a voter registration-themed spear-phishing campaign targeting U.S. local government organizations. The spear-phishing emails contained a Microsoft Word document trojanized with a Visual Basic script which, when opened, would spawn a PowerShell instance

Declassify On: 20420505

TOP SECRET//SI//ORCON/REL TO USA, FVEY/FISA

DIRNSA

and beacon out to malicious infrastructure. In October 2016, the actors also created a new email address that was potentially used to offer election-related products and services, presumably to U.S.-based targets. Lastly, the actors sent test emails to two non-existent accounts ostensibly associated with absentee balloting, presumably with the purpose of creating those accounts to mimic legitimate services.

Campaign Against U.S. Company 1 and Voter Registration-Themed Phishing of U.S. Local Government Officials (S//SI//REL TO USA, FVEY/FISA)

Russian Cyber Threat Actors Target U.S. Company 1 (S//REL TO USA, FVEY/FISA)

(TS//SI//OC/REL TO USA, FVEY/FISA) Cyber threat actors ██████████████████████ ███ executed a spear-phishing campaign from the email address noreplyautomaticservice@gmail.com on 24 August 2016 targeting victims that included employees of U.S. Company 1, according to information that became available in April 2017.[1] This campaign appeared to be designed to obtain the end users' email credentials by enticing the victims to click on an embedded link within a spoofed Google Alert email, which would redirect the user to the malicious domain ████████████████████.[2] The following potential victims were identified:

- U.S. email address 1 associated with U.S. Company 1,
- U.S. email address 2 associated with U.S. Company 1,
- U.S. email address 3 associated with U.S. Company 1,
- U.S. email address 4 associated with U.S. Company 1,
- U.S. email address 5 associated with U.S. Company 1,
- U.S. email address 6 associated with U.S. Company 1, and
- U.S. email address 7 associated with U.S. Company 1.

(TS//SI//OC/REL TO USA, FVEY/FISA) Three of the malicious emails were rejected by the email server with the response message that the victim addresses did not exist. The three rejected email addresses were U.S. email address 1 to 3 associated with U.S. Company 1.

---

1. (TS//SI//OC/REL TO USA, FVEY/FISA) *The GRU* ████████████████████████ *is also rendered as military unit* ██

2. (TS//SI//OC/REL TO USA, FVEY/FISA) *For additional information on* ██████ *and its cyber espionage mandate, specifically directed at U.S. and foreign elections, see* ████████████████████████

Page 2

TOP SECRET//SI//ORCON/REL TO USA, FVEY/FISA

TOP SECRET//SI//ORCON/REL TO USA, FVEY/FISA

████████████████ DIRNSA

(TS//SI//OC/REL TO USA, FVEY) COMMENT: The ████████ actors were probably trying to obtain information associated with election-related hardware and software applications. It is unknown whether the aforementioned spear-phishing deployment successfully compromised all the intended victims, and what potential data from the victim could have been exfiltrated. However, based upon subsequent targeting, it was likely that at least one account was compromised.

Cyber Threat Actors Create Spoofed Account and Voter Registration-Themed Targeting of Local Government Officials (TS//SI//OC/REL TO USA, FVEY/FISA)

(TS//SI//OC/REL TO USA, FVEY/FISA) The ████████ cyber threat actors created a new operational email account vr.elections@gmail.com with the username "U.S. Company 1" on 27 October 2016. (COMMENT: It is likely that the cyber threat actors created this email address to appear as if they were an employee of U.S. Company 1.) The cyber threat actors had in the email account two trojanized Microsoft Word documents with the titles "New_EViD_User_Guides.docm" and "NEW_Staging_Checklist_AIO_Style_EViD.docm". Both of these documents had identical content and hash values, and contained the same malicious Visual Basic script. The body of the trojanized documents contained detailed instructions on how to configure EViD software on Microsoft Windows machines. According to EViD's FAQ website (UNCLASSIFIED), EViD software allows poll workers to quickly check a voter's registration status, name and address. (END OF COLLATERAL)

(TS//SI//OC/REL TO USA, FVEY/FISA) Subsequently, the cyber threat actors used the vr.elections@gmail.com account to contact U.S. email addresses 1 to 122 associated with named local government organizations. (COMMENT: It possible that the targeted email addresses were obtained from the previously compromised account(s) of U.S. Company 1.) The "NEW_Staging_Checklist_AIO_Style_EViD" document was last modified on 31 October 2016 and the "New_EViD_User_Guides" document was last modified on 1 November 2016. (COMMENT: This likely indicates that the spear-phishing campaign occurred either on 31 October or 1 November , although th e exact date of the spear-phishing campaign was not confirmed.)

(TS//SI//REL TO USA, FVEY) COMMENT: Given the content of the malicious email it was likely that the threat actor was targeting officials involved in the management of voter registration systems. It is unknown whether the aforementioned spear-phishing deployment successfully compromised the intended victims, and what potential data could have been accessed by the cyber actor.

Technical Analysis of the Trojanized Documents (U//FOUO)

(TS//SI//OC/REL TO USA, FVEY/FISA) Both trojanized Microsoft Word documents contained a malicious Visual Basic script that spawns PowerShell and uses it to execute a series of commands to retrieve and then

Page 3

TOP SECRET//SI///ORCON/REL TO USA, FVEY/FISA

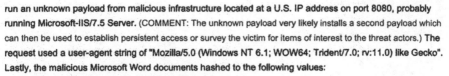

run an unknown payload from malicious infrastructure located at a U.S. IP address on port 8080, probably running Microsoft-IIS/7.5 Server. (COMMENT: The unknown payload very likely installs a second payload which can then be used to establish persistent access or survey the victim for items of interest to the threat actors.) **The request used a user-agent string of "Mozilla/5.0 (Windows NT 6.1; WOW64; Trident/7.0; rv:11.0) like Gecko".** Lastly, the malicious Microsoft Word documents hashed to the following values:

- MD5 Hash:5617e7ffa923de3a3dc9822c3b01a1fd,
- SHA-1 Hash:602aa899a6fadeb6f461112f3c51439a36ccba40, and
- SHA-256 Hash:f48c9929f2de895425bdae2d5b232a726d66b9b2827d1a9ffc75d1ea37a7cf6c.

Operational Accounts Spoofing Legitimate Elections-Related Services (S//REL TO USA, FVEY)

Spoofing Email Address Associated With U.S. Company 2 (U//FOUO)

(TS//SI//OC/REL TO USA, FVEY/FISA) In parallel to the aforementioned campaign, the ▮▮▮▮▮▮ cyber threat actors created another new operational email account elevationsystem@outlook.com on 19 October 2016. They then used this email address to send a test message to another known ▮▮▮▮ operational email account. In that test email, which was written in English, the threat actors spoofed U.S. Company 2, and offered election-related products and services. All emails associated with this account were later deleted, and it was unknown if there was any targeting using this email account. (COMMENT: G iven that the email body was written in English and prepared less than 1 month before the 2016 U.S. Presidential election, it was likely intended for U.S.-based targets.)

Spoofing Absentee Ballot Email Addresses (U//FOUO)

(TS//SI//OC/REL TO USA, FVEY/FISA) Additionally, the ▮▮▮▮▮▮ cyber threat actors sent what appeared to be a test email to two other accounts, requestabsentee@americansamoaelectionoffice.org and r-questabsentee@americansamoaelectionoffice.org. In both cases the actors received a response from the mail server on 18 October stating that the message failed to send, indicating that the two accounts did not exist.

> (TS//SI//REL TO USA, FVEY) COMMENT: Given that the test email did not contain any malicious links or attachments, it appeared the threat actors' intent was to create the email accounts rather than compromise them, presumably with the purpose of mimicking a legitimate absentee ballot-related service provider.

TOP SECRET//SI///ORCON/REL TO USA, FVEY/FISA

WHO REALLY IGNITED THE NATIONWIDE PROTESTS?

After the murder of George Floyd in my home city of Minneapolis ignited worldwide outrage and protest. mostly peaceful, yet sometimes violent, Trump and Attorney General William Barr claimed that chaos and disorder were being sown by anti-fascist "domestic terrorists" under the banner of Antifa.

But this was not the scenario that law enforcement reports around the country were privately sharing. Thanks to Blueleaks, which made the documents public in July 2020, we now know that it was really far-right extremists—such as the heavily armed "boogaloo boys"—that were hoping to trigger civil war through confrontations with the police.

Here's what the Department of Homeland Security (DHS) knew:

UNCLASSIFIED//FOR OFFICIAL USE ONLY

Username: NationalRevivalist
Statistics: As of 29 May 2020, channel had 3,493 subscribers and posted 1,536 photos, 296 videos, 74 files, 79 audio files, 499 shared links, and 20 voice messages. (See Attachment.)

2. (U//FOUO) On 27 May 2020, Source shared multiple messages about recent riots and protests posted by other users, including a photo showing damage to Minneapolis Police Department property. Following these, Source shared a message from another account that stated, "multiple gunshots". Then, Source replied to the post and stated, "The use of firearms greatly influences the scale and intensity of these events. Equally it is a deterance as well as a lethal measure". As of 29 May 2020, the post had approximately 1,220 views.

3. (U//FOUO) Soon after, on 28 May 2020, Source replied to the previous reply and stated, "When Riot Police employs the generic and common pulse tactic for arrests the important thing is to break their lines with cocktails, chainsaws, and firearms. Pig armor is made for bricks and blades. The pig knows his only advantage is equipment and training. Take away the equipment advantage and outnumber their training and you have an equal fight". As of 29 May 2020, the post had approximately 1,740 views.

4. (U//FOUO) On 29 May 2020, Source shared two images posted by another user that stated, "Reminder that looting and shoplifting are both cool and whites should be doing it way more" and "[...] When the laws no longer benefit you, break them for personal gain. If you don't feel like buying something, steal it. If you don't feel like driving slow, drive fast. If you don't like someone, hurt them." Source replied to this post and stated, "We ought to revel in the destruction of the police state. It is just as necessary to break down the police state and the system of control as it is to spread racial hatred". As of 29 May 2020, the post had approximately 507 views.

(U//FOUO) COMMENTS:
1. (U//FOUO) "Cocktail" in this context likely is short for Molotov Cocktail, a handheld, flammable liquid-based, improvised incendiary device. A Molotov Cocktail was reportedly thrown at a New York Police Department vehicle during violent activity in Crown Heights Brooklyn shortly after 10:30 PM local time.

2. (U//FOUO) Some white supremacist extremists adhering to accelerationism also incite violence against law enforcement and critical infrastructure in hopes of sparking the "boogaloo"--a term used by some violent extremists to refer to the start of a second Civil War.

3. (U//FOUO) Spelling, grammar, capitalization, and punctuation within quotations are unique to original material.

(U//FOUO) PREP: OSRN-052

(U//FOUO) POC: Direct feedback, evaluations, comments, and follow on collection requests to the Current and Emerging Threats Center (CETC), Open Source Collection Operations (OSCO) by accessing the OSIR evaluation link at Intelink-U (https://intelshare.intelink.gov/sites/dhs-osco/), Intelink-S (https://intelshare.intelink.sgov.gov/sites/dhs-osco/), or Intelink-TS (https://intelshare.intelink.ic.gov/sites/dhs-osco/). Contact CETC OSCO at 202-447-3688 or via e-mail at: CETC.OSCO@hq.dhs.gov, CETC.OSCO@dhs.sgov.gov, or CETC.OSCO@dhs.ic.gov.

==============================DISSEMINATION==============================

UNCLASSIFIED//FOR OFFICIAL USE ONLY

UNCLASSIFIED//FOR OFFICIAL USE ONLY

(U//FOUO) AGENCY: FBI

(U//FOUO) DHS COMPONENTS: CBP; CIS; FEMA; ICE; TSA; USCG; USSS

(U//FOUO) STATE/LOCAL: All Field Ops
==

(U//FOUO) ATTACHMENTS: See attached.

--------------------------BEGIN TEARLINE------------------------------------

UNCLASSIFIED//REL TO USA, FVEY

(U) WARNING: The following information is releasable to the governments of
Australia, Canada, United Kingdom, and New Zealand. It may be discussed with
appropriately cleared members of the Australian, Canadian, British, and New
Zealand governments who have a need to know this information in accordance
with their official duties. Further dissemination to other countries is not
authorized without prior approval of the originator.

(U) SERIAL: 04001-0669-20

(U//REL USA, FVEY) An extremist encrypted instant messaging channel incites
others to use "cocktails, chainsaws, and firearms" against riot police.
Source also states breaking down "the police state and the system of control"
is just as necessary as spreading "racial hatred".

(U) INTELLIGENCE PURPOSES ONLY: This information is provided only for
intelligence purposes and is intended for developing potential investigative
leads. It may not be used in any way that will expose intelligence sources or
methods. Any attachments separated from this report are publicly available
information and are not classified.

UNCLASSIFIED//REL TO USA, FVEY

--------------------------END TEARLINE---------------------------------------

CLIMATE CHANGE: THE NATIONAL SECURITY THREAT

We can all see it plain-as-day. The hurricanes and tornadoes are becoming stronger, the flooding and drought conditions are getting worse. The glaciers, the permafrost, and the polar ice caps are melting away. Sea levels are rising, mass migrations are happening, and the current power brokers are intent on further pumping more fossil fuels, sending carbon emissions to skyrocketing levels.

I'm proud to say that the military, in which I served six years as a Navy Frogman, isn't afraid to tell it like it is. As grim as the scenario is, an 86-page report released in February 2020 lays out the national security threat posed by allowing climate change to continue unchecked. Here's what we all need to realize as we move as fast as we can toward a clean energy future.

EXECUTIVE SUMMARY

As national security, military and intelligence professionals with decades of experience, we have dedicated our careers to anticipating, analyzing and addressing security threats to the United States, with the goal of protecting all citizens from harm. That includes threats ranging from the proliferation and use of nuclear weapons, to the likelihood of terrorist attacks striking our shores.

With this report, we set out together to fully assess one of the most pressing threats to both national and global security in the 21st Century - climate change.

Climate change is an evolving and multidimensional threat, caused by no single actor, but perpetuated by current human systems of energy, transportation, agriculture, and resource use. According to the world's top empirical research, the impacts of climate change have the potential to destabilize human life at all levels. Using our unique expertise in the national security, military and intelligence fields, we assess the risks posed by climate change through a security lens.

Based on our research, we have determined that even at scenarios of low warming, each region of the world will face severe risks to national and global security in the next three decades. Higher levels of warming will pose catastrophic, and likely irreversible, global security risks over the course of the 21st century.

KEY FINDINGS

- If global emissions are not reigned in, the world will experience destabilizing changes in both the near and medium-to-long terms which pose significant threats to security environments, infrastructure, and institutions.

- At low levels of warming, the areas hit the hardest are those that are already the most vulnerable: dry and arid regions, least-developed countries, small island states, and the Arctic polar region. These are areas of significant military engagement, and climate impacts threaten to further destabilize these fragile regions.

- Northern, industrialized regions will also face significant threats at all levels of warming. In longer term, high emissions warming scenarios, these countries could experience catastrophic security risks, including high levels of migration and a breakdown of key infrastructure and security institutions.

- The world is currently on track for a high level of global average warming, and our emission trajectory is proceeding. Even proposed international commitments, like those made under the Paris Climate Agreement, are not nearly commensurate to contain the threat.

- Without concerted efforts at both climate change mitigation and adaptation, we risk high-impact and catastrophic threats to our collective and national security.

The Center for Climate and Security, an institute of The Council on Strategic Risks
1025 Connecticut Ave., NW · Suite 1000 · Washington, DC 20036
www.climateandsecurity.org · www.councilonstrategicrisks.org

On current, high-end emissions trajectories, warming levels could reach between 2.3 and 4.1°C / 5.0 and 7.4°F above pre-industrial temperature levels by the end of the century. Even if all existing climate policies are implemented, we are on track to increase global temperatures by as high as 3.2°C/5.8°F by the end of the century.[1][2][3]

These ranges represent a wide span of potential climate futures, in which humans could mitigate emissions to contain warming to the lower end of the threat spectrum or allow relatively unabated actions to warm the planet to even more dangerous thresholds. On current emissions trajectories, global warming levels could reach 2°C/3.6°F as soon as mid-century and 4°C/7.2°F as soon as the end of the century.[4][5]

Climate change will have significant impacts on security across the globe but is dependent on our actions in the decades ahead. Thus, it is vital that the security and policy-making communities begin to analyze the implications of various warming levels, comparing the effects expected in near-term, low warming scenarios with long-term, high warming scenarios.

This report synthesizes the latest in both climate science and security analyses to offer **a threat assessment of global climate change.** Its key products include:

1. An overview of how climate change interacts with physical, social and political systems to create or intensify security threats ("The Climate Security Nexus," p. 18).

2. A synthesis of the climate security threats impacting each region of the globe ("Regional Climate Security Threat Assessments," p. 24), divided by U.S. Geographic Combatant Commands.

3. An assessment of intersecting global threats ("Global Climate Security Threat Assessment," p. 64), and a threat profile for global climate change ("Global Climate Security Threat Profile," p. 71).

These analyses present a detailed, sobering picture of the future of global security under climate change. We hope that these scenarios will energize the security community to immediately mitigate these risks, and support policies that: achieve net-zero global emissions as quickly as possible; build resilience to current and expected impacts; and integrate climate considerations across all areas of security planning.

CLIMATE SECURITY THREAT PROFILES AND ASSESSMENTS

This report compiles separate threat profiles and threat assessments for each region of the world, under two scenarios of warming in the 21st Century – 'Near Term' and 'Medium-Long Term.'

NEAR TERM SCENARIO (1-2°C WARMING)	MEDIUM-LONG TERM SCENARIO (2-4+°C WARMING)
Temperature: Global average temperature rises between 1 - 2°C / 1.8 - 3.6°F.	**Temperature:** Global average temperature rises between 2 - 4°C / 3.6 - 7.2°F, or higher.
Timeframe: Between now and 2050; reaching high-end of spectrum as soon as mid-century.	**Timeframe:** Between 2050-2100, reaching high-end of spectrum as soon as end of century.

Scientists believe that the implementation of current mitigation policies would put us on track for between 2.8 and 3.2°C / 5.0 and 5.8°F of warming by the end of the century. However, worst case scenarios of rapid emissions could lead to over 4°C/7.2°F by the end of the century.[6] Thus, we have based our two scenarios on the warming that is possible on this high-emissions trajectory, in which the planet warms an average of 2°C/ by mid-century, and 4°C/7.2°F or higher by the end of the century.

These two scenarios illustrate potential effects of warming impacts tied to bounded levels of temperature rise and time scales. They represent descriptive risk scenarios of possible futures, and *not* predictions or likelihoods of certain events occurring. Each regional assessment can be read on its own for a snapshot of climate security risks facing human populations.

Following our synthesis of the climate impacts expected for each region, we used our collective security experience and knowledge to assess and then rank all scenarios by their risk to security environments, infrastructure, and institutions, on a scale from "Low" to "Catastrophic."

> **LOW:** some material risk to human social and security systems
>
> **MEDIUM:** consequential risk to human social and security systems
>
> **HIGH:** severe risk to human social and security systems
>
> **VERY HIGH:** severe and systemic risk to human social and security systems
>
> **CATASTROPHIC:** disastrous and irreversible risk to human social and security systems

Based on this scale, we determine the following threat profiles and threat assessments for each climate scenario. These are an aggregation of conclusions drawn from separate regional and intersecting risk assessments, detailed in-depth throughout this report. The threat profile explains the overall risk level associated with the scenario, and the threat assessment gives more detail on the specific impacts expected under those conditions.

The Center for Climate and Security, an institute of The Council on Strategic Risks
1025 Connecticut Ave., NW · Suite 1000 · Washington, DC 20036
www.climateandsecurity.org - www.councilonstrategicrisks.org

GLOBAL CLIMATE SECURITY THREATS

NEAR-TERM SCENARIO (1-2°C WARMING): HIGH - VERY HIGH THREAT

Threat Profile: According to our analysis, climate change presents a **"high-very high"** risk level, and significant threat to both global and homeland security at 1-2°C/1.8-3.6°F of global average warming. Urgent and comprehensive prevention and preparation actions are recommended to avoid this significantly destabilizing security scenario.

Threat Assessment: At 1-2°C/1.8-3.6°F of global average warming, the world is very likely to experience more intense and frequent climate shocks that could swiftly destabilize areas already vulnerable to insecurity, conflict, and human displacement, as well as those regions whose stability is brittle due to underlying geographic and natural resource vulnerabilities. Under this scenario, all regions will experience **high levels of climate security threats** that will disrupt key security environments, institutions, and infrastructure. The resulting resource scarcity, population migration, and social and political disasters are likely to interact at the international level, alongside the creation of new areas of great power competition and potential conflict.

LOW	MEDIUM	HIGH	VERY HIGH	CATASTROPHIC

MEDIUM-LONG TERM SCENARIO (2-4+°C WARMING): VERY HIGH - CATASTROPHIC THREAT

Threat Profile: At 2-4+°C/3.6-7.2+°F of global average warming, climate change presents a **potentially unmanageable, "very high-catastrophic" global security threat** – such that this scenario must be avoided unequivocally. Avoiding this scenario will require comprehensive and urgent global actions to reduce the scale and scope of climate change, and to adapt to unavoidable threats.

Threat Assessment: At 2-4+°C/3.6-7.2+°F of global average warming, the world is very likely to experience significant insecurity and destabilization at the local, national, regional, and international levels. All regions will be exposed to potentially **catastrophic levels of climate security threats,** the consequences of which could lead to a breakdown of security and civilian infrastructure, economic and resource stability, and political institutions at a large scale.

LOW	MEDIUM	HIGH	VERY HIGH	CATASTROPHIC

The Center for Climate and Security, an institute of The Council on Strategic Risks
1025 Connecticut Ave., NW · Suite 1000 · Washington, DC 20036
www.climateandsecurity.org - www.councilonstrategicrisks.org

NORTHCOM:
NORTH AMERICA AND POLAR REGIONS

THREAT PROFILE

Based on the regional threat assessment for the two warming scenarios below, we have determined the following regional threat profile of climate change for the NORTHCOM area of responsibility.

NORTHCOM Climate Security Threat Profile

Near Term Scenario
(1-2°C Warming)

Medium - High

Extreme Weather
Drought and Food Stress
Regional Migration

Medium-Long Term Scenario
(2-4+°C Warming)

High - Catastrophic

Rising Seas
Frequent Extreme Weather
Intense Drought and Wildfires
Border Securitization

NEAR-TERM SCENARIO (1-2°C WARMING): MEDIUM - HIGH THREAT

At 1-2°C/1.8-3.6°F of global average warming, the NORTHCOM area of responsibility will experience more intense, extreme events like storms and wildfires, with significant impacts on life and property. These effects will reduce the readiness of security infrastructure, and undermine democratic and international institutions on which major power security relations depend.

MEDIUM-LONG TERM SCENARIO (2-4+°C WARMING): VERY HIGH THREAT - CATASTROPHIC

At 2-4+°C/3.6-7.2+°F of global average warming, the NORTHCOM area of responsibility will experience extreme heat, sea level rise, and disaster events that severely impact infrastructure critical for protecting the homeland. Increasing divisions within society -- including rising ethno-nationalist, anti-democratic and isolationist views -- could fracture historic security agreements, and great power competition over resources in the melting Arctic may become acute.

The Center for Climate and Security, an institute of The Council on Strategic Risks
1025 Connecticut Ave., NW · Suite 1000 · Washington, DC 20036
www.climateandsecurity.org - www.councilonstrategicrisks.org

THREAT ASSESSMENT

The threat profile of climate change for the NORTHCOM area is determined by an assessment of how climate change will affect the regional security landscape at both warming scenarios.

CLIMATE IMPACT ON REGIONAL SECURITY	THREAT ASSESSMENT
Risks to Security Environment	Near Term Scenario (1-2°C Warming): Medium - Very High Threat Medium-Long Term Scenario (2-4+°C Warming): Very High - Catastrophic Threat
Risks to Security Infrastructure	Near Term Scenario (1-2°C Warming): Medium - High Threat Medium-Long Term Scenario (2-4+°C Warming): High - Very High Threat
Risks to Security Institutions	Near Term Scenario (1-2°C Warming): Medium - High Threat Medium-Long Term Scenario (2-4+°C Warming): Very High Threat

BASELINE

For the U.S., Canada, and Mexico, climate change is contributing to risks of rising extremes across the continent, in heat, precipitation, drought, sea levels, wildfires, and storms. Few areas of the region are unaffected, even at low levels of warming, and all experience rising economic and social costs from intensified disasters. Melting Arctic conditions also newly define the region, as summers become ice free and tensions brew in the region over competing commercial interests.

RISKS TO SECURITY ENVIRONMENT

Warming across the North American region is projected to be swift, particularly for more Northern latitudes. On high end trajectories, temperature rise could exceed a regional average of 2°C by the middle of the century.[201] This warming will bring with it more frequent extreme heat and precipitation events, droughts, and earlier winter melting, as well as a host of localized impacts likely to stress the foundations of communities across the continent. The IPCC identifies this region as under particular risk from wildfires, extreme heat, and storms.[202]

NEAR TERM SCENARIO (1-2°C WARMING)

An increased intensity of tropical storms will inundate the Eastern coasts of the North American continent, bringing with them extreme economic and health impacts for communities affected. Recent research suggests that hurricanes will be both more intense and have higher rainfall rates as a result of coming climate change.[203] Together with increasingly high storm surges, flooding, and high wind effects, these hurricanes will threaten important coastal infrastructure and could lead to higher damages for those not able to escape a storm's path, particularly vulnerable and elderly communities.[204]

The Center for Climate and Security, an institute of The Council on Strategic Risks
1025 Connecticut Ave., NW · Suite 1000 · Washington, DC 20036
www.climateandsecurity.org - www.councilonstrategicrisks.org

As the East is hit by historic storms off the Atlantic, the Western areas of the continent will experience new patterns of severe wildfires that will increase under near to mid-term warming scenarios. Fires are burning hotter, larger, and for longer periods throughout the year, and lead to loss of homes, infrastructure, agriculture, and lives. Areas along the dry Western coast of the continent are at particular risk, but wildfires will increasingly threaten the Northern Plains, Rocky Mountains, and Southeast Pacific coast in summer and fall months.[205] These dangerous conditions have health impacts for nearby communities even if not directly impacted by fires, as smoke and air conditions can cause injury and respiratory impacts.[206]

The United States has seen mounting costs of such events, with climate and weather-related disasters costing over $400 billion in just 2014-18, and trends towards increased exposure and intensity of events are worrisome.[207] There are also direct security implications of more frequent storm and disaster events, as military bases, ships, aircraft, equipment, and troops must be moved out of harm's way, at great expense, or face significant and expensive damage.[208] [209]

Southwestern North America already faces conditions of water scarcity, through a combination of warming temperatures, drying, and decreased precipitation. In near-term projections, these conditions will deteriorate as water stress and drought become more acute in the arid regions of Western U.S., Canada, and Mexico, with negative implications for crop irrigation in these regions.[210] [211] The communities along the U.S.-Mexico border face particularly dire drought conditions, reported as the most extreme the region has experienced in the past century, along with consistently high temperatures.[212]

Water availability is not the only growing tension across the dry border regions. As record numbers of migrants from Central and South America attempt to cross the southern Mexican and U.S. borders, tensions have risen as political leaders have grown increasingly polarized on how to manage the situation. In both countries, military forces have been called on to respond to the migration flows, enforcement and vetting has increased, and asylum policies have become more restrictive.[213] Efforts to more strictly limit immigration could have labor implications for border economies, particularly in the agriculture and industrial sectors. With climate impacts including heat and drought diminishing crop yields across the region, migrants are citing lack of food as their primary impetuous for migration to Northern latitudes.[214]

In the Arctic region, warming is being experienced nearly twice as fast as the rest of the planet, with record-breaking temperatures every year since 2014 exceeding all previous records.[215] This fast-paced warming is expected to continue, with new light being shed on how warmer polar temperatures impact extreme weather conditions at midlatitudes, amplifying dryness and heat along the west coast of North America, and cold, wet weather along the East.[216]

The Arctic region is likely to begin experiencing ice-free summers within the next decade, with summers likely to be completely free of sea ice by mid-century, opening up valuable new territory for shipping lanes and resource extraction.[217] Such commercial activities are not without serious security implications for the variable and harsh conditions of the region, and lack of many permanent infrastructures, will require continual high-capability Navy and Coast Guard presence for search-and-rescue and ice breaking purposes. With the warming Arctic comes a rush of interest from other countries and commercial actors to the region, seeking these opportunities and drastically lowered shipping times. Currently addressed by the Arctic Council institution, as the region becomes more navigable relations

The Center for Climate and Security, an institute of The Council on Strategic Risks
1025 Connecticut Ave., NW · Suite 1000 · Washington, DC 20036
www.climateandsecurity.org - www.councilonstrategicrisks.org

among Arctic Council and official "Arctic Council Observer" states may be fraying.[218] While the Arctic Council currently has purview only over non-security issues, this may evolve in future years as security issues come to the fore.

MEDIUM-LONG TERM SCENARIO (2-4+°C WARMING)

Over a long-term, high-warming scenario, North America is projected to see large increases in extreme heat, with Southern latitudes experiencing decreases in annual precipitation and Northern latitudes experiencing an increase. Warming will be most pronounced in the North, with a 4°C temperature increase by the end-of-century translating to 6°C and greater in Northern Canada and Alaska.[219]

Rising sea levels under this scenario could be extreme and will threaten inundation of much of the heavily populated coastal regions, intense floods, storm surges, and groundwater disruptions. At the higher end emissions scenarios, 1.2 meters (4 feet) of sea level rise by end of century is likely, and high as 1.8-2.4m (6-8 feet) is possible, which could sink as much as $507 billion in coastal infrastructure and force large scale coastal resettlements.[220] While many North American cities have high adaptive capacity to such extremes, the density of population and infrastructure make damages and evacuations more costly. Critical coastal infrastructure, such as electricity grids, transportation lines, ports, and military bases, will be further threatened by sea levels, floods, and extreme events, and would likely need to be expensively retrofitted or relocated by the century's end.[221]

Extreme heat projections are increasingly dangerous in high-end, long term scenarios, in which the increased intensity and duration of heat waves will pose severe risks to human health. By mid-to-late 21st century, half of all North American summers are projected to be hotter than the maximum summer temperatures experienced at the end of the 20th century.[222] These extreme temperatures will put populations at risk of heat stresses across the continent, with particular risks in under-adapted northern areas. Across Mexico and the Western and Southeastern United States, extreme heat will define the majority of all summers and drought conditions will severely decrease water availability.[223]

While moderate levels of climate change could benefit some agricultural products, increased warming will have severe impacts on key staple crops including corn, soy, and cotton as temperature thresholds for growing conditions are surpassed. This could have drastic consequences for regional agriculture by the end of the century, with crop yields affected by as much as 63-82% by 2099 in high-emissions scenarios.[224] Livestock will also face heat-induced stressors, with implications for those agricultural sectors. Without reliable water sources and damaged by extreme summer temperatures, the agricultural regions of the American Great Plains will see good growing conditions move further and further north.

In the polar regions, severe scenarios will likely bring about wholly unprecedented climates, with fall seasonal temperatures as high as 13°C above pre-industrial levels projected by 2100.[225] These temperatures in high-emissions scenarios mean that the Arctic region could be free of ice well into September by the end of the century.[226] Changing conditions will make regions like the Arctic increasingly viable for commercial activity, leading to increased competition for the sea routes and resources available. As countries like Russia bolster their military presence in the Arctic, ice-free routes could push belligerent governments to act outside of cooperative institutions on both poles

The Center for Climate and Security, an institute of The Council on Strategic Risks
1025 Connecticut Ave., NW · Suite 1000 · Washington, DC 20036
www.climateandsecurity.org - www.councilonstrategicrisks.org

to unilaterally stake and protect their claims. Tensions among North American countries could also strain, as Canada pushes its existing claims on the Northwest Passage, and indigenous settlements face harsh impacts on ecosystems and fish stocks in the Northern Atlantic.

As these harsh climate effects overwhelm communities reliant on stable weather and resources, the governments of North America may be increasingly unable to respond to mounting disasters and help communities rebuild. As the United States has experienced following the weather events of 2017, damage costs compound quickly and legislative delays can hold resources from communities in need of aid and response.[227] With extremes increasing across all regions, even wealthy governments and trained security services of the U.S. and Canada will find it difficult to provide overlapping responses, and unstable local governance institutions across the continent could collapse under the strain.

Recent cases suggest that citizens with unmet needs following natural disasters resent unresponsive government institutions going forward, and these negative sentiments could shape public life over the next century.[228] [229] If Northern American countries are to manage severe climate change, alongside expected increases in migration flows, food price increases, trade shocks, and health impacts influenced by climate events across the world, public policy and funding on levels never seen before would be required to prepare this relatively wealthy continent to adapt to the extremes in store.

RISKS TO SECURITY INFRASTRUCTURE

The U.S. military has undertaken several extensive reviews of its homeland military installations and infrastructure, identifying the destructive risks that climate change will pose to mission readiness. On its bases, the Department of Defense sees sea level rise, drought, dust, fire, and heat negatively impacting its infrastructure and training ranges.[230] The most evident example is the infrastructure at Hampton Roads which, low-lying along the Atlantic Ocean, faces serious risks to military operations, readiness, and strategy."[231]

Military aircraft utility itself is negatively impacted, with decreased performance on hot and humid days.[232] In the complicated environment of the Arctic, new ice-breaking and search-and-rescue infrastructure is required to protect security and commercial interests from dangerous events.[233]

Civilian infrastructure, on which security operations also depend, is increasingly insecure. Electric grids and transportation lines are vulnerable to high winds, storms, fires, floods, and heat, causing new inefficiencies in logistical chains that impede the military's ability to respond.[234] Military forces are also being called on more than ever to perform rescue and humanitarian response to climate-induced disasters on their own soil, depleting budgets, readiness, and training time. When domestic critical infrastructure like agricultural and water systems are increasingly stressed, both the civilian and military communities dependent on them are weakened in turn.

RISKS TO SECURITY INSTITUTIONS

The stability of U.S. security institutions rests not only on the readiness of its military, but also on the stability of its communities and political institutions. As climate risks increase across the North American continent, this strength and safety becomes more difficult to uphold.

Climate threats in neighboring regions such as SOUTHCOM will drive migrants further north, potentially sparking increased political tensions over U.S. borders. Impacts of weakened social support systems and strengthened transnational crime networks in Central America and the Caribbean also can harm the U.S. homeland.[235] These risks communicated through incendiary political rhetoric, to an increasingly concerned public, can engender nationalist, isolationist, anti-democratic and authoritarian responses. These could limit future American responses to contain crises outside its border, just as those insecurities increasingly threaten to spill over into U.S. territory.

Relationships with historic allies are newly tested in the face of climate impacts. Within institutions from the Arctic Council and to the U.S.-Mexico-Canada Agreement (USMCA), climate stressors are creating new tensions among formerly friendly neighbors.[236] Undermining security agreements across the Atlantic and Pacific with negative rhetoric or decreasing financial commitments could also weaken the posture of institutions against great power adversaries.

With homeland populations living in more vulnerable conditions, threatened by floods, storms, fires, and droughts, the American public is less secure financially and physically.[237] Increasing political divisions across parties and locations, including a widening rural-urban divide, make policymaking across these communities more difficult, and crisis response slower and weaker. Widening economic and health inequalities across social spheres encourage populist rhetoric and mistrust in existing government institutions, further undermining their ability to address the climate situation in a concerted manner.

WILL OUR PENTAGON FINALLY COME CLEAN ABOUT UFOS?

The Pentagon has been claiming to have disbanded a once-covert program to investigate unidentified flying objects. But a Senate committee budget report released in July 2020 said there was indeed an Unidentified Aerial Phenomenon Task Force to "standardize collection and reporting" on sightings. The Office of Naval Intelligence is in charge of studying these close encounters with military pilots.

Luis Elizondo, who used to run the task force before retiring in 2017, told the *New York Times* he's convinced "that objects of undetermined origin have crashed on earth with materials retrieved for study." Harry Reid, who used to be the Senate Majority Leader, said he also became convinced after looking into this "that there were actual materials that the government and the private sector had in their possession" from crashed alien crafts.

The documents presented here are a Defense Department assessment of a 2004 incident called "Tic-Tac," and a list of thirty-eight strange projects that they're funding in the Advanced Aerospace Threat and Identification Program.

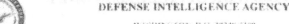

UNCLASSIFIED//FOR OFFICIAL USE ONLY

DEFENSE INTELLIGENCE AGENCY

WASHINGTON, D.C. 20340-5100

U-18-0001/OCC1

JAN 09 2018

The Honorable John McCain
Chairman
The Honorable Jack Reed
Ranking Member
Committee on Armed Services
United States Senate
228 Russell Senate Office Building
Washington, DC 20510

Dear Chairman McCain and Ranking Member Reed,

(U//FOUO) Based on interest from your staff regarding the Defense Intelligence Agency (DIA)'s role in the Advanced Aerospace Threat and Identification Program (AATIP) please find attached a list of all products produced under the AATIP contract for DIA to publish. The purpose of AATIP was to investigate foreign advanced aerospace weapon threats from the present out to the next 40 years.

(U//FOUO) There are 38 reports associated with DIA's involvement in the program documented in the list. All are UNCLASSIFIED//FOR OFFICIAL USE ONLY except for attachment 37 which is a SECRET//NOFORN version of attachment 38 *State of the Art and Evolution of High Energy Laser Weapons.* All are available for Congressional staff access on the Capitol Network (CapNet) except for attachments 12 and 15, respectively titled *Field Effects on Biological Tissues* and *An Introduction to the Statistical Drake Equation.* We are also happy to provide them directly upon request.

(U) Should you have any questions, please contact my Congressional Operations Lead, (b)(6) (b)(6)

Sincerely,

Christine Kapnisi
Chief
DIA Congressional Relations Division

UNCLASSIFIED//FOR OFFICIAL USE ONLY

(U) List of Attachments

1. *Inertial Electrostatic Confinement Fusion*, Dr. George Miley, Univ. Of Illinois (Product is classified UNCLASSIFIED//FOR OFFICIAL USE ONLY)

2. *Advanced Nuclear Propulsion for Manned Deep Space Missions*, Dr. F. Winterberg, Univ. of Nevada – Reno (Product is classified UNCLASSIFIED//FOR OFFICIAL USE ONLY)

3. *Pulsed High-Power Microwave Technology*, Dr. James Wells, JW Enterprises (Product is classified UNCLASSIFIED//FOR OFFICIAL USE ONLY)

4. *Space Access*, Dr. P. Czysz, HyperTech (Product is classified UNCLASSIFIED//FOR OFFICIAL USE ONLY)

5. *Advanced Space Propulsion Based on Vacuum (Spacetime Metric) Engineering*, Dr. Hal Puthoff, EarthTech International (Product is classified UNCLASSIFIED//FOR OFFICIAL USE ONLY)

6. *BioSensors and BioMEMS*, Dr. Bruce Towe, Univ. of Arizona (Product is classified UNCLASSIFIED//FOR OFFICIAL USE ONLY)

7. *Invisibility Cloaking*, Dr. Ulf Leonhardt, Univ. of St. Andrews (Product is classified UNCLASSIFIED//FOR OFFICIAL USE ONLY)

8. *Traversable Wormholes, Stargates, and Negative Energy*, Dr. Eric Davis, EarthTech International (Product is classified UNCLASSIFIED//FOR OFFICIAL USE ONLY)

9. *High-Frequency Gravitational Wave Communications*, Dr. Robert Baker, GravWave (Product is classified UNCLASSIFIED//FOR OFFICIAL USE ONLY)

10. *Role of Superconductors in Gravity Research*, Dr. George Hathaway, Hathaway Consulting (Product is classified UNCLASSIFIED//FOR OFFICIAL USE ONLY)

11. *Antigravity for Aerospace Applications*, Dr. Eric Davis, EarthTech International (Product is classified UNCLASSIFIED//FOR OFFICIAL USE ONLY)

12. *Field Effects on Biological Tissues*, Dr. Kit Green, Wayne State Univ. (Product is classified UNCLASSIFIED//FOR OFFICIAL USE ONLY)

13. *Positron Aerospace Propulsion*, Dr. Gerald Smith, Positronics Research (Product is classified UNCLASSIFIED//FOR OFFICIAL USE ONLY)

UNCLASSIFIED//FOR OFFICIAL USE ONLY

14. *Concepts for Extracting Energy from the Quantum Vacuum*, Dr. Eric Davis, EarthTech International (Product is classified UNCLASSIFIED//FOR OFFICIAL USE ONLY)

15. *An Introduction to the Statistical Drake Equation*, Dr. Claudio Maccone, International Academy of Astronautics (Product is classified UNCLASSIFIED//FOR OFFICIAL USE ONLY)

16. *Maverick Inventor Versus Corporate Inventor*, Dr. George Hathaway, Hathaway Consulting (Product is classified UNCLASSIFIED//FOR OFFICIAL USE ONLY)

17. *Biomaterials*, Dr. Bruce Towe, Univ. of Arizona (Product is classified UNCLASSIFIED//FOR OFFICIAL USE ONLY)

18. *Metamaterials for Aerospace Applications*, Dr. G. Shvets, Univ. of Texas – Austin (Product is classified UNCLASSIFIED//FOR OFFICIAL USE ONLY)

19. *Warp Drive, Dark Energy, and the Manipulation of Extra Dimensions*, Dr. R. Obousy, Obousy Consultants (Product is classified UNCLASSIFIED//FOR OFFICIAL USE ONLY)

20. *Technological Approaches to Controlling External Devices in the Absence of Limb-Operated Interfaces*, Dr. R. Genik, Wayne State Univ. (Product is classified UNCLASSIFIED//FOR OFFICIAL USE ONLY)

21. *Materials for Advanced Aerospace Platforms*, Dr. J. Williams, Ohio State Univ. (Product is classified UNCLASSIFIED//FOR OFFICIAL USE ONLY)

22. *Metallic Glasses*, Dr. T. Hufnagel, John Hopkins Univ. (Product is classified UNCLASSIFIED//FOR OFFICIAL USE ONLY)

23. *Aerospace Applications of Programmable Matter*, Dr. W. McCarthy, Programmable Matter Corporation (Product is classified UNCLASSIFIED//FOR OFFICIAL USE ONLY)

24. *Metallic Spintronics*, Dr. M. Tsoi, Univ. of Texas - Austin (Product is classified UNCLASSIFIED//FOR OFFICIAL USE ONLY)

25. *Space-Communication Implications of Quantum Entanglement and Nonlocality*, Dr. J. Cramer, Univ. of Washington (Product is classified UNCLASSIFIED//FOR OFFICIAL USE ONLY)

UNCLASSIFIED//FOR OFFICIAL USE ONLY

~~UNCLASSIFIED//FOR OFFICIAL USE ONLY~~

26. *Aneutronic Fusion Propulsion I*, Dr. V. Teofilo, Lockheed Martin (Product is classified UNCLASSIFIED//FOR OFFICIAL USE ONLY)

27. *Cockpits in the Era of Breakthrough Flight*, Dr. G. Millis, Tau Zero (Product is classified UNCLASSIFIED//FOR OFFICIAL USE ONLY)

28. *Cognitive Limits on Simultaneous Control of Multiple Unmanned Spacecraft*, Dr. R.Genik, Wayne State Univ. (Product is classified UNCLASSIFIED//FOR OFFICIAL USE ONLY)

29. *Detection and High Resolution Tracking of Vehicles at Hypersonic Velocities*, Dr. W. Culbreth, Univ. of Nevada – Las Vegas (Product is classified UNCLASSIFIED//FOR OFFICIAL USE ONLY)

30. *Aneutronic Fusion Propulsion II*, Dr. W. Culbreth, Univ. Of Nevada – Las Vegas (Product is classified UNCLASSIFIED//FOR OFFICIAL USE ONLY)

31. *Laser Lightcraft Nanosatellites*, Dr. E. Davis, EarthTech International (Product is classified UNCLASSIFIED//FOR OFFICIAL USE ONLY)

32. *Magnetohydrodynamics (MHD) Air Breathing Propulsion and Power for Aerospace Applications*, Dr. S. Macheret, Lockheed Martin (Product is classified UNCLASSIFIED//FOR OFFICIAL USE ONLY)

33. *Quantum Computing and Utilizing Organic Molecules in Automation Technology*, Dr. R. Genik, Wayne State Univ. (Product is classified UNCLASSIFIED//FOR OFFICIAL USE ONLY)

34. *Quantum Tomography of Negative Energy States in the Vacuum*, Dr. E. Davis, EarthTech International (Product is classified UNCLASSIFIED//FOR OFFICIAL USE ONLY)

35. *Ultracapacitors as Energy and Power Storage Devices*, Dr. J. Golightly, Lockheed Martin (Product is classified UNCLASSIFIED//FOR OFFICIAL USE ONLY)

36. *Negative Mass Propulsion*, Dr. F. Winterberg, Univ. of Nevada – Reno (Product is classified UNCLASSIFIED//FOR OFFICIAL USE ONLY)

37. *State of the Art and Evolution of High Energy Laser Weapons*, J. Albertine, Directed Technologies (Product is classified ~~SECRET//NOFORN~~)

38. *State of the Art and Evolution of High Energy Laser Weapons*, J. Albertine, Directed Technologies (Product is classified UNCLASSIFIED//FOR OFFICIAL USE ONLY)

Executive Summary

During the period of approximately 10-16 November 2004, the Nimitz Carrier Strike Group (CSG) was operating off the western coast of the United States in preparation for their deployment to the Arabian Sea. The USS Princeton on several occasions detected multiple Anomalous Aerial Vehicles (AAVs) operating in and around the vicinity of the CSG. The AAVs would descend "very rapidly" from approximately 60,000 feet down to approximately 50 feet in a matter of seconds. They would then hover or stay stationary on the radar for a short time and depart at high velocities and turn rates. On 14 November after again detecting the AAV, the USS Princeton took the opportunity of having a flight of two F/A-18Fs returning from a training mission to further investigate the AAV. The USS Princeton took over control of the F/A-18s from the E-2C Airborne Early Warning aircraft and vectored in the F/A-18s for intercept leading to visual contact approximately one mile away from the AAV, which was reported to be "an elongated egg or a 'Tic Tac' shape with a discernable midline horizontal axis". It was "solid white, smooth, with no edges. It was "uniformly colored with no nacelles, pylons, or wings." It was approximately 46 feet in length. The F/A-18Fs radar could not obtain a 'lock' on the AAV; however it could be tracked while stationary and at slower speeds with the Forward Looking Infrared (FLIR). The AAV did take evasive actions upon intercept by the F/A-18 demonstrating an advanced acceleration (G), aerodynamic, and propulsion capability. The AAV did not take any offensive action against the CSG; however, given its ability to operate unchallenged in close vicinity to the CSG it demonstrated the potential to conduct undetected reconnaissance leaving the CSG with a limited ability to detect, track, and/or engage the AAV.

Key Assessments

- The Anomalous Aerial Vehicle (AAV) was no known aircraft or air vehicle currently in the inventory of the United States or any foreign nation.
- The AAV exhibited advanced low observable characteristics at multiple radar bands rendering US radar based engagement capabilities ineffective.
- The AAV exhibited advanced aerodynamic performance with no visible control surfaces and no visible means to generate lift.
- The AAV exhibited advanced propulsion capability by demonstrating the ability to remain stationary with little to no variation in altitude transitioning to horizontal and/or vertical velocities far greater than any known aerial vehicle with little to no visible signature.
- The AAV possibly demonstrated the ability to 'cloak' or become invisible to the human eye or human observation.
- The AAV possibly demonstrated a highly advanced capability to operate undersea completely undetectable by our most advanced sensors.

WHY YOU NEED TO READ THIS BOOK

"There is little value in insuring the survival of our nation if our traditions do not survive with it. And there is very grave danger that an announced need for increased security will be seized upon by those anxious to expand its meaning to the very limits of official censorship and concealment."

—JOHN F. KENNEDY

This book is titled *63 Documents the Government Doesn't Want You to Read*, lest we forget that 1963 was the year that claimed the life of our 35th president. The conspiracy that killed JFK, and the cover-up that followed, is the forerunner for a lot of what you're going to read about in these pages. In fact, the idea behind this book came out of writing my last one, *American*

Conspiracies. There I presented a close look at whether or not our historical record reflects what really went on, based on facts that most of the media have chosen to ignore—from the Kennedy assassination through the tragedy of September 11th and the debacle on Wall Street. In poring through numerous documents, many of them

available through the Freedom of Information Act (FOIA), I came to realize the importance of the public's right to know. And I decided to see what new picture might be revealed if you laid out certain documents that the powers that be would just as soon stay buried.

Everything in this book is in the public domain and, for the most part, downloadable from the Internet. I'm not breaking any laws by putting these documents in book form, although some of them were classified "secret" until WikiLeaks published them. I'll get to my view on WikiLeaks in a moment, but let me begin by saying how concerned I am that we're moving rapidly in the direction President Kennedy tried to warn us about.

According to a recent article in the *Washington Post*, there are now 854,000 American citizens with top secret clearances. The number of new secrets rose 75 percent between 1996 and 2009, and the number of documents using those secrets went from 5.6 million in 1996 to 54.6 million last year. There are an astounding 16 million documents being classified top secret by our government every year! Today, pretty much everything the government *does* is presumed secret. Isn't it time we asked ourselves whether this is really necessary for the conduct of foreign affairs or the internal operation of governments? Doesn't secrecy actually protect the favored classes and allow them to continue to help themselves at the expense of the rest of us? Isn't this a cancer growing on democracy?

After Barack Obama won the 2008 presidential election, I was heartened to see him issue an Open Government Initiative on his first full day in office. "I firmly believe what Justice Louis Brandeis once said, that sunlight is the best disinfectant," Obama said, "and I know that restoring transparency is not only the surest way to achieve results, but also to earn back the trust in government without which we cannot deliver changes the American people sent us here to make." After eight years of Bush and Cheney's secretive and deceitful ways, that sounded like a welcome relief. Obama ordered all federal agencies to "adopt a presumption in favor" of FOIA requests and so laid the groundwork to eventually release reams of previously withheld government information on the Internet.

Well, so far it hasn't turned out the way Obama set forth. An audit released in March 2010 by the nonprofit National Security Archive found that less than one-third of ninety federal agencies that process FOIA requests had changed their practices in any significant way. A few departments—Agriculture, Justice, Office of Management and Budget, and the Small Business Administration—got high marks for progress. But the State Department, Treasury, Transportation, and NASA had fulfilled fewer requests and denied more in the same time period. "Most agencies had yet to walk the walk," said the Archive's director Tom Blanton.

Things went downhill from there. In June 2010, the *New York Times* carried a page-one story detailing how Obama's administration was even more aggressive than Bush's in looking to punish people who leaked information to the media. In the course of his first seventeen months as president, Obama had already surpassed *every* previous president in going after prosecutions of leakers. Thomas A. Drake, a National Security Agency employee who'd gone to the *Baltimore Sun* as a last resort because he knew that government eavesdroppers were squandering hundreds of millions of taxpayer dollars on failed programs, is today facing years in prison on ten felony charges including mishandling of classified information. An FBI translator received a twenty-month sentence for turning over some classified documents to a blogger. A former CIA officer, Jeffrey Sterling, has been indicted for unauthorized disclosure of national defense information. And the Pentagon arrested Bradley Manning, the twenty-two-year-old Army intelligence analyst, who for openers had passed along to WikiLeaks the shocking video footage of a U.S. military chopper gunning down Baghdad civilians.

In September 2010, the Obama Justice Department cited the so-called "state secrets doctrine" in successfully getting a federal judge to throw out a lawsuit on "extraordinary rendition" (a phrase that really means we send suspected terrorists to other countries to get held and tortured). In fact, Attorney General Eric Holder was hell-bent on upholding the Bush administration's claims in two major cases involving illegal detention and torture.

Also in September, the Pentagon spent $47,300 of taxpayer dollars to buy up and destroy all 10,000 copies of the first printing of *Operation Dark Heart*, a memoir about Afghanistan by ex-Defense Intelligence Agency (DIA) officer Anthony A. Shaffer. We first interviewed Lt. Colonel Shaffer for *American Conspiracies* because his outfit (Able Danger) had identified Mohammed Atta as a terrorist threat long before he became the supposed lead hijacker on 9/11.

With *Operation Dark Heart*, publishing executives and intelligence outfits couldn't remember another instance where a government agency set out to get rid of a book that was already printed. Some months earlier, the Army reviewers who'd asked for and received some changes and redactions said they had "no objection on legal or operational security grounds" to the final version. But when the DIA saw the manuscript and showed it around to some other spy operations, they came up with 200-plus passages that might cause "serious damage to national security." By that time, several dozen copies of the book had already gone out to reviewers and online booksellers. (Those went on sale on eBay for between $1,995 and $4,995.)

So *Operation Dark Heart* was hastily reprinted with a number of paragraphs blanked out and, guess what, it became a best seller. Here are a few of the things that got canned, which the *New York Times* first pointed out. Everybody's known for years that the nickname for the NSA headquarters at Fort Meade is "the Fort." Censor that one! Another big secret—the CIA training facility is located at Camp Peary, Virginia. You can find that on Wikipedia but not anymore in this book! And did you know that SIGINT stands for "Signals Intelligence?" You don't see that anymore in *Operation Dark Heart*. (I can't wait for the censors to pull my book from the shelves for revealing all this.) Oh, and they removed a blurb from a former DIA director who called Shaffer's "one terrific book." Shaffer has now gone to court looking to have the book's complete text restored when the paperback comes out.

To Obama's credit, early in November 2010 he issued an Executive Order establishing a program to manage unclassified information that rescinded a Bush-era order designed to keep still more documents away from public scrutiny by putting new labels on them ("For Official Use Only" and "Sensitive But Unclassified.")

But soon thereafter came WikiLeaks' first releases of a claimed trove of 251,287 secret State Department cables. This followed the group's disclosures

earlier last year of 390,136 classified documents about the Iraq War and 76,607 documents about Afghanistan. As everybody knows, the politicians and the media commentators went ballistic over the cables being in the public domain—even though the *New York Times*, among others, was running front-page stories every day about their contents.

Julian Assange, the founder of WikiLeaks, was for a moment our biggest bogeyman since Osama. Sarah Palin says he's "an anti-American operative with blood on his hands" who should be pursued "with the same urgency we pursue al Qaeda and Taliban leaders." She stopped short of saying he should be hunted down like the caribou she shoots in Alaska. Hillary Clinton calls what he's done "an attack on the international community." (I've never known Palin and Clinton to be this cozy in the same bed, so to speak.) Mike Huckabee called for the execution of whoever leaked the cables to WikiLeaks. Newt Gingrich referred to Assange as an "enemy combatant." Joe Biden described him as "closer to being a hi-tech terrorist" than a whistleblower, and some liberal democrats would like to see Assange sent to prison for life. He's also been labeled an old-fashioned anarchist, mastermind of a criminal enterprise and, at best, a control freak and a megalomaniac.

This smacks of worse than McCarthyism—we're in a lynch-mob moment, folks. Didn't Thomas Jefferson say that "information is the currency of democracy" and that, if he had to choose between government and a free press, he'd take the latter? Ron Paul is one of the only folks to have spoken up on Assange's behalf. Paul made quite a statement on the floor of the House, when he asked his colleagues what had caused more deaths—"lying us into war or the release of the WikiLeaks papers?" He added, "What we need is more WikiLeaks….In a free society, we're supposed to know the truth. In a society where truth becomes treason, then we're in big trouble. And now, people who are revealing the truth are getting into trouble for it."

Paul's point is important. Nobody has died as a result of WikiLeaks' disclosures, but maybe we've forgotten that the whole Iraq War was based on fake evidence manufactured by the Bush-Cheney White House and the Brits, resulting in 4,430 American troops dead and about 32,000 wounded as of early December 2010. In Afghanistan, the toll is climbing fast—close to 1,500 Americans dead and almost 10,000 wounded. This doesn't take into account, of course, the hundreds of thousands of civilian casualties. Do you think it's possible, as one Internet columnist has written, that Julian Assange is the scapegoat for arrogant American officials who'd rather point the finger at someone else than admit the blood on their own hands?

Personally, I think Julian Assange is a hero. It's a classic case of going after the messenger. Our diplomats get caught writing derogatory remarks and descriptions of foreign leaders, then turn around and accuse WikiLeaks of putting our country in danger. WikiLeaks is exposing our government officials for the frauds that they are. They also show us how governments work together to lie to their citizens when they are waging war.

Here are a few things we've learned from WikiLeaks' document releases that we didn't know before: The CIA has a secret army of 3,000 in Afghanistan, where the U.S. Ambassador in Kabul says there's no way to fix corruption because our ally is the one that's corrupt (one Afghan minister was caught carrying $52 million out of the country). In Iraq, there are another 15,000 civilian casualties that haven't been brought into the light, and our troops were instructed not to look into torture tactics that our Iraqi allies were using. U.S. Special Operations forces are in Pakistan without any public knowledge, and our Pakistani "allies" are the main protectors of the Taliban in Afghanistan!

I mean, let's face it: WikiLeaks exists because the mainstream media haven't done their job. Instead of holding government accountable as the "fourth branch" the founders intended, I guess the corporate media's role today is to protect the government from embassassment. Assange has pioneered "scientific journalism" (his term)—a news story is accompanied by the document it's based upon and the reader can make up his own mind. WikiLeaks' small team of reporters has unveiled more suppressed information than the rest of the world press combined!

Assange is the *publisher*, not the one who revealed the "classified information." That's apparently Private Bradley Manning, who somehow found a security loophole and now is being held in solitary confinement at our Quantico, Virginia base facing up to fifty-two years in prison. Are we surprised that the United Nations' special investigator on torture is looking into whether Manning has been mistreated in custody? As for Assange, how our government wants to try him under the Espionage Act of 1917 is beyond me. Come on, he's an Australian citizen and his Internet domain is in Switzerland. (By the way, he also received the Sam Adams Award for Integrity in 2010, and the Amnesty International Media Award in 2009.)

And what about these cyberspace sabotage attacks against WikiLeaks that are being carried out across national borders by our government? As far as I can determine, these are illegal under both U.S. law and international treaties. Meantime, it blows my mind that students at Columbia and Boston University and probably other institutions of "higher learning" are being warned not to read any of these documents if they want to get a government job in the future. The Office of Management and Budget sent out a memo that forbids unauthorized federal employees and contractors from accessing WikiLeaks. The Library of Congress has blocked visitors to its computer system from doing the same. The Air Force started blocking its personnel from using work computers to look at the websites of the *New York Times* and other publications that had posted the cables. Instead, a page came up that said: "ACCESS DENIED. Internet Usage is Logged & Monitored." Over in Iraq, our troops who'd like to even read *articles* about all this get a "redirect" notice on their government network telling them they're on the verge of breaking the law. And a lot of these same soldiers have security clearances that would have allowed them to see the cables *before* they were leaked.

Given the close ties between the government and large corporations, I can't say I'm surprised that Amazon, PayPal, Mastercard, Visa, and Bank of America took action to make sure that WikiLeaks could no longer receive any money through their channels. And I can't say I'm upset that a group of young "hacktavists" calling themselves Anonymous have taken retaliatory action against some of those same companies. They call it Operation Payback. "Websites that are bowing down to government pressure have become targets," a fellow named Coldblood posted. "As an organization we have always taken a strong stance on censorship and freedom of expression on the internet and come out against those who seek to destroy it by any means. We feel that WikiLeaks has become more than just about leaking of documents, it has become a war ground, the people vs. the government."

More than 500 "mirror sites" now possess all the cables, and Assange has said we ain't seen nothin' yet if he meets an untimely demise. As I write this a couple of weeks before the New Year in 2011, he's living in a friend's mansion in England and fighting extradition charges. I'm sure a whole lot more will have developed by the time this book is published. I say let the chips fall where they may as WikiLeaks puts the truth out there. If our State Department is asking diplomats to steal personal information from UN officials and human rights groups, in violation of international laws, then shouldn't the world know about it and demand corrective action? Maybe if they know they're potentially going to be exposed, the powers that hide behind a cloak of secrecy will think twice before they plot the next Big Lie.

I agree with Daniel Ellsberg, the former military analyst who leaked the Pentagon Papers during the Vietnam War. He faced charges, too, back in 1971, but they were thrown out by a judge. He's called Private Manning a "brother" who committed "a very admirable act" if he's the one who provided the documents to WikiLeaks. "To call them terrorists is not only mistaken, it's absurd," Ellsberg said.

The book you're about to read is undertaken in the same spirit. I've divided the book into five parts, starting out first to show links between deeds our government perpetrated in the past and what's going on today. If you don't know your own history, you're doomed to repeat it. Part One focuses on postwar deceptions, revealing some pretty scandalous behavior, including:

- The CIA's secret assassination manual and experiments to control human behavior with hypnosis, drugs, and other methods.
- The military's Operation Northwoods, a chilling attempt by the Joint Chiefs of Staff to stage a terror attack on our own citizens and make it look like Cuba was behind it—using a hijacked airliner, no less!
- After President Kennedy was trying to get our troops out of Vietnam, the military faked the Gulf of Tonkin attacks in order to expand the war.
- Our chemical and biological warfare capability back in 1969, leading you to wonder about the real origin of things like AIDS and lyme disease.

Part Two delves into a series of government, military, and corporate secrets, opening with excerpts from two recent reports on how our military and intelligence outfits put Nazi war criminals to work after World War Two. From there, you'll see some eye-opening documents, including:

- The CIA's "Propaganda Notes" designed to shore up the Warren Commission's lone-gunman conclusion.
- How Oliver North collaborated with Panama's drug-running dictator Manuel Noriega.
- What America knew, and ignored, about the genocide happening in Rwanda in the mid-1990s.
- How we still turn a blind eye to Gulf War Illness and our veterans.
- The frightening background for our military to intervene in domestic affairs, set up "emergency relocation facilities" for our citizens, and establish a Civilian Inmate Labor Program.
- How failed inspections and ignored science are impacting our food supply and our bees, while we push to promote Monsanto's biotech agenda.
- What our military really knows about the dangers of climate change.
- How companies like Koch Industries promote their political agendas at the expense of the rest of us.

Part Three I've called *Shady White Houses*, starting with "Tricky Dick" Nixon and his astounding plan to bring peace to Vietnam by pretending to nuke the Soviet Union! You'll also learn about:

- How the Bush White House stole the presidential elections in 2000 and again in 2004.
- The Obama State Department's call for our own diplomats to spy on the United Nations.
- Whether "cybersecurity" could mean the end of the Internet as we know it.

Part Four focuses in on a subject I've explored a great deal in recent years, and that's whether we've been told the truth about the terrible events of September 11, 2001.

- A think tank called the Project for a New American Century anticipating "a new Pearl Harbor" to promote its agenda for "Rebuilding America's Defenses."
- Clear warnings the Bush administration ignored that something was coming.
- The "Stand Down" order that kept our military from responding on 9/11.
- Evidence that Building 7 was taken down by a controlled demolition.
- The role of insider stock trading in advance of 9/11.

And finally, Part Five examines the so-called "war on terror" and the terrible price we're paying in terms of our liberties and the lives being lost in Iraq and Afghanistan. You'll first read excerpts from a long memo by Bush's Justice Department that subverts the Constitution by shredding a number of civil rights, followed by Bush's justification for America's torture of "unlawful combatants."

- The "Media Ground Rules" that keep the truth hidden at Guantanamo.
- The torture techniques, and medical experiments, being conducted there and the paper trail on the CIA's destruction of ninety-two torture videos.
- Decapitation of a detainee in Iraq, by our own troops!
- How the CIA "spins" the war in Afghanistan, and the fact that drugs are fueling that country's economy.
- A report by the Rand Corporation showing that military force has never worked in combating terrorism.

Following the 63 documents, you'll find an epilogue of Internet resources to use in your own pursuit of the truth about what's going on behind the scenes.

Here's what should concern us all: if you look back at the U.S. Patriot Act that Congress passed almost unanimously in the wake of 9/11, the Bill of Rights was already in peril. Let me offer a brief outline of how things changed:

The First Amendment is about freedom of speech, freedom of the press, and the right to assemble. The Patriot Act says that the government is free to monitor religious and political institutions without any suspicion of criminal activity. The government can also prosecute librarians or the keepers of any other records (including journalists) related to a "terror investigation."

The Fourth Amendment speaks to our right to be secure "against unreasonable searches and seizures." The Patriot Act says the government can search and seize Americans' papers and effects without probable cause.

The Sixth Amendment entitles anyone accused of a crime to "a speedy and public trial, by an impartial jury." The Patriot Act says the government can jail Americans indefinitely without a trial.

The Sixth Amendment says an accused person has "compulsory process for obtaining witnesses in his favor, and to have the assistance of counsel for his defense." The Patriot Act says the government can monitor conversations between attorneys and clients in federal prisons and even deny lawyers to Americans accused of crimes.

The Sixth Amendment also says an accused criminal must "be confronted with the witnesses against him." The Patriot Act says Americans can be jailed without even being charged, let alone face any witnesses.

What troubles me more than anything is how Congress can simply vote to supersede the Constitution. They're not allowed to do that, to vote in new rules arbitrarily. Changing the Constitution requires you to go through many hoops. How can we allow this kind of unprecedented change to happen? Now in response to WikiLeaks, Congress is considering a so-called Shield Bill, which would make it a crime for anybody to "knowingly and willfully" disseminate classified information "in any manner prejudicial to the safety or interest of the United

States." That includes not just the leaker, but anybody who publishes it! First Amendment, so long!

At the same time, it's recently been reported that our government is building up a huge domestic spying network to collect information on us all, involving local police, state and military authorities feeding information into a database on people who've never been accused of wrongdoing. Homeland Security has given billions of dollars in grants to state governments since 9/11, and there are now more than 4,000 organizations in the domestic apparatus. The FBI keeps the ultimate file, with profiles on tens of thousands of Americans reported to be "acting suspiciously." (I'm sure I'm one of them.) Also the technologies we've developed for the Iraq and Afghanistan wars are now being used by law enforcement agencies at home—handheld fingerprint scanners, biometric data devices, unmanned aircraft monitoring our borders with Mexico and Canada. And there are now 440,000 people on the goverment's secret terrorist watch list, with no recourse to petition to get yourself taken off it or even find out if you're listed on it.

In other words, we the taxpayers are funding our own government to keep tabs on what we do! This is outrageous, but it's been a long time coming. Our tax dollars have paid for mind control experiments and assassination attempts and fake attacks to draw us into war. Our tax dollars have funded drug runners and "extraordinary rendition" of detainees. And they've *not* been used in places where they should be going—like to help our veterans cope with Gulf War Syndrome and to keep the nation of Rwanda from mass genocide. What right does the government have to abuse *our money* like that? This is diabolical!

I've put together this book because it's become crystal clear that our democracy has been undermined from within and it's been going on for a long time. We the people have got to wake up and start demanding accountability! Let's never forget the words of Patrick Henry: "The liberties of a people never were, nor ever will be, secure, when the transactions of their rulers may be concealed from them."

PART ONE

OUR SCANDALOUS POSTWAR HISTORY

33 USA

The Vietnam War

ASSASSINATIONS

The CIA's Secret Assassination Manual

What follows are excerpts from a nineteen-page CIA document that was prepared as part of a coup against the Guatemalan government in 1954 and declassified in 1997. Maybe they should change the name to the CIA's "secret-first degree murder manual." How is that we are allowed to kill other people if we're not in a declared war with them? Clearly this is a premeditated conspiracy involving more than one person. My big question is, who makes the call on this? To arbitrarily go out in the world and kill someone without their being charged with a crime!

The thought of taking out another country's leadership is so despicable, it makes me ashamed that I'm an American. But it later was revealed that, during the Cold War, the CIA plotted against eight foreign leaders, and five of them died violent deaths. The CIA's "Executive Action" arm was involved for years in planning with the Mob and others to murder Fidel Castro.

Are we all to believe this is simply James Bond, where agents can arbitrarily knock off people and walk away? They actually had a manual that promotes throwing people from high buildings, with "plausible denial"! One paragraph in particular gives me pause, when I think back to what happened in Dallas on November 22, 1963. "Public figures or guarded officials may be killed with great reliability and some safety if a firing point can be established prior to an official occasion," the manual instructed.

Here is the original document.

A STUDY OF ASSASSINATION

DEFINITION

Assassination is a term thought to be derived from "Hashish", a drug similar to marijuana, said to have been used by Hassan-Ban-Sabah to induce motivation in his followers, who were assigned to carry out political and other murders, usually at the cost of their lives.

It is here used to describe the planned killing of a person who is not under the legal jurisdiction of the killer, who is not physically in the hands of the killer, who has been selected by a resistance organization for death, and whose death provides positive advantages to that organization.

EMPLOYMENT

Assassination is an extreme measure not normally used in clandestine operations. It should be assumed that it will never be ordered or authorized by any U. S. Headquarters, though the latter may in rare instances agree to its execution by members of an associated foreign service. This reticence is partly due to the necessity for committing communications to paper. No assassination instructions should ever be written or recorded. Consequently, the decision to employ this technique must nearly always be reached in the field, at the area where the act will take place. Decision and instructions should be confined to an absolute minimum of persons. Ideally, only one person will be involved. No report may be made, but usually the act will be properly covered by normal news services, whose output is available to all concerned.

1.   Manual.

It is possible to kill a man with the bare hands, but very few are skillful enough to do it well. Even a highly trained Judo expert will hesitate to risk killing by hand unless he has absolutely no alternative. However, the simplest local tools are often much the most efficient means of assassination. A hammer, axe, wrench, screw driver, fire poker, kitchen knife, lamp stand, or anything hard, heavy and handy will suffice. A length of rope or wire or a belt will do if the assassin is strong and agile. All such improvised weapons have the important advantage of availability and apparent innocence. The obviously lethal machine gun failed to kill Trotsky where an item of sporting goods succeeded.

In all safe cases where the assassin may be subject to search, either before or after the act, specialized weapons should not be used. Even in the last cases, the assassin may accidentally be searched before the act and should not carry an incriminating device if any sort of lethal weapon can be improvised at or near the site. If the assassin normally carries weapons because of the nature of his job, it may still be desirable to improvise and implement at the scene to avoid disclosure of his identity.

Here is a transcript of the most frightening excerpts:

CLASSIFICATIONS

The techniques employed will vary according to whether the subject is unaware of his danger, aware but unguarded, or guarded. They will also be affected by whether or not the assassin is to be killed with the subject. Hereafter, assassinations in which the subject is unaware will be termed "simple"; those where the subject is aware but unguarded will be termed "chase"; those where the victim is guarded will be termed "guarded."

If the assassin is to die with the subject, the act will be called "lost." If the assassin is to escape, the adjective will be "safe." It should be noted that no compromises should exist here. The assassin must not fall alive into enemy hands.

A further type division is caused by the need to conceal the fact that the subject was actually the victim of assassination, rather than an accident or natural causes. If such concealment is desirable the operation will be called "secret"; if concealment is immaterial, the act will be called "open"; while if the assassination requires publicity to be effective it will be termed "terroristic."

Following these definitions, the assassination of Julius Caesar was safe, simple, and terroristic, while that of Huey Long was lost, guarded and open. Obviously, successful secret assassinations are not recorded as assassination at all. [*Illeg*] of Thailand and Augustus Caesar may have been the victims of safe, guarded and secret assassination. Chase assassinations usually involve clandestine agents or members of criminal organizations.

THE ASSASSIN

In safe assassinations, the assassin needs the usual qualities of a clandestine agent. He should be determined, courageous, intelligent, resourceful, and physically active. If special equipment is to be used, such as firearms or drugs, it is clear that he must have outstanding skill with such equipment.

Except in terroristic assassinations, it is desirable that the assassin be transient in the area. He should have an absolute minimum of contact with the rest of the organization and his instructions should be given orally by one person only. His safe evacuation after the act is absolutely essential, but here again contact should be as limited as possible. It is preferable that the person issuing instructions also conduct any withdrawal or covering action which may be necessary.

In lost assassination, the assassin must be a fanatic of some sort. Politics, religion, and revenge are about the only feasible motives. Since a fanatic is unstable psychologically, he must be handled with extreme care. He must not know the identities of the other members of the organization, for although it is intended that he die in the act, something may go wrong. While the assassin of Trotsky has never revealed any significant information, it was unsound to depend on this when the act was planned.

PLANNING

When the decision to assassinate has been reached, the tactics of the operation must be planned, based upon an estimate of the situation similar to that used in military operations. The preliminary estimate will reveal gaps in information and possibly indicate a need for special equipment which must be procured or constructed. When all necessary data has been collected, an effective tactical plan can be prepared. All planning must be mental; no papers should ever contain evidence of the operation.

In resistance situations, assassination may be used as a counter-reprisal. Since this requires advertising to be effective, the resistance organization must be in a position to warn high officials publicly that their lives will be the price of reprisal action against innocent people. Such a threat is of no value unless it can be carried out, so it may be necessary to plan the assassination of various responsible officers of the oppressive regime and hold such plans in readiness to be used only if provoked by excessive brutality. Such plans must be modified frequently to meet changes in the tactical situation.

TECHNIQUES

The essential point of assassination is the death of the subject. A human being may be killed in many ways but sureness is often overlooked by those who may be emotionally unstrung by the seriousness of this act they intend to commit. The specific technique employed will depend upon a large number of variables, but should be constant in one point: Death must be absolutely certain. The attempt on Hitler's life failed because the conspiracy did not give this matter proper attention.

Techniques may be considered as follows:

1. Manual.
It is possible to kill a man with the bare hands, but very few are skillful enough to do it well. Even a highly trained Judo expert will hesitate to risk killing by hand unless he has absolutely no alternative.

However, the simplest local tools are often much the most efficient means of assassination. A hammer, axe, wrench, screwdriver, fire poker, kitchen knife, lamp stand, or anything hard, heavy and handy will suffice. A length of rope or wire or a belt will do if the assassin is strong and agile. All such improvised weapons have the important advantage of availability and apparent innocence. The obviously lethal machine gun failed to kill Trotsky where an item of sporting goods succeeded.

In all safe cases where the assassin may be subject to search, either before or after the act, specialized weapons should not be used. Even in the lost case, the assassin may accidentally be searched before the act and should not carry an incriminating device if any sort of lethal weapon can be improvised at or near the site. If the assassin normally carries weapons because of the nature of his job, it may still be desirable to improvise and implement at the scene to avoid disclosure of his identity.

2. Accidents.
For secret assassination, either simple or chase, the contrived accident is the most effective technique. When successfully executed, it causes little excitement and is only casually investigated.

The most efficient accident, in simple assassination, is a fall of 75 feet or more onto a hard surface. Elevator shafts, stair wells, unscreened windows and bridges will serve. Bridge falls into water are not reliable. In simple cases a private meeting with the subject may be arranged at a properly cased location. The act may be executed by sudden, vigorous [*excised*] of the ankles, tipping the subject over the edge. If the assassin immediately sets up an outcry, playing the "horrified witness", no alibi or surreptitious withdrawal is necessary. In chase cases it will usually be necessary to stun or drug the subject before dropping him. Care is required to ensure that no wound or condition not attributable to the fall is discernible after death.

Falls into the sea or swiftly flowing rivers may suffice if the subject cannot swim. It will be more reliable if the assassin can arrange to attempt rescue, as he can thus be sure of the subject's death and at the same time establish a workable alibi.

If the subject's personal habits make it feasible, alcohol may be used [2 *words excised*] to prepare him for a contrived accident of any kind.

Falls before trains or subway cars are usually effective, but require exact timing and can seldom be free from unexpected observation.

Automobile accidents are a less satisfactory means of assassination. If the subject is deliberately run down, very exact timing is necessary and investigation is likely to be thorough. If the subject's car is tampered with, reliability is very low. The subject may be stunned or drugged and then placed in the car, but this is only reliable when the car can be run off a high cliff or into deep water without observation.

Arson can cause accidental death if the subject is drugged and left in a burning building. Reliability is not satisfactory unless the building is isolated and highly combustible.

3. Drugs.

In all types of assassination except terroristic, drugs can be very effective. If the assassin is trained as a doctor or nurse and the subject is under medical care, this is an easy and rare method. An overdose of morphine administered as a sedative will cause death without disturbance and is difficult to detect. The size of the dose will depend upon whether the subject has been using narcotics regularly. If not, two grains will suffice.

If the subject drinks heavily, morphine or a similar narcotic can be injected at the passing out stage, and the cause of death will often be held to be acute alcoholism.

Specific poisons, such as arsenic or strychine, are effective but their possession or procurement is incriminating, and accurate dosage is problematical. Poison was used unsuccessfully in the assassination of Rasputin and Kolohan, though the latter case is more accurately described as a murder.

4. Edge Weapons.

Any locally obtained edge device may be successfully employed. A certain minimum of anatomical knowledge is needed for reliability.

Puncture wounds of the body cavity may not be reliable unless the heart is reached. The heart is protected by the rib cage and is not always easy to locate.

Abdominal wounds were once nearly always mortal, but modern medical treatment has made this no longer true.

Absolute reliability is obtained by severing the spinal cord in the cervical region. This can be done with the point of a knife or a light blow of an axe or hatchet.

Another reliable method is the severing of both jugular and carotid blood vessels on both sides of the windpipe.

EXECUTIVE ACTION

U.S. Assassination Plots against Foreign Leaders

The pages that follow are an excerpt from the Church Committee's 1977 congressional report on "Alleged Assassination Plots Involving Foreign Leaders." You'll see that they'd refined the title into "Executive Action," except the project code name is ZR/RIFLE. The full report is online at www.maryferrell.org.

The key CIA players here are Richard Bissell, William Harvey, and Richard Helms. They were all heavily involved in Cuban affairs and the targeting of Fidel Castro. (Bundy is apparently McGeorge Bundy, who was Kennedy's national security adviser.) The CIA guys tried to make it look like they had approval of the White House all through the Kennedy years (1960–63), but in fact the Kennedys put a stop to any such talk and the CIA kept right on going in secret. Harvey eventually got canned. Some researchers think he then turned the tables on JFK and helped organize an "Executive Action" to get rid of the president.

C. INSTITUTIONALIZING ASSASSINATION: THE "EXECUTIVE ACTION" CAPABILITY

In addition to investigating actual assassination plots, the Committee has examined a project known as Executive Action which included, as one element, the development of a general, standby assassination capability. As with the plots, this examination focused on two broad questions: What happened? What was the extent and nature of authorization for the project?

1. INTRODUCTION

Sometime in early 1961, Bissell instructed Harvey, who was then Chief of a CIA Foreign Intelligence staff, to establish an "executive action capability," which would include research into a capability to assassinate foreign leaders.[1] (Bissell, 6/9/75, p. 51; Harvey, 6/25/75, pp. 36-37) At some point in early 1961 Bissell discussed the Executive Action capability with Bundy. The timing of that conversation and whether "the White House" urged that a capability be created were matters on which the evidence varied widely, as is discussed in section (2) below.

Bissell, Harvey and Helms all agreed that the "generalized" capability was never used. (Bissell 6/9/75, p. 87; Harvey 6/25/75; p. 45; Helms 6/13/75, p. 52)

---

[1] During the late spring or early summer of 1960, Richard Bissell had requested his Science Advisor, Mr. Joseph Scheider, to review the general "capability of the clandestine service in the field of incapacitation and elimination." Scheider testified that assassination was one of the "capabilities" he was asked by Bissell to research. (Scheider, 10/9/75, pp. 5-6, 24-25)

Scheider indicated that Bissell turned to him because he was knowledgeable about "substances that might be available in CIA laboratories" and because Bissell would have considered it part of my job as his technical aide." (*id.*, 6).

Also prior to this time, there had been an internal CIA committee which passed on proposals involving the operational use of drugs, chemicals and biological agents. The purpose of this Committee is suggested by the following incident:

In February 1960, CIA's Near East Division sought the endorsement of what the Division Chief called the "Health Alteration Committee" for its proposal for a "special operation" to "incapacitate" an Iraqi Colonel believed to be "promoting Soviet bloc political interests in Iraq." The Division sought the Committee's advice on a technique, "which while not likely to result in total disablement would be certain to prevent the target from pursuing his usual activities for a minimum of three months," adding:

"We do not consciously seek subject's permanent removal from the scene; we also do not object should this complication develop." (Memo, Acting Chief N.E. Division to DC/CI, 2/25/60).

In April, the Committee unanimously recommended to the DDP that a "disabling operation" be undertaken, noting that Chief of Operations advised that it would be "highly desirable." Bissell's deputy, Tracy Barnes, approved on behalf of Bissell. (Memo, Deputy Chief CI to DDP, 4/1/62)

The approved operation was to mail a monogrammed handkerchief containing an incapacitating agent to the colonel from an Asian country. Scheider testified that, while he did not now recall the name of the recipient, he did remember mailing from the Asian country, during the period in question, a handkerchief "treated with some kind of material for the purpose of harassing that person who received it." (Scheider Affidavit. 10/20/75; Scheider, 10/9/75, pp. 52-55; 10/18/75, pp. 55-56.)

During the course of this Committee's investigation, the CIA stated that the handkerchief was "in fact never received (if, indeed, sent)." It added that the colonel:

"Suffered a terminal illness before a firing squad in Baghdad (an event we had nothing to do with) not very long after our handkerchief proposal was considered." (Memo, Chief of Operations, N.E. Division to Assistant to the SA/DDO. 9/26/75.)

"Executive Action" was a CIA euphemism, defined as a project for research into developing means for overthrowing foreign political leaders, including a "capability to perform assassinations." (Harvey, 6/25/75, p. 34) Bissell indicated that Executive Action covered a "wide spectrum of actions" to "eliminate the effectiveness" of foreign leaders, with assassination as the "most extreme" action in the spectrum. (Bissell, 7/22/75, p. 32) The Inspector General's Report described executive action as a "general standby capability" to carry out assassination when required. (I.G. Report, p. 37) The project was given the code name ZR/RIFLE by the CIA.[1]

A single agent ("asset") was given the cryptonym QJ/WIN, and placed under Harvey's supervision for the ZR/RIFLE project. He was never used in connection with any actual assassination efforts. Helms described QJ/WIN's "capability":

If you needed somebody to carry out murder, I guess you had a man who might be prepared to carry it out. (Helms, 6/13/75, p. 50)

Harvey used QJ/WIN, to spot "individuals with criminal and underworld connections in Europe for possible multi-purpose use." (Harvey, 6/25/75, p. 50) For example, QJ/WIN reported that a potential asset in the Middle East was "the leader of a gambling syndicate" with "an available pool of assassins." (CIA file, ZR/RIFLE/Personality Sketches) However, Harvey testified that:

During the entire existence of the entire ZR/RIFLE project * * * no agent was recruited for the purpose of assassination, and no even tentative targeting or target list was ever drawn. (Harvey, 6/25/75, p. 45)

In general, project ZR/RIFLE involved assessing the problems and requirements of assassination and developing a stand-by assassination capability; more specifically, it involved "spotting" potential agents and "researching" assassination techniques that might be used. (Bissell, 7/17/75, p. 11 and 6/9/75, p. 73; Harvey, 6/25/75, pp. 37-A, 45) Bissell characterized ZR/RIFLE as "internal and purely preparatory." (Bissell, 7/22/75, p. 32) The 1967 Inspector General's Report found "no indication in the file that the Executive Action capability of ZR/RIFLE-QJ/WIN was ever used," but said that "after Harvey took over the Castro operation, he ran it as one aspect of ZR/RIFLE." (I.G. Report, pp. 40-41)

SECRET EXPERIMENTS

U.S. Public Health Service Exposed Guatemalan Prostitutes, Prisoners, Soldiers to Sexually Transmitted Disease

This one boggles my mind. We knew about the horrifying Tuskegee Syphilis Experiment when the U.S. Public Health Service (USPHS) "observed" and experimented on 399 poor African-American men in the late stages of syphilis—basically watching them die over a forty-year period starting in 1932. This came to light in 1972.

Yet another study has been uncovered. In 2010, a researcher named Susan Reverby of Wellesley College discovered that the USPHS was also busy in Guatemala from 1946–1948, infecting nearly 1,000 Guatemalan citizens with venereal diseases. Why? To test antibiotics. Don't believe me— here are excerpts from *Findings from a CDC Report on the 1946–1948 U.S. Public Health Service Sexually Transmitted Disease (STD) Inoculation Study*. If you want to view it yourself, go to www.hhs.gov/1946incoulationstudy/findings.html.

Summary

From 1946-48, the U.S. Public Health Service (USPHS) Venereal Disease Research Laboratory (VDRL) and the Pan American Sanitary Bureau collaborated with several government agencies in Guatemala on U.S. National Institutes of Health-funded studies involving deliberate exposure of human subjects with bacteria that cause sexually transmitted diseases (STD). Guatemalan partners included the Guatemalan Ministry of Health, the National Army of the Revolution, the National Mental Health Hospital, and the Ministry of Justice. Studies were conducted under the on-site direction of John C. Cutler, MD in Guatemala City, under the supervision of R.C. Arnold MD and John F. Mahoney, MD of the USPHS VDRL in Staten Island, New York; the primary local collaborator was Dr. Juan Funes, chief of the VD control division of the Guatemalan Sanidad Publica.

The work by Dr. Cutler and VDRL colleagues was recently brought to light by Professor. Susan Reverby of Wellesley College as a result of archival work conducted as part of the research of her 2009 book on PHS syphilis studies, *Examining Tuskegee...* Upon learning of Professor Reverby's work, staff from the Centers for Disease Control and Prevention (CDC) conducted a review of materials in the papers of John Cutler, archived at the University of Pittsburgh, including several summary reports, experimental logs, correspondence between Dr. Cutler and professional colleagues, and subject-specific records...

According to materials in the archives, **the primary purpose of the studies was to develop human models of transmission of Treponema pallidum, the bacteria that causes syphilis, by sexual transmission and cutaneous and mucous membrane inoculation in order to assess effectiveness of potential chemoprophylactic regimens. Additional studies were conducted to assess potential for reinfection of persons with untreated latent syphilis or of those with recent treatment of syphilis with penicillin; to compare performance of various serologic tests for syphilis; and to develop human models of transmission and chemoprophylaxis of the agents of gonorrhea (Neisseria gonorrhoeae) and chancroid (Hemophilus ducreyi).**

Subjects for the transmission studies included female commercial sex workers (CSWs), prisoners in the national penitentiary, patients in the national mental hospital, and soldiers. These subjects were also involved in comparative serologic studies. Transmission studies initially included sexual exposure of prisoners to female CSWs experimentally infected with either syphilis or gonorrhea. Later, subjects underwent direct inoculation, primarily of skin and mucous membranes, by viable *T. pallidum. N. gonorrhoeae, and H. ducreyi.* The design and conduct of the studies was unethical in many respects, including deliberate exposure of subjects to known serious health threats, lack of knowledge of and consent for experimental procedures by study subjects, and the use of highly vulnerable populations. According to a "Syphilis Summary Report" and experimental logs in the archives, syphilis studies included CSWs, prisoners, and patients in the mental hospital.

In the series of syphilis studies, a total of 696 subjects of individual experiments (some representing the same patients involved in several experiments) were exposed to infection (by sexual contact or inoculation)... Gonorrhea studies included CSWs, prisoners, soldiers, and mental hospital patients. In the series of gonorrhea studies, a total of 772 subjects of individual experiments (some apparently representing the same patients involved in several experiments) were exposed to infection (by sexual contact or inoculation)... Chancroid studies included soldiers and mental hospital patients. A total of 142 subjects were exposed to infection by inoculation...

The study appears to have ended in 1948, although some follow-up laboratory testing and patient observation continued until the early 1950s. There is no indication that results of the STD inoculation experiments were ever published in the scientific literature or another forum.

4 & 5 & 6

MIND CONTROL

The CIA's Project ARTICHOKE and MKULTRA

A t the same time the Guatemalan experiments were taking place, the just-formed Central Intelligence Agency (CIA) was borrowing another page from 1930s Germany. I'd like to say that's where these next documents originated, but no, this is our own government using people as guinea pigs. Their behavior-control programs were known as Project ARTICHOKE and MKULTRA.

Why the perpetrators were not brought to trial and justice is beyond me. If anyone in the private sector did something like this, they would go to jail and throw away the key. But I guess governments are immune from the same standards. Laws that apply to the general populace don't apply to them. Lest we forget, isn't the government made up of people too?

Nothing was publicly known about these grisly experiments until the mid-1970s, and guess who in the Ford administration was involved in helping keep the lid on the worst of what went on? None other than Donald Rumsfeld and his deputy, Dick Cheney. It seems the torture of detainees at Guantanamo—which we'll examine later in this book—has deep roots in our secret history.

The three documents that follow are an excerpt from a 1975 CIA memo on some of what ARTICHOKE involved, a 1951 ARTICHOKE report on Sensory Integration (SI) and Hypnosis (H) on two unwitting girls, and a 1963 CIA "Report of Inspection of MKULTRA."

31 JAN 1975

MEMORANDUM FOR THE RECORD

SUBJECT: Project ARTICHOKE

ARTICHOKE is the Agency cryptonym for the study and/or use of "special" interrogation methods and techniques. These "special" interrogation methods have been known to include the use of drugs and chemicals, hypnosis, and "total isolation," a form of psychological harassment.

A review of available file information obtained from Office of Security resources failed to reflect a comprehensive or complete picture of the ARTICHOKE program as participated in by the Office of Security. Fragmentary information contained in a variety of files previously maintained by the Security Research Staff (SRS) reflected several basic papers which described, in general terms, the program known as ARTICHOKE. Information contained therein indicated that prior to 1952, the Office of Security had studied the use of drugs and chemicals in "unconventional interrogation." These studies were evidently coordinated with the Agency unit which was then called OSI. OSI at that time apparently was the coordinating unit within CIA.

One paper reflected that an Office of Security team, as early as 1949-50 experimented with drugs and hypnosis under a project called BLUEBIRD. This paper also reflected that by 1951 actual interrogations utilizing drugs were conducted by a combined team of Office of Security and Office of Medical Services personnel, but few details were available.

File information indicated that in 1952, overall responsibility for Project ARTICHOKE passed from OSI to the Office of Security. References to operational use of drugs as an aid to interrogation since that time were found in various files, but few details concerning these experiments were reflect HOKE, cted

...

One of the few areas where detailed information was available was concerned with hypnotic experimentations. A log of hypnotic experiments conducted by Office of Security personnel was reviewed. The log reflected that numerous (probably several hundred) experiments with hypnotism were conducted in Agency buildings, apparently utilizing the staff employee volunteers as subjects. In some instances, representatives from Agency components other than the Office of Security were present. The log reflected hypnotic experimentations during 1951, 1952, and 1953. It could not be determined from available file information when the hypnotic experiments actually began or were caused to be ceased.

A/B, 3, 2/112

To: Files

Subject: SI and H Experimentation (25 September 1951)

On 25 September 1951, ▓▓▓▓▓▓▓▓ and the writer conducted SI and H experimentation with ▓▓▓▓▓▓▓▓ and ▓▓▓▓▓▓▓▓ ▓▓ as subjects.

In view of the successful experimentation of Tuesday, 18 September 1951 with ▓▓▓▓▓▓ and ▓▓▓▓▓▓▓▓ it was decided to continue experiments along more or less related lines during this session. However, prior to actually beginning the more complex experiments, several simple post H were worked with both of the girls participating. In this connection, it is interesting to note that whereas ▓▓▓▓▓▓▓ was capable on each test tried of producing the desired post H effect, ▓▓▓▓▓▓ was unable to do so. No explanation was offered for this, but it should be noted for the record that ▓▓▓▓▓▓ and the writer did not make continuous and serious efforts to produce the desired effect for these simple post H tests.

The first major experiment of the evening was set up as follows without previous explanation to either ▓▓▓▓▓ or ▓▓▓▓▓ child. Both subjects were placed in a very deep trance state and while in this state, the following instructions were given:

    (A) ▓▓▓▓▓▓ was instructed that when she awakened, she was to procede to ▓▓▓▓▓'s room. She was told that while there, she would receive a telephone call from an individual whom she would know only as "Joe". This individual would engage her in a normal telephone conversation. During this conversation, this individual would give her a code word and upon mentioning the code word, ▓▓▓▓▓ would go into a deep SI trance state but would be "normal" in appearance with her eyes open. ▓▓▓▓▓▓ was then told that upon the conclusion of the telephone conversation, she would procede to the ladies room where she would meet a girl who was unknown to her. She was told that she would strike up a conversation with this girl and during the conversation she would mention the code word "New York" to this other girl who, in turn, would give her a device and further instructions which were to be carried out by ▓▓▓▓▓▓. She was told that after she carried out the instructions, she was to return to the Operations Room, sit on the sofa and go immediately into a deep sleep state.

    (D) ▓▓▓▓▓▓ was instructed that upon awakening, she would procede to ▓▓▓▓▓ room where she would wait at the desk for a telephone call. Upon receiving the call, a person known as "Jim" would engage her in normal conversation. During the course of the conversation, this individual would mention a code word to ▓▓▓▓▓▓▓ When she heard this code word

she would pass into an SI trance state, but would not close her
eyes and remain perfectly normal and continue the telephone conversation. She was told that thereafter upon conclusion of the
telephone conversation, she would then carry out the following
instructions:

▇▇▇▇▇▇▇▇▇▇ being in a complete SI state at this
time, was then told to open her eyes and was shown an electric
timing device. She was informed that this timing device
was an incendiary bomb and was then instructed how to attach
and set the device. After ▇▇▇▇▇▇▇▇▇ had indicated that
she had learned how to set and attach the device, she was
told to return to a sleep state and further instructed
that upon concluding the aforementioned conversation, she
would take the timing device which was in a briefcase and
procede to the ladies room. In the ladies room, she would
be met by a girl whom she had never seen who would identify
herself by the code word "New York". After identifying
herself, ▇▇▇▇▇▇▇▇▇▇ is then to show this individual
how to attach and set the timing device and further instructions would be given the individual by ▇▇▇▇▇▇▇
that the timing device was to be carried in the briefcase
to ▇▇▇▇▇ room, placed in the nearest empty electric-
light plug and concealed in the bottom, left-hand drawer
of ▇▇▇▇ desk, with the device set for 82 seconds and
turned on. ▇▇▇▇▇▇▇▇▇ was further instructed to tell
this other girl that as soon as the device had been set
and turned on, she was to take the briefcase, leave ▇
▇▇▇▇▇ room, go to the operations room and go to the sofa
and enter a deep sleep state. ▇▇▇▇▇▇▇▇▇ was further
instructed that after completion of instructing the other
girl and the transferring to the other girl of the incendiary bomb, she was to return at once to the operations
room, sit on the sofa, and go into a deep sleep state.

For a matter of record, immediately after the operation was begun it was noted that a member of the charforce was cleaning the floor
▇▇▇▇ in the ladies room and subsequently, both ▇▇▇▇▇▇▇
and ▇▇▇▇▇▇ had to be placed at once again in a trance state and
instructions changed from the ladies room to Room 3.

It should be noted that even with the change of locale in the
transfer point, the experiment was carried off perfectly without any
difficulty or hesitation on the part of either of the girls. Each
girl acted out her part perfectly, the device was planted and set
as directed and both girls returned to the operations room, sat on
the sofa and entered a deep sleep state. Throughout, their moove-
ments were easy and natural and the member of the charforce and the
guard were, to all intents and purposes, completely unaware of what
was taking place although they could clearly observe the movements
of ▇▇▇▇▇▇▇ and ▇▇▇▇▇▇

Before the girls were awakened, they were given instructions
▇▇▇▇▇▇▇▇▇▇▇▇▇▇▇▇▇▇▇▇▇▇▇▇▇▇▇▇▇▇

26 July 1963

MEMORANDUM FOR: Director of Central Intelligence

SUBJECT   : Report of Inspection of MKULTRA

1. In connection with our survey of Technical Services Division, DD/P, it was deemed advisable to prepare the report of the MKULTRA program in one copy only, in view of its unusual sensitivity.

2. This report is forwarded herewith.

3. The MKULTRA activity is concerned with the research and development of chemical, biological, and radiological materials capable of employment in clandestine operations to control human behavior. The end products of such research are subject to very strict controls including a requirement for the personal approval of the Deputy Director/Plans for any operational use made of these end products.

4. The cryptonym MKULTRA encompasses the R&D phase and a second cryptonym MKDELTA denotes the DD/P system for control of the operational employment of such materials. The provisions of the MKULTRA authority also cover [   ] The administration and control of this latter activity were found to be generally satisfactory and are discussed in greater detail in the main body of the report on TSD.

5. MKULTRA was authorized by the then Director of Central Intelligence, Mr. Allen W. Dulles, in 1953. The TSD was assigned responsibility thereby to employ a portion of its R&D budget, eventually set at 20%, for research in behavioral materials and [   ] under purely internal and compartmented controls, (further details are provided in paragraph 3 of the attached report). Normal procedures for project approval, funding, and accounting were waived. However, special arrangements for audit of expenditures have been evolved in subsequent years.

Ser A 0 286,
185209/1

6. The scope of MKULTRA is comprehensive and ranges from the search for and procurement of botanical and chemical substances, through programs for their analysis in scientific laboratories, to progressive testing for effect on animals and human beings. The testing on individuals begins under laboratory conditions employing every safeguard and progresses gradually to more and more realistic operational simulations. The program requires and obtains the services of a number of highly specialized authorities in many fields of the natural sciences.

7. The concepts involved in manipulating human behavior are found by many people both within and outside the Agency to be distasteful and unethical. There is considerable evidence that opposition intelligence services are active and highly proficient in this field. The experience of TSD to date indicates that both the research and the employment of the materials are expensive and often unpredictable in results. Nevertheless, there have been major accomplishments both in research and operational employment.

8. The principal conclusions of the inspection are that the structure and operational controls over this activity need strengthening; improvements are needed in the administration of the research projects; and some of the testing of substances under simulated operational conditions was judged to involve excessive risk to the Agency.

9. Attached for the signature of the Deputy Director of Central Intelligence is a memorandum transmitting the report to the Deputy Director/Plans requesting a summary of action taken or comments on the recommendations contained therein.

J. S. Earman
Inspector General

Attachments - as stated

- 2 -

a. Scope of the MKULTRA charter:

(1) Over the ten-year life of the program many additional avenues to the control of human behavior have been designated by the TSD management as appropriate to investigation under the MKULTRA charter, including radiation, electro-shock, various fields of psychology, psychiatry, sociology, and anthropology, graphology, harrassment substanc s, and paramilitary devices and materials.

(2) Various projects do not appear to have been sufficiently sensitive to warrant waiver of normal Agency procedures for authorization and control.

(3) Other secure channels for establishment and funding of Agency-sterile activities have been evolved over the past ten years by Deputy Director/Support (DD/S) and in some cases could reasonably be employed by TSD in lieu of MKULTRA procedures. In view of these developments there is substantial agreement among all parties concerned that redefinition of the scope of MKULTRA is now appropriate.

b/ MKULTRA management policies:

(1) The original charter documents specified that TSD maintain exacting control of MKULTRA activities.

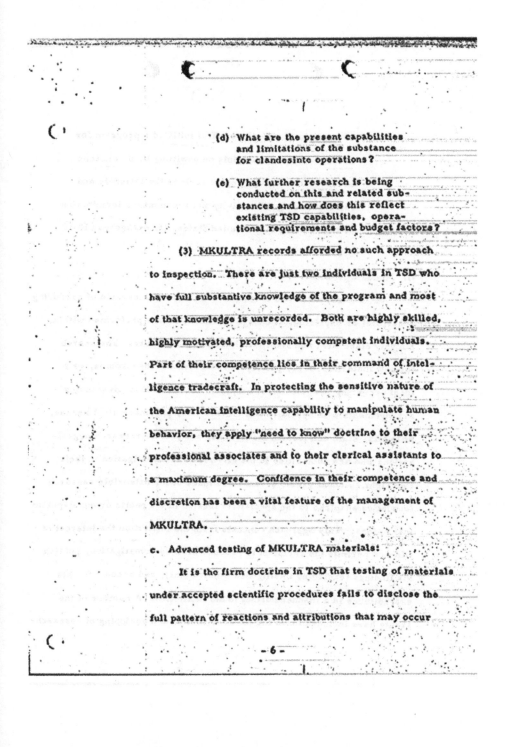

(d) What are the present capabilities
and limitations of the substance
for clandesinte operations?

(e) What further research is being
conducted on this and related substances and how does this reflect
existing TSD capabilities, operational requirements and budget factors?

(3) MKULTRA records afforded no such approach

to inspection. There are just two individuals in TSD who

have full substantive knowledge of the program and most

of that knowledge is unrecorded. Both are highly skilled,

highly motivated, professionally competent individuals.

Part of their competence lies in their command of intel-

ligence tradecraft. In protecting the sensitive nature of

the American intelligence capability to manipulate human

behavior, they apply "need to know" doctrine to their

professional associates and to their clerical assistants to

a maximum degree. Confidence in their competence and

discretion has been a vital feature of the management of

MKULTRA.

c. Advanced testing of MKULTRA materials:

It is the firm doctrine in TSD that testing of materials

under accepted scientific procedures fails to disclose the

full pattern of reactions and attributions that may occur

-6-

in operational situations. TSD initiated a program for
covert testing of materials on unwitting U. S. citizens
in 1955. The present report reviews the rationale and
risks attending this activity and recommends termination
of such testing in the United States, cf: paragraphs 10-18
below.

II. Modus Operandi

6. The research and development of materials capable of producing
behavioral or physiological change in humans is now performed within
a highly elaborated and stabilized MKULTRA structure. The search
for new materials; e. g., psilocybin from Mexican mushrooms, or a
fungi occurring in agricultural crops, is conducted through standing
arrangements with specialists in universities, pharmaceutical houses,
hospitals, state and federal institutions, and private research organizations who are authorities in the given field of investigation in their
own right. Annual grants of funds are made under ostensible research
foundation auspices to the specialists located in the public or quasi-public
institutions. This approach conceals from the institution the interest of
CIA and permits the recipient to proceed with his investigation, publish
his findings (excluding intelligence implications), and account for his
expenditures in a manner normal to his institution. A number of the
grants have included funds for the construction and equipping of research

- 7 -

A FAKE TERRORIST ATTACK

Operation Northwoods

At the end of April 2001, a little more than four months before 9/11, the startling fact that the American military had planned fake terrorist attacks on our own citizenry first came to light. The book *Body of Secrets*, by James Bamford, called it the "most corrupt plan ever created by the U.S. government." This was Operation Northwoods, which was approved by all the Joint Chiefs of Staff in 1962 for action against Cuba.

Here was the background: at a White House meeting on February 26, 1962, when various covert action plans seemed to be going nowhere, Robert Kennedy ordered a stop to all such anti-Castro efforts. General Lyman Lemnitzer, the holdover chairman of the Joint Chiefs from the Eisenhower years, decided the only option was to trick the American public and world opinion into a justifiable war.

The document you're about to read was presented to President Kennedy's Secretary of Defense, Robert McNamara, that March. Three days later, JFK told Lemnitzer that there was virtually no possibility of our using overt force to take Cuba. Within a few months, Lemnitzer had been transferred to a different job.

So Operation Northwoods remained secret for thirty-five years. Now you can download a PDF from the National Security Archive website, and it makes for pretty chilling reading. You could even think about it as establishing a precedent for the future. If something like this was on the table in

1962, wouldn't it likewise have been in 2001? What Northwoods had on the drawing board, I believe 9/11 was.

It seems that all through history, wars and takeovers are started with false flag operations: the Reichstag fire, the Chinese supposedly attacking Japan, the Gulf of Tonkin incident with Vietnam. The list goes on and on. History has a way of repeating itself, like that old cliché: if it works once, let's try it again.

~~TOP SECRET SPECIAL HANDLING NOFORN~~

THE JOINT CHIEFS OF STAFF
WASHINGTON 25, D.C.

UNCLASSIFIED   13 March 1962

MEMORANDUM FOR THE SECRETARY OF DEFENSE

Subject: Justification for US Military Intervention
in Cuba (TS)

1. The Joint Chiefs of Staff have considered the attached Memorandum for the Chief of Operations, Cuba Project, which responds to a request of that office for brief but precise description of pretexts which would provide justification for US military intervention in Cuba.

2. The Joint Chiefs of Staff recommend that the proposed memorandum be forwarded as a preliminary submission suitable for planning purposes. It is assumed that there will be similar submissions from other agencies and that these inputs will be used as a basis for developing a time-phased plan. Individual projects can then be considered on a case-by-case basis.

3. Further, it is assumed that a single agency will be given the primary responsibility for developing military and para-military aspects of the basic plan. It is recommended that this responsibility for both overt and covert military operations be assigned the Joint Chiefs of Staff.

For the Joint Chiefs of Staff:

SYSTEMATICALLY REVIEWED
BY JCS ON ___27 May 84___
CLASSIFICATION CONTINUED

L. L. LEMNITZER
Chairman
Joint Chiefs of Staff

1 Enclosure
Memo for Chief of Operations, Cuba Project   EXCLUDED FROM GDS

EXCLUDED FROM AUTOMATIC
REGRADING; DOD DIR 5200.10
DOES NOT APPLY

~~TOP SECRET SPECIAL HANDLING NOFORN~~

SECRET SPECIAL HANDLING   NOFORN

APPENDIX TO ENCLOSURE A

DRAFT   UNCLASSIFIED

MEMORANDUM FOR CHIEF OF OPERATIONS, CUBA PROJECT

Subject: Justification for US Military Intervention
in Cuba (TS)

1. Reference is made to memorandum from Chief of Operations, Cuba Project, for General Craig, subject: "Operation MONGOOSE", dated 5 March 1962, which requested brief but precise description of pretexts which the Joint Chiefs of Staff consider would provide justification for US military intervention in Cuba.

2. The projects listed in the enclosure hereto are forwarded as a preliminary submission suitable for planning purposes. It is assumed that there will be similar submissions from other agencies and that these inputs will be used as a basis for developing a time-phased plan.   The individual projects can then be considered on a case-by-case basis.

3. This plan, incorporating projects selected from the attached suggestions, or from other sources, should be developed to focus all efforts on a specific ultimate objective which would provide adequate justification for US military intervention.   Such a plan would enable a logical build-up of incidents to be combined with other seemingly unrelated events to camouflage the ultimate objective and create the necessary impression of Cuban rashness and irresponsibility on a large scale, directed at other countries as well as the United States.   The plan would also properly integrate and time phase the courses of action to be pursued.   The desired resultant from the execution of this plan would be to place the United States in the apparent position of suffering defensible grievances from a rash and irresponsible government of Cuba and to develop an international image of a Cuban threat to peace in the Western Hemisphere.

UNCLASSIFIED   5   Appendix to
Enclosure A

UNCLASSIFIED

4. Time is an important factor in resolution of the Cuban problem. Therefore, the plan should be so time-phased that projects would be operable within the next few months.

5. Inasmuch as the ultimate objective is overt military intervention, it is recommended that primary responsibility for developing military and para-military aspects of the plan for both overt and covert military operations be assigned the Joint Chiefs of Staff.

TOP SECRET SPECIAL HANDLING   NOFORN

ANNEX TO APPENDIX TO ENCLOSURE A

PRETEXTS TO JUSTIFY US MILITARY INTERVENTION IN CUBA

(Note: The courses of action which follow are a preliminary
submission suitable only for planning purposes. They are
arranged neither chronologically nor in ascending order.
Together with similar inputs from other agencies, they are
intended to provide a point of departure for the development
of a single, integrated, time-phased plan. Such a plan would
permit the evaluation of individual projects within the context
of cumulative, correlated actions designed to lead inexorably
to the objective of adequate justification for US military
intervention in Cuba).

1. Since it would seem desirable to use legitimate
provocation as the basis for US military intervention in Cuba
a cover and deception plan, to include requisite preliminary
actions such as has been developed in response to Task 33 c,
could be executed as an initial effort to provoke Cuban
reactions. Harassment plus deceptive actions to convince the
Cubans of imminent invasion would be emphasized. Our military
posture throughout execution of the plan will allow a rapid
change from exercise to intervention if Cuban response justifies.

2. A series of well coordinated incidents will be planned
to take place in and around Guantanamo to give genuine
appearance of being done by hostile Cuban forces.

a. Incidents to establish a credible attack (not in
chronological order):

(1) Start rumors (many). Use clandestine radio.

(2) Land friendly Cubans in uniform "over-the-fence"
to stage attack on base.

(3) Capture Cuban (friendly) saboteurs inside the
base.

(4) Start riots near the base main gate (friendly
Cubans).

7   Annex to Appendix
                           to Enclosure A

UNCLASSIFIED

TOP SECRET SPECIAL HANDLING NOFORN

UNCLASSIFIED

(5) Blow up ammunition inside the base; start fires.

(6) Burn aircraft on air base (sabotage).

(7) Lob mortar shells from outside of base into base. Some damage to installations.

(8) Capture assault teams approaching from the sea or vicinity of Guantanamo City.

(9) Capture militia group which storms the base.

(10) Sabotage ship in harbor; large fires -- napthalene.

(11) Sink ship near harbor entrance. Conduct funerals for mock-victims (may be lieu of (10)).

b. United States would respond by executing offensive operations to secure water and power supplies, destroying artillery and mortar emplacements which threaten the base.

c. Commence large scale United States military operations.

3. A "Remember the Maine" incident could be arranged in several forms:

a. We could blow up a US ship in Guantanamo Bay and blame Cuba.

b. We could blow up a drone (unmanned) vessel anywhere in the Cuban waters. We could arrange to cause such incident in the vicinity of Havana or Santiago as a spectacular result of Cuban attack from the air or sea, or both. The presence of Cuban planes or ships merely investigating the intent of the vessel could be fairly compelling evidence that the ship was taken under attack. The nearness to Havana or Santiago would add credibility especially to those people that might have heard the blast or have seen the fire. The US could follow up with an air/sea rescue operation covered by US fighters to "evacuate" remaining members of the non-existent crew. Casualty lists in US newspapers would cause a helpful wave of national indignation.

4. We could develop a Communist Cuban terror campaign in the Miami area, in other Florida cities and even in Washington.

8

Annex to Appendix to Enclosure A

UNCLASSIFIED

TOP SECRET SPECIAL HANDLING NOFORN

The terror campaign could be pointed at Cuban refugees seeking haven in the United States. We could sink a boatload of Cubans enroute to Florida (real or simulated). We could foster attempts on lives of Cuban refugees in the United States even to the extent of wounding in instances to be widely publicized. Exploding a few plastic bombs in carefully chosen spots, the arrest of Cuban agents and the release of prepared documents substantiating Cuban involvement also would be helpful in projecting the idea of an irresponsible government.

5. A "Cuban-based, Castro-supported" filibuster could be simulated against a neighboring Caribbean nation (in the vein of the 14th of June invasion of the Dominican Republic). We know that Castro is backing subversive efforts clandestinely against Haiti, Dominican Republic, Guatemala, and Nicaragua at present and possible others. These efforts can be magnified and additional ones contrived for exposure. For example, advantage can be taken of the sensitivity of the Dominican Air Force to intrusions within their national air space. "Cuban" B-26 or C-46 type aircraft could make cane-burning raids at night. Soviet Bloc incendiaries could be found. This could be coupled with "Cuban" messages to the Communist underground in the Dominican Republic and "Cuban" shipments of arms which would be found, or intercepted, on the beach.

6. Use of MIG type aircraft by US pilots could provide additional provocation. Harassment of civil air, attacks on surface shipping and destruction of US military drone aircraft by MIG type planes would be useful as complementary actions. An F-86 properly painted would convince air passengers that they saw a Cuban MIG, especially if the pilot of the transport were to announce such fact. The primary drawback to this suggestion appears to be the security risk inherent in obtaining or modifying an aircraft. However, reasonable copies of the MIG could be produced from US resources in about three months.

Annex to Appendix
to Enclosure A

UNCLASSIFIED

7. Hijacking attempts against civil air and surface craft
should appear to continue as harassing measures condoned by the
government of Cuba. Concurrently, genuine defections of Cuban
civil and military air and surface craft should be encouraged.

8. It is possible to create an incident which will demonstrate
convincingly that a Cuban aircraft has attacked and shot down
a chartered civil airliner enroute from the United States to
Jamaica, Guatemala, Panama or Venezuela. The destination would
be chosen only to cause the flight plan   route to cross Cuba.
The passengers could be a group of college students off on a
holiday or any grouping of persons with a common interest to
support chartering a non-scheduled flight.

a. An aircraft at Eglin AFB would be painted and
numbered as an exact duplicate for a civil registered
aircraft belonging to a CIA proprietary organization in the
Miami area. At a designated time the duplicate would be
substituted for the actual civil aircraft and would be
loaded with the selected passengers, all boarded under
carefully prepared aliases. The actual registered
aircraft would be converted to a drone.

b. Take off times of the drone aircraft and the actual
aircraft will be scheduled to allow a rendezvous south of
Florida. From the rendezvous point the passenger-carrying
aircraft will descend to minimum altitude and go directly
into an auxiliary field at Eglin AFB where arrangements will
have been made to evacuate the passengers and return the
aircraft to its original status. The drone aircraft
meanwhile will continue to fly the filed flight plan. When
over Cuba the drone will being transmitting on the international distress frequency a "MAY DAY" message stating he
is under attack by Cuban MIG aircraft. The transmission
will be interrupted by destruction of the aircraft which will
be triggered by radio signal. This will allow ICAO radio

10   Annex to Appendix
                                      to Enclosure A

UNCLASSIFIED

stations in the Western Hemisphere to tell the US what
has happened to the aircraft instead of the US trying to
"sell" the incident.

9. It is possible to create an incident which will make it
appear that Communist Cuban MIGs have destroyed a USAF aircraft
over international waters in an unprovoked attack.

a. Approximately 4 or 5 F-101 aircraft will be dispatched
in trail from Homestead AFB, Florida, to the vicinity of Cuba.
Their mission will be to reverse course and simulate fakir
aircraft for an air defense exercise in southern Florida.
These aircraft would conduct variations of these flights at
frequent intervals. Crews would be briefed to remain at
least 12 miles off the Cuban coast; however, they would be
required to carry live ammunition in the event that hostile
actions were taken by the Cuban MIGs.

b. On one such flight, a pre-briefed pilot would fly
tail-end Charley at considerable interval between aircraft.
While near the Cuban Island this pilot would broadcast that
he had been jumped by MIGs and was going down. No other
calls would be made. The pilot would then fly directly
west at extremely low altitude and land at a secure base, an
Eglin auxiliary. The aircraft would be met by the proper
people, quickly stored and given a new tail number. The
pilot who had performed the mission under an alias, would
resume his proper identity and return to his normal place
of business. The pilot and aircraft would then have
disappeared.

c. At precisely the same time that the aircraft was
presumably shot down a submarine or small surface craft
would disburse F-101 parts, parachute, etc., at approximately
15 to 20 miles off the Cuban coast and depart. The pilots
returning to Homestead would have a true story as far as
they knew. Search ships and aircraft could be dispatched
and parts of aircraft found.

Annex to Appendix
to Enclosure A

11

UNCLASSIFIED

TOP SECRET SPECIAL HANDLING NOFORN

THE VIETNAM SHAM

Kennedy's Plans to Withdraw Troops from Vietnam

I enlisted in the Navy on September 11, 1969, at the height of the Vietnam War. As part of the Frogmen Underwater Demolition Team, I spent time off the coast of Hanoi waiting with a Marine division for a Normandy-type invasion that never happened. Altogether I served seventeen months overseas, never questioning how we ended up in Vietnam to begin with.

Today, I know different. It was a sham from the get-go, trumped up by the military industrial complex. If President Kennedy had lived, we'd have started withdrawing troops by late 1963 and had all our servicemen out of there by the end of 1965. The idea that JFK was responsible for having escalated the war is simply bogus. It's obvious his plans were to pull us out, but he'd said behind the scenes he had to wait until after the next election to do it.

When the Joint Chiefs of Staff (JCS) official file from those years was declassified in 1997, it contained a memorandum concerning the Secretary of Defense (SECDEF in the document) conference on May 6, 1963, held at CINCPAC headquarters in Camp Smith, Hawaii. Let's start with key excerpts from that one, and a follow-up memo from late October (less than a month before JFK was assassinated) that clearly show we were starting to get out of Vietnam and leave matters in the hands of the South Vietnamese, where they belonged. Unfortunately, this is again a case of misleading the people for years, by keeping the true thoughts of John F. Kennedy out of the public realm.

09180

MESSAGE

DEPARTMENT OF THE A?
STAFF COMMUNICATIONS OFFICE

PRECEDENCE		TYPE MSG (Check)			PROC. STAMP	ORIG OR REFERRED		CLASSIFIC OF REFER
ACTION PRIORITY	BOOK	MULTI	SINGLE		DA		TIME	
INFO PRIORITY		X						

FROM:
  JCS

SPECIAL INSTAL.

TO: CINCPAC

INFO: COMUSMACV   DECLASSIFIED BY JCS

      AMEM SAIGON   DATE _____ 11 May 89

      ~~JCS~~ JCS   9820   From JCS

Regular
Distribu

CINCPAG
102300Z
DA IN 28

JACE's n
necessar

SACSA

GenKeu

Actions Resulting SECDEF Conference 6 May

Refs: a. CINCPAC DTG 102300Z Nov 62; b. DEF 921892 DTG

210001Z Nov 62

   This msg in five parts:

PART I. US Medical Civic Action Team in RVN. SECDEF

expressed concern that US Medical Civic Action person-

nel are apparently involved more in treatment of Viet-

namese population than training indigenous medical

civic actions teams. Request you institute and report

on a program which will provide for training of RVN

medical personnel to accomplish medical civic action

program.

④

DATE 9	TIME 18
MONTH MAY	YEAR 1

SYMBOL J-3		SIGNATURE *Herbert D. Riley*
TYPED NAME AND TITLE (Signature, if required) E. G. Glidden, Col, USMC	R E L E A S E R	TYPED (or stamped) NAME AND TITLE HERBERT D. RILEY Vice Admiral, USN Director
PHONE 57909	PAGE NR. 1	NR. OF PAGES 4
SECURITY CLASSIFICATION ~~SECRET~~		

JCS 9820   091805Z MAY 63

PAGE 0000

SCO FORM 35-3
6 JUN 58

MESSAGE

DEPARTMENT OF THE ARMY
STAFF COMMUNICATIONS OFFICE

CINCPAC for the years FY 65 through FY 69 is at least
$270 million higher than an acceptable program; (4) US,
as we withdraw, should consider leaving behind for GVN
use where latter can absorb, materials such as C-123's,
helicopters, AC&W equipment, and troposcatter communication equipment.

b. Accordingly, request you prepare a new plan for the
period FY 65-69 inclusive. The plan should include for
each of the years FY 65-69, the following info: (1)
personnel strength of each of the South Vietnamese forces;
(2) the weapons inventory of SVN forces shown as a listing of major items, cumulative thru 30 Jun 61 and as of
the end each 6 month period thereafter with indication
amount remaining to be delivered, copy of format desired
will be forwarded under separate cover; (3) the Defense
budget to be funded by RVN; (4) supplementary assistance
to be furnished by US; (5) MAP both in dollars and in
terms of principal items of equipment per (2) above;
(6) US forces broken down by function. Further funding
guidance for FY 64 will be furnished by OSD ASAP. PART V
of this message is also pertinent.

PART IV. Withdrawal US forces. As a matter of urgency a
plan for the withdrawal of about 1,000 US troops before
the end of the year should be developed based upon the
assumption that the progress of the counterinsurgency

JCS 9820

SCD FORM 35-3
6 JUN 56

MESSAGE

DEPARTMENT OF THE A'
STAFF COMMUNICATIONS C. ICE

campaign would warrant such a move. Plans should be based upon withdrawal of US units (as opposed to individuals) by replacing them with selected and specially trained RVNAF units.

PART V. Phase-out of US forces. SECDEF advised that the phase-out program presented during 6 May conference appeared too slow. In consonance with PART III request you develop a revised plan to accomplish more rapid phase-out of US forces. SECDEF expressed special interest in the development of training plans which would accelerate replacement of US by GVN units, such as an accelerated training program for VNAF. GP -4.

(7)

DISTR: CJCS-2, DJS-3, SJCS-3, J1-1, J3-5, J4-2, J5-1, SACSA-1, DIA/CIIC-3, NMCC-2, RRA-1, SAMAA-1, CNO, CSAF, CMC, DCSOP, ACSFOR, DCSLOG, MED, TC, DCSPER

JCS 9820

PAGE 0000

SCO FORM 35-3
4 JUN 58

THE JOINT CHIEFS OF STAFF
WASHINGTON 25, D.C.

CM-985-63

3 1 OCT 1963

MEMORANDUM FOR THE DIRECTOR, JOINT STAFF +1

Subject: 1,000 U.S. Military Withdrawal from Vietnam

Reference: DJSM-1793-63 dated 28 October 1963

1. In compliance with the request contained in paragraph 4 of
reference, the Chairman queried the Secretary of Defense on
30 October concerning the latter's having provided altered guidance
to COMUSMACV regarding subject withdrawal.

2. The Secretary of Defense recalled having given no additional
guidance on this subject during his most recent trip to Vietnam.
The Secretary stated that in his opinion the JCS should pursue that
plan for withdrawal which the Chiefs consider most advantageous.

3. In discussing this subject with the undersigned, the Chairman
took note of the fact that CINCPAC (i) concurs with COMUSMACV's
estimate that the latter's new plan will have less impact on operational
effectiveness, and (ii) recommends the revised mix (70%/30%) be
approved.

FOR THE CHAIRMAN:

Bernard W. Rogers

BERNARD W. ROGERS
Colonel, USA
Executive to the Chairman

O.C.
SACSA
J-1
SJCS

Taylor Box 7 1

(S84)

DECLASSIFIED BY JOINT STAFF
DATE: JUL 0 1 1997

FLAWED INTELLIGENCE

What Really Happened at the Gulf of Tonkin

The official line was that, in August 1964, the North Vietnamese twice attacked U.S. ships in the Gulf of Tonkin. That was the incident that led to Congress passing the Tonkin Gulf Resolution and President Johnson's dramatic buildup of our forces. As it turns out, according to top secret documents finally released by the National Security Agency (NSA) in 2005, the second attack never happened. Somebody involved in SIGINT (Signals Intelligence) skewed the data to make it look that way.

Some 58,000 of my generation were killed in the Vietnam War, and no telling how many Vietnamese, probably over a million but who knows? Again, all based upon fraudulence. How can our government have any credibility whatsoever when it's always caught in these major lies?

An article in *Naval History*, a magazine published by the U.S. Naval Institute, first revealed the story in 1999 of Operation Plan 34A, a highly classified program of covert attacks against North Vietnam, including the raids on two offshore islands that forced their one (and only) retaliation against the USS *Maddox*.

As far back as 1972, the Senate Foreign Relations Committee was pushing the NSA to release what its files contained on the Gulf of Tonkin. They stonewalled, even as late as 2004 when a FOIA request pushed for it. According to the *New York Times*, high-level officials at the NSA were "fearful that [declassification] might prompt uncomfortable comparisons with the flawed intelligence used to justify the war in Iraq." Oh really?

TOP SECRET//COMINT//X1   Cryptologic Quarterly

(U) Skunks, Bogies, Silent Hounds, and the Flying Fish: The Gulf of Tonkin Mystery, 2-4 August 1964

ROBERT J. HANYOK

(C//SI) The Gulf of Tonkin incidents of 2 to 4 August 1964 have come to loom over the subsequent American engagement in Indochina. The incidents, principally the second one of 4 August, led to the approval of the Gulf of Tonkin Resolution by the U.S. Congress, which handed President Johnson the carte blanche charter he had wanted for future intervention in Southeast Asia. From this point on, the American policy and programs would dominate the course of the Indochina War. At the height of the American involvement, over a half million U.S. soldiers, sailors, airmen, and marines would be stationed there. The war would spread across the border into Cambodia and escalate in Laos. Thailand assumed a greater importance as a base for supporting the military effort, especially for the air war, but also for SIGINT purposes of intercept and direction finding.

(U) At the time, the Gulf of Tonkin incidents of August were not quite so controversial. According to the Johnson administration, the issue of the attacks was pretty much cut and dried. As the administration explained, our ships had been in international waters – anywhere from fifty to eighty miles from the DRV coastline by some calculations, during the alleged second attack – and were attacked twice, even though they were innocent of any bellicose gestures directed at North Vietnam. Secretary of Defense Robert McNamara had assured the Senate that there had been no connection between what the U.S. Navy was doing and any aggressive operations by the South Vietnamese.[1] Washington claimed that the United States had to defend itself and guarantee freedom of navigation on the high seas.

(U) However, within the government, the events of 4 August were never that clear. Even as the last flare fizzled in the dark waters of the South China Sea on that August night, there were conflicting narratives and interpretations of what had happened. James Stockdale, then a navy pilot at the scene, who had "the best seat in the house from which to detect boats," saw nothing. "No boats," he would later write, "no boat wakes, no ricochets off boats, no boat impacts, no torpedo wakes – nothing but black sea and American firepower."[2] The commander of the *Maddox* task force, Captain John J. Herrick, was not entirely certain what had transpired. (Captain Herrick actually was the commander of the destroyer division to which the *Maddox* belonged. For this mission, he was aboard as the on-site commander.) Hours after the incident, he would radio the Commander-in-Chief, Pacific (CINCPAC) telling them that he was doubtful of many aspects of the "attack."

(U) It would be years before any evidence that an attack had not happened finally emerged in the public domain, and even then, most reluctantly. Yet, remarkably, some of the major participants in the events still maintained that the Gulf of Tonkin incident had occurred just as it had been originally reported. Secretary of Defense Robert McNamara, in his memoirs *In Retrospect*, considered the overall evidence for an attack still convincing.[3] The U.S. Navy's history of the Vietnam conflict, written by Edward J. Marolda and Oscar P. Fitzgerald (hereafter referred to as the "Marolda-Fitzgerald history"), reported that the evidence for the second attack, especially from intelligence, including a small amount of SIGINT, was considered conclusive.[4]

Derived From: NSA/CSSM 123-2
            24 February 1998
Declassify On: X1   TOP SECRET//COMINT//X1   Page 1

Cryptologic Quarterly

(U) The public literature on the Gulf of Tonkin for years has been overwhelmingly skeptical about the 4 August battle. Articles that appeared in magazines within a few years illustrated the general inconsistency in the descriptions of the incident of 4 August by simply using the conflicting testimony from the officers and crews of both ships. The first major critical volume was Joseph Goulden's *Truth Is the First Casualty*, published in 1969. The most complete work to date is Edwin Moise's *Tonkin Gulf and the Escalation of the Vietnam War*. Moise's work has the dual advantage of using some Vietnamese sources, as well as small portions of a few SIGINT reports released to the author under a Freedom of Information Act request. Yet, even what few scraps he received from NSA were enough to raise serious questions about the validity of the SIGINT reports cited by the administration which related to the 4 August incident.[5]

(S//SI) The issue of whether the available SIGINT "proved" that there had been a second attack has been argued for years. In 1968, Robert McNamara testified before Senator William Fulbright's Foreign Relations Committee's hearings on the Gulf of Tonkin that the supporting signals intelligence was "unimpeachable." On the other hand, in 1972 the deputy director of NSA, Louis Tordella, was quoted as saying that the 4 August intercepts pertained to the 2 August attacks. In a 1975 article in the NSA magazine *Cryptolog*, the Gulf of Tonkin incident was retold, but the SIGINT for the night of August 4 was not mentioned, except for the "military operations" intercept, and even then without comment.[6] The Navy's history of the Vietnam War would misconstrue the SIGINT (disguised as unsourced "intelligence") associating portions of two critical intercepts and implying a connection in the evidence where none could be established.[7]

(C//SI) Except for the sizable collection of SIGINT material within NSA, and a much smaller amount from the archives of the Naval Security Group (which essentially duplicates portions of the NSA holdings), almost all relevant material relating to the Gulf of Tonkin incidents has been released. Although the questions about what happened in the Gulf of Tonkin on the night of 4 August have been fairly well answered by the evidence from all of the other sources – radar, sonar, eyewitness, and archival – the SIGINT version needs to be told. This is because of the critical role that SIGINT played in defining the second attack in the minds of Johnson administration officials. Without the signals intelligence information, the administration had only the confused and conflicting testimony and evidence of the men and equipment involved in the incident. It is difficult to imagine the 5 August retaliatory air strikes against North Vietnamese naval bases and installations being ordered without the SIGINT "evidence."[8] Therefore, it is necessary to recount in some detail what signals intelligence reported.

(S//SI) For the first time ever, what will be presented in the following narrative is the *complete* SIGINT version of what happened in the Gulf of Tonkin between 2 and 4 August 1964. Until now, the NSA has officially maintained that the second incident of 4 August occurred. This position was established in the initial SIGINT reports of 4 August and sustained through a series of summary reports issued shortly after the crisis. In October 1964, a classified chronology of events for 2 to 4 August in the Gulf of Tonkin was published by NSA which furthered the contention that the second attack had occurred.

(S//SI) In maintaining the official version of the attack, the NSA made use of surprisingly few published SIGINT reports – fifteen in all. The research behind the new version which follows is based on the discovery of an enormous amount of never-before-used SIGINT material. This included *122* relevant SIGINT products, along with watch center notes, oral history interviews, and messages among the various SIGINT and military command centers involved in the Gulf of Tonkin incidents. Naturally, this flood of new information changed dramatically the story of that night of 4/5 August. The most important element is that it is now known what the North Vietnamese Navy was doing that night. And with this information a nearly complete story finally can be told.

(S//SI) Two startling findings emerged from the new research. First, it is not simply that there is a different story as to what happened; it is that *no attack* happened that night. Through a compound of analytic errors and an unwillingness to consider contrary evidence, American SIGINT elements in the region and at NSA HQs reported Hanoi's plans to attack the two ships of the Desoto patrol. Further analytic errors and an obscuring of other information led to publication of more "evidence." In truth, Hanoi's navy was engaged in nothing that night but the salvage of two of the boats damaged on 2 August.

(S//SI) The second finding pertains to the handling of the SIGINT material related to the Gulf of Tonkin by individuals at NSA. Beginning with the period of the crisis in early August, into the days of the immediate aftermath, and continuing into October 1964, SIGINT information was presented in such a manner as to preclude responsible decisionmakers in the Johnson administration from having the complete and objective narrative of events of 4 August 1964. Instead, only SIGINT that supported the claim that the communists had attacked the two destroyers was given to administration officials.

(S//SI) This mishandling of the SIGINT was not done in a manner that can be construed as conspiratorial, that is, with manufactured evidence and collusion at all levels. Rather, the objective of these individuals was to support the Navy's claim that the Desoto patrol had been deliberately attacked by the North Vietnamese. Yet, in order to substantiate that claim, all of the relevant SIGINT could not be provided to the White House and the Defense and intelligence officials. The conclusion that would be drawn from a review of all SIGINT evidence would have been that the North Vietnamese not only did not

attack, but were uncertain as to the location of the ships.

(S//SI) Instead, three things occurred with the SIGINT. First of all, the overwhelming portion of the SIGINT relevant to 4 August was kept out of the post-attack summary reports and the final report written in October 1964. The withheld information constituted nearly 90 percent of all available SIGINT. This information revealed the actual activities of the North Vietnamese on the night of 4 August that included salvage operations of the two torpedo boats damaged on 2 August, and coastal patrols by a small number of DRV craft. As will be demonstrated later in this chapter, the handful of SIGINT reports which suggested that an attack had occurred contained severe analytic errors, unexplained translation changes, and the conjunction of two unrelated messages into one translation. This latter product would become the Johnson administration's main proof of the 4 August attack.

(S//SI) Second, there were instances in which specious supporting SIGINT evidence was inserted into NSA summary reports issued shortly after the Gulf of Tonkin incidents. This SIGINT was not manufactured. Instead, it consisted of fragments of legitimate intercept lifted out of its context and inserted into the summary reports to support the contention of a premeditated North Vietnamese attack on 4 August. The sources of these fragments were not even referenced in the summaries. It took extensive research before the original reports containing these items could be identified.

(S//SI) Finally, there is the unexplained disappearance of vital decrypted Vietnamese text of the translation that was the basis of the administration's most important evidence – the so-called Vietnamese after-action report of late 4 August. The loss of the text is important because the SIGINT record shows that there were critical differences in the English translations of it issued both by the navy intercept site in the Philippines and

Cryptologic Quarterly   ~~TOP SECRET//COMINT//X1~~

NSA. Without the individual texts (there were two of them), it is difficult to determine why there are critical differences in the translations and more importantly, to understand why two separate North Vietnamese messages were combined into one translation by NSA.

• • •

We have discussed earlier that, for the most part, the NSA personnel in the crisis center who reported the second Gulf of Tonkin incident believed that it had occurred. The problem for them was the SIGINT evidence. The evidence that supported the contention that an attack had occurred was scarce and nowhere as strong as would have been wanted. The overwhelming body of reports, if used, would have told the story that no attack had happened. So a conscious effort ensued to demonstrate that the attack occurred.

(S//SI) The exact "how" and "why" for this effort to provide only the SIGINT that supported the claim of an attack remain unknown. There are no "smoking gun" memoranda or notes buried in the files that outline any plan or state a justification. Instead, the paper record speaks for itself on what happened: what few product (six) were actually used, and how 90 percent of them were kept out of the chronology; how contradictory SIGINT evidence was answered both with speculation and fragments lifted from context; how the complete lack of Vietnamese C3I was not addressed; and, finally, how critical original Vietnamese text and subsequent product were no longer available. From this evidence, one can easily deduce the deliberate nature of these actions. And this observation makes sense, for there was a purpose to them: This was an active effort to make SIGINT fit the claim of what happened during the evening of 4 August in the Gulf of Tonkin.

(S//SI) The question why the NSA personnel handled the product the way they did will probably never be answered. The notion that they were under "pressure" to deliver the story that the administration wanted simply cannot be supported. If the participants are to be believed, and they were adamant in asserting this, they did not bend to the desires of administration officials. Also, such "environmental" factors as overworked crisis center personnel and lack of experienced linguists are, for the most part, not relevant when considering the entire period of the crisis and follow-up. As we have seen, the efforts to ensure that the only SIGINT publicized would be that which supported the contention that an attack had occurred continued long after the crisis had passed. While the product initially issued on the 4 August incident may be contentious, thin, and mistaken, what was issued in the Gulf of Tonkin summaries beginning late on 4 August was deliberately skewed to support the notion that there had been an attack. What was placed in the official chronology was even more selective. That the NSA personnel believed that the attack happened and rationalized the contradictory evidence away is probably all that is necessary to know in order to understand what was done. They walked alone in their counsels.

AGENT ORANGE?

U.S. Capabilities in Chemical and Biological Warfare

It's hard to imagine today's Congress holding this kind of hearing in anything but a closed-door top-secret session. But there seemed to be a lot more openness in our government as the sixties came to a close. I found the transcript of this House Subcommittee to be a real eye-opener. Not only in terms of the R&D going on at the time—and I realize this was during the Cold War with the Russians—but of how "innocently" we were using herbicides in Vietnam. You won't see Agent Orange mentioned, but clearly that's what they're talking about. The other part that blew my mind was how acceptable it was to dump "obsolete chemical agents" into the ocean.

It's just appalling to know that we have this capability to use as we so desire. Is it truly survive-at-any-cost, where we have no moral high ground on anything? Maybe so. Because, as my Special Forces friend Dick Marcinko has said, at the end of the day it's all about who's still alive. That seems to be the mind-set here: we can have every weapon imaginable at our disposal but nobody else is allowed to be that way. I find it kind of ironic that the very thing we attacked Saddam Hussein over, we'd maintained in our arsenal for many years! The hypocrisy would be laughable if this weren't such a serious matter.

Pay particular attention to the little section on "Synthetic Biological Agents." Molecular biology was then just beginning and they're saying here: "eminent biologists believe that within a period of 5 to 10 years it would be possible to produce a synthetic biological agent, an agent that does not naturally exist and for which no natural immunity could have been acquired."

When did people start to die from AIDS? Ten years later, the early 1980s. What about lyme disease? The first cluster of cases occurred in 1976 at a Naval Medical Hospital in Connecticut, not far from the military's Plum Island facility engaged in secret biochemical warfare experiments.

I don't want to jump to any conclusions here. But after reading the transcript of this congressional hearing—and I've included most of it—I sure as heck wonder how far all this has developed over the last forty years.

CONGRESS. | HOUSE   / (Appropriations. Committee on

DEPARTMENT OF DEFENSE APPROPRIATIONS FOR 1970

HEARINGS
BEFORE A
SUBCOMMITTEE OF THE
COMMITTEE ON APPROPRIATIONS
HOUSE OF REPRESENTATIVES
NINETY-FIRST CONGRESS
FIRST SESSION

SUBCOMMITTEE ON DEPARTMENT OF DEFENSE APPROPRIATIONS

GEORGE H. MAHON, Texas, *Chairman*

ROBERT L. F. SIKES, Florida	GLENARD P. LIPSCOMB, California
JAMIE L. WHITTEN, Mississippi	WILLIAM E. MINSHALL, Ohio
GEORGE W. ANDREWS, Alabama	JOHN J. RHODES, Arizona
DANIEL J. FLOOD, Pennsylvania	GLENN R. DAVIS, Wisconsin
JOHN M. SLACK, West Virginia	
JOSEPH P. ADDABBO, New York	
FRANK E. EVANS, Colorado [1]	

R. L. MICHAELS, RALPH PRESTON, JOHN GARRITY, PETER MURPHY, ROBERT NICHOLAS, AND ROBERT FOSTER, *Staff Assistants*

[1] Temporarily assigned.

...

MONDAY, JUNE 9, 1969

CHEMICAL AND BIOLOGICAL WARFARE

WITNESSES

DR. D. M. MacARTHUR, DEPUTY DIRECTOR (RESEARCH AND TECH-
NOLOGY), D.D.R. & E.

DR. B. HARRIS, DEPUTY ASSISTANT DIRECTOR (CHEMICAL TECH-
NOLOGY), D.D.R. & E.

DR. K. C. EMERSON, ACTING DEPUTY ASSISTANT SECRETARY OF
THE ARMY (R. & D.)

BRIG. GEN. W. S. STONE, JR., DIRECTOR OF MATERIEL REQUIRE-
MENTS, HEADQUARTERS, U.S. ARMY MATERIEL COMMAND

COL. J. J. OSICK, CHIEF, SYSTEMS AND REQUIREMENTS DIVISION,
DIRECTORATE OF CBR AND NUCLEAR OPERATIONS, OFFICE OF
THE ASSISTANT CHIEF OF STAFF FOR FORCE DEVELOPMENT

Mr. MAHON. We have before us this afternoon Dr. Donald M.
MacArthur. Dr. MacArthur at this point we will place in the record
your biographical sketch.

(The biographical sketch follows:)

Dr. Donald M. MacArthur was born in Detroit, Mich. in 1931. He received a
B. Sc. (Honors) degree from St. Andrews University, Scotland, in 1954, and a
Ph. D. in X-ray crystallography from Edinburgh University in 1957.

Afterward Dr. MacArthur taught for a year at the University of Connecticut.
In 1958 he joined Melpar, a subsidiary of Westinghouse Air Brake. When he
left he was manager of the Chemistry and Life Sciences Research Center. In
this position he was responsible for the management and direction of a large
number of defense and space programs representing a broad spectrum of
disciplines from instrumentation engineering to biology. These programs
represented applied research in the physical and life sciences, in addition to

development programs in space instrumention, life support equipment, chemical and biological detection and warning equipment, and the development of large-scale atmospheric diffusion experiments.

In July 1966 he was designated Deputy Director (Research and Technology), Defense Research and Engineering in the Office of the Secretary of Defense.

As Deputy Director (Research and Technology) he is responsible for management of the DOD overall research and technology programs. The programs which he directs cover such diverse fields as rocket and missile propulsion, materials technology, medical and life sciences, social and behavioral sciences, environmental sciences, and chemical technology. He also oversees the 70 DOD in-house laboratories for development of policies, and improved management systems to insure that they are organized most effectively to meet current and future military weapons needs.

INTRODUCTORY REMARKS

Mr. MAHON. I take note of the fact that prior to the beginning of the formal hearing we have had an informal discussion about some of the matters which are to be covered in your presentation.

We are very much interested in all aspects of our defense program.

This subcommittee and the Congress has, over a period of years, supported the appropriation of funds for chemical and biological warfare. This has not been a program of great magnitude but it has been a program of considerable significance.

I think there is probably considerable misconception about the nature of the program.

I am not sure what portion of your testimony can appropriately be put in the record, or we would want to have in the record. We would not want to have in the record anything that would be damaging to the security of the United States, but otherwise we feel that the Congress and the American public are entitled to know all the basic facts.

Now, Dr. MacArthur, do you have a written statement or how do you propose to proceed?

Dr. MACARTHUR. Mr. Chairman, I do not have a prepared statement. The way I proposed to proceed was to pose the questions that seemed to be of most concern to Members of the Congress, the press, and to the public at large, and try to answer them.

Mr. MAHON. I think that is a good way to proceed.

Dr. MACARTHUR. I believe I know most of the facts about this area but when it comes to areas of national policy and the policy that has been espoused by certain individuals, I would want the privilege of reading specifically for the record what they have said.

In addition I have a discussion paper here, which discusses various issues in this area and I will be happy to distribute this. It is unclassified.

Some of the material I will speak about will be classified, but as I go along I will indicate the level of classification.

Mr. MAHON. You have been authorized by the Department of Defense to make the presentation.

Dr. MACARTHUR. Yes, Mr. Chairman.

Mr. SIKES. Who is the author of the paper on the U.S. position?

Dr. MacArthur. This position paper was prepared in the Office of the Secretary of Defense and already is in the record.

Mr. Sikes. But not in this committee's record.

Dr. MacArthur. It is in the Congressional Record of April 21, 1969, pages E3167–3169.

Mr. Mahon. You may insert the position paper in the record.

(The information follows:)

"U.S. POSITION WITH REGARD TO CHEMICAL AND BIOLOGICAL WARFARE

"In recent weeks there has been increased comment and conjecture regarding the involvement of the United States in chemical and biological (CB) warfare, and speculation concerning the policies and purposes governing such involvement.

"It is the policy of the United States to develop and maintain a defensive chemical-biological (CB) capability so that U.S. military forces could operate for some period of time in a toxic environment if necessary; to develop and maintain a limited offensive capability in order to deter all use of CB weapons by the threat of retaliation in kind; and to continue a program of research and development in this area to minimize the possibility of technological surprise. This policy on CB weapons is part of a broader strategy designed to provide the United States with several options for response against various forms of attack. Should their employment ever be necessary, the President would have to authorize their use. The United States does not have a policy that requires a single and invariable response to any particular threat. In the field of CB warfare, deterrence is the primary objective of the United States.

"CB weapons, in many situations, may be more effective than conventional (high explosive and projectile) weapons. Accordingly, it is believed wise to deter their use. If two approximately equally effective military forces were engaged in combat, and one side initiated a CW operation, it would gain a significant advantage even if the opposing side has protective equipment. This advantage cannot be neutralized with conventional weapons.

"As a matter of policy the United States will not be the first to use lethal chemical or biological weapons, but we are aware of the capabilities these weapons place in the hands of potential adversaries. For this reason it is important to carry on our R. & D. program in CB, not only to provide necessary equipment, such as detection and warning devices, but to define and quantify more fully the potential threat to our country from these weapons, and the hazards involved if they are ever used against the United States.

"The threat to the U.S. civil population from CB attack has been studied by the Department of Defense, and these analyses are periodically updated. It is clear that the threat of CB attack is less significant than that of nuclear attack. For this reason, more emphasis has been placed in civil defense on the nuclear threat.

"For logistic reasons, chemical agents do not appear to pose a major strategic threat against the United States. For example, it would require many tons of nerve agent munitions to carry out an effectiv attack against a city of a few million people. This may appear incon sistent with the high toxicity of the nerve agents, but for many tech nical reasons, such as the difficulty in disseminating the agents i vapor or aerosol form, the dilution of the agent in the atmosphere and their impingement on ground and vegetation, it is correct. Fo this reason, stockpiles of therapeutic materials for nerve agents ar not maintained. Although the possibility of the employment of bio logical weapons against U.S. population centers cannot be ruled ou entirely, it does not presently warrant the priority given to defens against the effects of nuclear weapons. Research on methods of detect ing and warning, identifying, and defending against biological attac are continuing, as is review of the magnitude and nature of the threat

"The Office of Civil Defense has developed an inexpensive but effec tive protective mask for civilian use, and a limited production run was made to test production quality. No large-scale production wa undertaken because of the low estimate of the threat as describe above. Should the threat to our population increase, this mask coul be produced quite rapidly and, together with other necessary defen sive measures, would afford protection against both chemical and bio logical attack. Filtration systems have been designed and tested, an these could be added to fallout shelters to afford collective protection for groups of people. In addition, many of the emergency plans devel oped by the Department of HEW for post-nuclear attack medical support would be applicable. The emergency packaged hospitals, for example, provide for expansion of hospital facilities by the equiva lent of 2,500 hospitals of 200-bed size.

"Large stockpiles of medical supplies such as antibiotics and vaccines are not maintained against the possibility of biological attack. There is no specific antibiotic therapy available for most BW agents. As for vaccines, there are more than 100 possible BW agents, and production and administration of 100 vaccines to the U.S. population is not prac tical. There is medical reason to believe that such a program would be generally injurious to health in addition to requiring prohibitive expenditures.

"Chemical detection and warning instruments which could provide the components for a national alarm system have been developed, but it has not seemed wise to expend the large sums to deploy them to build such a system. As noted above, we believe that the threat of strategic chemical attack is not great. Warning against biological at tack is much more difficult technologically. Recently there has been success with a prototype instrument which would provide some bio logical warning capability. R. & D. efforts in this area will be con tinued.

U. S. forces have the equipment required for protection against CB attack with the exception of a biological warning and detection device which is under development. Soldiers and sailors overseas have masks and protective clothing; and collective protection equipment for vans and communication centers is being developed and supplied.

"Statements have been made that there is enough nerve gas to kill 100 billion people. This kind of general statement is as "true" as saying that a test tube in a hospital laboratory can contain enough disease microorganisms to kill 100 billion people. Neither statement is true in any real sense, and there is no way in which the human race could be destroyed with nerve agents. The United States could not launch an immediate, massive retaliatory chemical or biological attack. The technical capability to do this has been developed, but it has not been judged necessary or desirable to procure and install the weapon systems for this purpose. The carefully controlled U.S. inventories are adequate for tactical response against enemy military forces, but not for strategic, nationwide attack.

"The total U.S. expenditure in the CB field, including smoke, flame and incendiary weapons, is $350 million for fiscal year 1969. There is no procurement of lethal chemical agents or of biological agents. Details of expenditures are given in the table below.

CB expenditures, fiscal year 1969

Procurement:	Million
Smoke, flame and incendiary	$139
Riot control munitions	81
Herbicides	5
Defensive equipment	15
Total	240

R.D.T. & E.:	
General and basic R. & D	9
Offensive R. & D	31
Defensive R. & D	30
Test and evaluation	20
Total	90
Operation and maintenance	20

"Of the $90 million in R. & D., about $26 million is spent on contracts, primarily with industry; $2 million is contracted to universities for basic defensive investigations. Every attempt is made to use discretion in selection of contractors, and not to ask institutions to do work which might be contrary to their policies and purposes. For example, some years ago the advice of the Smithsonian Institution was sought in identifying a suitable institute to perform an ecological and medical survey of the Central Pacific area. As a result, they submitted a proposal, which was accepted. As a direct consequence of this work, there have been 45 papers written by Smithsonian scientists and published in the scientific literature. This has been a remarkably productive scientific investigation brought about by a coincidence of interests in the fauna of the area.

"The Smithsonian Institution was never asked to do, nor did they do, any "military" chemical or biological warfare research. It carried out scientific investigations appropriate to its charter and objectives, and published the significant findings in the scientific literature. These results are available for use by any Government agency, or by any nation or scientist wishing to do so.

"U.S. forces have used riot control agents and defoliants (herbicides) in the Vietnamese conflict. These materials do not cause lethalities in humans, and, as former Secretary Rusk said, are not considered to be the type of materials prohibited by the Geneva protocol of 1925.

"The only riot control agent in use by U.S. forces in Vietnam is CS, although CN was also authorized some years ago. Both are tear gases. There are no known verified instances of lethality by CS, either in Vietnam or anywhere else in the world where it has been used to control disturbances by many governments.

"Of the herbicidal chemicals, there are none used in Vietnam to destroy vegetation which have not been widely used in the United States in connection with clearing areas for agricultural or industrial purposes.

"The term 'defoliants' is often used because it properly describes the purpose of its use; that is, to remove leaves from jungle foliage to reduce the threat of ambush and to increase visibility for U.S. and Allied troops. This use of defoliants has saved many American and South Vietnamese lives.

"Herbicides are also used in a carefully limited operation in South Vietnam to disrupt the enemy's food supply. It is limited to the attack of small and usually remote jungle plots which the VC or NVA are known to be using. Usually these plots are along trails or near their base camp areas. Each such operation is approved by the U.S. Embassy and the Government of the Republic of Vietnam. Enemy caches of food, principally rice, are also destroyed when it cannot be used by the South Vietnamese. These limited Allied activities have never, in any single year, affected as much as 1 percent of the annual food output of South Vietnam.

"To date surveys have shown no evidence of substantial permanent or irreparable damage from the viewpoint of the future development of South Vietnam, attributable to the defoliation effort. The Department of Defense has supported the Department of Agriculture in studies of herbicides in analogous areas, and in a base line study of the forests of Vietnam. Recently a study, "Assessment of Ecological Effects of Extensive or Repeated Use of Herbicides," was done by Midwest Research Institute, and reviewed by a special committee of the National Academy of Sciences. It was judged by them to be an accurate and competent report. Last fall, the Department of State, with Department of Defense participation, made a survey of the ecology of defoliated areas. One of the scientists who made this survey, Dr. Fred Tschirley from the Department of Agriculture, published his report in *Science*, volume 163, pages 779–786, February 21, 1969.

"At the end of active combat, it appears probable that there will be agricultural and forestry activities and other programs which will aid the South Vietnamese people. The Department of Defense would cooperate with the Department of State and the U.S. Agency for International Development as necessary in accomplishing these. The Department of Defense supports the concept of a comprehensive study of the long-term effects of the limited defoliation program, and has

endorsed   principle, proposals by the American Association for the
Advance.   .t of Science for such a scientific study.

"Every effort is made to assure that activities in CB do not pose
hazards to the U.S. population. Strict safety practices are enforced
at laboratories which do research on CB agents. Elaborate systems
of air-tight hoods, air filtration and waste decontamination are employed. These precautions and procedures are reviewed by the U.S.
Public Health Service as well as by our own safety experts. The
equipment and building designs developed at the U.S. Army Biological Laboratories, for example, have been generally accepted throughout the world as the ultimate in safety for the investigation of infectious diseases.

"With regard to the extremely unfortunate Skull Valley incident in
which a number of sheep died, the exact chain of events is still not
completely understood. A freak meteorological situation was probably
a major contributing factor. This matter has been carefully reviewed
by a special advisory committee appointed by the Secretary of the
Army and chaired by the Surgeon General of the U.S. Public Health
Service. This committee has made a number of recommendations
concerning test limitations, toxicological and environmental investigations, added meteorological facilities, and a permanent safety
committee. All of these recommendations are being followed.

• • •

EFFECTIVENESS OF CHEMICAL WARFARE AGENTS

I would like for a moment to dwell on the types of chemical and
biological systems we have. On the chemical side, in addition to mus-

tard, we have lethal chemicals of the same types as the chemical warfare agents developed by the Germans prior to World War II. These
are more powerful than several of our well-known insecticides, and
about 10 times more potent than the most toxic of World War I gases.

A lethal dose of these agents is about 1 milligram per person.

Mr. FLOOD. Would you touch upon delivery systems?

Dr. MacARTHUR. Yes. There are various ways of delivery. You can
deliver in artillery shells or bombs, rockets, or you can deliver them
from spray tanks.

Mr. MINSHALL. How much of a drop is a milligram?

Dr. MacARTHUR. One-fiftieth of a drop.

I would like to elaborate on that.

There has been a lot of misunderstanding, not so much about toxicity, but about its effectiveness.

Mr. SIKES. The story has gone around that there is enough of this
material on hand to kill everybody in the world.

Dr. MacARTHUR. Thirty times over.

Mr. SIKES. This might be true if you lined them up and injected them
one by one.

Would you get into the practicality of this statement?

Dr. MacARTHUR. I would be happy to, sir.

As you indicated, if you simply do the arithmetic you arrive at the
conclusion that that could be accomplished if you line them up and
inject them one by one with the minimum amount of agent.

But that is just like saying we have enough bullets to kill the population of the world 50 times over, or 100 times over if you equate one
bullet with one individual.

It is totally impossible to get 1 milligram inhaled by every person
in any practical situation.

Due to atmospheric dilution, absorption by the terrain, and destruction in deployment (when I say destruction I mean part of the agent
is physically burned up as the munition bursts), the quantity required
is much higher. In fact, a typical nerve agent—I am talking right now
about GB—requires 1 ton of agent dispersed in the air to produce 50
percent casualties to unprotected personnel over an area of about 1
square mile. Now this is more effective than high explosives but certainly not as effective as nuclear weapons and most certainly not as
effective as some self-ordained experts who write and talk about it
would have us believe.

Does that answer your question?

Mr. SIKES. I think so.

Dr. MacARTHUR. One ton, 50 percent casualties among unprotected
personnel per square mile.

Mr. MINSHALL. What kind of a gas was that?

Dr. MacARTHUR. It is called GB.

Mr. MINSHALL. What is that?

Dr. MacARTHUR. It is a nerve agent. It is one of the most toxic ones
we have.

Talking about effectiveness, I would like to extrapolate a little
further and say, to attack a complete city of many millions of people—

let's sa   lensely populated city like New York—it would take 300 to 400 tons efficiently dispersed to immobilize the city.

Mr. MINSHALL. How would you disperse it?

Dr. MacArthur. Effective dispersal is difficult. That is why you require that number of tons. It would have to be dispersed in the air from aircraft or missiles. which would have to fly over the city and deliver it fairly uniformly over the entire area.

Mr. ADDABBO. We do not have a stockpile that large.

Dr. MacArthur. Yes, we do.

I just wanted to bring out that the weapon, though effective, is not as effective as many people today make it out to be.

From the example I gave, the high logistics burden imposed, makes chemical warfare weapons clearly tactical rather than strategic.

INCAPACITATING AGENTS

Mr. FLOOD. Wouldn't it be more effective to disable than to kill troops? Wouldn't it cause the enemy more trouble to disable him than to kill him.

Dr. MacArthur. Yes, it imposes a greater logistic burden on the enemy when he has to look after the disabled people. And we do R. & D. on chemical warfare agents that are not lethal but incapacitate.

For clarification, incapacitating agents are agents that incapacitate troops by either physical or mental effects (or a combination of both) so that they constitute no effective threat. We have to insist, by definition, that the lethal dose of such an agent is so high that the risk of death is minimal. We have one standard agent of this kind called BZ, and it is effective up to 2 or 3 days.

Mr. EVANS. What does it do?

EFFECTS OF BZ

Dr. MacArthur. BZ brings about complete mental disorientation as well as sedation which induces sleep.

Mr. SIKES. Explain that in more detail.

Dr. MacArthur. First of all the individual is completely confused as to what he is doing or what he is supposed to do and in addition he has hallucinations.

Mr. SIKES. He cannot concentrate on the task in front of him.

Dr. MacArthur. He cannot carry out his assigned duties nor can he remember what his assigned duties were.

Mr. FLOOD. Isn't there a nausea and temporary physical disability?

Dr. MacArthur. From BZ?

Mr. FLOOD. Yes.

General STONE. I don't think there is any nausea.

Dr. MacArthur. You are correct, General Stone. There is physical incapacitation but vomiting is not a usual symptom.

Mr. SIKES. Is there complete recovery?

Dr.MacArthur. Yes, there is.

Mr. SIKES. It is automatic?

Dr. MacArthur. Yes. It takes 2 or 3 days. He does not need any therapy, if I understand the sense of your question.

(Note: Current cost of BZ is $20 per pound.)

Mr. FLOOD. Where do your raw materials come from, Continental United States?

Dr. MacArthur. Yes, sir.

Mr. SIKES. Compared to other chemical or biological weapons, is it expensive?

Could you give us some of the range of cost on these?

Dr. MacArthur. The nerve agent GB is $1 to $2 a pound. VX is $2 to $3 a pound.

Mr. ANDREWS. What is VX?

Dr MacArthur. That is a nerve agent similar to GB, but in addition to being effective through inhalation it can also be effective through the skin—that is why we call it a percutaneous agent.

PRODUCTION OF BZ

Mr. MINSHALL. What is the lead time for manufacturing these incapacitating agents? How long would it take for you to make 10 tons of BZ?

Dr. MacArthur. Six to 9 months.

Mr. MINSHALL. With the plants that you have going, or the standby's?

Dr. MacArthur. Our three chemical plants which are in stand-by are for nerve gases. BZ would be procured from industry; however, there is no requirement for additional production.

Mr. SIKES. Can you switch to an industrial chemical operation?

Dr. MacArthur. Yes, for an incapacitant.

Mr. SIKES Quicker than you can put your own plants back in operation?

Dr. MacArthur. For incapacitants we would go to industry. For lethal agents, we could recondition our plants more rapidly than we could procure from industry.

LETHAL VERSUS INCAPACITATING AGENTS

Mr. FLOOD. Why do you emphasize and lay so much stress on the stockpile and speak so highly of the killer rather than the disabling agent? You have so much of the killer and you are so concerned about it and so interested in it and you beat your chest about it. Why not the disabling agent? Why not that first?

Dr. MacArthur. We have had lethal agents for a long time and they are the ones that comprise our stockpile. I merely want to get the record straight on what the agents can and cannot do. Incapacitating agents are a more recent development and are largely in the R. & D. phase. In fact, the prime emphasis in agent R. & D. is on developing better incapacitating agents. We are not emphasizing new lethal agents at all.

In fact, we have not in this country developed any new classes of lethal agents. They were developed by other countries and we have just adopted them. As far as R. & D. is concerned, the amount of R. & D. dollars we are spending on developing more toxic lethal agents is no more than $500,000 per year. We are concentrating on incapacitants.

Mr. FLOOD. If you are talking about a lethal agent, it does not matter how many you have. If you are killed by one it doesn't matter what it is called. And it does not matter whether the Germans or British created it. We have it.

Mr. SIKES. When you speak of the development of incapacitants, what do you include? How many different agents?

Dr. MACARTHUR. We are looking at various types on the chemical side. In addition to chemical incapacitants you can have biological incapacitants.

On the chemical side we are looking at four classes of compounds.

Mr. SIKES. You say looking at them, what does that mean?

Dr. MACARTHUR. We are synthesizing new compounds and testing them in animals. I should mention that there is a rule of thumb we use. Before an agent can be classified as an incapacitant we feel that the mortality must be very low. Therefore, the ratio of the lethal dose to the incapacitating dose has to be very high. Now this is a very difficult technical job. We have had some of the top scientists in the country working for years on how to get more effective incapacitating agents. It is not easy.

. . .

DEVELOPMENT OF NEW INCAPACITANTS

Mr. SIKES. Are we seeking to develop new incapacitants or to improve the ones that we have?

Dr. MACARTHUR. We are seeking to develop new incapacitants.

Mr. SIKES. Will you provide for the record some information on what we are doing in that field? What can you tell us about the Russian capability in the field of chemical incapacitants?

Dr. MACARTHUR. I am not personally aware, and I do not think anybody here is, about what the Russians are doing in the field of chemical incapacitants. Whether they are doing R. & D. or have incorporated them in military weapons, we do not know. I will submit for the record information on our program.

(The information follows:)

Chemical incapacitants are substances which cause incapacitation with an extremely small risk of death or permanent injury to personnel. They would be used in weapons with very little risk to personnel, such as pyrotechnic grenades. Possible uses include attack of mixed population of enemy and civilians, capture of prisoners, and similar actions where the intent is to reduce the scale of violence with minimum risk to target personnel. Compounds investigated include LSD, which was discarded as unsuitable in view of deleterious side effects, including possible genetic effects. We have one standard agent, known as BZ, which has the effect of causing confusion, disorientation, and slowing of mental and physical activity. Research is under way on several classes of compounds of greater promise.

DEVELOPMENT OF BIOLOGICAL WEAPONS

Mr. SIKES. Tell us something about the biological weapons, both lethal and incapacitants. Tell us what we are doing and what the Russians are doing.

Dr. MACARTHUR. I am sure all of you know biologicals are micro-organisms.

We have had a policy that the biological agents that we would try to develop would be noncontagious; that is, that it could not be passed on directly from individual to individual.

Mr. FLOOD. Would they be effective if not contagious?

Dr. MACARTHUR. They could be infectious from the standpoint that they would be used as a primary aerosol and infect people inhaling it. After that they could be carried from me to you, say by an insect vector—a mosquito, for example.

Mr. FLOOD. Could they be effective and contagious?

Dr. MACARTHUR. No.

Mr. FLOOD. I doubt that. I doubt that.

Dr. MACARTHUR. A contagious disease would not be effective as a biological warfare agent, although it might have devastating effects. It lacks the essential element of control which I alluded to earlier since there would be no way to predict or control the course of the epidemic that might result.

Mr. SIKES. Tell us the story of our progress and our capability.

Dr. MACARTHUR. I want to reemphasize that our policy has been not to develop any contagious agents so that we could control the effects so that they would not "boomerang" on our own people if ever we were forced to use them. Typical examples of diseases caused by agents we have worked on are tularemia, Rocky Mountain spotted fever, "Q" fever, Venezuelan equine encephalitis. These agents are different from the chemicals in that they are naturally occurring diseases.

Mr. SIKES. Are all of these lethal?

Dr. MACARTHUR. No. Some of these are lethal and others are non-lethal.

Mr. FLOOD. Could any be inherent by transmission? One generation to another?

Dr. MACARTHUR. If you are talking about genetic effects, no.

I would like to dwell a moment on the limitations of biological weapons which most people don't fully understand and consequently lead to a great deal of public misunderstanding. They are just not as effective as they are made out to be by many people.

LETHAL AND INCAPACITATING AGENTS

Mr. FLOOD. Break out for the record which are lethal and which are incapacitants.

(The information follows:)

121

BIOLOGICAL AGENTS

The following potential biological agents are among those that have been studied for offensive and defensive purposes:

Incapacitating:
Rickettsia causing Q-fever
Rift Valley fever virus
Chikungunya disease virus
Venezuelan equine encephalitis
    virus

Lethal:
Yellow fever virus
Rabbit fever virus
Anthrax bacteria
Psittacosis agent
Rickettsia of Rocky Mountain
    spotted fever
Plague

* * *

General STONE. Yes, sir.

Mr. SIKES. Will you provide information on the actual quantities of different kinds of chemical weapons that have been used in Vietnam, so we will have some comparison of the effectiveness?

(The quantities of CS used in Vietnam by type of weapon has been provided to the committee and is classified.)

Mr. MINSHALL. Have you had sufficient supply of these tear gases to take care of the commanders' needs in Vietnam?

General STONE. Yes, quite well. The quantities of production have been stepped up several times and I believe at the present time we are satisfying all requirements.

Mr. MINSHALL. Has there been a time when you have been in short supply?

General STONE. Yes, there was initially as we were getting going.

Mr. MINSHALL. When was that?

General STONE. About 3 years ago. I think we should supply this for the record.

Mr. MINSHALL. Fine.

(The information follows:)

PROCUREMENT OF RIOT-CONTROL AGENT CS (ALL SERVICES)

[In thousands of pounds]

Fiscal year	CS in weapons	Bulk CS-1	Bulk CS-2
1964	233	142	
1965	93	182	
1966	458	1,217	
1967	509	770	
1968 (programed)	869	3,504	931
1969 (programed)	2,334	192	3,884
Total	4,496	6,007	4,815

MACE

Mr. MINSHALL. I would like to know a little bit more about Mace. Are you qualified to tell us about that? We have read so much in the papers about it, whether it is harmful. or whether it is not harmful. One report said it was harmful and another said it is not harmful. What are the facts?

Dr. EMERSON. We ran some experiments with Mace as it is commercially available, at Edgewood Arsenal.

Mr. FLOOD. Many police departments will use it and many are against it.

Dr. EMERSON. On rabbits, which was the only test animal we used it on, we found that in some cases there was some damage, very slight damage to the eye.

Mr. MINSHALL. Permanent damage to the eye?

Dr. EMERSON. No.

Mr. FLOOD. There are reports to the contrary.

Dr. EMERSON. I know it.

Mr. MINSHALL. What do you mean damage to the eye? How temporary was it? Describe that damage a little more.

Dr. EMERSON. The lens on the eye became opaque. Our experiments only ran for 30 days. The Food and Drug Administration at the same time ran some experiments. They did not duplicate the damage that we got. By that time we had determined that we wanted to go with CS rather than CN, which is the product in Mace. It was no longer of any interest to the Army and we dropped our experiments at that point. Food and Drug continued.

Mr. MINSHALL. What is the fact in your opinion? Is Mace harmful or isn't it?

Dr. EMERSON. In the form you buy it today it is dissolved in a petroleum base and there is some question as to whether it is the petroleum base or the CN. We haven't determined that because we were not interested in it.

Mr. MINSHALL. What is your opinion, Dr. MacArthur?

Dr. MACARTHUR. I would like to comment on the way the experiment was made. The rabbit's eyes were kept open and the material was dropped in.

Many people feel that if anything is squirted at the eye the automatic response is for the eyelid to close, so that it is unlikely that the same concentration that was used in the experiment will get into the eye.

Mr. MINSHALL. If you get enough soap in your eye in a heavy concentrate, it will do some damage, won't it?

Dr. MACARTHUR. Yes.

Mr. SIKES. Was it really a harmful effect?

Dr. MACARTHUR. Yes, during the experiment. The question is how much will get into the eye in a practical situation.

● ● ●

POSSIBILITY OF PERMANENT EYE DAMAGE

Mr. MINSHALL. Would you recommend to a police department based on the experiments that you have conducted, that Mace is safe, or is it unsafe to use, as far as permanent eye damage?

Dr. MACARTHUR. Based on my personal knowledge of experiments conducted at Edgewood, I think no definitive conclusions can be drawn. I do not believe I am in a position to say whether it would be safe or unsafe. The indications from the experiment were that it might be unsafe. However, we have to look carefully at how the experiment was conducted in terms of whether it represents a true simulation of a practical situation before we come out with a definitive answer saying it is safe or unsafe.

I myself as an individual, couldn't in all good conscience say whether it was safe or unsafe.

Mr. SIKES. Now would you get into herbicides as used in Vietnam?

· · ·

HERBICIDES

USE IN VIETNAM

Mr. SIKES. Herbicides in Vietnam, now, please.

Dr. MACARTHUR. Herbicides are plant control chemicals and they are used in many countries throughout the world by millions of pounds a year. Domestic use is 50 to 70 million pounds per year in the United States. People continually say, "You are not using herbicides, you are using defoliants." Defoliants and herbicides are one and the same. We call them defoliants because we use them to defoliate the jungles. We use them to defoliate the jungle along the sides of roads to reduce ambush and save lives, and along enemy trails to reveal enemy traffic and camps, and for very limited anticrop use along infiltration routes on rice plots used by the enemy.

In fact, when we started using it, the ambush rate on roads—main roads leading out of Saigon—was reduced by 90 percent while the ambush rate in other areas of the country remained the same. So that is an indicator that its use was successful.

Secondly, when we use it, the vertical visibility through the jungle is increased by 80 percent and the horizontal visibility through the jungle is increased by 40 to 60 percent.

Mr. SIKES. Does that mean you can also take pictures if necessary of what is under the jungle cover when you could not while the leaves were on the trees?

Dr. MACARTHUR. That is exactly the reason we use it to detect the enemy, in addition to ambush prevention.

Mr. FLOOD. This can only be delivered by air?

Dr. MACARTHUR. No. If you want to put your herbicides on a rice plot that is known to have been planted along the trail by VC for later use you just take a little sprayer. But the most effective way for large area coverage is aerial delivery.

• • •

SYNTHETIC BIOLOGICAL AGENTS

There are two things about the biological agent field I would like to mention. One is the possibility of technological surprise. Molecular biology is a field that is advancing very rapidly, and eminent biologists believe that within a period of 5 to 10 years it would be possible to produce a synthetic biological agent, an agent that does not naturally exist and for which no natural immunity could have been acquired.

Mr. SIKES. Are we doing any work in that field?

Dr. MACARTHUR. We are not.

Mr. SIKES. Why not? Lack of money or lack of interest?

Dr. MACARTHUR. Certainly not lack of interest.

Mr. SIKES. Would you provide for our records information on what would be required, what the advantages of such a program would be, the time and the cost involved?

Dr. MACARTHUR. We will be very happy to.

(The information follows:)

The dramatic progress being made in the field of molecular biology led us to investigate the relevance of this field of science to biological warfare. A small group of experts considered this matter and provided the following observations:

1. All biological agents up to the present time are representatives of naturally occurring disease, and are thus known by scientists throughout the world. They are easily available to qualified scientists for research, either for offensive or defensive purposes.

2. Within the next 5 to 10 years, it would probably be possible to make a new infective microorganism which could differ in certain important aspects from any known disease-causing organisms. Most important of these is that it might be refractory to the immunological and therapeutic processes upon which we depend to maintain our relative freedom from infectious disease.

3. A research program to explore the feasibility of this could be completed in approximately 5 years at a total cost of $10 million.

4. It would be very difficult to establish such a program. Molecular biology is a relatively new science. There are not many highly competent scientists in the field, almost all are in university laboratories, and they are generally adequately supported from sources other than DOD. However, it was considered possible to initiate an adequate program through the National Academy of Sciences-National Research Council (NAS-NRC).

The matter was discussed with the NAS-NRC, and tentative plans were made to initiate the program. However, decreasing funds in CB, growing criticism of the CB program, and our reluctance to involve the NAS-NRC in such a controversial endeavor have led us to postpone it for the past 2 years.

It is a highly controversial issue, and there are many who believe such research should not be undertaken lest it lead to yet another method of massive killing of large populations. On the other hand, without the sure scientific knowledge that such a weapon is possible, and an understanding of the ways it could be done, there is little that can be done to devise defensive measures. Should an enemy develop it there is little doubt that this is an important area of potential military technological inferiority in which there is no adequate research program.

• • •

When the Air Force identified certain items as being excess, we then looked at what were the methods of disposal. We had on three different occasions disposed of unserviceable items by taking them to sea and dumping them. The Maritime Administration makes available an old hulk from the Reserve fleet; it is stripped of anything usable in shipyards and then they literally have holes cut in the hulk and patched. The hulk is then filled with these unserviceable munitions, towed to a site, the patches are pulled off and literally the hulk sinks as a container.

Since we had done three of these in the past and it has proven to be the cheapest and safest——

Mr. SIKES. When was this done?

Colonel OSICK. The last one was done in 1967. I have the exact dates here.

Mr. SIKES. Provide it for the record.

(The information follows:)

There have been three previous CHASE operations involving chemical munitions:

Date of operation	Material involved
June 15, 1967	Concrete coffins of M–55 rockets, 1-ton containers of mustard
June 19, 1968	Concrete coffins of M–55 rockets, 1-ton containers of mustard
Aug. 7, 1968	Contaminated 1-ton containers (water filled)

DISPOSAL LOCATION

Mr. FLOOD. Where?

Colonel OSICK. At the same site we planned to do this one. The figure 250 miles east of Atlantic City has been used, but I will not use that. It turned out to be incorrect.

Mr. FLOOD. What is peculiar about that site? With all the seacoast we have, why pick on the same site three times?

Colonel OSICK. That particular site is one of two on the east coast that is identified on maritime maps as a disposal area.

Mr. FLOOD. That doesn't answer my question.

Colonel OSICK. I will get to it, sir.

The geography of it, the depth at which we will drop this, the marine life and what we know about what is on the bottom there is ideal for this type of dump. It is in 1,200 fathoms of water, roughly 7,200 feet.

We have dumped other munitions there before and therefore shipping stays away from it. It is off the Continental Shelf.

•••

COST OF LAND VERSUS SEA DISPOSAL

Mr. MINSHALL. To revert back to my question about disposing of it or storing it in some desert area; is that feasible?

Colonel OSICK. I guess everything is feasible. Yes, sir. We have gone through it. In the land burial we estimated that to prepare the ground, fill the pit with concrete, move the items there, make sure the ground is blocked off or fenced so that animals or human beings would not traverse the top of it, and insure there would be no percolation up; about $11 million and about 39 months to do it.

Mr. SIKES. Compared with what cost for disposal by sea?

Colonel OSICK. About $3.9 million and 3 months.

Mr. MINSHALL. How much area would be required to dispose of this and to bury it? How many acres, square miles or whatever it might be?

Colonel OSICK. I would have to provide that.

Mr. SIKES. Provide the details for the comparison for the record.

(The information follows:)

It is estimated that approximately 25 acres of land would be required to bury on land the items in Project Chase.

...

Mr. SIKES. We have not completed all of the items that are before us. For instance, there is the problem of the sheep kill.

Let me suggest, doctor, that you provide a paper for the record in which you will spell out in detail any items that we have not discussed that were to have been covered.

Dr. MACARTHUR. We will be happy to do that.

(The information follows:)

ESCAPED NERVE AGENTS FROM TESTING AREA AT DUGWAY PROVING GROUND, UTAH

On March 13, 1968, a spray mission using a high performance aircraft was conducted at Dugway Proving Ground using liquid persistent nerve agent VX. One spray tank malfunctioned, so that the agent continued to trail out of the tank as the plane rose to a higher altitude (about 1,500 feet) enroute to the area in which the tank was jettisoned. The meterological conditions at the time of test were such that all agent would have been deposited within the test area, miles from the Proving Ground border. Subsequent to the test the meteorology changed abruptly and in an unpredicted and anomalous manner. Subsequent analysis reveals that less than 20 pounds of agent remained airborne.

On March 14 range sheep began sickening and some died later. This was not reported to the Army until March 17 at which time investigations were started. These ultimately involved the Utah State Departments of Health and Agriculture, the U.S. Public Health Service, and the U.S. Department of Agriculture as well as many elements of the U.S. Army Materiel Command. Extensive investigations finally revealed that the sheep probably ingested very low dosages of the agent VX. In later experiments on sheep, the symptoms exhibited by the range sheep were reproduced at much higher dosages, leading to the conclusion that the range sheep were more susceptible for some reason or reasons, as yet unknown. There might have been such factors as physical condition due to overwintering, and the presence on the range of various toxic plants. In view of the fact that the agent VX was apparently involved, the Army has agreed to the compensation of the owners of the sheep in accordance with established claims procedures.

In July of 1968 Secretary of the Army Stanley Resor established an advisory panel of experts from the groups mentioned above and others, and chaired by Dr. William Stewart, Surgeon General of the U.S. Public Health Service. This panel recommended certain additional restrictions on open-air testing at Dugway Proving Ground which were immediately ordered by the Secretary of the Army and are now in effect. A permanent chemical safety advisory committee has now been established to oversee testing in the future. This committee is composed of representatives of U.S. Public Health Service, Departments of Interior, Commerce and Agriculture, Utah State Department of Health, and two members representing the public at large, one of whom is the chairman.

PART TWO

GOVERNMENT, MILITARY, AND CORPORATE SECRETS

Honoring
ThoseWhoServed

USA
29

Desert Shield ★ Desert Storm

12

NAZIS IN THE U.S.

Putting War Criminals
to Work for America

If you believe in things like making a pact with the devil, you might say that our intelligence agencies did just that at the end of World War Two. That's when we started giving many of Hitler's top henchmen not only sanctuary in our country, but putting these same Nazis to work for us. The Cold War with the Soviet Union was beginning—and the excuse was that we needed every bit of expertise, scientific and otherwise, that we could get.

It almost seems to me that the Cold War was staged so the weapons manufacturers and others could make money off it. Otherwise, how could we go from being allies with the Russians all through the war to their becoming our bitter enemies almost overnight? As Colonel Fletcher Prouty once said, "Nothing just happens, everything is planned."

And I find it outrageous that some of the leading Nazis were brought over here because it was apparently more important to fight the Cold War than to hold them responsible for what they'd done. I don't understand how the people making those decisions look only at the "big picture" and forget about collateral damage underneath. If they were absolutely sure no war crimes or atrocities had been committed, fine and dandy. But there should have been a thorough vetting done by this country—and not secretly but in public—so the American people knew which Nazis were coming and why.

The Justice Department's Office of Special Investigations put together a massive 600-page report about all this, which they completed in 2006. A few years later, the National Security Archive (a nonprofit in Washington, D.C.) filed a Freedom of Information Act request. This got turned down, the excuse being that the report was only a "draft." That was despite the Obama administration supposedly being committed to an "unprecedented" level of transparency. What could possibly be so sensitive after all these years?

Anyway, the National Security Archive filed suit in a federal district court, and the Justice Department then began to "process" the document for release. Well, they must have bought up pretty much all the Wite-Out left in the office supply. They could've issued a CD titled "My Blank Pages." After the redacted report got turned over to the National Security Archive, somebody inside the Justice Department took matters into their own hands and leaked a complete copy to the *New York Times*.

If you want to read the whole thing, or compare the two versions, check out the National Security Archive website at www.gwu.edu/~nsarchiv/NSAEBB/NSAEBB331/index.htm. I'm including here a one-page sampler of the censored version with the actual—an example of the lengths our government will go to keep "secrets" under wraps more than sixty years after-the-fact. This is followed by a few of the more telling pages from the Office of Special Investigations' report.

1

2   ] Ex.
                                                                      85,
3   B6

4   The SLU attorneys were invited to transfer *en masse* and all but one made the move. The

5   students and archivist, who had been hired on a temporary part-time basis, were given pink slips

6   and had to reapply for a permanent position. All those who did were chosen. Mendelsohn was

7   named Deputy Director of the unit.

8

9

10
11
12
13
14
15
16   Ex. 86
17
18
19
20
21
22
23
24
25
26
27
28   ]
29   Rockler, as Mendelsohn before him, also traveled to the U.S.S.R. and Israel to speak with his

30   counterparts.

31   [   ] Ex.
                                                              86

arrangement would last six to eight months, by which time the office would be established and a new director in place. Rockler's firm too was accommodating, agreeing to provide his full partnership draw, less only what he earned from the government.[77]

The SLU attorneys were invited to transfer *en masse* and all but one made the move. The students and archivist, who had been hired on a temporary part-time basis, were given pink slips and had to reapply for a permanent position. All those who did were chosen. Mendelsohn was named Deputy Director of the unit. Rockler wanted him to oversee litigation while Rockler would assess new cases and deal with the mechanics of establishing the section. As Rockler described his own responsibilities:

> I had to waste an awful lot of time seeing delegations of groups, the Baltics, the Ukrainians. I had delegations descend on me to plead the case of their countrymen. They were all being potentially persecuted. I didn't know anything about it. I would listen to them and be fairly non-committal. After a while I got fairly impatient with them and I said look, we're not going to pursue anybody because they are Latvian, Lithuanian or Ukrainian. It ain't a nationality designation. If we find they've engaged in anything, why don't you help us instead of criticizing us? Why don't you come forward with stuff so we'll get done with it? And I was short tempered and I didn't understand public relations. I didn't understand the job is a public relations job. Meanwhile the Jewish groups were descending on me and they had a different pitch, which I found extremely irritating too, which was: Where the hell have you been for 30 years? How come you haven't hung anybody? I thought to myself, they're all nuts. I mean people are totally polarized. They don't know what the hell goes on and they were annoying. Some of the particular Jewish groups had particular targets in mind. They wanted us to go after Mr. X, Mr. Y or Mr. Z. So I was wasting an awful lot of time on things like that. I had a couple of public appearances. I didn't want the public relations part of it anyhow, but there was no way to avoid it.[78]

Rockler, as Mendelsohn before him, also traveled to the U.S.S.R. and Israel to speak with his counterparts.

Holtzman, meanwhile, kept her eye on the new section and periodically summoned

Otto von Bolschwing – An Eichmann Associate Who Became a CIA Source

Otto von Bolschwing worked with Adolf Eichmann and helped devise programs to persecute and terrorize Germany's Jewish population. As the chief SS intelligence officer, first in Romania and then in Greece, he was the highest ranking German prosecuted by OSI.

• • •

In 1946, von Bolschwing was hired by the Gehlen organization, a group of former Nazi intelligence operatives who came under the aegis of the U.S. Army after the war. The group had provided Germany with data and sources useful in the war on the Eastern front; the U.S. wanted to develop and expand this material for use during the Cold War. Gehlen needed von Bolschwing to provide contacts among ethnic Germans and former Iron Guardsmen in Romania.[5]

In 1949, the CIA hired some members of the Gehlen organization; von Bolschwing was among those chosen.[6] The CIA knew about his Nazi party and SD connections. They also knew that he had supported the Iron Guard uprising and had helped leaders of that rebellion escape from Romania. He portrayed himself, however, as a Nazi gadfly[7] and the agency apparently accepted this characterization.[8] The agency was unaware that he had worked in the Jewish Affairs Office and that he had been associated with Eichmann.[9]

Although he never developed into a "first-class agent," the CIA was sufficiently grateful to help him emigrate to the United States in 1954.[10] The CIA advised INS about his past as they understood it. INS agreed to admit him nonetheless.[11] He entered under the INA as part of the German quota. Once here, he worked as a high-ranking executive for various multi-national corporations; he did no further work for U.S. intelligence agencies.[12]

Even before von Bolschwing emigrated, however, the CIA was concerned that he might have difficulty obtaining citizenship.

> Grossbahn [von Bolschwing's code name] has asked a question which has us fairly well stumped. What should his answer be in the event the question of NSDAP [Nazi party] membership arises <u>after</u> his entry into the U.S., for example,

on the citizenship application forms? We have told him he is to deny any party, SS, SD, Abwehr [German military intelligence], etc. affiliations. Our reason for doing so runs as follows: his entry into the U.S. is based on our covert clearance. In other words, in spite of the fact he has an objectionable background, [   ] is willing to waive their normal objections based on our assurance that Grossbahn's services . . . have been of such a caliber as to warrant extraordinary treatment. Should Grossbahn later, overtly and publicly, admit to an NSDAP record, it strikes us that this might possibly leave [   ] with little recourse than to expel him from the U.S. as having entered under false pretenses. . . . At the same time, we feel such instructions might give Grossbahn a degree of control against us, should he decide he wants our help again at some future date – an altogether undesirable situation. What has Headquarters' experience been on this point? Have we instructed Grossbahn incorrectly? Cabled advice would be appreciated, as time to the planned departure date is running short.[13]

The response urged that von Bolschwing tell the truth.

Assuming that he has not denied Nazi affiliations on his visa application form, he should definitely not deny his record if the matter comes up in dealing with US authorities and he is forced to give a point-blank answer. Thus, if asked, he should admit membership, but attempt to explain it away on the basis of extenuating circumstances. If he were to make a false statement on a citizenship application or other official paper, he would get into trouble. Actually Grossbahn is not entering the US under false pretenses as [   ] will have information concerning his past record in a secret file.[14]

Arthur Rudolph – An Honored Rocket Scientist

As early as July 1945, the U.S. War Department brought selected German and Austrian scientists to the United States under military custody for "short-term exploitation." The immediate goal was to have them pursue military research in an effort to shorten the war with Japan. The longer term goal was to keep the Soviet Union and other countries from gaining access to the information and skills of many elite members of the scientific community.

With the direct approval of the president of the United States, the program was extended after the close of hostilities:

> in order to permit the Armed Services of the United States to take advantage of German scientific and technical progress in such fields as guided missiles and aerodynamics, pending formulation of governmental policy to permit legal entry of these and other specialists. . . to pursue research and development projects for both military and civilian agencies.

Ultimately codenamed "Operation Paperclip," the program was designed to exclude anyone who was more than a "nominal participant" in Nazi party activities or had been an "active supporter of Nazism or militarism." Those scientists who wished to settle permanently in the United States could, "at a later date . . . be granted regular status under the immigration laws."[1]

Eventually, hundreds of scientists came to the United States under the program. Those seeking permanent residence had to apply for a visa. Once it was issued, they had to leave the country and then "formally" reenter. They generally did so through a Mexican border city.

During the war, Arthur Rudolph had served as Operations Director at the massive Mittelwerk underground V-2 rocket manufacturing facility. The factory was part of the Dora-Nordhausen concentration camp complex and used prisoners of war and slave laborers. The latter group included thousands of Czech, Polish, Russian, and French political prisoners, as well as Jewish and Jehovah's Witness inmates.[2] The laborers, wearing striped concentration camp uniforms, came from Nazi camps including Auschwitz and Buchenwald. They were guarded by armed SS men as well as kapos, and worked 12-hour shifts in cold, damp, and dusty tunnels. Thousands perished, generally from malnutrition, exhaustion and overwork; some were murdered. Until Dora got its own crematorium, the dead were burned at Buchenwald.

Rudolph was one of the first Germans to come to the United States under Operation Paperclip; he arrived in December 1945. Although INS knew that he had been a member of the Nazi party and that he had worked at Mittelwerk, there is no indication that they had any information about his use of slave labor.[3] On the contrary, there was much to recommend Rudolph. The number two official at the Department of Justice urged INS (an agency then under the jurisdiction of the Justice Department) to admit him. Based on information from the Joint Chiefs of Staff and the Department of the Army, the official opined that failure to do so "would be to the detriment of the national interest."[4]

In 1949, Rudolph went to Ciudad Juarez, Mexico, where he received a visa and then formally reentered the United States under the INA. Although the "assistance in persecution" provisions of the DPA and RRA were inapplicable, State Department visa regulations prohibited the entry of an alien "who has been guilty of, or has advocated or acquiesced in, activities or conduct contrary to civilization and human decency on behalf of the Axis countries."

Rudolph became a naturalized U.S. citizen in 1954 and worked in the U.S. rocket program until his retirement from NASA in 1969. He was considered the father of the Saturn V rocket which enabled the United States to make its first manned moon landing. At his retirement, NASA awarded him the Distinguished Service Award, its highest honor.

13 & 14 & 15

NAZI WAR CRIMES

More on U.S. Intelligence and the Nazis

Not long after the Justice Department's 2006 report came out, along came another from the National Archives. This is based on 1.3 million Army files and another 1,110 CIA files. The *New York Times* had this to say about it: "After World War II, American counterintelligence recruited former Gestapo officers, SS veterans and Nazi collaborators to an even greater extent than had been previously disclosed and helped many of them avoid prosecution or looked the other way when they escaped..."

I'm including here the 100-page report's introduction and conclusion, and sandwiched in between are three documents that caught my eye. One is an interview with a personal secretary to Hitler, who took his last will and testament, and who also related how the armored car carrying Martin Bormann was blown up. The second is about how the Germans supported a number of Arab leaders during the war, apparently based on expecting to later establish pro-German governments in the Middle East. And the third, signed by CIA Director Allen Dulles in 1952, shows the Agency looking to head off a criminal investigation into a Ukrainian nationalist leader that it wanted to keep using.

INTRODUCTION

At the end of World War II, Allied armies recovered a large portion of the written or filmed evidence of the Holocaust and other forms of Nazi persecution. Allied prosecutors used newly found records in numerous war crimes trials. Governments released many related documents regarding war criminals during the second half of the 20th century. A small segment of American-held documents from Nazi Germany or about Nazi officials and Nazi collaborators, however, remained classified into the 21st century because of government restrictions on the release of intelligence-related records.

Approximately 8 million pages of documents declassified in the United States under the 1998 Nazi War Crimes Disclosure Act added significantly to our knowledge of wartime Nazi crimes and the postwar fate of suspected war criminals. A 2004 U.S. Government report by a team of independent historians working with the government's Nazi War Criminal Records Interagency Working Group (IWG), entitled *U.S. Intelligence and the Nazis*, highlighted some of the new information; it appeared with revisions as a 2005 book.[1] Our 2010 report serves as an addendum to *U.S. Intelligence and the Nazis*; it draws upon additional documents declassified since then.

The latest CIA and Army files have: evidence of war crimes and about the wartime activities of war criminals; postwar documents on the search for or prosecution of war criminals; documents about the escape of war criminals; documents about the Allied protection or use of Nazi war criminals; and documents about the postwar political activities of war criminals. None of the declassified documents conveys a complete story in itself; to make sense of this evidence, we have also drawn on older documents and published works.

The Timing of Declassification

Why did the most recent declassifications take so long? In 2005–07 the Central Intelligence Agency adopted a more liberal interpretation of the 1998 Nazi War Crimes Disclosure Act. As a result, CIA declassified and turned over to the National Archives and Records Administration (NARA) additional documents from pre-existing files as well as entirely new CIA files, totaling more than 1,100 files in all. Taken together, there were several thousand pages of new CIA records that no one outside the CIA had seen previously.

A much larger collection came from the Army. In the early postwar years, the Army had the largest U.S. intelligence and counterintelligence organizations in Europe; it also led the search for Nazi war criminals. In 1946 Army intelligence (G-2) and the Army Counterintelligence Corps (CIC) had little competition—the CIA was not established until a year later. Even afterwards, the Army remained a critical factor in intelligence work in central Europe.

Years ago the Army facility at Fort Meade, Maryland, turned over to NARA its classified Intelligence and Security Command Records for Europe from the period (approximately) 1945–63. Mostly counterintelligence records from the Army's Investigative Records Repository (IRR), this collection promised to be a rich source of information about whether the United States maintained an interest in war crimes and Nazi war criminals.

After preserving these records on microfilm, and then on a now obsolete system of optical disks, the Army destroyed many of the paper documents. But the microfilm deteriorated, and NARA could not read or recover about half of the files on the optical disks, let alone declassify and make them available. NARA needed additional resources and technology to solve the technological problems and transfer the IRR files to a special computer server. Declassification of these IRR files only began in 2009, after the IWG had gone out of existence.

This new Army IRR collection comprises 1.3 million files and many millions of pages. It will be years before all of these Army files are available for researchers.

For this report we have drawn selectively upon hundreds of these IRR files, amounting to many thousands of pages, which have been declassified and are already available at NARA.

Intelligence Organizations and War Crimes

American intelligence and counterintelligence organizations each had its own raison d'être, its own institutional interests, and its own priorities. Unfortunately, intelligence officials generally did not record their general policies and attitudes toward war crimes and war criminals, so that we hunted for evidence in their handling of individual cases. Despite variations, these specific cases do show a pattern: the issue of capturing and punishing war criminals became less important over time. During the last months of the war and shortly after it, capturing enemies, collecting evidence about them, and punishing them seemed quite consistent. Undoubtedly, the onset of the Cold War gave American intelligence organizations new functions, new priorities, and new foes. Settling scores with Germans or German collaborators seemed less pressing; in some cases, it even appeared counterproductive.

In the months after the war in Europe ended Allied forces struggled to comprehend the welter of Nazi organizations. Allied intelligence agencies initially scrutinized their German intelligence counterparts for signs of participation in underground organizations, resistance, or sabotage. Assessing threats to the Allied occupation of Germany, they thought first of Nazi fanatics and German intelligence officials. Nazi officials in the concentration camps had obviously committed terrible crimes, but the evidence about the Gestapo was not as striking. The Allies started by trying to find out who had been responsible for what.

NOTES

1 Richard Breitman, Norman J.W. Goda, Timothy Naftali, and Robert Wolfe, *U.S. Intelligence and the Nazis* (New York: Cambridge University Press, 2005).

(15) When did you first and last see Rattenhuber durin-
the escape from the chancellery? What did he say about the fate
of Bormann? What else do you know, or have you heard, about the
of Bormann and Stumpfegger?

ANSWER: I went north by foot, hoping to come into unoccupied
German territory, but until the Elbe everything was still occupi
by Russians and made it impossible to get into the American Zone

I continued to wander along the demarcation line, and also there I
could not pass the Russians. Then I went back to Berlin, where a
woman had offered an apartment to me.

On my refuge in the vicinity of Berlin in the little spot Bykwitz
on approximately the 15th May I met the Chauffeur of Hitler,
Sturmbannführer Kempka in civilian clothes. He told me that he
had left with a smaller group together with Bormann, Dr Naumann,
and Dr Stumpfegger the Reichschancellery later than I did. When
crossing the Weidendamm Bridge the enemy fire was so strong,
Kempka told me, that many died. An armoured car, in which
Bormann, Naumann and Stumpfegger tried to cross the bridge, received a full target shell, just before Kempka wanted to jump
on it. He was thrown back, was blind for a short time, and saw,
after he had gained consciousness, that Bormann and Stumpfegger
were lying dead in their blood. I do not remember whether he
claimed that Naumann was dead too.

      3. For your information.

Tel Garmisch Mil 160, 161   KARL SUSSMANN
                                             Special Agent, CIC

Gertrude (Traudl) Junge, one of Hitler's personal secretaries, stayed in the Reichschancellery bunker to take Hitler's last will and testament before his suicide. Junge describes the perils in working her way through the Russian lines surrounding Berlin. She relates meeting Hitler's chauffeur Kemka and of the deaths of Martin Bormann, Stumpfegger, and Naumann, when their armored car was blown up. *RG 319, Records of the Army Staff.*

Early in 1945 Geheim Rat MELCHERS, head of Pol VII, told REKOWSKI that he had reached an agreement with Raschid Ali EL GAILANI to be put into effect 1 Apr 45. It provided that all sums paid by the Reich to EL GAILANI were to be repaid after the conquest of Iraq. Beginning 1 Apr 45, probably under provisions of the same contract, the monthly cash payments to EL GAILANI were to be raised to RM 85,000. REKOWSKI does not know if this increase was ever approved by the Foreign Minister; nor does he know if a similar agreement was reached with the Grand Mufti or whether the contract of 1941 remained in force unchanged.

By decree of the Foreign Office both Arab leaders enjoyed equal standing and were treated as potentates. Since all their expenses were paid by Germany, they used the monthly cash payments, certainly large parts and possibly all of them, to support their Arab followers. EL GAILANI maintained an office solely for the purpose of paying his followers and thereby prevented his men from going directly to the Foreign Office.

The following Arabs in Germany were supported by EL GAILANI: Kamil EL GAILANI, Jempi SULETAN, Maj SALMAN of the Iraq Army Hikemet SAMI, and the widow and two children of the executed former Air Minister of Iraq, Mohud SALMAN.

The Grand Mufti, Amin EL HUSSEINI, supported his Staff consisting of two other HUSSEINI's (fnu), Dr JANDALI, Dr WAKIL, and Dr ALLMAIER, as well as the Islamisches Institut in BERLIN and a number of other Arabs unknown to REKOWSKI.

The foreign exchange funds received by both leaders were used to support appr 150 students in PARIS and some Arabs living outside of Germany, and to finance trips abroad to purchase articles not easily obtained in Germany.

The Foreign Office made monthly payments directly to Prince Mansour DOUD (RM 1,000), Junes BAHRI (RM 600), the Cheriff CHARAF (RM 1,000), Dr Tahib NASSER (RM 750), Fauci EL KAUDCI (RM ?), and to the Minister of War of Iraq, name unknown, then living in VIENNA, The last named may have been Ibrahim PASDIA. Tahib NASSER also received a monthly sum (RM 750), from Rundfunk VII.

REKOWSKI learned from Dr SCHOERBEL, head of Presse VII, a subordinate division of Dept VII of the Foreign Office, that Chakib AROLAN received payments from Presse VII for his contributions to the magazine La Nation Arabe. REKOWSKI does not know the amounts or the methods of paying. The magazine was printed in French and dealt with Arab questions of a political nature. It was planned as a monthly publication of Presse VII but appeared infrequently or irregularly because not enough suitable writers could be found.

b. German Intentions Towards the Arab Countries

Through casual conversations with Dr GROBBA, REKOWSKI learned that the German plan was to charge the Mufti and EL GAILANI with the establishment of pro-German governments in their respective countries and to exploit these countries in due time. The currency to be used under the new regime in Iraq was printed in Germany as early as 1942, and a set of new uniforms was ready for Raschid Ali EL GAILANI.

German financial support of Arab leaders during the entire war was astonishing. The Grand Mufti Amin el Husseini and Raschid Ali El Gailani financed their operations with funding from the German Foreign Ministry from 1941–45. German intention in the Arab countries was based on an expectation of establishing pro-German governments in the Middle East. *RG 319, Records of the Army Staff.*

CENTRAL INTELLIGENCE AGENCY

WASHINGTON 25, D. C.

OFFICE OF THE DIRECTOR

6 MAY 1952

RECEIVED
MAY 9 1952
INVESTIGATION
SECTION

Mr. Argyle R. Mackey
Commissioner of Immigration
  and Naturalization
Department of Justice
Washington 25, D.C.

     SUBJECT: Mykola LEBED

Dear Sir:

    inestimable value to this Agency in its operations. In connection
with future Agency operations of the first importance, it is
urgently necessary that subject be able to travel in Western
Europe. Before subject undertakes such travel, however, this
Agency must be in a position to assure his reentry into the United
States without investigation or incident which would attract undue
attention to his activities. Your Service has indicated that it
cannot give such assurance because of the fact that subject was
convicted in 1936 of complicity in the 1934 Assassination of the
Polish Minister of the Interior and sentenced to death, later
commuted to life imprisonment. Subject's trial by the Polish
court was largely influenced by political factors and this Agency
has no reason to disbelieve subject's denial of complicity in this
assassination. However, the conviction of a crime involving moral
turpitude raises the question of subject's admissibility to the
United States under the Immigration laws. Your Service has indicated that, if the subject reenters the United States on a reentry
permit, an investigation must then be conducted. Such investiga-

    In order to remove the obstacles to the fulfillment of this
Agency's projected operations and pursuant to the authority granted
under Section 8 of the CIA Act of 1949, I approve and recommend for
your approval, the entrance of this subject into the United States
for permanent residence under the above Act because such entry is
essential to the furtherance of the national intelligence mission
and is in the interest of national security. In accordance with
previous correspondence in Section 8 cases, it is understood that
you will present this matter to the Attorney General for his
approval. There is attached a memorandum of biographical information and Form I-125 in duplicate.

    In line with the suggestion made in your letter of 31 March
1952, it will be appreciated if you will record the subject's
admission for permanent residence as of the date of his original
entry, 4 October 1949, to coincide with date of entry of his
wife and daughter.

    In view of the urgency in this case, it would be appreciated
if you would give it your expeditious consideration.

              Sincerely,

              Allen W. Dulles
              Deputy Director

*DECLASSIFIED AND REL
CENTRAL INTELLIGENCE
SOURCES METHODS EXEMPT
NAZI WAR CRIMES DISCLO
DATE 2002 2005*

*DECLASSIFIED
Nazi War Crimes Disclosure Act
PL 105-246*

ABLE COPY

LABLE COPY

The CIA moved to protect Ukranian nationalist leader Mykola Lebed from criminal investigation by the Immigration and Naturalization Service in 1952. *RG 263, Records of the Central Intelligence Agency.*

CONCLUSION

This report discusses only a sample of newly released records, hinting at their overall richness. The 1.3 million Army files include thousands of titles of many more issues regarding wartime criminals, their pursuit, their arrest, their escape, and occasionally, their use by Allied and Soviet intelligence agencies. These include files on German war criminals, but also collaborators from the Baltic States, Belarus, Ukraine, Romania, Hungary, Croatia, and elsewhere. These files also include information on Allied and non-aligned states that had an interest in Axis personalities, including Great Britain, France, Italy, Argentina, and Israel.

The 1,110 re-released or newly released CIA name files are in most cases far more detailed than the files of the initial CIA release in 2001 and after. They contain a trove of information on Nazis who eventually worked for the Gehlen Organization or as Soviet spies after the war. They hold information about important Nazi officials who escaped and became figures of security interest in other countries spanning the globe from the Middle East to South America. Together, the Army and CIA records will keep scholars of World War II and the Cold War busy for many years.

The new files also have postwar intelligence on other subjects. The CIC kept close watch on other suspect groups, such as German communists, and kept thousands of files on them. They kept watch on politically active Jewish refugees in displaced persons camps. Indeed, there are many hundreds of newly released files concerning the remnant of European Jews who searched for a new life in Palestine or the United States. Thus the new records are of great interest to those researching a very broad range of topics from international Communism to the Jewish diaspora to the history of mass migration.

The declassification of intelligence-related material is a controversial subject, involving as it does the release of records formerly of national security interest. The current releases show, however, that the passage of years lessens the information's sensitivity while providing researchers access to raw information that is simply not available elsewhere. By their very nature, intelligence agencies attain and record information that other government or non-government organizations cannot. None of the chapters in this report could have been written without declassified intelligence records, nor could the many articles and books that will emerge as a result of the current release. The funding for declassification and the assurance that intelligence records are opened to the public thus preserve key aspects of world history. In the interest of understanding our past Congress should, in our view, ensure that such openness continues.

UNCLASSIFIED

WARREN COMMISSION

CIA "Propaganda Notes" on the Kennedy Assassination

This CIA memo of "Propaganda Notes" from 1964 is self-explanatory. They were going to make sure the Warren Report that concluded President Kennedy was assassinated by a lone nut named Lee Harvey Oswald got disseminated far and wide. The intention was to bury suspicions of conspiracy, part of a systematic government-promoted distribution of—they said it, not me—propaganda.

A great deal of the CIA's job seems to be to "spin" whatever happens in the best light they can. And for the most part, spinning is done to cover up the truth: If we've done it, then it has to be right.

OUTGOING TELEGRAM   Department of State

C   38249   CONFIDENTIAL   C
O   O
P   ACTION: CIRCULAR   505   18 Sept 1964   P
Y   ALL AMERICAN DIPLOMATIC POSTS, Except LUXEMBOURG   Y
          and USUN, LISTED CONSULAR POSTS

          JOINT STATE-USIA

          FOR PRINCIPAL OFFICERS AND PAO's

          Arrangements made to air pouch to addressees presentation and staff
copies one-volume Warren Commission Report which extremely sensitive prior formal
release by White House. Copies will be separately packaged, labeled "EYES ONLY
PRINCIPAL OFFICER", registered and individually pouched. Essential that each
Principal Officer be responsible personally for integrity of package containing
copies from receipt until formal release. Dispatch from Washington by unaccom-
panied pouch being timed so no copies will reach addressees earlier than two
days prior to Washington release. Some addressees necessarily will receive copies
following formal release.

          You will receive specific notice of release time and identifying pouch
containing reports.

          Report should be selectively presented to editors, jurists, Government
officials, and other opinion-leaders at post discretion immediately after repeat
after formal release time.

          USIA preparing in addition: newsreel clips, newspix, illustrated
pamphlet of highlights of Report in language versions through RSC's and principal posts. Wireless File and VOA will backstop with interviews, panels, official
comment, domestic and foreign editorial comments, columns and commentaries. Also
possibly later 30 minutes TV documentary, and 16mm film for direct projection.
Maximum post effort needed to assure foreign recognition that truth concerning
assassination fully set forth in Commission's findings.

                                                     RUSK
TO:
ADANA   DOUALA   KADUNA   PALERMO
AREQUIPA   DUSSELDORF   KHORRAMSHAHR   PARAMARIBO
ASMARA   ELIZABETHVILLE   LAHORE   PORTO ALEGRE
BELEM   ENUGU   LOURENCO MARQUES   RECIFE
BENGHAZI   FLORENCE   LUANDA   SALISBURY
BOMBAY   FRANKFURT   LUSAKA   SALVADOR BAHIA
BUKAVU   GEORGETOWN   MADRAS   SANTIAGO DE LOS
BELO HORIZONTE   GENOA   MARACAIBO   CABALLEROS
BRASILIA   GUADALAJARA   MARTINIQUE   SAO PAULO
CALCUTTA   GUAYAQUIL   MELBOURNE   SINGAPORE
CALI   HAMBURG   MESHED   STUTTGART
CASABLANCA   HONG KONG   MILAN   SYDNEY
COCHABAMBA   IBADAN   MONTERREY   TABRIZ
CONSTANTINE   ISFAHAN   MUNICH   TANGIER
CORDOBA   ISTANBUL   NAPLES   THESSALONIKI
CURITIBA   IZMIR   ORAN   TURIN
DACCA   ZAGREB

                              CS COPY
                    CONFIDENTIAL   201-289248 200 5-41

PROPAGANDA NOTES

Series A :   BULLETINS

OX-274
67 (A)   22 September 1964

WARREN COMMISSION REPORT — Policy recommendations
as stated in Propaganda Notes issue of 22 Sept

1. The long awaited Warren Commission Report, on its exhausive
investigation into the assassination of President Kennedy on November
22, 1963 and the subsequent murder of Lee Oswald by Jack Ruby, will be
sent to the White House on Thursday September 24th and will probably be
released sometime over the weekend. The Department of State is air pouch-
ing copies of the Report (based on some 20 volumes of hearings) to posts
for selective presentation (upon formal release) to "editors, jurists,
Government officials, other opinion-leaders" after the formal release.
(See attachment, State Circular 505, 19 September 1964, joint State-USIA
message, with list of recipients). Copies of this Government Printing
Office edition will be sent to field stations from headquarters.

2. Reports from around the world indicate that there is a strong
belief in many countries that the assassination of the President was the
result of a "political plot"; the unwarranted interpretation that Ruby's
murder of Oswald was committed to prevent Oswald from revealing the purported conspiracy adds to this belief. Communist regimes have used both
murders to denigrate American society and the release of the Report will
undoubtedly be used as a new peg for the same purpose.

3. Covert assets should explain the tragedy wherever it is genuinely
misunderstood and counter all efforts to misconstrue it intentionally --
provided the depth of impact warrants such action. Communists and other
extremists always attempt to prove a political conspiracy behind violence.
In countries accustomed to assassination by political conspiracy, American
dedication to institutions of law and government with stable administrative
procedures can be described; and American Presidents can be shown to have
been the victims (with the exception of Lincoln) of single, fanatical individuals.

4. Three commercial editions will be published as soon as possible
after the formal release. KUWOLF/PROP has ordered 150 of Bantam's publication but will evaluate the introductions of all three and inform operating Divisions of any drawbacks. Divisions should make bulk purchases for
field use through regular channels.

CS COPY

200-5-41
201-289248

NORIEGA AND THE U.S.

Running Drugs
with Dictators

The Reagan years are remembered, of course, for the Iran-Contra scandal that made a notorious celebrity (and future political hero to many) of Colonel Oliver North. He claimed that John Kerry's 1988 Senate Foreign Relations subcommittee report on the interplay between U.S. support for the Nicaraguan Contras and the drug trade was all wrong. "The fact is nobody in the government of the United States...ever had anything to do with running drugs to support the Nicaraguan resistance...I will stand on that to my grave."

Well, North may still be standing but his credibility sure isn't. His diary entries actually had numerous reports of drug smuggling among the Contras, none of which North alerted the DEA or other law enforcement agencies about. One mentions $14 million in drug money being funneled into an operation.

I have to laugh and, in the immortal words of Nancy Reagan, "just say no" to drugs. The hypocrisy of the double standard is ludicrous. All you can do is laugh, or cry. I guess it's okay to deal drugs if it's for the cause of war.

I'm including here an exchange between North and his boss, Admiral John Poindexter, about Manuel Noriega, the Panamian dictator who our government later overthrew. Noriega is still doing time for drug-running, and it turns out that he and North had "a fairly good relationship." Poindexter said he had "nothing against him other than his illegal activities." (He misspells "assassination.")

For more details on all this, check out National Security Archive Electronic Briefing Book No. 113 on-line (February 26, 2004).

This sets the stage for an extraordinary exchange between the NSC and Noriega. After the *New York Times* story, other press coverage of Noriega's criminal activities sprouts like mushrooms after rain. Noriega needs public relations help, so who does he call? — the White House. On August 23, 1986, Oliver North writes his boss, Adm. John Poindexter: "You will recall that over the years Manuel Noriega in Panama and I have developed a fairly good relationship." North describes an overture from Noriega: "In exchange for a promise from us to 'help clean up his [Noriega's] image' and a commitment to lift our ban on FMS [Foreign Military Sales] to the Panamanian Defense [Force, he would] undertake to 'take care of' the Sandinista leadership for us."

```
ᵀO: NSJMP    /--CPUA
      /
••• Reply to note of 05/08/86 10:54
NOTE FROM: OLIVER NORTH
Subject: Iran
```

```
      NICARAGUA:You will recall that over the years Manuel Noriega in Pana
ma and I have developed a fairly good relationship. It was Noriega who had
told me that Panama wd be willing to accept Marcos - a plan that got fouled up
by a bungled approach to DelValle. Last night Noriega called and asked if I wd
met w/ a man he trusts - a respected Cuban American - the president of a
college in Florida. He flew in this morning and he outlined Noriega's
proposal: In exchange for a promise from us to "help clean up his (Noriega's)
image" and a commitment to lift our ban on FMS sales to the Panamanian Defense

      ...u undertake to "take care of" the Sandinista leadership for
us. I told the messenger that such actions were forbidden by our law and he
countered that Noriega had numerous assets in place in Nicaragua that could
accomplish many things that wd be essential and that after all, Noriega had
helped us w/ the operation last year that resulted in the EPS arsenal
explosion and fire in Managua and that w/o many more of these kinds of
actions, a contra victory was out of the question. I thanked the emissary for
his message and told him that we wd get back to him. The emissary told me
that I should go directly to Noriega if there were any msgs back, that his
instructions were limited to delivering the msg to me. I have checked w/ our
█████ friends who ran the Managua Op and they now inform me (but had not at the
time) that they did indeed use a Panamanian civilian ordnance expert as the
means of access to the storgage facility. Interesting. My sense is that this
is a potentially very useful avenue, but one which wd have to be very
carefully handled. A meeting w/ Noriega could not be held on his turf - the
potential for recording the meeting is too great (you will recall that he was
head of intelligence for the PDF before becoming CG). My last mtg w/ Noriega
was in June on a boat on the Potomac. Noriega travels frequently to Europe this
time of year and a meeting could be arranged to coincide w/ one of my
other trips. My sense is that this offer is sincere, that Noriega does indeed
have the capabilities proffered and that the cost could be borne by Project
Democracy (the figure of $1M was mentioned) if other PC activities do indeed
proceed as planned. If, as in the past, Noriega refuses to deal w/ the CIA, we
might have available a very effective, very secure means of doing some of the
things" which must be done if the Nicaragua project is going to succeed. The
way it is being approached now, these kind of internal actions will not
materialize until late next year - far too late to be effective when they are
needed now. The proposal seems sound to me and I believe we could make the
appropriate arrangements w/ reasonable OPSEC and deniability. Beg advise.
```

about the human North had "a fairly good relationship," Poindexter said. he had "nothing against him other than his illegal activities." He accepts

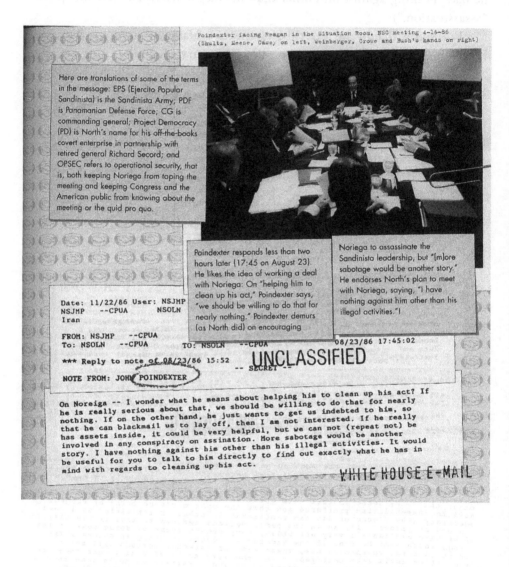

Poindexter facing Reagan in the Situation Room, NSC meeting 4-16-86
(Shults, Meese, Casey on left, Weinberger, Crowe and Bush's hands on right)

Here are translations of some of the terms in the message: EPS (Ejercito Popular Sandinista) is the Sandinista Army; PDF is Panamanian Defense Force; CG is commanding general; Project Democracy (PD) is North's name for his off-the-books covert enterprise in partnership with retired general Richard Secord; and OPSEC refers to operational security, that is, both keeping Noriega from taping the meeting and keeping Congress and the American public from knowing about the meeting or the quid pro quo.

Poindexter responds less than two hours later (17:45 on August 23). He likes the idea of working a deal with Noriega. On "helping him to clean up his act," Poindexter says, "we should be willing to do that for nearly nothing." Poindexter demurs (as North did) on encouraging

Noriega to assassinate the Sandinista leadership, but "[m]ore sabotage would be another story." He endorses North's plan to meet with Noriega, saying, "I have nothing against him other than his illegal activities."[1]

Date: 11/22/86 User: NSJHP
NSJHP --CPUA NSOLN
Iran

FROM: NSJHP --CPUA
To: NSOLN --CPUA   TO: NSOLN --CPUA   08/23/86 17:45:02

*** Reply to note of 08/23/86 15:52 -- SECRET -- UNCLASSIFIED

NOTE FROM: JOHN POINDEXTER

On Noreiga -- I wonder what he means about helping him to clean up his act? If he is really serious about that, we should be willing to do that for nearly nothing. If on the other hand, he just wants to get us indebted to him, so that he can blackmail us to lay off, then I am not interested. If he really has assets inside, it could be very helpful, but we can not (repeat not) be involved in any conspiracy on assination. More sabotage would be another story. I have nothing against him other than his illegal activities. It would be useful for you to talk to him directly to find out exactly what he has in mind with regards to cleaning up his act.

WHITE HOUSE E-MAIL

18 & 19

RWANDA ATROCITIES

America's Blind Eye to Genocide

The callousness of our government—and how we'll only put something on the line when our own self-interest is involved (think oil in Iraq)—is shockingly clear when you look back at the Clinton administration's position on the genocide that took place in Rwanda in 1994. For a three-month period starting in April that year, Hutu death squads slaughtered an estimated 800,000 Tutsis and moderate members of their own tribe.

A few years later, when Clinton visited the Rwandan capital of Kigali, the president said: "It may seem strange to you here, especially the many of you who lost members of your family, but all over the world there were people like me sitting in offices, day after day after day, who did not fully appreciate the depth and speed with which you were being engulfed by this unimaginable terror."

I visited Clinton in the White House after I was elected governor of Minnesota, and we played golf together and enjoyed each other's company. But I've got to be blunt: that statement he made in Rwanda was a bald-faced lie. The CIA's national intelligence daily, a secret briefing that went to Clinton and Vice President Gore and hundreds of senior officials, had almost daily reports on what was happening in Rwanda. But let's face it, this was a small country in central Africa with no minerals or strategic value.

Clearly, there was nothing in Rwanda for corporate America to profit from, and it seems today that's the only time we get involved. If there's no oil or lithium or what-have-you, we really don't have time. Humanitarian reasons aren't good enough, there's got to be financial gain. So we turned our backs on one of the worst mass murders in history. Even our support for the United Nations' initiatives was less than lukewarm.

In 2004, again thanks to a FOIA lawsuit by the National Security Archive, the government released a set of documents related to our Rwanda policy ten years earlier. These are highly educational, as to how things work in D.C., beginning with some talking points by the State Department for a dinner engagement with Henry Kissinger! This spells out, early on, how *not-far* we were willing to go—even though it was likely that "a massive (hundreds of thousands of deaths) bloodbath will ensue." But be sure not to mention genocide, or we might be committed to "actually 'do something.'"

The second memo takes up the subject of "Has Genocide Occurred in Rwanda?" (you bet!) and how best to keep our international credibility while doing zip.

I-94/16533

EXECUTIVE SUMMARY/COVER BRIEF

MEMORANDUM FOR UNDER SECRETARY OF DEFENSE FOR POLICY

THROUGH: Assistant Secretary of Defense for International Security
                Affairs

FROM: Deputy Assistant Secretary of Defense for Middle East
                Africa
                Prepared by: LtCol Harvin:MEA:x78824

SUBJECT: Talking Points On Rwanda/Burundi (U)

PURPOSE: INFORMATION--Talking points for your dinner
                tonight with Mr. Kissinger.

DISCUSSION: (U) Action Officers in H&RA, PK/PE, and MEA
                collaborated on the attached talking points.

COORDINATION
ASD/SOLIC _____
ASD/SR&R _____

Atch: a/s

• • •

RWANDA/BURUNDI

• **What is State doing now?**
    Just beginning to look at next steps (DCM Leader will brief at
    State tomorrow).
    Expect little beyond diplomatic statements.

• • •

• We believe State will initially limit itself to diplomatic statements
in support of the UN, the French, the Belgians, and the necessity for
both sides to resume the peace process. Of note: this crisis will
likely raise questions at the UN about the wisdom of including lightly
armed troops in a Chapter VI PKO instead of only unarmed observers (who
would probably have been well-treated like most other un-armed ex-pats).

• Unless both sides can be convinced to return to the peace process, a
massive (hundreds of thousands of deaths) bloodbath will ensue that
would likely spill over into Burundi. In addition, millions of refugees
will flee into neighboring Uganda, Tanzania, and Zaire, far exceeding
the absorptive capacity of those nations. Since neither the French nor
the Belgians have the trust of both sides in the conflict, they are
unlikely to be able to convince the parties to return to the peace
process--thus there will be role to play for the U.S. as the "honest
broker."

~~SECRET~~ UNCLASSIFIED

DISCUSSION PAPER
RWANDA

AOs from SOLIC, PA, FRMA, HRA, PK/PE, MEA, and J5 met this morning and prepared these comments for today's DC discussion on Rwanda.

IWG's Six Short Term Policy Objectives:
We have the following suggestions/problems:
1. to stop the on-going massacres as quickly as possible through contacts with the GOR and RPF leaders and demarches for similar representations with neighboring states, France, Belgium, and others.
    OK, but include the OAU and influential political figures in Africa.

2. to support the UN and other in attempts to achieve a cease fire.
    Need to change "attempts" to "political efforts" -- without "political" there is a danger of signing up to troop contributions.

3. to encourage Tanzanian and other attempts to resume negotiations under the Arusha Framework.
    OK

4. to seek to prevent the violence from spreading outside Rwanda through contacts with neighboring states.
    OK

5. to push in the UN to launch an immediate expanded humanitarian assistance effort.
    NO. MUST ADD at end of sentence: effort in neighboring areas, and in securing areas within Rwanda. This effort should be expanded throughout Rwanda when security conditions permit.

6. to prevent a similar round of slaughter and disorder in Burundi by closely monitoring the situation there and staying in touch with the various elements in the country to dissuade.
    OK .

7. ADD: Urge all parties to keep borders open for refugee flows.

Issues For Discussion:

1. <u>Genocide Investigation:</u> Language that calls for an international investigation of human rights abuses and possible violations of the genocide convention.
    Be Careful. Legal at State was worried about this yesterday-- Genocide finding could commit USG to actually "do something"

~~SECRET~~

UNCLASSIFIED

~~SECRET~~ UNCLASSIFIED

2. __In country Protection of Refugees:__ Language that authorizes the use of UNAMIR military or civilian police to protect in-country refugee camps receiving UNHCR or ICRC relief.
    NO. Present force does not have the manpower or equipment to do so. No support at present for increasing either the size or equipment of the UN PKO force.

3. __Arms Embargo:__ language banning arms exports to Rwanda and would sanction the ongoing aid to RPF.
    YES.

4. __Counter-propaganda:__ should the US engage in additional propaganda activities to get a message into Rwanda to counter the radio stations that are urging killing.
    This is a significant increase in our role. Suggest that we offer equipment to neighbors and urge them to do it.

5. __Pressure to Punish Organizers of Killings:__
    NO. Hold till Ceasefire has been established--don't want to scare off the participants.

• • •

• State of Political Play:

    - The U.S. will continue to seek an embargo on Rwanda (i.e. weapons, ammo etc.) **we do not envision it will have a significant impact on the killings because machetes, knives and other hand implements have been the most common weapons.**

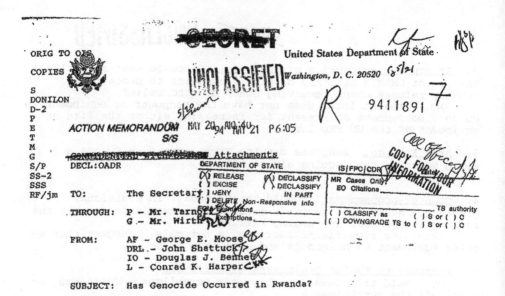

ORIG TO O~~I~~

COPIES

S
DONILON
D-2
P
E
T
M
G
S/P
SS-2
SSS
RF/jm

United States Department of State

UNCLASSIFIED Washington, D. C. 20520

R 9411891 7

ACTION MEMORANDUM   MAY 20 94 AM '40 MAY 21 P6:05
S/S

~~CONFIDENTIAL~~ Attachments

DECL:OADR

DEPARTMENT OF STATE

(X) RELEASE   (X) DECLASSIFY
( ) EXCISE   ( ) DECLASSIFY
( ) DENY   IN PART
( ) DELETE Non-Responsive Info
( ) Exemptions _____
( ) Exemptions _____

IS/FPC/CDR _____

MR Cases Only?
EO Citations _____

_____ TS authority
( ) CLASSIFY as ____ ( )S or ( )C
( ) DOWNGRADE TS to ( )S or ( )C

TO: The Secretary

THROUGH: P – Mr. Tarnoff
          G – Mr. Wirth

FROM: AF – George E. Moose
          DRL – John Shattuck
          IO – Douglas J. Bennet
          L – Conrad K. Harper

SUBJECT: Has Genocide Occurred in Rwanda?

ISSUES FOR DECISION

    Whether (1) to authorize Department officials to state
publicly that "acts of genocide have occurred" in Rwanda and
(2) to authorize U.S. delegations to international meetings to
agree to resolutions and other instruments that refer to "acts
of genocide" in Rwanda, state that "genocide has occurred"
there or contain other comparable formulations. (A resolution
posing this issue is expected at the May 24-25 Special Session
of the UN Human Rights Commission).

ESSENTIAL FACTORS

    Events in Rwanda have led to press and public inquiries
about whether genocide has occurred there. In light of the
stark facts in Rwanda (see INR's analysis, Tab 1) and L's legal
analysis (Tab 2), we believe that Department officials should
be authorized to state the Department's conclusion that "acts
of genocide have occurred" in Rwanda. This is the same
formulation that we use with respect to Bosnia.

    A Special Session of the UN Human Rights Commission will
meet May 24-25 in Geneva to consider the human rights situation
in Rwanda. The U.S. delegation will press for a strong

~~CONFIDENTIAL WITH SECRET~~ attachments)

SECRET
UNCLASSIFIED

UNCLASSIFIED
(with ~~B~~ attachments)

- 2 -

resolution condemning the violence and calling for action, including the appointment of a Special Rapporteur. We expect other delegations to seek language in the resolution that condemns events in Rwanda as "genocide." We believe that U.S. delegations to such international meetings should be authorized to agree to resolutions and other instruments that provide that "genocide" or "acts of genocide" have occurred in Rwanda, or contain other formulations that indicate that some, but not necessarily all, of the violence in Rwanda is "genocide" within the meaning of the 1948 Genocide Convention. (In the case of Bosnia, we have shown flexibility in international fora, e.g., the World Conference on Human Rights, where we joined in a consensus statement that genocide is "taking place" in Bosnia).

DISCUSSION

As defined in the 1948 Genocide Convention, the crime of "genocide" occurs when certain acts are committed against members of a national, ethnic, racial or religious group with the intent of destroying that group in whole or in part. Among the relevant acts are killing, causing serious bodily or mental harm and deliberately inflicting conditions of life calculated to bring about physical destruction of the group. In addition, conspiracy, direct and public incitement and attempts to commit genocide, as well as complicity in genocide, are offenses under the Convention.

INR's assessment of relevant activities in Rwanda since the April 6 crash of the airplane carrying the Rwandan President is attached (Tab 1). L believes (Tab 2) that there is a strong basis to conclude that some of the killings and other listed acts carried out against Tutsis have been committed with the intent of destroying the Tutsi ethnic group in whole or in part. Moreover, there is evidence that some persons in Rwanda have incited genocide or have been complicit in genocide, which would also constitute offenses under the Convention.

A USG statement that acts of genocide have occurred would not have any particular legal consequences. Under the Convention, the prosecution of persons charged with genocide is the responsibility of the competent courts in the state where the acts took place or an international penal tribunal (none has yet been established); the U.S. has no criminal jurisdiction over acts of genocide occurring within Rwanda unless they are committed by U.S. citizens or they fall under another criminal provision of U.S. law (such as those relating to acts of terrorism for which there is a basis for U.S. jurisdiction).

(with ~~CONFIDENTIAL~~ attachments)
UNCLASSIFIED

- 1 -

Although lacking in legal consequences, a clear statement that the USG believes that acts of genocide have occurred could increase pressure for USG activism in response to the crisis in Rwanda. We believe, however, that we should send a clear signal that the United States believes that acts of genocide have occurred in Rwanda. If we do not seize the opportunity presented by fora such as the UNHRC to use the genocide label to condemn events in Rwanda, our credibility will be undermined with human rights groups and the general public, who may question how much evidence we can legitimately require before coming to a policy conclusion.

20

SOLDIERS AS GUINEA PIGS

Military Experiments on Our Own Troops

As a veteran who served his country for six years (1969–75), I think I've earned the right to be outraged at how my fellow servicemen have been treated by our government. But I can't say this surprises me. Our patriotism toward our veterans is appalling and actually laughable. I mean, we honor them at sports events, say the Pledge, thank them up and down for their service. But those thank-you's ring pretty hollow when, behind the scenes, nothing much is done for the veteran who's put his life on the line.

It's been that way for every war in my lifetime. When we're done using the soldier, we give him lip service but everything else is hastily forgotten—the injuries, the diseases, all of that we want to bury and pretend that it doesn't exist. If you end up doing something for veterans, it costs money—and then we'd have to realize that there's more to war than just dying. There's a huge amount of collateral damage—of *living death*—that takes place after a war. Benefits, hospitalization, true care: all the things that should happen after a veteran is done serving, forget it! So all the praise for their service is, to me, utterly phony.

Take a look at the excerpt from a staff report prepared for the Senate Committee on Veterans' Affairs on December 8, 1994. I hope this turns your stomach, as it did mine. (You can access the full Senate 103-97 report at www.gulfwarvets.com/senate.htm.)

103d Congress, 2d Session - COMMITTEE PRINT - S. Prt. 103-97

HEALTH?   IS MILITARY RESEARCH HAZARDOUS TO VETERANS'
                              LESSONS SPANNING HALF A CENTURY

   A STAFF REPORT PREPARED FOR THE COMMITTEE ON VETERANS'
                            AFFAIRS

                      UNITED STATES SENATE
                       DECEMBER 8, 1994

    JOHN D. ROCKEFELLER IV, West Virginia, Chairman

          DENNIS DeCONCINI, Arizona
          FRANK H. MURKOWSKI, Alaska
          GEORGE J. MITCHELL, Maine
          STROM THURMOND, South Carolina
          BOB GRAHAM, Florida
          ALAN K. SIMPSON, Wyoming
          DANIEL K. AKAKA, Hawaii
          ARLEN SPECTER, Pennsylvania
          THOMAS A. DASCHLE, South Dakota
          JAMES M. JEFFORDS, Vermont
          BEN NIGHTHORSE CAMPBELL, Colorado

      Jim Gottlieb, Chief Counsel/Staff Director
  John H. Moseman, Minority Staff Director/Chief Counsel
     Diana M. Zuckerman, Professional Staff Member
      Patricia Olson, Congressional Science Fellow

FOREWORD

U.S. Senate,
Committee on Veterans' Affairs,
Washington, DC, December 8, 1994

During the last few years, the public has become aware of
several examples where U.S. Government researchers
intentionally exposed Americans to potentially dangerous
substances without their knowledge or consent. The Senate
Committee on Veterans' Affairs, which I have been privileged
to chair from 1993-94, has conducted a comprehensive
analysis of the extent to which veterans participated in
such research while they were serving in the U.S. military.
This resulted in two hearings, on May 6, 1994, and August 5,
1994.

This report, written by the majority staff of the Committee,
is the result of that comprehensive investigation, and is
intended to provide information for future deliberations by
the Congress. The findings and conclusions contained in this
report are those of the majority staff and do not
necessarily reflect the views of the members of the
Committee on Veterans' Affairs.

This report would not have been possible without the dedication and expertise of Dr. Patricia Olson, who, as a Congressional Science Fellow, worked tirelessly on this investigation and report, and the keen intelligence, energy, and commitment of Dr. Diana Zuckerman, who directed this effort.

John D. Rockefeller IV, Chairman

CONTENTS

- <u>I.</u> Records of anthrax vaccinations are not suitable to evaluate safety
- <u>J.</u> Army regulations exempt informed consent for volunteers in some types of military research
- <u>K.</u> DOD and DVA have repeatedly failed to provide information and medical followup to those who participate in military research or are ordered to take investigational drugs
- <u>L.</u> The Federal Government has failed to support scientific studies that provide information about the reproductive problems experienced by veterans who were intentionally exposed to potentially dangerous substances
- <u>M.</u> The Federal Government has failed to support scientific studies that provide timely information for compensation decisions regarding military personnel who were harmed by various exposures
- <u>N.</u> Participation in military research is rarely included in military medical records, making it impossible to support a veteran's claim for service-connected disabilities from military research
- <u>O.</u> DOD has demonstrated a pattern of misrepresenting the danger of various military exposures that continues today

IV. Recommendations

- A. Congress should deny the DOD request for a blanket waiver to use investigational drugs in case of war or threat of war
- B. FDA should reject any applications from DOD that do not include data on women, and long-term followup data
- C. Congress should authorize a centralized database for all federally funded experiments that utilize human subjects
- D. Congress should mandate all Federal agencies to declassify most documents on research involving human subjects
- E. Congress should reestablish a National Commission for the Protection of Human Subjects
- F. VA and DOD should implement regular site visits to review Institutional Review Boards
- G. The Feres Doctrine should not be applied for military personnel who are harmed by inappropriate human experimentation when informed consent has not been given

<u>Appendix</u> -- Survey of 150 Persian Gulf War Veterans

IS MILITARY RESEARCH HAZARDOUS TO VETERANS' HEALTH? LESSONS SPANNING HALF A CENTURY

I. INTRODUCTION

During the last 50 years, hundreds of thousands of military personnel have been involved in human experimentation and other intentional exposures conducted by the Department of Defense (DOD), often without a servicemember's knowledge or consent. In some cases, soldiers who consented to serve as human subjects found themselves participating in experiments quite different from those described at the time they volunteered. For example, thousands of World War II veterans who originally volunteered to "test summer clothing" in exchange for extra leave time, found themselves in gas chambers testing the effects of mustard gas and lewisite. (Note 1) Additionally, soldiers were sometimes ordered by commanding officers to "volunteer" to participate in research or face dire consequences. For example, several Persian Gulf War veterans interviewed by Committee staff reported that they were ordered to take experimental vaccines during Operation Desert Shield or face prison. (Note 2)

The goals of many of the military experiments and exposures were very appropriate. For example, some experiments were intended to provide important information about how to protect U.S. troops from nuclear, biological, and chemical weapons or other dangerous substances during wartime. In the Persian Gulf War, U.S. troops were intentionally exposed to an investigational vaccine that was intended to protect them against biological warfare, and they were given pyridostigmine bromide pills in an experimental protocol intended to protect them against chemical warfare.

However, some of the studies that have been conducted had more questionable motives. For example, the Department of Defense (DOD) conducted numerous "man-break" tests, exposing soldiers to chemical weapons in order to determine the exposure level that would cause a casualty, i.e., "break a man." (Note 3) Similarly, hundreds of soldiers were subjected to hallucinogens in experimental programs conducted by the DOD in participation with, or sponsored by, the CIA. (Note 4), (Note 5) These servicemembers often unwittingly participated as human subjects in tests for drugs intended for mind-control or behavior modification, often without their knowledge or consent. Although the ultimate goal of those experiments was to provide information that would help U.S. military and intelligence efforts, most Americans would agree that the use of soldiers as unwitting guinea pigs in experiments that were designed to harm them, at least temporarily, is not ethical.

Whether the goals of these experiments and exposures were worthy or not, these experiences put hundred of thousands of U.S. servicemembers at risk, and may have caused lasting harm to many individuals.

Every year, thousands of experiments utilizing human subjects are still being conducted by, or on behalf of, the DOD. Many of these ongoing experiments have very appropriate goals, such as obtaining information for preventing, diagnosing, and treating various diseases and disabilities acquired during military service. Although military personnel are the logical choice as human subjects for such research, it is questionable whether the military hierarchy allows for individuals in subordinate positions of power to refuse to participate in military experiments. It is also questionable whether those who participated as human subjects in military research were given adequate information to fully understand the potential benefits and risks of the experiments. Moreover, the evidence suggests that they have not been adequately monitored for adverse health effects after the experimental protocols end.

Veterans who become ill or disabled due to military service are eligible to receive priority access to medical care at VA medical facilities and to receive monthly compensation checks. In order to qualify, they must demonstrate that their illness or disability was associated with their military service. Veterans who did not know that they were exposed to dangerous substances while they were in the military, therefore, would not apply for or receive the medical care or compensation that they are entitled to. Moreover, even if they know about the exposure, it would be difficult or impossible to prove if the military has not kept adequate records. It is therefore crucial that the VA learn as much as possible about the potential exposures, and that the DOD assume responsibility for providing such information to veterans and to the VA.

II. BACKGROUND

A. CODES, DECLARATIONS, AND LAWS GOVERNING HUMAN EXPERIMENTATION

The Nuremberg Code is a 10-point declaration governing human experimentation, developed by the Allies after World War II in response to inhumane experiments conducted by Nazi scientists and physicians. The Code states that voluntary and informed consent is absolutely essential from all human subjects who participate in research, whether during war or peace. The Code states:

The person involved should have the legal capacity to give consent; should be so situated as to be able to exercise free power of choice, without the intervention of any element of force, fraud, deceit, duress, overreaching, or other ulterior form of constraint or coercion; and should have sufficient knowledge and comprehension of the elements of the subject matter involved as to enable him to make an understanding and enlightened decision. This latter element requires that before the acceptance of an affirmative decision by the experimental subject, there should be made known to him the nature, duration, and purpose of the experiment; the method and means by which it is to be conducted; all inconveniences and hazards reasonable to be expected; and the effects upon his health and person which may possibly come from his participation in the experiments. (Note 6)

There is no provision in the Nuremberg Code that allows a country to waive informed consent for military personnel or veterans who serve as human subjects in experiments during wartime or in experiments that are conducted because of threat of war. However, the DOD has recently argued that wartime experimental requirements differ from peacetime requirements for informed consent. According to the Pentagon, "In all peacetime applications, we believe strongly in informed consent and its ethical foundations.....But military combat is different." (Note 7) The DOD argued that informed consent should be waived for investigational drugs that could possibly save a soldier's life, avoid endangerment of the other personnel in his unit, and accomplish the combat mission.

More than a decade after the development of the Nuremberg Code, the World Medical Association prepared recommendations as a guide to doctors using human subjects in biomedical research. As a result, in 1964 the Eighteenth World Medical Assembly met in Helsinki, Finland, and adopted recommendations to be used as an ethical code by all medical doctors conducting biomedical research with human subjects. This code, referred to as the Declaration of Helsinki, was revised in 1975, 1983, and 1989. (Note 8) It differs from the Nuremberg Code in certain important respects. The Declaration of Helsinki distinguishes between clinical (therapeutic) and nonclinical (nontherapeutic) biomedical research, and addresses "proxy consent" for human subjects who are legally incompetent, such as children or adults with severe physical or mental disabilities. (Note 9) Proxy consent for legally competent military personnel who participate in military research is not considered appropriate under the Nuremberg Code or the Declaration of Helsinki.

On June 18, 1991, the Federal Government announced that 16 U.S. governmental agencies would abide by a set of regulations, referred to as the "Common Rule," designed to protect human subjects who participate in federally funded research. (Note 10) The provisions of the "Common Rule," first promulgated for the Department of Health and Human Services (DHHS) in 1974, described how federally funded research involving human subjects shall be conducted. However, local Institutional Review Boards (IRB's) may revise or exclude some or all consent elements if the research exposes subjects to no more than "minimal risk," meaning "that the probability and magnitude of harm or discomfort anticipated in the research are not greater in and of themselves than those ordinarily encountered in daily life or during the performance of routine physical or psychological examinations or tests." (Note 11) IRB's vary greatly in their interpretation of the risks of daily life.

There are three provisions governing research funded by DHHS that are intended to protect vulnerable populations, such as pregnant women and fetuses, prisoners, and children. (Note 12) There are no special Federal regulations to protect military personnel when they participate as human subjects in federally funded research, despite logical questions about whether military personnel can truly "volunteer" in response to a request from a superior officer.

Current law prevents the Department of Defense from using Federal funds for research involving the use of human experimental subjects, unless the subject gives informed consent in advance. This law applies regardless of whether the research is intended to benefit the subject. (Note 13)

WAR'S REAL COST

Gulf War Illness and Our Veterans

Bringing things up-to-date, here are parts of two documents from 2010. The first comes straight from the Department of Veterans Affairs, and it has some pretty shocking statistics on how many veterans of the first Gulf War have suffered adverse health consequences. The second is testimony from Paul Sullivan, Executive Director of Veterans for Common Sense, given before the House Committee on Veterans' Affairs on September 30. I found his statement heart-wrenching. What's it going to take for our leaders to consider the *real* cost of these endless wars?

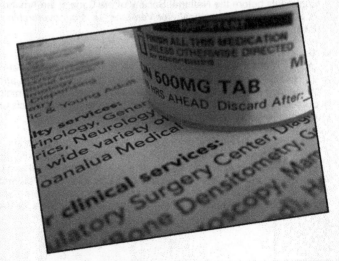

Final 2010 Report

of

Department of Veterans Affairs

Gulf War Veterans' Illnesses Task Force

to the

Secretary of Veterans Affairs

EXECUTIVE SUMMARY:

In August 2009, the Secretary of Veterans Affairs (VA) directed a comprehensive review of the Department's approach and practices in meeting the needs of Veterans of the 1990 – 1991 Gulf War. The intended outcome of this review was a set of action plans to ensure the needs of Gulf War Veterans are met and improve their level of satisfaction with VA services. More broadly, these efforts reflect the cultural and institutional change within VA as it transforms into a 21st century organization.

This report reflects the efforts of an interdisciplinary team of subject matter experts from across multiple work centers within VA – a task force led by the senior Gulf War Veteran within VA leadership. The Gulf War Veterans' Illnesses Task Force (GWVI-TF) was established to identify gaps in services as well as opportunities to better serve this Veteran community and in so doing help guide efforts at making the VA people-centric, results-driven, and forward-looking. The GWVI-TF target population is Veterans who were deployed on the Operation Desert Shield and/or Operation Desert Storm components of the 1990 – 1991 Gulf War period. The Persian Gulf War (hereinafter referred to as the Gulf War) is legally defined in 38 U.S.C. § 101(33) as beginning on August 2, 1990, and ending on the date thereafter prescribed by Presidential proclamation or by law. While the term "Gulf War Veterans" could refer to all Veterans of conflicts during this period, including Veterans of Operation Iraqi Freedom, and subsequent conflicts, this report will use the term "1990 – 1991 Gulf War Veterans" to mean those Veterans who served in Operation Desert Shield and/or Operation Desert Storm.

The GWVI-TF worked over several months to develop a comprehensive plan of action consistent with the challenge inherent in Secretary Shinseki's pledge to all Veterans in his comments before the National Society of the Sons of the American Revolution on January 9, 2010: *"At VA, we advocate for Veterans – it is our overarching philosophy and, in time, it will become our culture."*

The GWVI-TF identified seven areas where VA can – and will – improve services for this group. Among these improvements, VA will reconnect with Veterans from the "1990 – 1991 Gulf War Veterans," strengthen the training of clinicians and claims processors, and reenergize its research effort. VA will also strengthen partnerships and medical surveillance to proactively address the potential health impacts on Veterans from the environmental exposures on today's battlefields.

The report's action plans are an initial roadmap to transform the care and services we deliver to Veterans from the "1990 – 1991 Gulf War Veterans." Execution of these plans will deliver the critical tools for frontline staff to address real and perceived misunderstandings between VA and Gulf War Veterans, Veterans Service Organizations, Congressional Committees, and other external stakeholders. Specifically, this report establishes action plans to deliver new and improved tools for VA personnel to improve:

INTRODUCTION

Twenty years have passed since the start of the deployment and combat operations known as Operations Desert Shield and Desert Storm. Since then, many Veterans of that conflict have endured adverse health consequences from the war. Of the 696,842 Service members who served in the conflict, of which approximately 7% were women, 297,555 Veterans have filed Department of Veterans Affairs (VA) claims. As of March 2010, the VA has processed over 289,610 disability claims related to their service in these operations; 250,627 have been granted at least one service-connected condition, 38,983 claims were denied; and 7,945 claims from first time claimants are currently pending. Additionally, VA has treated over 146,445 combat Veterans, and has participated in federal research efforts on Gulf War illness totaling more than $152.1 million from VA and $400.5 million in total Federal commitment to date. Yet through these years, many Veterans have felt disenfranchised in these efforts, and underserved by the VA. Stakeholders have been critical of VA's culture and processes as well. The excess of unexplained medical symptoms reported by deployed 1990 – 1991 Gulf War Veterans cannot be reliably ascribed to any known psychological disorder. Veterans and stakeholders have noted that VA has historically failed to recognize that undiagnosed multisymptom illness suffered by Gulf War Veterans are distinct illnesses with potentially debilitating consequences and the large numbers of Veterans affected (an estimated 175,000 to 250,000 Veterans). They have also criticized VA emphasis in its research (before 2005) and in its clinician training materials and public statements (to date), that these illnesses were related to stress or other psychiatric disorders, when scientific research indicates otherwise. The Gulf War Veterans' Illness Task Force (GWVI-TF) was set up to respond to these criticisms.

Findings 3B: The "1990 – 1991 Gulf War Veterans" largely attribute their illnesses to environmental exposures that were undetected and/or not monitored during that conflict (i.e. oil fires, pesticides, sandstorms etc.). Based upon data gathered from DoD's Medical Surveillance Monthly Report, it is estimated that between 16 and 20 percent of active duty, and 28 and 35 percent of Reserve soldiers serving in the Operation Enduring Freedom/Operating Iraqi Freedom (OEF/OIF) conflicts have concerns about their own exposures to environmental hazards during their military service as several environmental exposure events are known to have occurred in the current conflicts. Although each VA Medical Center (VAMC) provides access to environmental health clinicians and coordinators, there is variability in knowledge and practice among VAMCs as to when and how to conduct exposure assessments. Primary care providers currently do an excellent job of providing patients with work-ups based on symptoms but do not always have the necessary tools to provide thorough exposure assessments. An initial seminar was developed in August 2009 in conjunction with Mount Sinai Medical Center and the New Jersey War Related Illness and Injury Study Center (WRIISC) to overcome this deficiency. The seminar was very successful because it provided clinicians with the information needed to expertly treat and discuss problems with their Gulf War patients, and for the first time presented it together at one time in a concise manner. The seminar not only addressed issues concerning 1990 – 1991 Gulf War Veterans' concerns (Sarin gas, Pyridostigmine, pesticides, oil fires) but also addressed several concerns from the current conflicts in Iraq and Afghanistan. Thus, lessons learned from prior conflicts are being coupled with the lessons learned at the August 2009 seminar to build a more comprehensive training program for VA staff. The Veterans Health Administration will conduct exportable workshops in exposure evaluation and assessment to update VA clinicians on the unique exposures of returning OEF/OIF Veterans and provide educational and clinical tools for evaluation of exposure risk and the health outcomes relevant to these risks. These workshops will be offered in two different geographic areas and there will be a satellite broadcast seminar accessible to most geographic areas and time zones.

Gulf War Illness: The Future for Dissatisfied Veterans

Statement of Paul Sullivan

Executive Director
Veterans for Common Sense

Veterans for Common Sense (VCS) thanks Subcommittee Chairman Mitchell, Ranking Member Roe, and members of the Subcommittee for inviting us to testify about our recommendations for improving government policies for our nation's 250,000 ill Gulf War veterans. Congress remains a loyal friend of our Gulf War veterans by holding hearings, passing legislation, and conducting vital oversight hearings.

With me today is my good friend Steve Robinson, a fellow Gulf War veteran and the former Executive Director at the National Gulf War Resource Center, a position I once held. Also with me is Thomas Bandzul, our VCS Associate Counsel. Steve, Thomas, and several ill Gulf War veterans assisted VCS with preparing this statement.

VCS is here today because Gulf War veterans are dissatisfied and disappointed with the actions of the Department of Veterans Affairs (VA). VA is not listening to our concerns about our illnesses associated with our deployment to the 1991 Gulf War. VA does not listen to advisory panels created by Congress or VA. VA does not listen to expert scientists. VA does not even listen to Congress. Two decades of inaction have already passed. Gulf War veterans urgently want to avoid the four decades of endless suffering endured by our Vietnam War veterans exposed to Agent Orange. VA's actions are unfortunate and disastrous for our nation's 250,000 ill Gulf War veterans.

Veterans for Common Sense sends up a red star cluster for Congress, VA, and America to see. In military terms, VCS asks VA for cease fire. VCS urges VA leadership to stop and listen to our veterans before time runs out, as VA is killing veterans slowly with bureaucratic delays and mismanaged research that prevent us from receiving treatments or benefits in a timely manner.

VCS is here urging VA to issue regulations so Gulf War veterans can learn why we are ill, obtain medical care, and receive disability benefits for our medical conditions scientists agree are associated with our Gulf War deployment during 1990 - 1991.

After twenty years of war, we are done waiting. VCS urges VA to act now and provide research, treatment, and benefits. As a Gulf War veteran, I have watched too many of my friends die without answers, without treatment, and without benefits. In a few cases, veterans completed suicide due to Gulf War illness and the frustration of dealing with VA. VCS asks Congress and VA to keep this in mind when evaluating VA policies.

Our statement contains a copy of our formal petition to VA Secretary Eric Shinseki urging to VA promulgate regulations under the Administrative Procedure Act (5 USC Section 551) so our veterans can obtain answers to the questions about why 250,000 veterans remain ill, treatment for veterans' conditions, and benefits so our veterans do not fall through the economic cracks due to disabilities.

VCS asks Congress to intervene if VA fails to act now. VCS asks Congress to continue holding oversight hearings and to pass legislation to implement our petition if VA continues ignoring the needs of our veterans, ignoring the laws passed by Congress, and ignoring the peer-reviewed and published findings of our nation's top scientists.

Gulf War Illness

VCS is here today urging action by Congress because the scope of the healthcare and disability challenges facing our Gulf War veterans is real and increasing in size. VA officially reports 265,000 of the veterans deployed between 1990 and 1991 sought medical care and 248,000 filed disability claims by 2008, the last time VA released official statistics about veterans from the 1991 conflict.

VCS estimates VA spends up to $4.3 billion per year for Gulf War veterans' medical care and benefits. However, VA has never actually revealed the financial costs, and VA has indicated no intention the agency plans to release those facts. VA's failure to release information about the human and financial costs of war reveal VA remains without the fundamental facts needed to monitor Gulf War veteran policies.

In 2008, VA's Research Advisory Committee on Gulf War Veterans' Illness (RAC) estimated as many as 210,000 Gulf War veterans suffer from multi-symptom illness.

In 2009, the Institute of Medicine (IOM) agreed the exposures and illnesses are real, impacting as many as 250,000 veterans of the 1991 invasion Iraq. Both the RAC and IOM studies were mandated by the "Persian Gulf Veterans Act of 1998."

Gulf War veterans are hoping for improvements with the new administration. In August 2009, VA created a new Gulf War Task Force under the leadership of Gulf War veteran and VA Chief of Staff John Gingrich. We look forward to VA's testimony today with the hope that VA will offer new, substantive regulations for our Gulf War veterans who need answers, healthcare, and benefits. We do thank VA for taking the precedent-setting initiative of proposing policy via the Federal Register on April 1, 2010. VCS submitted detailed comments to VA about the Draft Task Force report on May 3, 2010.

However, VCS recommendations to VA's Chief of Staff John Gingrich appear to have fallen on deaf ears. The only VA action since January 2009 was a paltry $2.8 million for stress research announced on July 21, 2010. Only VA's Research Office, in a vacuum without input, wants this research. VA's systemic failures reveal significant problems remain at VA. If VA Secretary Shinseki won't fix VA's Research Office, then Congress must intervene and place Gulf War research outside of their area of responsibility.

VCS also urges Secretary Shinseki to investigate the improper and arbitrary termination of essential Gulf War illness research. A July 15, 2009 VA IG report concluded $75 million in Gulf War illness research at the University of Texas Southwestern Medical Center (UTSW) was "impeded" by VA (page iv, IG "Review of Contract No. VA549-P-0027"). Without any reasonable scientific basis, VA arbitrarily terminated UTSW research, potentially undermining more

than 15 years of critical inquiry. VCS remains outraged VA's Research Office
has not been held accountable.

On November 19, 2009, VCS filed Freedom of Information Act (FOIA) requests
with VA to determine the extent of the VA internal sabotage.   VA has not
released any information about who "impeded" Gulf War illness research.   On
June 29, 2010, VCS filed a formal appeal under FOIA with VA's General Counsel
to obtain documents about the cabal of VA staff intentionally delaying
research and treatment for our veterans.

VCS also urges VA to investigate the adverse health impact of depleted
uranium, a radioactive toxic waste used as ammunition. On August 19, 1993,
then-Army Brigadier General Eric Shinseki signed a memorandum confirming that
on June 8, 1993, the Deputy Secretary of Defense ordered the Army Secretary
to "Complete medical testing of personnel exposed to DU contamination during
the Persian Gulf War." No medical testing was performed. VCS urges VA
Secretary Shinseki to take the rare opportunity for a second chance and
complete the research ordered 17 years ago.   In February 2010, VCS President
Dan Fahey requested DU research during a conference call with VA Chief of
Staff John Gingrich. To date, VA has not conducted DU research.

Third, other than a VA-VCS conference call in February 2010, VA has excluded
Veterans for Common Sense from participating in any meaningful, consistent
dialog on the issue of Gulf War illness. The communication from VA is almost
always one direction: telling veterans what VA will do with little or no
input from veterans until after VA has reached a final, irreversible
decision.   VA's continued insulation is the main reason why VCS urges VA to
create a permanent Gulf War Veteran Advocacy office.

Conclusion

The needs of our veterans are detailed in two decades of scientific research
reviewed by the RAC and IOM as well as countless Congressional
investigations, hearings, and reports. However, VA's Research Office has
failed Gulf War veterans for two decades. This absolutely vital hearing
represents VA's last chance to get it right so Gulf War veterans have a
reasonable chance at answers, treatments and benefits in our lifetime.

After 20 years of waiting, we refuse to wait on more empty promises from VA.
The first step is for Secretary Shinseki and Chief of Staff Gingrich to
immediately clean house of VA bureaucrats who have so utterly and miserably
failed our veterans for too long. Our bottom line is clear: we urge VA
Secretary Shinseki to quickly implement the recommendations we make in our
petition sent to VA today. If VA does not immediately take action, we urge
Congress to continue holding hearings and passing legislation so VA is held
accountable for taking care of our veterans. Our waiting must end now.

                                        Veterans for Common Sense
                                        Washington, DC.

MILITARY TAKEOVER

Operation Garden Plot: Our Military and "Civil Disturbances"

The curious thing is, a Civil Disturbance Plan called Garden Plot was in place more than ten years before 9/11. See if you agree whether this is a blueprint for the military taking over during any protest or "unrest" that might seem to be getting out of hand. In case you still think the Patriot Act couldn't be applied to *us*.

Turning the military loose in our country to take care of things: Isn't this what the National Guard is for, and doesn't that fall under the jurisdiction of the states and their governors? It seems that the feds shouldn't be coming in unless they're asked. Which maybe they'd have to be now, because the National Guard is off fighting in foreign countries. It's all ass-backwards. We've got the Guard in Iraq and they're trying to turn the regular military loose on our own citizens. Again we owe that role reversal to George W. Bush.

I can understand occasions when federal help is needed, but this shouldn't be top-down but bottom-up. You need to do this under great scrutiny, in very limited types of situations, to ensure that there are no abuses of power.

Headquarters, Department of the Army
Washington, D.C. 20310-0440
15 February 1991

PREFACE

1.   This operations plan (OPLAN) is entitled Department of
Defense Civil Disturbance Plan. Its nickname is GARDEN PLOT.
This OPLAN provides guidance and direction for participation by
all Department of Defense (DOD) components in civil disturbance
operations in support of civil authorities. All parts of this
OPLAN are unclassified.

2.   In accordance with (IAW) DOD Directive 3025.12, the Secretary
of the Army is the DOD Executive Agent for military operations in
response to domestic civil disturbances within the fifty states,
District of Columbia, Commonwealth of Puerto Rico, U.S. ter-
ritories and possessions, and any political subdivision thereof.
This OPLAN is published under the authority of this executive
agency. GARDEN PLOT applies to the military departments, the
unified and specified commands, the defense agencies, and other DOD
components for planning, coordinating, and executing military
operations during domestic civil disturbances.

3.   This OPLAN supercedes DA Civil Disturbance Plan dated 1 March
1984. This OPLAN is effective upon publication. All supporting
planning documents should be updated IAW with this revised OPLAN
within 180 days.

4.   Revision of GARDEN PLOT was prompted by the following
factors:

     a.   The Goldwater-Nichols Department of Defense Reorganiza-
tion Act of 1986.

     b.   The need to clearly establish a direct line of opera-
tional authority for domestic civil disturbance operations.

     c.   Various organizational changes and redesignations among
DOD components.

     d.   A general need to clarify and simplify GARDEN PLOT.

5.   The proponent for this OPLAN is the Director of Military
Support (DOMS). Recommended changes to this plan should be
submitted to the following address:

                    Headquarters, Department of the Army
                    ATTN: DAMO-ODS
                    Washington, D.C. 20310-0440

(2)   The DOMS is the Action Agent for the Executive
Agent. The DOMS plans for, coordinates, and directs the employment
of all designated federal resources for the Executive Agent in
civil disturbance operations and serves as the DOD point of contact
in all such matters. DOD components having cognizance over
military resources are responsible for supporting the Executive
Agent through the DOMS in matters concerning civil disturbances.

(3)   The Executive Agent--or the Under Secretary of the
Army as his designee--exercises direction of designated joint task
force (JTF) commanders through a designated commander-in-chief
(CINC) who serves as his Operating Agent. The Operating Agent is
a supported CINC and is responsible for all civil disturbance
operations involving federal military forces within his area of
responsibility (AOR). The potential operating Agents/Supported
CINCs for domestic civil disturbance opera-tions are: United
States Commander in Chief, Atlantic Command (USCINCLANT);
Commander in Chief, Forces Command (CINCFOR); and United States
Commander in Chief, Pacific Command (USCINCPAC). See Annex H for
diagrams depicting command relationships during civil disturbance
operations.

c.   Intelligence.

(1)   See Annex B.

(2)   Threat.

(a)   During domestic civil disturbance operations,
federal military forces will confront members of the civil populace participating in group acts of violence antagonistic to
authority. These acts can fall anywhere along a broad spectrum of
violence that encompasses individual acts of terrorism, riots, and
insurrection.

(b)   Civil disturbances may occur spontaneously, by
preplanning, or incidental to some other event. People participating in a civil disturbance may be members of any class, age
group, or part of the political spectrum. Their participation may
be motivated by economic, criminal, racial, religious, political, or
psychological considerations, or any combination thereof.

(c)   The capabilities of the participants will vary
widely. They may use planned or spontaneous tactics that are
nonviolent or violent. The technical sophistication of violent
participants can also vary widely, ranging from crude weapons to
sophisticated modern weapons. Participants' actions may be
governed by the forces of crowd behavior or by leaders exercising
command and control through advanced communications. While most
participants will typically be on foot, vehicles may be used.

FREEDOMS FOR SAFETY?

"Emergency" Detention Camps and Civilian Inmate Labor Program

Are we ready for martial law? I think we are, because everybody's sitting back and watching our freedoms being taken away and the handcuffs put on and "Newspeak" (read Orwell's *1984* again, folks) being slowly put into practice. We can all proudly stand up as Americans and say, Guess what? The terrorists are winning because our country has changed in the last decade, and not for the good. We're a country that's now living in fear and so are willing to trade our freedoms for safety—which I stand against and will go to my grave stating: "I'd rather face the terrorists on a daily basis than lose any of my freedoms."

So let's look at how the government has been intent on keeping us safe. First, a press release issued by KBR, a subsidiary of Halliburton (the company Cheney ran), early in 2006. It's a joint deal they made with Homeland Security and Immigration & Customs Enforcement (ICE), "in the event of an emergency influx of immigrants into the U.S., or to support the rapid development of new programs," whatever that means. Did you know that the ICE already had detention centers in place since it was established in March 2003?

Second, the Army went on to establish a Civilian Inmate Labor Program back in 2005. "This regulation provides Army policy and guidance for establishing civilian inmate labor programs *and civilian prison camps on Army installations.*" The italics are mine. Would somebody tell me what this means, so I don't have to worry so much about what it implies?

KBR Awarded U.S. Department of Homeland Security Contingency Support Project for Emergency Support Services

Arlington, Virginia - January 24, 2006 - KBR announced today that its Government and Infrastructure division has been awarded an Indefinite Delivery/Indefinite Quantity (IDIQ) contract to support the Department of Homeland Security's (DHS) U.S. Immigration and Customs Enforcement (ICE) facilities in the event of an emergency. KBR is the engineering and construction subsidiary of Halliburton (NYSE:HAL).

With a maximum total value of $385 million over a five-year term, consisting of a one-year based period and four one-year options, the competitively awarded contract will be executed by the U.S. Army Corps of Engineers, Fort Worth District. KBR held the previous ICE contract from 2000 through 2005.

"We are especially gratified to be awarded this contract because it builds on our extremely strong track record in the arena of emergency operations support," said Bruce Stanski, executive vice president, KBR Government and Infrastructure. "We look forward to continuing the good work we have been doing to support our customer whenever and wherever we are needed."

The contract, which is effective immediately, provides for establishing temporary detention and processing capabilities to augment existing ICE Detention and Removal Operations (DRO) Program facilities in the event of an emergency influx of immigrants into the U.S., or to support the rapid development of new programs. The contingency support contract provides for planning and, if required, initiation of specific engineering, construction and logistics support tasks to establish, operate and maintain one or more expansion facilities.

The contract may also provide migrant detention support to other U.S. Government organizations in the event of an immigration emergency, as well as the development of a plan to react to a national emergency, such as a natural disaster. In the event of a natural disaster, the contractor could be tasked with providing housing for ICE personnel performing law enforcement functions in support of relief efforts.

ICE was established in March 2003 as the largest investigative arm of the Department of Homeland Security. ICE is comprised of four integrated divisions that form a 21st century law enforcement agency with broad responsibilities for a number of key homeland security priorities.

KBR is a global engineering, construction, technology and services company. Whether designing an LNG facility, serving as a defense industry contractor, or providing small capital construction, KBR delivers world-class service and performance. KBR employs more than 60,000 people in 43 countries around the world.

CONTACT:
Halliburton Public Relations. Houston

Headquarters
Department of the Army
Washington, DC
14 January 2005

*Army Regulation 210-35

Effective 14 February 2005

Installations

Civilian Inmate Labor Program

By Order of the Secretary of the Army:

PETER J. SCHOOMAKER
General, United States Army
Chief of Staff

Official:

Sandra R. Riley

SANDRA R. RILEY
Administrative Assistant to the
Secretary of the Army

History. This publication is a rapid action revision. The portions affected by this rapid action revision are listed in the summary of change.

Summary. This regulation provides guidance for establishing and managing civilian inmate labor programs on Army installations. It provides guidance on establishing prison camps on Army installations. It addresses recordkeeping and reporting incidents related to the Civilian Inmate Labor Program and/or prison camp administration.

Applicability. This regulation applies to the Active Army, the Army National

Guard of the United States, and the U.S. Army Reserve unless otherwise stated. During mobilization, the Assistant Chief of Staff for Installation Management may modify chapters and policies contained in this regulation.

Proponent and exception authority. The proponent of this regulation is the Assistant Chief of Staff for Installation Management. The proponent has the authority to approve exceptions or waivers to this regulation that are consistent with controlling law and regulations. The proponent may delegate this approval authority, in writing, to a division chief within the proponent agency or a direct reporting unit or field operating agency of the proponent agency in the grade of colonel or the civilian equivalent. Activities may request a waiver to this regulation by providing justification that includes a full analysis of the expected benefits and must include formal review by the activity's senior legal officer. All waiver requests will be endorsed by the commander or senior leader of the requesting activity and forwarded through their higher headquarters to the policy proponent. Refer to AR 25-30 for specific guidance.

Army management control process.

This regulation contains management control provisions and identifies key management controls that must be evaluated.

Supplementation. Supplementation of this regulation and establishment of command and local forms are prohibited without prior approval from Assistant Chief of Staff for Installation Management (DAIM-ZA), 600 Army Pentagon, Washington, DC 20310-0600.

Suggested Improvements. Users are invited to send comments and suggested improvements on DA Form 2028 (Recommended Changes to Publications and Blank Forms) directly to Assistant Chief of Staff for Installation Management (DAIM-MD), 600 Army Pentagon, Washington, DC 20310-0600.

Distribution. This publication is available in electronic media only and is intended for command levels A, B, C, D, and E for the Active Army, Army National Guard of the United States, and the U.S. Army Reserve.

•••

Chapter 1
Introduction

1-1. Purpose
This regulation provides Army policy and guidance for establishing civilian inmate labor programs and civilian prison camps on Army installations. Sources of civilian inmate labor are limited to on- and off–post Federal corrections facilities, State and/or local corrections facilities operating from on–post prison camps pursuant to leases under Section 2667, Title 10, United States Code (10 USC 2667), and off–post State corrections facilities participating in the demonstration project authorized under Section 1065, Public Law (PL) 103–337. Otherwise, State and/or local inmate labor from off–post corrections facilities is currently excluded from this program.

1-2. References
Required and related publications and prescribed and referenced forms are listed in appendix A.

1-3. Explanation of abbreviations and terms
Abbreviations and special terms used in this regulation are explained in the glossary.

1-4. Responsibilities
a. The Assistant Secretary of the Army (Installations and Environment) (ASA(I&E)) will—

(1) Provide policy guidance and resolve policy issues.

(2) Provide overall program direction.

(3) Serve as approval authority for establishing civilian inmate labor programs and civilian inmate prison camps on Army installations.

(4) Provide procedural guidance on real property acquisition, management, and disposal relating to establishing prison camps on Army installations.

b. The Assistant Secretary of the Army (Financial Management and Comptroller) (ASA(FM&C)) will—

(1) Provide reimbursement policy guidance on interservice, interagency, and/or interdepartmental support agreements between installations and corrections facilities to establish civilian inmate prison camps on Army installations.

(2) Provide reimbursement policy for civilian inmate labor utilization, other than reimbursement for inmate labor itself.

(3) Review all actions pertaining to the Civilian Inmate Labor Program for compliance with Army financial management guidance.

c. The Chief of Public Affairs will—

(1) Monitor media coverage on installation civilian inmate labor programs and civilian inmate prison camps on Army installations.

(2) Coordinate all proposed media coverage of potential national interest concerning the Army Civilian Inmate Labor Program and civilian inmate prison camps with the Assistant Chief of Staff for Installation Management (ACSIM) prior to release.

d. The Assistant Secretary of the Army (Manpower and Reserve Affairs) (ASA(M&RA)) will—

(1) Provide policy guidance on inmate labor utilization issues pertaining to existing in–house resources.

(2) Provide policy guidance and procedures for apprising installation government employee labor unions of proposals to use civilian inmate labor and, for existing installation civilian inmate labor programs, apprising these unions of changes in agreements with corrections facilities governing inmate use.

e. The Assistant Chief of Staff for Installation Management will—

(1) Execute the Army Civilian Inmate Labor Program.

(2) Develop and implement policy and procedures for using civilian inmate labor and establishing civilian inmate prison camps on Army installations.

(3) Serve as the focal point for staff coordination on issues pertaining to the Civilian Inmate Labor Program and/or civilian inmate prison camps.

(4) Conduct a program review in accordance with AR 11–2 once every 5 years.

(5) Provide policy guidance on functions for which civilian inmate labor can be used.

(6) Review reports of availability pertaining to granting the use of Army real property.

(7) Immediately inform the Chief, Legislative Liaison of approval of civilian inmate labor programs and civilian inmate prison camps on Army installations to facilitate notification to interested members of Congress.

f. The General Counsel and the Judge Advocate General will review all actions pertaining to the Civilian Inmate Labor Program and civilian inmate prison camps for compliance with applicable laws and regulations.

g. The Chief of Engineers will, in those cases involving use of Army real property, handle all matters pertaining to granting the use of Army real property.

h. The Provost Marshal General will—

(1) Monitor reporting of serious incidents, that is, walkaways, escapes, riots, disturbances, and any criminal activity by civilian inmates occurring on the installation under AR 190–40.

(2) Provide policy on law enforcement operations on Army installations.

i. Heads of other Army Staff and Army Secretariat agencies will provide advice, as necessary, on aspects of the Civilian Inmate Labor Program within their functional areas of responsibility.

j. The Director, Headquarters, Installation Management Agency (HQ, IMA) will—

(1) Ensure that their installations participating in civilian inmate labor programs comply with 18 USC 4125(a) and other applicable laws governing civilian inmate labor, Executive Order (EO) 11755, and all provisions of this regulation.

(2) Review and endorse installation memoranda of agreement (MOA) and Inmate Labor Plans to establish civilian inmate labor programs and proposals to establish civilian inmate prison camps on Army installations, and forward such MOA, plans and proposals to Headquarters, Department of the Army (HQDA) for approval.

(3) Review and endorse installation requests for changes to Army Civilian Inmate Labor Program policy.

(4) Annually review installation civilian inmate labor programs against the key management controls listed in appendix D.

k. Installation commanders will—

(1) Comply with 18 USC 4125(a) and other applicable laws governing civilian inmate labor, EO 11755, and all provisions of this regulation.

(2) Submit the following through command channels to Headquarters, Installation Management Activity (SFIM–PL), 2511 Jefferson Davis Highway, Taylor Building, Arlington, VA 22202–3926:

(a) Memoranda of agreement and Inmate Labor Plans to establish civilian inmate labor programs.

(b) Proposals to establish civilian inmate prison camps.

(c) Written notification of termination of civilian inmate labor programs.

(d) Revisions to existing memoranda of agreement requiring changes to Army Civilian Inmate Labor Program policy.

(e) Requests for guidance on any Civilian Inmate Labor Program situation that is not addressed in this regulation.

(3) Annually review their civilian inmate labor programs to determine if their programs continue to generate cost avoidance.

(4) Annually review their civilian inmate labor programs against the key management controls identified in appendix D.

(5) Report all contacts with State or local corrections system on possible use of civilian inmate labor, facilities, land, or installation through command channels to Headquarters, Installation Management Activity (SFIM–PL), 2511 Jefferson Davis Highway, Taylor Building, Arlington, VA 22202–3926.

1–5. Civilian inmate labor programs

a. Civilian inmate labor programs benefit both the Army and corrections systems by—

(1) Providing a source of labor at no direct labor cost to Army installations to accomplish tasks that would not be possible otherwise due to the manning and funding constraints under which the Army operates.

(2) Providing meaningful work for inmates and, in some cases, additional space to alleviate overcrowding in nearby corrections facilities.

(3) Making cost–effective use of buildings and land not otherwise being used.

b. Except for the 3 exceptions listed in paragraph 2–1*d* below, installation civilian inmate labor programs may use civilian inmate labor only from Federal corrections facilities located either off or on the installation.

c. Keys to operating an effective civilian inmate labor program on Army installations include—

(1) Establishing a comprehensive lease agreement, interservice, interagency, and/or interdepartmental support agreement (ISA), and/or memoranda of agreement with the corrections facility.

(2) Developing a cooperative working relationship between installation personnel and corrections facility personnel.

(3) Working closely with installation government employee labor unions to ensure union leaders understand the program and have current information on program status.

(4) Training all installation personnel involved in the operation or administration of the program frequently.

(5) Developing a public affairs plan informing the installation and the surrounding local community of the program and work projects assigned to civilian inmate labor.

1–6. The process

Figure 1–1 diagrams the Army Civilian Inmate Labor Program process. The flowchart reads top down and left to right, starting with the decision to establish both a prison camp and an inmate labor program (the diamond–shaped box in the upper left corner of the diagram labeled "prison camp inmate labor?"). The diamond–shaped boxes are decision nodes; the rectangular boxes are steps in the process to establish a civilian inmate labor program, establish a civilian inmate prison camp on post, or do both. Follow the arrows through the flowchart. Chapters 2 and 3 address procedures for establishing a civilian inmate labor program and/or on–post civilian inmate prison camp.

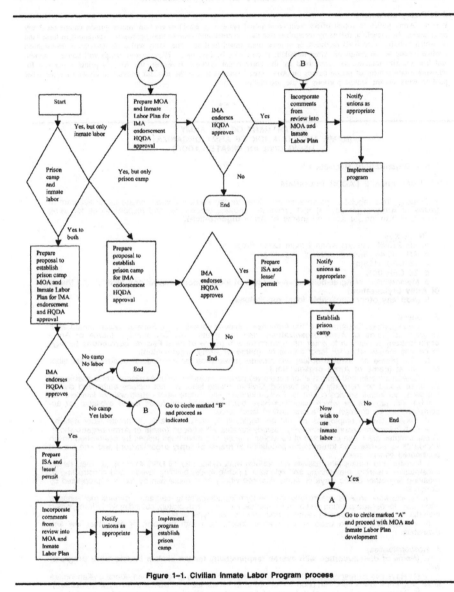

Figure 1–1. Civilian Inmate Labor Program process

Chapter 3
Establishing Civilian Inmate Prison Camps on Army Installations

3-1. Policy statement

It is not Army policy to solicit offers from correctional systems to establish civilian inmate prison camps on Army installations. Nevertheless, the Army recognizes that these correctional systems may approach installations to lease land on which to build corrections facilities, or to lease unoccupied facilities. The Army will evaluate requests to establish civilian inmate prison camps on Army installations on a case by case basis. These prison camps will house minimum and low security inmates, as determined by the correctional systems. However, the Army's primary purpose for allowing establishment of prison camps on Army installations is to use the resident nonviolent civilian inmate labor pool to work on the leased portions of the installation.

• • •

DEPARTMENT OF THE ARMY
(NAME AND LOCATION OF ARMY ORGANIZATION
USING CIVILIAN INMATE LABOR)

(Army Organization) Regulation No. _____

FEDERAL INMATE LABOR PROGRAM

1. Purpose. This regulation establishes guidelines for the Federal Civilian Inmate Labor Program at (name of Army organization) and prescribes policies, procedures, and responsibilities for using Federal civilian inmate labor on (name of Army organization).

2. References.
    a. AR 210-35, Army Civilian Inmate Labor Program.
    b. AR 190-40, Serious Incident Reporting.
    c. 18 USC 4125(a).
    d. 28 CFR 301.
    e. Memorandum of Agreement between (name of local Federal corrections facility) and (name of Army organization).
    f. (Add any other applicable local regulations).

3. General.
    a. Headquarters, Department of the Army has approved establishing a Federal civilian inmate labor program at (name of Army organization), and has granted the Commander, (name of Army organization) permission to enter into agreement with (name of local Federal corrections facility) to provide inmate labor for labor details on (name of Army organization).
    b. The (name of division/office) will provide stewardship for the Federal civilian inmate labor program at (name of Army organization).
    c. Civilian inmates and inmate labor details will perform tasks for which funding is not available and therefore would not normally be performed. Civilian inmate labor will not replace authorized civilian positions, nor impair service contracts. Civilian inmates and inmate labor details will not interfere nor conflict with projects for which resources have been allocated and funds made available for accomplishment by contract or Federal civilian labor force.
    d. Federal civilian employees will not be displaced by civilian inmates or inmate labor details.
    e. Only minimum security community custody inmates will work on (name of Army organization). These inmates are those convicted of nonviolent crimes who have been judged by established prison standards to represent no threat to the population at (name of Army organization) and who are not considered escape risks.
    f. Inmates and inmate labor details will perform work defined by 18 USC 4125(a), i.e. road repair/construction, clearing, maintaining and reforesting public lands, building levees, and constructing or repairing any other public ways or works financed wholly or in major part by funds appropriated by Congress.
    g. Typical work projects inmate labor can perform include painting, carpentry, general maintenance and repair, landscape planting and/or maintenance, mowing, trash pickup, custodial work, transporting material to and from recycling centers, and other similar type work.
    h. Inmates will not be used in any manner inconsistent with this plan or any other law and regulation.

4. Responsibilities.
    a. (Name of division/office with overall responsibility for the civilian inmate labor program) will:
        (1) Have overall responsibility for managing and coordinating action of the Federal civilian inmate labor program and will establish priorities for use of all inmate labor on (name of Army organization).
        (2) Maintain a current list of all (name of Army organization) personnel trained and certified by (name of local Federal corrections facility) to check on the quality of inmate labor being performed, provide necessary daily training related to tasks, safety, and proper use of equipment, materials, tools, and supplies for inmates working at (name of Army organization).
        (3) Provide/accomplish all inmate labor reporting requirements.
        (4) Ensure that training and licensing of inmates is accomplished in accordance with Army

Figure C-1. Sample Inmate Labor Plan—continued

regulations, as necessary, for inmates to operate government equipment/vehicles on **(name of Army organization)**.

(5) Coordinate training for **(name of Army organization)** personnel on **(name of local Federal corrections facility)** policies and procedures in such areas as inmate and inmate labor detail discipline, accountability, **(name of local Federal corrections facility)** staff conduct and safety. This training will be required for personnel who will serve as inmate labor detail monitors, or have any contact with inmates.

(6) Review and approve (or disapprove) each inmate labor work project request.

(Add additional paragraphs as appropriate).

b. The **(name of Army organization)** Public Affairs Office (PAO) will develop a plan to inform the installation and surrounding communities (to include family members) of the Federal civilian inmate labor program, projects inmate labor will perform, and community training regarding the presence of inmates on the installation.

c. The **(name of Army organization)** Staff Judge Advocate will review each inmate labor work project request to ensure that the work projects are within the parameters of 18 USC 4125(a). Factors other than those identified herein may be considered in the approval process.

d. Director and heads of other organizations will ensure that the provisions of this regulation are followed by personnel within their respective organizations.

e. Users of inmate labor will:

(1) Provide trained personnel for inmate labor details. Personnel provided must be trained and certified by **(name of local Federal corrections facility)** officials and be listed on the **(name of local Federal corrections facility)** record of training. Personnel will check on the quality of work being performed and provide necessary daily training related to tasks, safety, and proper use of equipment, materials, tools, and supplies. These personnel will not become directly involved with the operation of labor details, and in no event will perform custodial supervision of inmates or inmate labor details.

(2) Identify designated work break, lunch, restroom, and vending machine areas for use by inmates and inmate labor details.

(3) Submit written requests, **(specify type of written request)** to **(division/office having overall responsibility for the civilian inmate labor program)** for inmate labor support. All written requests must contain the following:

(a) Work location (building, area, place, etc.)

(b) Work period (days, hours, etc.)

(c) Duration of work required (weeks, months, indefinite, etc.)

(d) Names of **(name of local Federal corrections facility)** trained personnel who will be providing assistance at the work site.

(e) Names and telephone numbers of points of contact within the user's organization.

(f) Number of inmates required.

(g) Statement of work to be performed. This information should be simply stated but comprehensive enough to show expertise, training, qualifications, or any other knowledge/ skills inmates must possess to perform the work. Include physical requirements of the job.

(4) Ensure that inmates are used in accordance with guidelines and instructions provided by **(name of local Federal corrections facility)** officials, **(name of Army organization)** requirements, and job safety.

(5) Provide an escort at all times for inmate labor details working within controlled and restricted areas.

(6) Report the following to **(name of division/office with overall responsibility for the civilian inmate labor program):**

(a) Any walkaway, escape, riot, disturbances or similar incident involving inmates or the **(name of Army organization)** Federal civilian inmate labor program.

(b) Any criminal act by a **(name of local Federal corrections facility)** inmate against a military member or civilian assigned to, residing on, or traversing the installation.

(c) Any negative media coverage concerning the inmate labor program or **(name of local Federal corrections facility)** inmates.

(d) Accidents/injuries.

(7) Maintain records of hours worked and work performed.

(8) Provide a safe and humane work environment for inmate labor details.

(9) Provide all materials, supplies, equipment, tools, and personal protective equipment for inmates and inmate labor details in a safe and serviceable condition.

(10) Enforce inventory and control procedures for hand tools and other equipment provided for inmate labor details.

(11) Ensure that personnel in their organization who will be directly involved with inmates and inmate labor details are of good integrity, have no known criminal record, have no known history of drug or alcohol abuse, and have no prior nor present social or other relationship with inmates and members of inmate labor details.

Figure C-1. Sample Inmate Labor Plan—continued

26

CONTINGENCY PLANNING

The Army's Continuity of Operations Plan

Hours after the events of September 11, 2001, the Bush administration put "Continuity of Government" plans into operation for the first time in American history. These had actually been drawn up by Donald Rumsfeld earlier in the year, and when WikiLeaks published it, the document was affixed with a warning: "Destruction Notice: Destroy by any method that will prevent disclosure of contents or reconstruction of the document."

I guess something has changed since then, because the revised Army Regulation 500-3 issued in April 2008 is stamped UNCLASSIFIED. I'm ending this section with some excerpts, which seem like decent contingency planning on the face of it. Still, the emergency relocation facilities do give me pause, not unlike the KBR contract and the civilian prison camps.

In the wrong hands...I'd better stop there.

Army Regulation 500–3

Emergency Employment of Army and
Other Resources

U.S. Army
Continuity of
Operations
Program Policy
and Planning

Chapter 1
Introduction

Section I
General

1–1. Purpose
This regulation establishes responsibilities, policies, and planning guidance to ensure the effective execution of critical Army missions and the continuation of mission essential functions (MEFs) under all circumstances. All Department of the Army (DA) continuity-related activities will be coordinated and managed under the Army Continuity of Operations (COOP) Program. This regulation is the proponent policy document for the U.S. Army COOP program. If there is any conflict in this guidance with any other Army regulation, pamphlet, or other Army document, this regulation takes precedence. A COOP plan is complementary to other continuity programs and is a part of the foundation for Army COOP.

1–2. References
Required and related publications and prescribed and referenced forms are in appendix A.

1–3. Explanation of abbreviations and terms
Abbreviations and special terms used in this regulation are explained in the glossary.

Section II
Responsibilities

1–4. Heads of Headquarters, Department of the Army Secretariat, and Staff Agencies
The heads of HQDA Secretariat and Staff Agencies will—

a. Designate in writing a primary and alternate COOP point of contact (POC). The COOP POC will be directly responsible to the senior Army official of each agency. The head of HQDA Secretariat and Staff Agencies may delegate their COOP Program oversight authority and responsibility to their immediate deputy, but not to a lower echelon. COOP POC information will be provided to the Director, Force Protection Division (DAMO-ODA-F) not later than (NLT) 30 September of each year, or within 10 working days if the POC name or contact information changes. Names, telephone numbers, unclassified and classified Army Knowledge Online (AKO), and unclassified and classified non-AKO e-mail addresses will be provided to HQDA, Director, Force Protection Division, ATTN: DAMO-ODA-F, 3200 Army Pentagon, Washington, DC 20310-3200 or e-mailed to: armycoop@conus.army.mil.

b. Provide COOP primary POCs and alternates with individually assigned secret Internet protocol router network (SIPRNET) access/connectivity depending upon their organization's mission. It is recommended that the primary means for conducting COOP planning, correspondence, and communication be via SIPRNET.

c. Identify and prioritize MEFs in accordance with MEF definitions and guidance contained within this regulation to be performed as the basis for continuity planning, preparation, and execution. MEF should directly support HQDA, the Chairman of the Joint Chiefs of Staff (CJCS) MEFs and the Department of Defense (DOD) MEFs.

d. Review, re-evaluate, and provide their MEFs to the Director, Force Protection Division no later than 1 February of every odd year. As changes occur, agencies will provide updates to their MEFs for consideration and review at all times. Heads of HQDA Secretariat and Staff Agencies will sign their submission indicating their approval.

e. Establish COOP plans and procedures to ensure the execution of critical HQDA MEFs.

f. Identify and train their HQDA Emergency Relocation Group (ERG) personnel and provide electronic online roster updates to the Director, Force Protection Division (DAMO-ODA-F) as changes occur.

g. Identify critical requirements and procurement needs for command, control, communications & intelligence (C3I), prepositioned files, vital records, documents, software, databases, or other resources to be stored, protected and made available at their Emergency Relocation Facility (ERF) (also known as Emergency Relocation Site (ERS)) and alternate headquarters (AH) and alternate headquarters. Review prepositioned items and contingency procurement requests semiannually and update as changes occur. Priority should be given using electronic media storage vice paper files.

• • •

Section III
Requirements for the Army Continuity of Operations Program

1–9. General

The Army COOP Program represents an integrated set of Army policies, plans, and procedures that support the Defense Continuity Program. The Army COOP Program assures the capability exists to continue organization MEFs under all circumstances including crisis, attack, recovery, and reconstitution across a wide range of potential emergencies. This includes all planning and preparatory measures, alert and notification actions, response actions, and restoration activities for all hazards, including acts of nature, natural disasters, accidents, and technological and/or attack-related emergencies. The program encompasses HQDA Secretariat and Staff agencies, ACOMs, ASCCs, or DRUs, and subordinate commands performing COOP functions. A sample command inspection checklist is at appendix B.

• • •

j. Establish the capability to shelter-in-place essential personnel. Shelter-in-place may be declared by the senior Army official responsible for the organization or by the senior person present at the location where the threat and/or hazardous condition precludes safe egress from that facility. The duration for possible shelter-in-place conditions and preparation of the shelter including, but not limited to, stockage of food, water, bedding, hygiene supplies, will be determined by the senior Army official responsible for the organization. This determination should consider all-hazards the organization may possibly experience. Sheltering-in-place is considered a disaster response. Relevant regulations, such as AR 30-22 and DA Pam 30-22, for example, should be consulted. Organization's advisors such as legal, contractor, logistics, and others, as determined by the senior Army official responsible for the organization, should be consulted in advance when shelter-in-place plans, procedures, and preparation are being formulated.

• • •

q. Consider issuing military personnel, civilian and contractor employees with COOP responsibilities a Government Emergency Telecommunication Service (GETS) cards. The GETS is a national security and emergency preparedness service of the Federal Government. This system increases the probability of completing emergency calls worldwide when normal calling methods fail. For more information, see http://gets.ncs.gov.

• • •

r. Ensure emergency relocation facilities (ERF) comply with the Americans with Disabilities Act (ADA). Procedures for routine and emergency ingress and egress must consider handicap assigned and visiting personnel, including during power-out conditions

s. Ensure ERFs are capable of permitting ingress as well as egress during power-out conditions.

t. Ensure that Department of Army Civilians (DAC) position descriptions and statements of work for contractors with COOP responsibilities clearly reflect and/or specify what their nonroutine office duties are (for example, travel, 24-hour on-call duties, 24-hour exercise duties, and so on). Review current contract statements of work for COOP language. Some existing contracts may require a contract modification. Some DACs occupy positions that cannot be vacated during national emergency or mobilization without seriously impairing the capability of their organization. To ensure continuity in mission, commanders may designate these positions as key.

u. Consider designations on badges or other forms of identification to distinguish the COOP or other personnel exempt from movement restrictions during a COOP event.

v. Declare in their procedures that their COOP OPLAN automatically becomes an OPORD upon COOP declaration/ activation.

w. Ensure that ERG and other COOP Personnel who may carry classified information outside of their normal place of duty are issued and possess current Courier Cards upon appointment to these positions.

• • •

(9) Oversee programs such as the Government Emergency Telecommunications Service (GETS) for ERG members.

(10) Ensure ERG members exercise their computer equipment and software at ERF locations to ensure connectivity to their required files.

(11) Ensure procedures for telecommuting (also known as telework), work-at-home agreements, virtual offices, are established, as applicable.

(12) Ensure their agency's contracting requirements and agreements to support COOP are identified and in place in advance of COOP events.

(13) Prepare and maintain an agency COOP plan and oversee their subordinate agency's COOP plan development and maintenance.

(14) Ensure ERG members and agency principals are knowledgeable and informed of ERG member COOP OPLAN responsibilities.

• • •

Chapter 2
Continuity of Operations Planning Guidance

2-1. General

The Army COOP program assures that the capability exists to continue MEFs across the full spectrum of emergencies and prepares Army organizations for any contingency that potentially interrupts normal operations. The COOP Program supports the President, the Secretary of Defense, the CJCS, Department of the Army organizations, and other DOD components.

a. Developing flexible COOP plans and procedures for all possible events have become the new norm for the Army. Army COOP plans will be event neutral and consider capabilities, connectivity, and procedures that would provide Army organizations and leadership with the ability to ensure their MEFs continue to operate in all-hazards environments with minimum disruption, through and during the event, until normal operations are restored. Minor interruptions such as a short duration power failure, for example, that do not substantially disrupt an organization's MEFs potentially will not be considered by the organization's leadership as a declared COOP event.

• • •

2–9. Department of the Army Relocation Sites (DARS) Program

Selection and use of alternate headquarters (AH) and emergency relocation facilities (ERF).

a. An ERF is the location an organization moves to in order to continue operations. An AH is a subordinate command that takes over in case the headquarters is suddenly rendered incapable of commanding the organization.

(1) DOD centrally manages and documents ERFs and AH locations, to include COOP training and exercise locations. This is necessary to prevent potential interference with or compromise of sensitive locations or operations.

(2) Army organizations establishing an ERF or AH will coordinate the locations through the IMCOM, which is the office of primary responsibility (OPR) for the Army's day-to-day management of the AH/ERF program.

(3) The OPR will coordinate ERF or AH requests with the OCR. The OCR may overrule requests for mission deconfliction reasons and will advise the OPR of such. Once the facility is deconflicted, then site surveying, acquisition, and equipping the fixed or other assets will be the responsibility of the requesting organization and may require an MOA between the requesting and host organizations. Copies of MOAs will be provided to IMCOM. MOAs entered into prior to the April 2006 revision of this directive should be reviewed to ensure compliance with current directives and submitted through the Garrison Commander to HQ IMCOM for accountability purposes.

(4) AH and ERF information will be updated in accordance with DOD classification guidance and sent to IMCOM

AR 500–3 · 18 April 2008   11

• • •

2–10. Emergency relocation group

a. ERG members will be selected to provide the best mix of senior leaders and supporting staff to execute MEFs regardless of the type of emergency or crisis that causes execution of COOP plans. Recommend that COOP POCs, and Individual Mobilization Augmentees who are Civilian Servants with conflicting duties, not be members of the ERG. Personnel assigned to the ERG will be—

(1) Cleared for access to the ERF or AH and for the materials and equipment they are designated to use.

(2) Available through alert and notification recall procedures.

(3) Prepared to move to an alternate location when the primary location is threatened or no longer viable.

(4) Briefed on all aspects of relocating to and operating at designated facilities.

(5) Exercised at least annually.

(6) Prepared to activate the organization's shelter-in-place plans and procedures.

(7) Trained in COOP operations/execution to effectively support respective COOP plans.

b. As required, ERG members must be capable of—

(1) Providing organization-specific functional expertise.

(2) Providing essential planning and support.

(3) Coordinating with appropriate representatives of higher headquarters, other Services, other agencies, and civil governmental sectors, as applicable.

(4) Issuing and implementing decisions and directives.

(5) Ensuring execution of MEFs.

(6) Monitoring and reporting on the situation.

(7) Accounting for organizational personnel.

2–11. Prepositioned information and duplicate emergency files

a. With the advent of new data storage hardware (for example, storage area networks and network access storage devices), the use of electronic data files has replaced the use of paper copies. ERG organizations will coordinate with their information technology support element(s) to ensure the systems, applications, databases, and electronic files they require to execute and sustain their MEFs are available at their ERF.

b. However, if budget constraints prevent an organization from electronically storing and accessing its data from a data storage facility other than their primary place of business, paper copies, CD–Rs, or magnetic tape will be used and prepositioned at the ERF. In addition, if an organization is bound by Federal regulations to maintain paper records, it is incumbent upon that organization to implement those regulatory requirements.

EMBASSY CABLES

The State Department Cable on Russia as a "Mafia State"

No doubt by the time this book appears, there will be whole volumes being assembled based on the WikiLeaks slow-but-steady release of U.S. embassy cables. I haven't had time to do more than peruse some of the most intriguing of these, but I go back to what Congressman Ron Paul has to say about the whole WikiLeaks saga. What's caused more deaths—"lying us into war [in Iraq] or the release of the WikiLeaks papers? . . . In a society where truth becomes treason, then we're in big trouble." He says it so eloquently, I have nothing more to add.

Here is the first of several of the U.S. embassy cables that caught my eye. It's our State Department reporting about a senior Spanish prosecutor looking into organized crime, who says that Russia has become a virtual "Mafia state" with the Kremlin using mob bosses to carry out its wishes. I've only included excerpts here.

Monday, 08 February 2010, 11:00
S E C R E T SECTION 01 OF 05 MADRID 000154
NOFORN
SIPDIS
DEPARTMENT FOR EUR/WE (ALEX MCKNIGHT, STACIE ZERDECKI),
EUR/ERA (ALESSANDRO NARDI), INR/TNC (JENNIFER MCELVEEN,
STEPHEN WOROBEC), INL (ELIZABETH VERVILLE, SCOTT HARRIS), L
(KEN PROPP),
EMBASSY MOSCOW (THOMAS FIRESTONE)
DEPARTMENT PASS TO NSC (GREG GATJANIS)
DEPARTMENT PASS TO ODNI/NIC (JOHN REGAS, MAT BURROWS)
DEPARTMENT PASS TO FBI (BARRY M. BRAUN,KAREN GREENAWAY)
DEPARTMENT PASS TO DOJ (BRUCE SWARTZ, TOM OTT, BRUCE OHR,
LISA HOLTYN)
DEPARTMENT PASS TO TREASURY/OFFICE OF TERRORISM AND
FINANCIAL INTELLIGENCE (BOB WERNER)
EO 12958 DECL: 02/08/2035
TAGS KJUS, KHLS, PGOV, PREL, PTER, SP, PINS, KCOR, PINR,
XH, RS
SUBJECT: <u>SPAIN</u> DETAILS ITS STRATEGY TO COMBAT THE RUSSIAN

MAFIA

REF: A. MADRID 76 B. 09 MADRID 869 C. 09 MADRID 870 D. 09 MADRID 1003

MADRID 00000154 001.2 OF 005

Classified By: POLCOUNS William H. Duncan for reasons 1.4 (b) and (d)

1. (C) SUMMARY AND COMMENT: National Court Prosecutor Jose "Pepe" Grinda Gonzalez on January 14 gave a detailed, frank assessment of the activities and reach of organized crime (OC) in both Eurasia and Spain and Spain's strategy for how best to combat it in court. As he did so, he evaluated the levels of cooperation that Spain receives from numerous countries. Grinda presented his remarks on January 13 at the new US-Spain Counter-Terrorism and Organized Crime Experts Working Group meeting in Madrid (See Ref A). He provided a 17-page, English-language handout entitled, "The Organized Crime and the Russian Mafia," which he used as the basis for his remarks, which were more explicit than the document is. (NOTE: Post will send a copy of the handout to interested parties.) Grinda's comments are insightful and valuable, given his in-depth knowledge of the Eurasian mafia and his key role in Spain's pioneering efforts to bring Eurasian mafia leaders to justice. END SUMMARY AND COMMENT.

//Bio Info//

2. (S//NF) Grinda, a Special Prosecutor for Corruption and Organized Crime, in early December wrapped up his prosecution of the alleged OC network led by Zahkar Kalashov, the Georgian-born, Russian citizen who allegedly is a "vor v zakone," ("Thief in Law," the highest echelon of Russian OC leadership) and reportedly the most senior Russian mafia figure jailed outside <u>Russia</u>. The defendants were arrested as part of Operation Avispa (see Refs B and C). A verdict is expected by early February, according to Belen Suarez, Deputy Prosecutor for Corruption and Organized Crime and one of Grinda's superiors. Grinda is known to Post's Legat Office as a skilled and rigorous professional with deep subject matter expertise. He

is forward-leaning in his cooperation with the USG and grateful for USG assistance. His work places him under considerable stress, which make him suspicious of penetration attempts by intelligence services and causes him to have heightened sensitivities regarding his physical security. Grinda also will be the prosecutor in the trial for those arrested in Operation Troika (See Refs B and C).

•   •   •

4. (C//NF) *Grinda stated that he considers Belarus, Chechnya and Russia to be virtual "mafia states" and said that Ukraine is going to be one. For each of those countries, he alleged, one cannot differentiate between the activities of the government and OC groups.*

//Identifying The Scope of The Threat the Russian Mafia Poses//

5. (C) Grinda suggested that there are two reasons to worry about the Russian mafia. First, it exercises "tremendous control" over certain strategic sectors of the global economy, such as aluminum. He made a passing remark that the USG has a strategic problem in that the Russian mafia is suspected of having a sizable investment in XXXXXXXXXXXX 6. (S//NF) *The second reason is the unanswered question regarding the extent to which Russian PM Putin is implicated in the Russian mafia and whether he controls the mafia's actions. Grinda cited a "thesis" by Alexander Litvinenko, the former Russian intelligence official who worked on OC issues before he died in late 2006 in London from poisoning under mysterious circumstances, that the Russian intelligence and security services - Grinda cited the Federal Security Service (FSB), the Foreign Intelligence Service (SVR), and military intelligence (GRU) - control OC in Russia. Grinda stated that he believes this thesis is accurate.* (COMMENT: See Ref B on a reported meeting between Litvinenko and the Spanish security services shortly before his death.) Grinda said that he believes the FSB is "absorbing" the Russian mafia but they can also "eliminate" them in two ways: by killing OC leaders who do not do what the security services want them to do or by putting them behind bars to eliminate them as a competitor for influence. The crimelords can also be put in jail for their own protection.

7. (S//NF) *Grinda said that according to information he has received from intelligence services, witnesses and phone taps, certain political parties in Russia operate "hand in hand" with OC. For example, he argued that the Liberal Democratic Party (LDP) was created by the KGB and its successor, the SVR, and is home to many serious criminals. Grinda further alleged that there are proven ties between the Russian political parties, organized crime and arms trafficking. Without elaborating, he cited the strange case of the "Arctic Sea" ship in mid-2009 as "a clear example" of arms trafficking.*

8. (S//NF) Grinda said what he has read from 10-12 years' worth of investigations on OC has led him to believe that whereas terrorists aim to substitute the essence of the state itself, OC seeks to be a complement to state structures. He summarized his views by asserting that the GOR's strategy is

MADRID 00000154 003.2 OF 005

to use OC groups to do whatever the GOR cannot acceptably do as a government. As an example, he cited Kalashov, whom he said worked for Russian military intelligence to sell weapons to the Kurds to destabilize Turkey. Grinda claimed that the GOR takes the relationship with OC leaders even further by granting them the privileges of politics, in order to grant them immunity from racketeering charges.

Grinda described OC as "very powerful" in Georgia and claimed that the intertwined ties there between the government and OC began under former President Shevardnadze, when he alleges a paramilitary group served as a de facto shadow presidency. Although Grinda acknowledged improvements under current President Saakashvili, he said that there are still "limitations" in Georgia's efforts to combat OC. Citing his personal experience in trying to secure Georgian assistance in the prosecution of Kalashov's OC network in

Spain (See upcoming septel on the Kalashov trial), Grinda said that he feels "completely abandoned" and "betrayed" by Georgia and the explanations that he has received from Georgia regarding its lack of cooperation are "more pathetic than the betrayal itself."

THE FDA'S BLIND SIDE

Our Food Supply Imperiled by Lack of Inspections

I can't say I was surprised to read in this report how little attention is being paid to what's going on with our factory farms and feedlots. I've known about this problem since I was governor. The simple fact is, the Food and Drug Administration doesn't have the manpower. They tell you they're conducting these inspections, but nobody is actually out there checking to make sure.

The reality is, the conditions by which our food is being supplied to us are very dangerous. Consider that more than *half a billion* eggs were recalled last year and a salmonella outbreak in August made about 1,700 people sick. Preventable food-borne illness hits about 76 million Americans every year—325,000 become hospitalized and 5,000 die from eating tainted food!

It all comes back to the same old thing: this is what happens when corporations, in this case agribusiness, take over. It simply becomes bottom line, money, and profits—everything else be damned. There is a staph infection that's antibiotic-resistant and widely present in our vast hog and chicken factories. It's called ST398, and the reason it's a huge problem is because those animals are getting daily doses of antibiotics—which make them grow faster (more bang for the buck) and keep them alive in the stressful and unsanitary conditions where they're raised.

You'd think that the federal regulators would want to keep tabs on this, but for years the FDA looked the other way and wouldn't even calculate estimates of how much antibiotics the livestock industry is using. Finally, in December 2010, the Department of Health and Human Services Office of the Inspector General released a report—it turned out to be 29 million pounds of antibiotics in 2009! And that, my friends, is a veritable shitload. Here are a few excepts from "FDA Inspections of Domestic Food Facilities" (April 2010).

BACKGROUND

Each year, more than 300,000 Americans are hospitalized and 5,000 die after consuming contaminated foods and beverages. Recent high-profile outbreaks of foodborne illness have raised serious questions about FDA's inspections process and its ability to protect the Nation's food supply. The Senate Committee on Agriculture, Nutrition, and Forestry requested that the Office of Inspector General (OIG) review the extent to which FDA conducts food facility inspections and identifies violations.

FDA inspects food facilities to ensure food safety and compliance with regulations. During an inspection, FDA inspectors may identify potential violations of the Food, Drug, and Cosmetic Act as well as other applicable laws and regulations. Based on the outcome of the inspection, FDA assigns a facility one of three classifications: official action indicated (OAI), voluntary action indicated (VAI), or no action indicated (NAI). In addition, FDA may choose to change a facility's initial classification to another classification under certain circumstances.

FDA relies on several approaches to determine whether a facility corrected the violations found by inspectors. FDA may review evidence provided by a food facility describing any completed corrective actions. FDA may also reinspect a facility to verify that corrections were made.

FINDINGS

On average, FDA inspects less than a quarter of food facilities each year, and the number of facilities inspected has declined over time.
Between fiscal years (FY) 2004 and 2008, FDA inspected annually an average of 24 percent of the food facilities subject to its inspection. Except for a few instances, there are no specific guidelines that govern the frequency with which inspections should occur. Further, the number of food facilities that FDA inspected declined between FYs 2004 and 2008, even as the number of food facilities increased. In addition, the number of inspections of facilities that have been designated by FDA as "high risk" has also declined. FDA officials noted that the overall decline in FDA inspections was largely due to a decline in staffing levels.

Fifty-six percent of food facilities have gone 5 or more years without an FDA inspection. FDA identified 51,229 food facilities that were subject to inspection and were in business from the start of FY 2004 until the end of FY 2008. Of these, 56 percent were not inspected at all, 14 percent were inspected a single time, and the remaining 30 percent were inspected two or more times. If FDA does not routinely inspect food facilities, it is unable to guarantee that these facilities are complying with applicable laws and regulations.

The number of facilities that received OAI classifications has declined over time. The number of inspected facilities that received OAI classifications decreased from 614 in FY 2004 to 283 in FY 2008. The percentage of facilities that received OAI classifications also dropped from nearly 4 percent to nearly 2 percent during this 5-year period. In addition, nearly three-quarters of the facilities that received OAI classifications in FY 2008 had a history of violations. Two percent of facilities that received OAI classifications refused to grant FDA officials access to their records.

FDA took regulatory action against 46 percent of the facilities with initial OAI classifications; for the remainder, FDA either lowered the classification or took no regulatory action. In FY 2007, a total of 446 facilities initially received OAI classifications. FDA took regulatory action against 46 percent of these facilities. For the remainder, FDA lowered the OAI classification for 29 percent and took no regulatory action for 25 percent.

For 36 percent of the facilities with OAI classifications in FY 2007, FDA took no additional steps to ensure that the violations were corrected. In FY 2007, 280 facilities received OAI classifications that were not lowered by FDA. For 36 percent of these facilities, FDA did not reinspect them within a year of the inspection or review other evidence provided by facilities to ensure that the violations were corrected.

29

THE EPA'S BLIND SIDE

Pesticides and Honeybees

We all learned in grade school how important the honeybees are to our food production. And we know that they've been dying off in droves over the past several years. Nobody's yet determined exactly why, but the spraying of pesticides is one of the prime suspects.

At the end of 2010, some brave and outraged individual within the Environmental Protection Agency leaked an internal memo. It's a lengthy new EPA study of a tongue-twister pesticide called clothianidin, which is manufactured by the German agrichemical giant Bayer. Their Bayer CropScience division had applied to use this particular pesticide as a seed treatment on cotton and mustard. It's already widely used on corn, soy, wheat, sugar beets, sunflowers, and canola in the States. In 2009, Bayer took in about $262 million in sales of clothianidin.

This new study says flat out that the health of our nation's honeybees is imperiled by this product. That's actually been a concern for almost ten years, except the EPA under Bush granted "conditional registration" to clothianidin in 2003. Bayer's own study in 2007 was rubber-stamped by the EPA as "scientifically sound." And, in April 2010, the Obama administration's EPA granted *full* registration to the pesticide. So how come Bayer is being treated with kid gloves? Why are tens of millions of acres of farmland going to bloom with clothianidin-laced pollen this year? And what's this going to mean for the health of our little pollinator friends?

This ties in to something that happened when I took my TV show (*Conspiracy Theory*) to New Orleans to look into the Gulf oil spill. At the time, BP was applying a chemical called Corexit as a means of dispersing the millions of gallons of oil. A guy from BP looked at me and said, "Everything we've put into the water was approved by the EPA." I said, "So what?! Doesn't your common sense tell you that putting something in the water that has four lethal poisons in it, when you've already got all this oil, is not a good thing?" But his answer again was, "Everything we did was approved." That told me right there that the EPA can be bought and sold.

Here are some excerpts from the EPA's study on bees and pesticides, and you can read the whole thing at: www.panna.org/sites/default/files/Memo_Nov2010_Clothianidin.pdf.

UNITED STATES ENVIRONMENTAL PROTECTION AGENCY
WASHINGTON, D.C. 20460

Office of Chemical Safety and
Pollution Prevention

PC Code: 044309
Date: November 2nd, 2010
DP Barcodes: 378994, 377955

MEMORANDUM

• • •

This memo summarizes the Environmental Fate and Effects Division's (EFED) screening-level Environmental Risk Assessment for clothianidin. The registrant, Bayer CropScience, is submitting a request for registration of clothianidin to be used as a seed treatment on cotton and mustard (oilseed and condiment).

• • •

Clothianidin's major risk concern is to nontarget insects (that is, honey bees). Clothianidin is a neonicotinoid insecticide that is both persistent and systemic. Acute toxicity studies to honey bees show that clothianidin is highly toxic on both a contact and an oral basis. Although EFED does not conduct RQ based risk assessments on non-target insects, information from standard tests and field studies, as well as incident reports involving other neonicotinoids insecticides (e.g., imidacloprid) suggest the potential for long term toxic risk to honey bees and other beneficial insects. An incident in Germany already illustrated the toxicity of clothianidin to honeybees when allowed to drift off-site from treated seed during planting.

A previous field study (MRID 46907801/46907802) investigated the effects of clothianidin on whole hive parameters and was classified as acceptable. However, after another review of this field study in light of additional information, deficiencies were identified that render the study supplemental. It does not satisfy the guideline 850.3040, and another field study is needed to evaluate the effects of clothianidin on bees through contaminated pollen and nectar. Exposure through contaminated pollen and nectar and potential toxic effects therefore remain an uncertainty for pollinators.

EFED expects adverse effects to bees if clothianidin is allowed to drift from seed planting equipment. Because of this and the uncertainty surrounding the exposure and potential toxicity through contaminated pollen and nectar, EFED is recommending bee precautionary labeling.

• • •

Ecological Effects:
The database available for clothianidin to support the assessment was largely complete. The following ecological studies for clothianidin are still outstanding and need to be submitted.

Honey Bee Toxicity of Residues on Foliage (850.3030): This study is required for chemicals that have outdoor terrestrial uses in which honeybees will be exposed and exhibit an LD50 < 11μg a.i./bee. The study that was submitted to satisfy this guideline is supplemental but does not satisfy the guideline requirement. This study is not required for this assessment due to the lack of exposure to residues on foliage from the seed treatments. This study is placed in reserve pending future new uses.

Field Test for Pollinators (850.3040): The possibility of toxic exposure to nontarget pollinators through the translocation of clothianidin residues that result from seed treatments has prompted EFED to require field testing (850.3040) that can evaluate the possible chronic exposure to honey bee larvae and queen. In order to fully evaluate the possibility of this toxic effect, a field study should be conducted and the protocol submitted for review by the Agency prior to initiation. Another study had been submitted to satisfy this guideline requirement. While it had originally been classified as acceptable, after recent reevaluation it is classified as supplemental, and a field study is still being needed for a more refined risk assessment.

• • •

EFED Label Recommendations

Label Recommendations

Manufacturing Use Product
Do not discharge effluent containing this product into lakes, streams, ponds, estuaries, oceans, or other waters unless in accordance with the requirements of a National Pollutant Discharge Elimination System (NPDES) permit and the permitting authority has been notified in writing prior to discharge. Do not discharge effluent containing this product to sewer systems without previously notifying the local sewage treatment plant authority. For guidance contact your State Water Board or Regional Office of the EPA.

End Use Products
This product is toxic to aquatic invertebrates.

• • •

This chemical has properties and characteristics associated with chemicals detected in ground water. The use of this chemical in areas where soils are permeable, particularly where the water table is shallow, may result in ground water contamination.

This compound is toxic to birds and mammals. Treated clothianidin seeds exposed on soil surface may be hazardous to birds and mammals.

• • •

1.1   Potential Risk to Non-Target Organisms

• • •

Clothianidin's major risk concern is to nontarget insects (that is, honey bees). Clothianidin is a neonicotinoid insecticide that is both persistent and systemic. Acute toxicity studies to honey bees show that clothianidin is highly toxic on both a contact and an oral basis. Although EFED does not conduct RQ based risk assessments on non-target insects, information from standard tests and field studies, as well as incident reports involving other neonicotinoids insecticides (e.g., imidacloprid) suggest the potential for long term toxic risk to honey bees and other beneficial insects. An incident in Germany already illustrated the toxicity of clothianidin to honeybees when allowed to drift off-site from treated seed during planting.

A previous field study (MRID 46907801/46907802) investigated the effects of clothianidin on whole hive parameters and was classified as acceptable. However, after another review of this field study in light of additional information, deficiencies were identified that render the study supplemental. It does not satisfy the guideline 850.3040, and another field study is needed to evaluate the effects of clothianidin on bees through contaminated pollen and nectar. Exposure through contaminated pollen and nectar and potential toxic effects therefore remain an uncertainty for pollinators.

EFED expects adverse effects to bees if clothianidin is allowed to drift from seed planting equipment. Because of this and the uncertainty surrounding the exposure and potential toxicity through contaminated pollen and nectar, EFED is recommending bee precautionary labeling.

EMBASSY CABLES

America's Fight against Europe over Biotech Crops

In case you still imagine our government isn't completely in bed with the mega-corporations, this WikiLeaked cable ought to make you think twice. Our former ambassador to France was a guy named Craig Stapleton, who before that used to co-own the Texas Rangers baseball team with George W. Bush. In 2007, he called for "moving to retaliation" against France for having the gall to ban Monsanto's genetically modified corn, and against the whole European Union because they at the time had an anti-biotech policy. "In our view, Europe is moving backwards not forwards on this issue," Ambassador Stapleton determined, as if somehow we had the right to tell them how to think!

Reference ID	Created	Released	Classification	Origin
07PARIS4723	2007-12-14 16:04	2010-12-19 12:12	CONFIDENTIAL	Embassy Paris

```
VZCZCXRO2245
PP RUEHAG RUEHROV
DE RUEHFR #4723/01 3481623
ZNY CCCCC ZZH
P 141623Z DEC 07
FM AMEMBASSY PARIS
TO RUEHC/SECSTATE WASHDC PRIORITY 1495
RUCPDOC/USDOC WASHDC PRIORITY
RHEHAAA/WHITE HOUSE WASHDC PRIORITY
INFO RUCNMEM/EU MEMBER STATES COLLECTIVE
RUEHGV/USMISSION GENEVA 2786
C O N F I D E N T I A L SECTION 01 OF 02 PARIS 004723
```

SIPDIS

USTR FOR SUSAN SCHWAB
DEPARTMENT FOR E - REUBEN JEFFERY AND EB - DAN SULLIVAN
FROM AMBASSADOR STAPLETON

SIPDIS

E.O. 12958: DECL: 12/14/2017
TAGS: ECON ETRD EAGR PGOV SENV FR

SUBJECT: FRANCE AND THE WTO AG BIOTECH CASE

REF: A)PARIS 5364, B)PARIS 4255, C)PARIS 4170, D)PARIS 3970, E)PARIS

3967, F)PARIS 3853, G)PARIS 3429, H)PARIS 3399, I)PARIS 3429

Classified by Ambassador Craig Stapleton; reasons 1.4 (b), (d) and
(e).

¶1. (C) Summary: Mission Paris recommends that that the USG reinforce our
negotiating position with the EU on agricultural biotechnology by publishing
a retaliation list when the extend "Reasonable Time Period" expires. In our
view, Europe is moving backwards not forwards on this issue with France
playing a leading role, along with Austria, Italy and even the Commission. In
France, the "Grenelle" environment process is being implemented to circumvent
science-based decisions in favor of an assessment of the "common interest,"
Combined with the precautionary principle, this is a precedent with
implications far beyond MON 010 BT corn cultivation. Moving to retaliation
will make clear that the current path has real costs to EU interests and
could help strengthen European pro-biotech voices. In fact, the pro-biotech
side in France -- including within the farm union -- have told us retaliation
is the only way to begin to begin to turn this issue in France. End Summary.

¶2. (C) This is not just a bilateral concern. France will play a leading role
in renewed European consideration of the acceptance of agricultural
biotechnology and its approach toward environmental regulation more
generally. France expects to lead EU member states on this issue during the
Slovene presidency beginning in January and through its own Presidency in the
second half of the year. Our contacts have made clear that they will seek to
expand French national policy to a EU-wide level and they believe that they

are in the vanguard of European public opinion in turning back GMO's. They have noted that the member states have been unwilling to support the Commission on sanctioning Austria's illegal national ban. The GOF sees the ten year review of the Commission's authorization of MON 810 as a key opportunity and a review of the EFSA process to take into account societal preferences as another (reftels).

¶3. (C) One of the key outcomes of the "Grenelle" was the decision to suspend MON 810 cultivation in France. Just as damaging is the GOF's apparent recommitment to the "precautionary principle." Sarkozy publicly rejected a recommendation of the Attali Commission (to review France's competitiveness) to move away from this principle, which was added to the French constitution under Chirac.

¶4. (C) France's new "High Authority" on agricultural biotech is designed to roll back established science-based decision making. The recently formed authority is divided into two colleges, a scientific college and a second group including civil society and social scientists to assess the "common interest" of France. The authority's first task is to review MON 810. In the meantime, however, the draft biotech law submitted to the National Assembly and the Senate for urgent consideration, could make any biotech planting impossible in practical terms. The law would make farmers and seed companies legally liable for pollen drift and sets the stage for inordinately large cropping distances. The publication of a registry identifying cultivation of GMOs at the parcel level may be the most significant measure given the propensity for activists to destroy GMO crops in the field.

¶5. (C) Both the GOF and the Commission have suggested that their respective actions should not alarm us since they are only cultivation rather than import bans. We see the cultivation ban as a first step, at least by anti-GMO advocates, who will move next to ban or further restrict imports. (The environment minister's top aide told us that people have a right not to buy meat raised on biotech feed, even though she acknowledged there was no possible scientific basis for a feed based distinction.) Further, we should not be prepared to cede on cultivation because of our considerable planting seed business in Europe and because farmers, once they have had experience with biotech, become its staunchest supporters.

¶6. Country team Paris recommends that we calibrate a target retaliation list that causes some pain across the EU since this is a collective responsibility, but that also focuses in part on the worst culprits. The list should be measured rather than vicious and must be sustainable over the long term, since we should not expect an early victory.

¶7. (C) President Sarkozy noted in his address in Washington to the Joint Session of Congress that France and the United States are "allies but not aligned." Our cooperation with France on a range of issues should continue alongside our engagement with France and the EU on ag biotech (and the next generation of environmental related trade concerns.) We can manage both at the same time and should not let one set of priorities detract from the other.

PARIS 00004723 002 OF 002

Stapleton

MILITARY STUDIES CLIMATE

Climate Change as a Threat to National Security

Back in 2006, the Center for Naval Analyses (CNA), a federally funded R&D center for the Navy and Marine Corps, brought together a Military Advisory Board of eleven retired three-star and four-star admirals and generals. Their task was to examine the impact of global climate change for future national security. The report came out in April 2007, and I'm reprinting the Executive Summary here. Its conclusion is that climate change represents a "a serious threat" that is likely to create "instability in some of the most volatile regions of the world." (The entire report is viewable online at http://www.cna.org/reports/climate.)

I find it very chilling that the U.S. military would recognize this situation and begin preparations for how to deal with it, when many of our elected officials are still prepared to think climate change is some kind of hoax! I don't think it's such a good idea to have the military being out front on things like this, it isn't their proper role. We're the ones who should be leading them, not the other way around—unless we're like the proverbial ostrich with its head buried in the sand.

NATIONAL SECURITY
AND THE THREAT OF
CLIMATE CHANGE

SecurityAndClimate.cna.org

EXECUTIVE SUMMARY

The purpose of this study is to examine the national security consequences of climate change. A dozen of the nation's most respected retired admirals and generals have served as a Military Advisory Board to study how climate change could affect our nation's security over the next 30 to 40 years—the time frame for developing new military capabilities.

The specific questions addressed in this report are:

1. What conditions are climate changes likely to produce around the world that would represent security risks to the United States?

2. What are the ways in which these conditions may affect America's national security interests?

3. What actions should the nation take to address the national security consequences of climate change?

The Military Advisory Board hopes these findings will contribute to the call President Bush made in his 2007 State of the Union address to "...help us to confront the serious challenge of global climate change" by contributing a new voice and perspective to the issue.

FINDINGS

Projected climate change poses a serious threat to America's national security.
The predicted effects of climate change over the coming decades include extreme weather events, drought, flooding, sea level rise, retreating glaciers, habitat shifts, and the increased spread of life-threatening diseases. These conditions have the potential to disrupt our way of life and to force changes in the way we keep ourselves safe and secure.

In the national and international security environment, climate change threatens to add new hostile and stressing factors. On the simplest level, it has the potential to create sustained natural and humanitarian disasters on a scale far beyond those we see today. The consequences will likely foster political instability where societal demands exceed the capacity of governments to cope.

Climate change acts as a threat multiplier for instability in some of the most volatile regions of the world. Projected climate change will seriously exacerbate already marginal living standards in many Asian, African, and Middle Eastern nations, causing widespread political instability and the likelihood of failed states.

Unlike most conventional security threats that involve a single entity acting in specific ways and points in time, climate change has the potential to result in multiple chronic conditions, occurring globally within the same time frame. Economic and environmental conditions in already fragile areas will further erode as food production declines, diseases increase, clean water becomes increasingly scarce, and large populations move in search of resources. Weakened and failing governments, with an already thin margin for survival, foster the conditions for internal conflicts, extremism, and movement toward increased authoritarianism and radical ideologies.

The U.S. may be drawn more frequently into these situations, either alone or with allies, to help provide stability before conditions worsen and are exploited by extremists. The U.S. may also be called upon to undertake stability and reconstruction efforts once a conflict has begun, to avert further disaster and reconstitute a stable environment.

• • •

Projected climate change will add to tensions even in stable regions of the world. The U.S. and Europe may experience mounting pressure to accept large numbers of immigrant and refugee populations as drought increases and food production declines in Latin America and Africa. Extreme weather events and natural disasters, as the U.S. experienced with Hurricane Katrina, may lead to increased missions for a number of U.S. agencies, including state and local governments, the Department of Homeland Security, and our already stretched military, including our Guard and Reserve forces.

Climate change, national security, and energy dependence are a related set of global challenges. As President Bush noted in his 2007 State of the Union speech, dependence on foreign oil leaves us more vulnerable to hostile regimes and terrorists, and clean domestic energy alternatives help us confront the serious challenge of global climate change. Because the issues are linked, solutions to one affect the other. Technologies that improve energy efficiency also reduce carbon intensity and carbon emissions.

RECOMMENDATIONS OF THE MILITARY ADVISORY BOARD:

1. The national security consequences of climate change should be fully integrated into national security and national defense strategies.

As military leaders, we know we cannot wait for certainty. Failing to act because a warning isn't precise enough is unacceptable. The intelligence community should incorporate climate consequences into its National Intelligence Estimate. The National Security Strategy should directly address the threat of climate change to our national security interests. The National Security Strategy and National Defense Strategy should include appropriate guidance to military planners to assess risks to current and future missions caused by projected climate change. The next Quadrennial Defense Review should examine the capabilities of the U.S. military to respond to the consequences of climate change, in particular, preparedness for natural disasters from extreme weather events, pandemic disease events, and other related missions.

2. The U.S. should commit to a stronger national and international role to help stabilize climate change at levels that will avoid significant disruption to global security and stability.

Managing the security impacts of climate change requires two approaches: mitigating the effects we can control and adapting to those we cannot. The U.S. should become a more constructive partner with the international community to help build and execute a plan to prevent destabilizing effects from climate change, including setting targets for long term reductions in greenhouse gas emissions.

3. The U.S. should commit to global partnerships that help less developed nations build the capacity and resiliency to better manage climate impacts.

As President Bush noted in his State of the Union speech, "Our work in the world is also based on a timeless truth: To whom much is given, much is required." Climate forecasts indicate countries least able to adapt to the consequences of climate change are those that will be the most affected. The U.S. government should use its many instruments of national influence, including its regional commanders, to assist nations at risk build the capacity and resiliency to better cope with the effects of climate change. Doing so now can help avert humanitarian disasters later.

4. The Department of Defense should enhance its operational capability by accelerating the adoption of improved business processes and innovative technologies that result in improved U.S. combat power through energy efficiency.

Numerous Department of Defense studies have found that combat forces would be more capable and less vulnerable by significantly reducing their fuel demand. Unfortunately, many of their recommendations have yet to be implemented. Doing so would have the added benefit of reducing greenhouse gas emissions.

5. The Department of Defense should conduct an assessment of the impact on U.S. military installations worldwide of rising sea levels, extreme weather events, and other projected climate change impacts over the next 30 to 40 years.

Many critical defense installations are located on the coast, and several strategically important ones are on low-lying Pacific islands. Sea level rise and storm surges will threaten these facilities. Planning and action can make these installations more resilient. Lack of planning can compromise them or cause them to be inundated, compromising military readiness and capability.

CORPORATE INFLUENCE

Koch Industries Seminars for the Rich and Powerful

E ver since the Supreme Court decided last year (*Citizens United v. FEC*) to override Congress and allow unlimited secret cash from corporations—and even foreign governments—to influence American elections, following the money has gotten difficult. One mega-player, though, that we've found out a lot about is Koch Industries.

The Koch brothers, Charles and David from Wichita, Kansas, are each worth more than $21.5 billion. Charles has come right out and admitted that their major goal is to eliminate 90 percent of all laws and government regulations, so as to further the "culture of prosperity." The Kochs are the biggest funder of right-wing front groups in the country.

Twice a year they bring together all the wealthy donors to talk about their game plan. A website called ThinkProgress somehow got hold of a memo that outlines what happened the last time Koch and company got together for a secret election-planning meeting, in June 2010 in Aspen, Colorado. You'll notice that the agenda included a fair number of the conservative media stars like Glenn Beck.

CHARLES G. KOCH
CHAIRMAN AND
CHIEF EXECUTIVE OFFICER

September 24, 2010

"If not us, who? If not now, when?"

That question was posed by a member of our network of business and philanthropic leaders, who are dedicated to defending our free society. We cannot rely on politicians to do so, so it is up to us to combat what is now the greatest assault on American freedom and prosperity in our lifetimes.

Twice a year our network meets to review strategies for combating the multitude of public policies that threaten to destroy America as we know it. These meetings have been critical in improving and expanding our efforts.

Our next meeting will be held January 30-31, 2011, at the Rancho Las Palmas Resort in Rancho Mirage, California. You would be a valuable addition to our gathering, and we hope you can join us.

In Palm Springs, we will assemble an exceptional group of leaders along with a strong line-up of speakers. Together, we will develop strategies to counter the most severe threats facing our free society and outline a vision of how we can foster a renewal of American free enterprise and prosperity.

At our most recent meeting in Aspen, our group heard plans to activate citizens against the threat of government over-spending and to change the balance of power in Congress this November. In response, participants committed to an unprecedented level of support. The important work being done with these initiatives continues. However, even if these efforts succeed, other serious threats demand action.

Everyone benefits from the prosperity that emerges from free societies. But that prosperity is under attack by the current Administration and many of our elected officials. Their policies threaten to erode our economic freedom and transfer vast sums of power to the state. We must stop – and reverse – this internal assault on our founding principles.

316.828.5201 Tel
P.O. Box 2256
Wichita, Kansas 67201

Fighting back with incremental changes will only lead to a slower rate of decline. We must dedicate ourselves to making major advances in the direction of economic freedom. Our goal for these meetings must be to advance ideas that strengthen that freedom, beat back the unrelenting attacks and hold elected leaders accountable.

To give you a better idea of the nature of this event, I have enclosed the program from our Aspen meeting. While we will have great speakers and a beautiful setting, our ultimate goal is not "fun in the sun." This is a gathering of *doers* who are willing to engage in the hard work necessary to advance our shared principles. Success in this endeavor will require all the help we can muster.

Your active participation would increase our probability of success during this pivotal time in our nation's history. We hope to see you in Palm Springs, January 30-31.

Sincerely,

GOALS & MISSIONS

At our seminars, we work to understand and address the threats to American free enterprise and prosperity. These meetings provide an opportunity to discuss these threats and the appropriate strategies to counter them. To that end, we focus on four main objectives:

- Attracting principled leaders and investors who will effectively defend our free society

- Sharing best practices and opportunities to defend our free enterprise system from destructive public policies

- Fashioning the message and building the education channels to reestablish widespread belief in the benefits of the principles of a free and prosperous society

- Building principled, effective institutions that identify, educate and mobilize citizens in pursuit of a free and prosperous society

Our seminars bring together business and philanthropic leaders who possess the vision and knowledge to develop innovative strategies to achieve results. The combination of knowledgeable speakers and motivated participants produces a dynamic environment that inspires creative approaches to advancing a free society.

CONFIDENTIALITY AND SECURITY

In order to understand issues and develop strategies more effectively, the proceedings of this meeting are confidential. The meetings are closed to the public, including media. Please be mindful of the security and confidentiality of your meeting notes and materials, and do not post updates or information about the meeting on blogs, social media such as Facebook and Twitter, or in traditional media articles. These meetings are invitation-only and nametags should be worn for all meeting functions.

THINK

AGENDA

1:00 – 1:40 pm GRAND BALLROOM LOWER LEVEL	**The Threats to American Freedom and Prosperity** We are undergoing the greatest internal assault on American freedom and prosperity in our lifetimes. Rather than cede ground to more government, we must strengthen economic freedom. Business leaders have an important role to play in promoting prosperity, countering the dangerous attacks on our founding principles, and reversing this trend. Charles Koch, Koch Industries
1:40 – 2:10 pm GRAND BALLROOM	**What's the Outlook for Future Prosperity?** Government spending continues to climb to dangerously high levels, putting our economy at risk. This session will explore the precarious path that we are on, led by one of the analysts best known for predicting the financial crisis. Peter Schiff, Euro Pacific Capital
2:10 – 2:30 pm GRAND BALLROOM	**Q&A with Charles Koch and Peter Schiff**
2:30 – 2:50 pm	**Break**
2:50 – 3:50 pm GRAND BALLROOM	**Understanding the Persistent Threats We Face** The current administration swept into office with a promise to "fundamentally transform America." From the nationalization of healthcare to the rising power of unions, as well as a push for major new climate and energy regulations, financial regulation, and even more government spending, there is no lack of significant threats for us to understand and address. Moderated by Steve Moore, *The Wall Street Journal* Phil Kerpen, Americans for Prosperity Ramesh Ponnuru, *National Review* Peter Wallison, American Enterprise Institute

AGENDA

3:50 - 4:30 pm
GRAND BALLROOM

An Integrated Strategy to Address These Threats
While the threats we face are significant, we have seen progress. Building on the lessons learned from the past and capitalizing on several unique opportunities we face this year, we believe there is a way to reverse this present course and build a more prosperous future.

Richard Fink, Koch Industries

4:30 – 6:30 pm

Free Time

6:30 – 9:00 pm
FOUNTAIN COURTYARD

Reception and Dinner at the St. Regis

Is America on the Road to Serfdom?

Glenn Beck

9:00 – 10:15 pm
RESTAURANT BAR
MAIN LEVEL

Cocktails and Dessert Reception hosted by DonorsTrust
Conclude your evening with a cocktail or dessert at the St. Regis' Restaurant Bar.

Monday, June 28

7:30 – 8:30 am
FOUNTAIN COURTYARD

Breakfast Buffet and Presentation

7:50 – 8:30 am
FOUNTAIN COURTYARD

We're Spending Too Much
Americans are increasingly concerned with the growth of government, but we also need a positive vision of what smaller government means, a vision that goes beyond lower taxes and economic efficiency. Without that positive vision, the appeal of liberty is limited. This presentation provides a vision of how we can regain the moral high ground and make a new case for liberty and smaller government that appeals to all Americans, rich and poor.

Russ Roberts, Mercatus Center

AGENDA

8:30 – 8:45 am	Break and Transition to Grand Ballroom

8:45 – 9:30 am
GRAND BALLROOM

Understanding This Electorate
This spring's primaries have produced many surprises
and upsets. What is causing this electorate to vote
the way they are? What does this mean for the
November elections? This session will offer insight
into the mood of this year's electorate.

Michael Barone, *The Almanac of American Politics*

9:30 – 10:30 am
GRAND BALLROOM

Framing the Debate on Spending
Polls show that the American public is deeply
concerned about government growth and spending –
and they are making their frustrations known. In this
session, we will better understand if this is a fleeting
circumstance or one that holds opportunities for
advocates of free enterprise into the future.

Nancy Pfotenhauer
Jeff Crank, Americans for Prosperity - Colorado
Veronique de Rugy, Mercatus Center
Gretchen Hamel, Public Notice

10:30 – 10:50 am   Break

10:50 am – 11:50 pm
GRAND BALLROOM

Mobilizing Citizens for November
Is there a chance this fall to elect leaders who are
more strongly committed to liberty and prosperity?
This session will further assess the landscape and
offer a strategic plan to educate voters on the
importance of economic freedom.

Sean Noble
Karl Crow, Themis
Mark Mix, National Right to Work
Tim Phillips, Americans for Prosperity

8

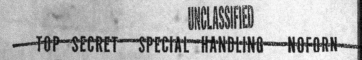

PART THREE

SHADY WHITE HOUSES

NUKE THE RUSSIANS?

Nixon's Vietnam Peace Plan

"Tricky Dick" had his own version of Operation Northwoods, and if this one had backfired, we would've been in a nuclear war. Lining up the bombers to look like we were attacking Russia is so far-fetched it was like reading a comic book when I first came across this. Amazingly enough, during Nixon's first year in office, he and his national security adviser, Henry Kissinger, cooked up a plan to end the Vietnam War by pretending to launch a nuclear strike against the Soviet Union.

They code-named the operation Giant Lance; I'm going to avoid speculating whether the sub-title was "Mine's Bigger than Yours." they set the whole thing in motion on October 10, 1969, when the Strategic Air Command received an urgent order to ready our most powerful thermonuclear weapons for immediate potential use against the Russkies.

According to an article in *Wired* magazine (February 25, 2008), on the morning of October 27, 1969, a squadron of 18 B-52s "began racing from the western U.S. toward the eastern border of the Soviet Union. The pilots flew for 18 hours without rest, hurtling toward their targets at more than 500 miles per hour. Each plane was loaded with nuclear weapons hundreds of times more powerful than the ones that had obliterated Hiroshima and Nagasaki…The aircraft were pointed toward Moscow, but the real goal was to change the war in Vietnam."

This was one of a bunch of military measures aimed at putting our nuclear forces on a higher state of readiness. We had destroyers, cruisers, and aircraft carriers doing all kinds of maneuvers in the Atlantic, Mediterranean, Gulf of Aden, and Sea of Japan. This was all executed secretly but designed to be detectable—but supposedly not alarming—to the leadership of the Kremlin. And our commanders-in-chief (CINCs) had no idea why Nixon had ordered the "Joint Chiefs of Staff (JCS) Readiness Test," also to become known as the "madman theory."

You can find the following document at the National Security Archive website (Electronic Briefing Book No. 81).

JOINT MESSAGEFORM

SECURITY CLASSIFICATION
TOP SECRET-EYES ONLY-SENSITIVE-EYES ONLY.

TYPE MSG — BOOK | MULTI X | SINGLE

OCT 10 22 05 269

PRECEDENCE
ACTION IMMEDIATE
INFO

FROM: GEN WHEELER, CHAIRMAN, JCS

SPECIAL INSTRUCTIONS
CJCS
J-3

TO: GEN HOLLOWAY, CINCSAC
ADM MCCAIN, CINCPAC
GEN GOODPASTER, CINCEUR
ADM HOLMES, CINCLANT
GEN MCKEE, CINCNORAD/CONAD
GEN THROCKMORTON, CINCSTRIKE
GEN MATHER, CINSO
LGEN RUEGG, CINCAL

TOP SECRET-EYES ONLY SENSITIVE JCS   12650   OCT 69

1. WE HAVE BEEN DIRECTED BY HIGHER AUTHORITY TO INSTITUTE A SERIES OF ACTIONS DURING THE PERIOD 130000Z - 250000Z OCT, TO TEST OUR MILITARY READINESS IN SELECTED AREAS WORLD-WIDE TO RESPOND TO POSSIBLE CONFRONTATION BY THE SOVIET UNION. THESE ACTIONS SHOULD BE DISCERNIBLE TO THE SOVIETS, BUT NOT THREATENING IN THEMSELVES. THEY MAY INCLUDE, BUT ARE NOT NECESSARILY LIMITED TO, THE FOLLOWING TYPE ACTIONS:

ZFF-3

EYES ONLY

A. STAND-DOWN OF FLYING OF COMBAT AIRCRAFT IN SELECTED AREAS OR COMMANDS, TO IMPROVE OPERATIONAL READINESS.

DATE 10 | TIME 1800
MONTH OCT | YEAR 1969
PAGE NO. 1 | NO. OF PAGES 2

DRAFTER
TYPED NAME AND TITLE
RADM F. A. BARDSHAR, USN
VDIR J3
PHONE 56243

RELEASER
SIGNATURE Paul Kearney
TYPED (or stamped) NAME AND TITLE
Paul M Kearney
Administrative Assistant

SECURITY CLASSIFICATION
TOP SECRET-EYES ONLY SENSITIVE

REGRADING INSTRUCTIONS, J.C.S.
GP-1

DD FORM 173
1 NOV 63

REPLACES EDITION OF 1 MAY 63 WHICH WILL BE USED.

ABBREVIATED JOINT MESSAGEFORM
and/or CONTINUATION SHEET

SECURITY CLASSIFI...

PRECEDENCE	RELEASED BY	DRAFTED BY	PHONE
ACTION IMMEDIATE			
INFO			

B. IMPLEMENTATION OF RADIO AND/OR OTHER
COMMUNICATIONS SILENCE IN SELECTED AREAS OR COMMANDS.

C. INCREASED SURVEILLANCE OF SOVIET SHIPS EN ROUTE
TO NORTH VIETNAM.

D. INCREASED GROUND ALERT RATE OF SAC BOMBERS AND
TANKERS.

2. TO INITIATE ACTIONS WITHIN THE TIME FRAME SPECIFIED,
CERTAIN COMMANDERS HAVE BEEN DIRECTED TO STAND-DOWN
TRAINING FLIGHTS AND INTRODUCE VARYING DEGREES OF EMCON.
THESE INITIAL ACTIONS WILL COVER THE FIRST FOUR DAYS OF
THE 14-DAY PERIOD.

3. I REQUEST THAT YOU NOMINATE FURTHER ACTIONS COMPATIBLE
WITH THE GUIDANCE HEREIN, AND COGNIZANT OF LOCAL PROBLEMS
PECULIAR TO YOUR AREAS, ALLIES, AND ENVIRONMENT. THESE
NOMINATIONS ARE REQUIRED NLT 122300Z. ACTIONS PROPOSED
SHOULD BE COMPATIBLE WITH PROJECT 703.

4. WARM REGARDS. GP-1

SSO NOTE: DELIVER DURING WAKING HOURS.

CONTROL NO.	TOR/TOD	PAGE NO.	NO. OF PAGES	MESSAGE IDENTIFICATION	INITIALS
		2	2		

REGRADING INSTRUCTIONS	SECURITY CLASSIFICATION
GP-1	TOP SECRET SENSITIVE EYES ONLY

DD FORM 173-1   REPLACES EDITION OF 1 MAY 65 WHICH WILL BE USED.

34

THE CIA VS THE PRESIDENT

Nixon's Pursuit of the CIA's Secret Files

In December 2010, a new release of documents relating to the Nixon years transpired at the National Archives. One that I found especially telling was this "Memorandum for the Record" by John Ehrlichman, Nixon's deputy chief of staff, about the president's attempt to pry out secret CIA files related to the Vietnam coup that overthrew Diem in 1963 as well the Bay of Pigs and Cuban Missile Crisis. Just why Nixon wanted all this material remains unknown to this day, but it seems he definitely wanted to get some "goods" on the Kennedy administration. And he may have had another motive—to find out what the CIA might have on why JFK was killed. Or on Nixon's own involvement in the attempts to kill Castro, for example. There are a lot of redactions in these three pages, but one thing comes through crystal clear: there was a small war going on between Nixon and Richard Helms, director of the CIA.

Again, what people need to understand is that it appears the CIA answers to no one. They're supposed to be the president's arm on foreign intelligence, but the best way I can put it is: There's been an amputation. That body part is not attached anymore. Time and again, the CIA thumbs its nose even at presidents. So who runs this agency if the president doesn't?

III.   Filing.

It is the judgment of each CIA man that I talked to that next to nothing is
thrown away at CIA. A copy of anything that comes out as finished intelligence
is kept. There are definitely files containing every report, bulletin, survey,
etc. that is published by the Office of Current Intelligence (OCI). This would
also seem to be the case with all cables, back channel and regular. Cross
division memoranda are also kept and the only instance in which there may not
be copies on file is with internal subdivision memoranda. In brief, all finished   25X1
intelligence should be available.

CIA slang for a memorandum from the Director to the President or Secretaries
of State or Defense is "nugget."

IV.   Personnel.

After John McCone, the Director was Admiral Rayburn and Helms was his
Deputy. When Rayburn left, Helms was moved up.

Bay of Pigs

The Deputy Director of Plans was Bissell who took the responsibility
for the Bay of Pigs fiasco, and when he was moved out as a result,
Helms   was made Deputy Director of Plans. During the actual invasion,
however, Helms was Chief of Operations under Bissell but apparently was
not implicated in the failure because it was run by para-military staff of the
DDP.

-2-

25X1

V. Positioning.

Our net objective is to get all materials relating to the Diem Coup in 1963, and the Cuban crises (Bay of Pigs & Missiles). In this connection we may cite:

(1) Our announced intention to move ahead with the declassification of documents surrounding particular crises (Korea, Lebanon and Cuba) which provides the grounds for reviewing these materials. What's the best way? Rehnquist Committee? New committee?

(2) The President's statement to the press last week indicating the need for us to review the coup period materials.

(3) The President's obvious right to see any and all CIA materials without giving any reason.

In order to extract these without a confrontation, it will be necessary to avoid giving Helms any grounds for saying that we are trying to use the CIA for political purposes. My sense is that Helms, having been around the bureaucracy for some time, may be a tough in-fighter when push comes to shove.

Helms' power base is first the White House and secondly the Congress. In the former he relies quite heavily on Kissinger and is, therefore, imperative that we line up Kissinger before we confront Helms and Helms gets to him. As far as Congress goes, Helms' support would probably come from the likes of Jackson, Stennis, Margaret Chase Smith, Fulbright, Symington, Kennedy, McGovern, etc. and of course all Armed Services Committee members in both Houses.

We also must gauge the probability of there being considerable press in favor of Helms if he should be fired and claim that we tried to use the Agency for political ends.

Addendum :

25X1

LAW

The National Security Act of 1947 provides "that the Director of the CIA shall be responsible for protecting intelligence sources and methods from unauthorized disclosure."

- 3 -

David Young

35

RESTLESS YOUTH

How Nixon Wanted the CIA and FBI to Crack Down on Youthful Dissidence

I can't leave the Nixon years without another tidbit released at the end of 2010. This shows clearly how Nixon was looking to bring the CIA and FBI together in 1970 to crack down on the antiwar protesters and other "restless youth." Keep in mind that the CIA was forbidden by statute from taking part in such domestic operations, but that didn't seem to make any difference. This is the basis of what later became known as the Huston Plan, after the author of the memorandum, Tom Charles Huston.

Having grown up in that era, though, this doesn't really surprise me. Not when you learn about all the people the government had under surveillance, from Dr. King to Malcolm X to John Lennon. I thought we'd left those times behind, but everything seems to be circular. It's worse than ever today, since 9/11, and we'll get to that in a bit.

CENTRAL INTELLIGENCE AGENCY

WASHINGTON, D.C. 20505

OFFICE OF THE DIRECTOR

2 5 JUN 1970

MEMORANDUM FOR: The Honorable Henry A. Kissinger
                  Assistant to the President for
                  National Security Affairs

SUBJECT   : Restless Youth (June 1970)

Attached is the most recent issue of this Agency's study on Restless Youth.

We have updated this study periodically in an effort to keep it current. While some of the original background information on individual countries has been retained, the country chapters concentrate on developments since March 1969 when the previous issue was distributed.

This paper illustrates the striking similarities in youthful dissidence, especially in the more advanced countries of the world. Most important, I believe, is the paper's conclusion that among militants, and less committed youth alike, there is a growing belief in the efficacy of violence as a political device.

Richard Helms
Director

cc: The Honorable Robert H. Finch
     Counselor to the President

     Mr. Tom Charles Huston
     Staff Assistant to the President

     The Honorable John N. Mitchell
     The Attorney General

THE WHITE HOUSE

WASHINGTON

June 16, 1970

SECRET

MEMORANDUM FOR H. R. HALDEMAN

SUBJECT: Domestic Intelligence Review

      I thought you might like to know that the review is moving along extraordinarily well with full cooperation by all agencies. Frankly, I have been amazed at the quality of the initial contributions to this study and the unity of purpose displayed by all involved. Dick Helms has submerged his personal hostility to Mr. Hoover and has afforded a degree of cooperation unexpected from CIA.

      We are concentrating on three areas of interest: (1) assessment of the current internal security threat; (2) operational restrictions on intelligence collection; and (3) inter-community cooperation and coordination.

      This is the first time since World War II that the President has directed CIA and the FBI to work together on a specific project and the first time in history that the entire intelligence community has been directed to pool its resources in the domestic intelligence area. The opportunity thus afforded to the community to move aggressively in an area where it has felt frustrated in the past is not lost on those involved, and each agency is determined to make the most of this opportunity.

      The finished report of this committee will be the most sensitive intelligence document to come into the White House in years. Details of the clandestine operations of the intelligence community which have never before been reduced to paper will be included, and I would like to urge that we take every possible step to insure that its disimination is as limited as possible within the White House. I strongly believe that the most rigid "need to know" requirement should be instituted.

FBI REVIEW
COMPLETED

ON-FILE NSC
RELEASE
INSTRUCTIONS APPLY

SECRET

-2-

SECRET

I would appreciate it if you would let me know how you wish
to have this report staffed and the names of those whom you believe
should have access to the report.

I have emphasized the importance of reviewing the intelligence
role of the military services, but I must confess that there is
virtually unanimous opinion among all concerned that it would be
a mistake to expand their role in any significant manner. However,
we will lay out the options for the President's decision.

TOM CHARLES HUSTON

SECRET

STOLEN 2000 ELECTION

The GES Emails
and a CBS News Analysis

We all know how the Supreme Court awarded the disputed 2000 election to George W. Bush. What's often forgotten is how, on election night, a computer "error" made it look like Al Gore had lost Florida—and prompted the media to announce prematurely that Bush was the winner. This happened in Volusia County, where an electronic voting machine company called Global Election Systems (GES) was tabulating things. GES turns out to have been run by Republicans who were only too eager to see Bush take over after eight years of Clinton. All of a sudden that night, 16,022 votes for Gore got subtracted from his total in Volusia County. It wasn't until 2003, when a bunch of internal Global Election Systems memos got leaked, that it became clear company officials knew all about this at the time. "The problem precinct had two memory cards uploaded," according to GES tech guy Tab Iredale in one memo. "There is always a possibility that 'the second memory card' came from an unauthorized source." These emails follow.

I cry out to stop the electronic ballots, because any computer can be hacked into, as evidence clearly shows. I say, stick with handwritten ballots. If you can't fill in the blank circle with a pencil, then you shouldn't be voting because we've been doing that since the first grade! Maybe the ballots still need to be hand-counted, but at least you'd have a paper trail.

After perusing the emails, you'll read a couple of pages from a report that CBS News prepared about the coverage of election night 2000—an apology, really, for going with the rest of the herd and calling the victory for Bush. This could be solved if something I've advocated was put in place, to allow no media coverage until the final polls close in Hawaii. Hell, they're already predicting winners when it's two o'clock in the afternoon in California. The polls are still open, but why do I need to go vote if I'm already told who's going to be president? I suppose what I'm proposing infringes greatly on the First Amendment but what the heck, with all the documents you're seeing in this book, what's wrong with that?

THE GES MEMOS

-----Original Message-----
From: Lana Hires
Sent: Wednesday, January 17, 2001 8:07 AM
To: jmglobal Glanca

Cc: Deanie Lowe
Subject: 2000 November Election

Hi Nel, Sophie & Guy (you to John),

I need some answers! Our department is being audited by the County.

I have been waiting for someone to give me an explanation as to why Precinct 216 gave Al Gore a minus 16022 when it was uploaded. Will someone please explain this so that I have the information to give the auditor instead of standing here "looking dumb".

I would appreciate an explanation on why the memory cards start giving check sum messages. We had this happen in several precincts and one of these precincts managed to get her memory card out of election mode and then back in it, continued to read ballots, not realizing that the 300+ ballots she had read earlier were no longer stored in her memory card . Needless to say when we did our hand count this was discovered.

Any explantations you all can give me will be greatly appreciated.

Thanks bunches,

Lana

· · ·

From: owner-"Support" [mailto:owner-"Support"]On Behalf Of Guy Lancaster
Sent: Thursday, January 18, 2001 1:41 PM

Now to Lana's questions. The above should answer everything other than why erroneous data managed to upload. I see two possible explanations. One is that the data was corrupted after the checksums were validated. In this case the errors would show the next time the checksums were checked. The other possibility is the [60k to 1] chance that the erroneous data managed to add up to the correct checksum.

My understanding is that the card was not corrupt after (or before) upload. They fixed the problem by clearing the precinct and re-uploading the same card. So neither of these explainations washes. That's not to say I have any idea what actually happened, its just not either of those.

So John, can you satisfy Lana's request from this? I can't without more details.

The problem is its going to be very hard to collect enough data to really know what happened. The card isn't corrupt so we can't post-mortem it (its not mort). Guy if you can get the exact counter numbers that were uploaded into the races (not just president) perhaps you could guess the nature of the corruption at least, but if I had to bet the numbers were just garbage and you won't be able to tell.

About the only constructive suggestion I have is to insert a line in the AV upload code to check that candvotes + undervotes = votefor*timescounted. If it happens, punt. That would have at least prevented the embarrassment of negative votes, which is really what this is all about. Then John can go to Lana and tell her it has never happened before and that it will never happen again.

Ken

• • •

John,

Here is all the information I have about the 'negative' counts.

Only the presidential totals were incorrect. All the other races the sum of the votes + under votes + blank votes = sum of ballots cast.

The problem precinct had two memcory cards uploaded. The second one is the one I believe caused the problem. They were uploaded on the same port approx. 1 hour apart. As far as I know there should only have been one memory card uploaded. I asked you to check this out when the problem first occured but have not heard back as to whether this is true.

When the precinct was cleared and re-uploaded (only one memory card as far as I know) everything was fine.

Given that we transfer data in ascii form not binary and given the way the data was 'invalid' the error could not have occured during transmission. Therefore the error could only occur in one of four ways:

1. Corrupt memory card. This is the most likely explaination for the problem but since I know nothing about the 'second' memory card I have no ability to confirm the probability of this.

2. Invalid read from good memory card. This is unlikely since the candidates results for the race are not all read at the same time and the corruption was limited to a single race. There is a possiblilty that a section of the memory card was bad but since I do not know anything more about the 'second' memory card I cannot validate this.

3. Corruption of memory, whether on the host or Accu-Vote. Again this is unlikely due to the localization of the problem to a single race. Invalid memory card (i.e. one that should not have been uploaded).

4. There is always the possiblity that the 'second memory card' or 'second upload' came from an un-authorised source.

If this problem is to be properly answered we need to determine where the 'second' memory card is or whether it even exists. I do know that there were two uploads from two different memory cards (copy 0 (master) and copy 3).

Tab

CBS NEWS COVERAGE OF ELECTION NIGHT 2000

Investigation, Analysis, Recommendations

Analysis of the Call for Bush

The call was based entirely on the tabulated county vote. There were several data errors that were responsible for that mistake. The most egregious of the data errors has been well documented. Vote reports from Volusia County severely understated Gore's actual total when a faulty computer memory card reported votes that were off by thousands. That precinct, Number 216, *subtracted* more than 16,000 votes from Gore's total and added votes to Bush's total. In addition, an apparent reporting error in Brevard County reduced Gore's total by an additional 4,000 votes.

The mistakes, both of which originated with the counties, were critical, since there were only about 3 percent of the state's precincts outstanding at this time. They incorrectly increased Bush's lead in the tabulated vote from about 27,000 to more than 51,000. Had it not been for these errors, the CBS News call for Bush at 2:17:52 AM would not have been made. While the errors should have been caught by VNS and CBS News analysts through a comparison of VNS data with data from the AP or the Florida Secretary of State, VNS computers could also have had a more sophisticated program that would have constantly compared one set of numbers with the others and raised a warning signal.

(Unlike the television networks, the Associated Press never called Florida for Bush, and, as we mentioned earlier, neither did VNS.)

There was another problem: the VNS end-of-the-night model uses a straightforward projection of the number of precincts yet to report in each county. It assumes that the outstanding precincts in each county will be of average size and will vote in the same way as the precincts that have already reported from that county. However, at 2:17 AM there were more as-yet-uncounted votes than the model predicted. In fact, in Palm Beach County, a heavily Democratic area, there were three times as many votes yet to be reported as the model predicted. Some of that appears to be accounted for by the late release by county election officials of a large absentee vote.

Conclusion

As we have seen above, the first Florida call for Gore was probably unavoidable, given the current system of projecting winners. Early in the evening, the sample that VNS selected to represent voters statewide overestimated Gore's lead, and a call was made for him. As the tabulated vote started accumulating, Gore lost his apparent lead, and a decision was made to take back the call. The ongoing VNS reviews have determined that the exit-poll sample of precincts in this election did not adequately represent the state. The exit-poll sample estimated a significant Gore lead that never materialized. That fact remained unknown until the actual vote count. The sampling data and exit polling did not take into account the 12 percent of the Florida vote that was cast by absentee ballot, which also affected the quality of the data. The CBS News Decision Desk could not have known about these problems.

However, the second Florida call, the one for Bush, could have been avoided. It was based, as we have seen, on a combination of faulty tabulations entered into the total Florida vote, with an especially large error from Volusia County that exaggerated Bush's lead. Later, in the early morning hours, reports from large precincts in Palm Beach were recorded, along with a surge of absentee ballots from that county. When the Volusia County numbers were corrected and the new numbers from Palm Beach taken into account, the Bush lead shrank, and a decision was made to take back the Bush call. The call might have been avoided, if there had been better communication between the CBS News Decision Desk and the CBS News studio and newsgathering operations, which had been reporting ballot irregularities and large numbers of potentially Democratic votes still outstanding, and if the VNS vote totals had been checked against the ones from the AP and the Florida Secretary of State's Web site. The AP corrected the Volusia County error 35 minutes before VNS did, and one minute before CBS News made its call.

And, despite all the understandable focus on the Florida calls, they were not the only mistaken calls of the night.

STOLEN 2004 ELECTION

Fixing the Vote in Ohio

Ohio, as everyone knows, was the state that put George W. Bush over the top in the 2004 election. A comfortable 118,000-plus vote official margin in Ohio gave him a victory over John Kerry and a second term as president. There were plenty of rumors that Ohio Secretary of State Kenneth Blackwell had connived with the Bush people to fix the vote, but Kerry's people were unwilling to pursue this too far.

The story of what went on behind the scenes started to surface in a lawsuit brought by a group of citizens against Ohio officials in the summer of 2006. A well-known voting rights attorney named Cliff Arnebeck set out to charge Blackwell and his cronies with "election fraud, vote dilution, vote suppression, recount fraud and other violations."

The first document you're going to read here is a deposition taken of Stephen Spoonamore, an expert in computer systems who knew plenty about how electronic voting machines can be manipulated. The company he refers to, Diebold, bought the GES outfit that was involved in the Florida debacle in 2000. And the fellow he mentions at the end, Mike Connell, was Karl Rove's IT guy. Connell was involved in developing important parts of the computer network, including the election results reporting server systems. The second document is a contract with the Ohio secretary of state's office, dated November 20, 2003.

The Computer C "man in the middle" that Spoonamore is talking about was the property of a Chattanooga company called SMARTech. They were the subcontractor of GovTech Solutions, Mike Connell's company, for purposes of hosting a "mirror site" on election night. This ensured that the Ohio election results could be observed and changed, using remote access through high-speed Internet.

If this were the private sector and something got diverted to an intermediary in Chattanooga that was clearly illegal, there would be an investigation for sure. Why does this situation get a pass? Again, I call for handwritten ballots!

The contract I mentioned that follows is somewhat complicated, but it's back-up for what Spoonamore was talking about. Eventually Connell would most likely have talked about all this. Except that on December 19, 2008, Connell's private single-engine plane crashed on the way back to his home in Akron. The man who could've blown the whistle on the biggest election fraud in American history was dead. I guess, as always, we're supposed to attribute that to bad timing. Let me quote Colonel Fletcher Prouty again: "Nothing just happens, everything is planned." If you're interested in all the details, take a look at my previous book, *American Conspiracies*.

In regard to the system set up to tabulate the vote in Ohio in 2004.

1) The vote tabulation and reporting system, as initially designed, was supposed to allow each   county central tabulator (Computer A) to add up local information locally, and then, via a lightly encrypted system, send the information to the Sec. of State statewide tabulator (Computer B). This system, while using public Internet and public information carrying capacity, could be compromised at the level of one county (Computer A is hacked) or in the transmission of any one county to the central state tabulator (Computer A talking to Computer B). However, it would only be possible to compromise the vote on a statewide basis by a compromise at the state level tabulator (Computer B is hacked). Alternately I have been told that these processes were replaced at the last minute by fax transmitted results.

It is relatively simple to establish if the security of the transmissions, whether sent by fax, or by electronic transmission, by reviewing the network architecture as operated on election night, and review the session logs of the secretary of states central tabulation computer to determine the IP address and times of communication by other machines to the the Secretary. The variable nature of the story of what occurred, and lack of documentation available, would be cause to launch an immediate fraud investigation in any of my banking clients.

2) The vote tabulation and reporting system, as modified at the direction of Mr. Blackwell, allowed the introduction of a single computer in the middle of the pathway. This computer located at a company principally managing IT Systems for GOP campaign and political operations (Computer C) received all information from each county computer (Computer A) BEFORE it was sent onward to Computer B. This centralized collection of all incoming statewide tabulations would make it extremely easy for a single operator, or a preprogrammed single "force balancing computer" to change the results in any way desired by the team controlling Computer C. In this case GOP partisan operatives. Again, if this out of state system had ANY digital access to the Secretary of States system it would be cause for immediate investigation by any of my banking clients.

3) If scenario #2 described above is true, Computer C, was placed functionally in a central control position in the network, for Computer C to have even updated instructions for various tabulators at the county level (Computers A) to change their results at the county level. If this had happened, in order to cover up this fact, the hard drives of the county level tabulators would have to be pulled and destroyed, as they would have digital evidence of this hacking from Computer C. The efforts by the company in charge of these computers to pull out hard drives and destroy them in advance of the Green Party Recount from the 2004 election is a clear signal something was deliberately amiss with the county tabulators (Computers A).

If even the presence of such a Computer C was found in a banking system, it would be cause to launch an immediate fraud investigation. This computer placement, in the middle of the network, is a defined type of attack. It is called a MIM (Man in the Middle) Attack. It is a common problem in the banking settlement space. A criminal gang will introduce a computer into the outgoing electronic systems of a major retail mall, or smaller branch office of a bank. They will capture the legitimate transactions and then add fraudulent charges to the system for their benefit.

Another common MIM is the increasingly common "false" website attack. In this MIM, errors in the computers that feed the Digital Name Service are exploited directing an unsuspecting user to a site that looks like the one they wished to visit, but is in fact an "evil twin" which then exploits them for various purposes for a portion of the time, and then in many cases passes them on the CORRECT web site they wanted. Once passed on, the operators of the evil twin site may continue to exploit the user, or later duplicate the session and exploit them in another manner. Any time all information is directed to a single computer for consolidation, it is possible, and in fact likely, that single computer will exploit the information for some purpose.

In the case of Ohio 2004, the only purpose I can conceive for sending all county vote tabulations to a GOP managed Man-in-the-Middle site in Chattanooga BEFORE sending the results onward to the Sec. of State, would be to hack the vote at the MIM.

IN REGARD TO THE DIEBOLD SYSTEMS, Formerly Global, DESI and now called Premier.

In my opinion, there is NO POSSIBLE WAY to make a secure touch screen voting system. None. Secure systems are predicated on establishing securely the identity of every user of the system. Voting is predicated on being anonymous. It is impossible to have a system that does both.

It is possible to design relatively secure optical scan machines, but even these can be hacked in even the best of cases. In the case of optical scan you have the ability to recount manually the paper ballot itself, and the ability to spot check the machines for errors against a sample of hand recounting.

Even considering no secure system for touch screen machines can be designed, ever, the Diebold system is riddled with exploitable errors. The SAIC report on the system architecture, commissioned by Maryland Gov. Erlich, outlined over 200 concerns. Many of these concerns are almost comical from the perspective of a computer architect. One example of this:

The existence of negative fields being possible in some number fields. Voting machines as custom built computers which should be designed to begin at the number Zero, no votes, and advance only in increments of 1, one vote, until they max out at the most possible votes cast in one day. Perhaps 3000 voters could use a machine in one day, but more realistically 400 or so. There is no possible legitimate reason that NEGATIVE votes should ever be entered. And yet these machines are capable of having negative numbers programmed in, injected, or preloaded.

IN REGARD to Mr. Mike Connell.

Mr. Connell and I share a mutual interest in democracy building, freedom of speech and religion worldwide. We have mutually participated in activity to forward this goal. At a meeting in London last year, and again at a Lunch in Washington, DC, Mike and I briefly discussed voting security. While he has not admitted to wrongdoing, and in my opinion he is not involved in voting theft, Mike clearly agrees that the electronic voting systems in the US are not secure. He further made a statement that he is afraid that some of the more ruthless partisans of the GOP, may have exploited systems he in part worked on for this purpose.

Mr. Connell builds front end applications, user interfaces and web sites. Knowing his team and their skills, I find it unlikely they would be the vote thieves directly. I believe however he knows who is doing that work, and has likely turned a blind eye to this activity. Mr. Connell is a devout Catholic. He has admitted to me that in his zeal to 'save the unborn' he may have helped others who have compromised elections. He was clearly uncomfortable when I asked directly about Ohio 2004.

I declare under penalty of perjury that the foregoing is true and correct.

Executed this 17th day of September 2008.

Stephen Spoonamore

STATEMENT OF WORK

UNDER STATE TERM SCHEDULE NUMBER 533384-1

Secretary of State Contract Number 180

This Statement of Work is between the **Office of the Ohio Secretary of State** (hereinafter the "Secretary"), located at 180 E. Broad Street, 16th Floor, Columbus, Ohio 43215, and **GovTech Solutions, LLC,** an Ohio limited liability company, with offices at 3046 Brecksville Road, Suite D, Richfield, Ohio 44286 (hereinafter "GovTech") (Secretary and GovTech each referred to herein as a "Party" and collectively as the "Parties").

RECITALS

WHEREAS, Secretary currently maintains an election night system; however, the current system requires an updated customer facing presentation layer (hereinafter the "Application").

WHEREAS, Secretary wishes to update it's Application with a browser based and user friendly interface that does not require the installation of software on the end-user's machine.

WHEREAS, GovTech is in the business of providing Internet World Wide Web development, programming and related services, including technical and creative services;

WHEREAS, Secretary wishes to retain the services of GovTech to perform certain Application planning and design related services, including, providing technical and creative services in connection with the development of the new interactive Election Night Web site as described more fully herein; and

WHEREAS, GovTech wishes to provide Secretary with such services;

THEREFORE, the parties, for good and valuable consideration and based on the mutual promises recited herein, do agree as follows:

Article I.   STATE TERM SCHEDULE

1.01   This Statement of Work ("SOW") is entered into under the authority of State Term Schedule **533384-1** (the "STS") and incorporates by reference the Terms & Conditions of the STS.

(a)   Meet the expectations of typical Internet users and will not require any additional software installation;

(b)   Comply with all requirements stated in section 3517.106 and divisions (C)(6)(b) and (D)(6) of section 3517.10 of the Revised Code;

(c)   Be based on the known data structures and relationships in the Secretary's existing Election Night Database;

(d)   Provide for appropriate authentication procedures; and

(e)   Be in accordance with the other requirements listed in Exhibit A.

3.06   Installation Phase Upon completion and Acceptance of the Application, GovTech shall install the Application on a Server owned and designated by the Secretary.

(a)   GovTech shall provide an onsite resource for the Installation of the Application.

(b)   GovTech shall provide stress testing of the Installed Application by simulating the number of hits expected during election night. Should the initial tests have negative results, GovTech will work with the Secretary's IT Department to arrive at an acceptable solution to allow for this traffic level.

(c)   GovTech shall also provide an onsite resource on the day and night of the election, November 4, 2003, to assist the Secretary to troubleshoot the Application, if necessary.

3.07   Mirror Application GovTech shall install and host (as set forth in Exhibit B) a Mirror site of the Application to provide a failover solution in the event of failure of the primary installation on Election Day.

(a)   GovTech shall perform stress testing of the Mirror site.

(b)   The Parties agree that GovTech shall subcontract its hosting responsibilities under this SOW to SMARTech Corporation, with offices located at 801 Broad Street, Suite 220, Chattanooga, TN 37402. GovTech may subcontract to another entity, but must first receive Secretary approval.

3.08   In addition to the Planning Phase Deliverables, the Application Design Deliverables, and the Installation and Mirroring Deliverables, GovTech shall provide timely status reports to Secretary.

EXHIBIT B

To Statement of Work (Secretary of State Contract Number 180)

Mirror Site Hosting

SMARTech proposes to provide the State of Ohio SOS with a backup offsite hosting configuration shown as follows:

EMBASSY CABLES

Hillary Clinton's Call for Diplomats to Spy on the UN

Who knew? Under Hillary Clinton, our State Department has been asking American diplomats around the world and at the UN to provide detailed technical information, including passwords and personal encryption keys, for communications networks used by UN officials. And we're trying to take down WikiLeaks and throw Julian Assange in the clinker for life? The hypocrisy, once again, boggles the mind.

US embassy cables: Washington calls for intelligence on top UN officials

28 November 2010

Friday, 31 July 2009, 20:24 S E C R E T SECTION 01 OF 24 STATE 080163 NOFORN
SIPDIS EO 12958 DECL: 07/31/2034 TAGS PINR, KSPR, ECON, KPKO, KUNR SUBJECT:
(S) REPORTING AND COLLECTION NEEDS: THE UNITED NATIONS REF: STATE
048489 Classified By: MICHAEL OWENS, ACTING DIR, INR/OPS. REASON: 1.4(C).

1. (S/NF) This cable provides the full text of the new National HUMINT Collection Directive
(NHCD) on the United Nations (paragraph 3-end) as well as a request for continued DOS
reporting of biographic information relating to the United Nations (paragraph 2).

A. (S/NF) The NHCD below supercedes the 2004 NHCD and reflects the results of a recent
Washington review of reporting and collection needs focused on the United Nations. The review
produced a comprehensive list of strategic priorities (paragraph 3) and reporting and collection
needs (paragraph 4) intended to guide participating USG agencies as they allocate resources and
update plans to collect information on the United Nations. The priorities should also serve as a
useful tool to help the Embassy manage reporting and collection, including formulation of
Mission Strategic Plans (MSPs).

B. (S/NF) This NHCD is compliant with the National Intelligence Priorities Framework (NIPF),
which was established in response to NSPD-26 of February 24, 2003. If needed, GRPO can
provide further background on the NIPF and the use of NIPF abbreviations (shown in
parentheses following each sub-issue below) in NHCDs.

C. (S/NF) Important information often is available to non-State members of the Country Team
whose agencies participated in the review of this National HUMINT Collection Directive.
COMs, DCMs, and State reporting officers can assist by coordinating with other Country Team
members to encourage relevant reporting through their own or State Department channels.

2. (S/NF) State biographic reporting:

A. (S/NF) The intelligence community relies on State reporting officers for much of the
biographical information collected worldwide. Informal biographic reporting via email and other
means is vital to the community's collection efforts and can be sent to the INR/B (Biographic)
office for dissemination to the IC.

B. (S/NF) Reporting officers should include as much of the following information as possible
when they have information relating to persons linked to : office and

organizational titles; names, position titles and other information on business cards; numbers of
telephones, cell phones, pagers and faxes; compendia of contact information, such as telephone
directories (in compact disc or electronic format if available) and e-mail listings; internet and

intranet "handles", internet e-mail addresses, web site identification-URLs; credit card account numbers; frequent flyer account numbers; work schedules, and other relevant biographical information.

*   *   *

4) Telecommunications Infrastructure and Information Systems (INFR-5H). — Current technical specifications, physical layout, and planned upgrades to telecommunications infrastructure and

STATE 00080163 024 OF 024

information systems, networks, and technologies used by top officials and their support staffs. — Details on commercial and private VIP networks used for official communications, to include upgrades, security measures, passwords, personal encryption keys, and types of V P N versions used. — Telephone numbers and e-mail addresses of key officials, as well as limited distribution telephone numbers/directories and public switched networks (PSTN) telephone directories; dialing numbers for voice, datalink, video teleconferencing, wireless communications systems, cellular systems, personal communications systems, and wireless facsimiles. — Information on hacking or other security incidents involving UN networks. — Key personnel and functions of UN entity that maintains UN communications and computer networks. — Indications of IO/IW operations directed against the UN. — Information about current and future use of communications systems and technologies by officials or organizations, including cellular phone networks, mobile satellite phones, very small aperture terminals (VSAT), trunked and mobile radios, pagers, prepaid calling cards, firewalls, encryption, international connectivity, use of electronic data interchange, Voice-over-Internet protocol (VoIP), Worldwide interoperability for microwave access (Wi-Max), and cable and fiber networks.

Countries: Austria, Burkina Faso, China, Costa Rica, Croatia, France, Japan, Libya, Mexico, Russia, Turkey, Uganda, Vietnam International Organizations: UN CLINTON

41

PROTECTING CYBERSPACE

An Internet "Kill Switch"?

A bill—"Protecting Cyberspace as a National Asset Act of 2010"—was introduced in the Senate last June by Joe Lieberman. Note particularly the part under section 4: "Authorizes the President to issue a declaration of a national cyber emergency to covered critical infrastructure." Would this give Obama, or any future president, the right to basically pull a "kill switch" on the Internet? Could, say, a huge leak of classified documents serve as a justification?

Because the bill is so long and convoluted, I only include part of it. Here also is a summary of the bill, written by the Congressional Research Service, a well-respected nonpartisan arm of the Library of Congress.

6/10/2010--Protecting Cyberspace as a National Asset Act of 2010-Establishes in the Executive Office of the President an Office of Cyberspace Policy, which shall: (1) develop a national strategy to increase the security and resiliency of cyberspace; (2) oversee, coordinate, and integrate federal policies and activities relating to cyberspace security and resiliency; (3) ensure that all federal agencies comply with appropriate guidelines, policies, and directives from the Department of Homeland Security (DHS), other federal agencies with responsibilities relating to cyberspace security or resiliency, and the National Center for Cybersecurity and Communications (established by this Act); and (4) ensure that federal agencies have access to, receive, and appropriately disseminate law enforcement, intelligence, terrorism, and any other information relevant to the security of specified federal, military, and intelligence information infrastructure.

Authorizes the President to issue a declaration of a national cyber emergency to covered critical infrastructure. Requires the President to then notify the owners and operators of the infrastructure of the nature of the emergency, consistent with the protection of intelligence sources and methods. Requires the NCCC Director to take specified steps, including immediately directing the owners and operators to implement required response plans and to ensure that emergency actions represent the least disruptive means feasible to operations. Terminates such an emergency measure or action 30 days after the President's declaration, with 30-day extensions authorized if the NCCC Director or the President affirms that such measure or action remains neces-

sary to address the continuing emergency. Requires
each owner or operator of covered critical infrastructure to certify to the NCCC Director whether
the owner or operator has developed and implemented approved security measures and any applicable
emergency measures or actions required for any
cyber vulnerabilities and national cyber emergencies. Sets forth civil penalties for violations.
Requires the DHS Secretary and the private sector
to develop, periodically update, and implement a
supply chain risk management strategy designed to
ensure the security of the federal information infrastructure. Sets forth provisions regarding the
information security authority and functions of the
NCCC Director and executive agency responsibilities. Requires NCCC to annually oversee, coordinate, and develop guidance for the effective implementation of operational evaluations of the federal
information infrastructure and agency information
security programs and practices to determine their
effectiveness. Authorizes the NCCC Director to order the isolation of any component of the federal
information infrastructure if: (1) an agency does
not implement measures in an approved risk-based
plan; and (2) the failure to comply presents a significant danger to the federal information infrastructure. Establishes in the executive branch a
Federal Information Security Taskforce, which shall
be the principal interagency forum for collaboration regarding best practices and recommendations
for agency information security and the security of
the federal information infrastructure.

HEN10553   S.L.C.

111TH CONGRESS
2D SESSION

To amend the Homeland Security Act of 2002 and other laws to enhance the security and resiliency of the cyber and communications infrastructure of the United States.

IN THE SENATE OF THE UNITED STATES

Mr. LIEBERMAN (for himself, Ms. COLLINS, and Mr. CARPER) introduced the following bill; which was read twice and referred to the Committee on

---

A BILL

To amend the Homeland Security Act of 2002 and other laws to enhance the security and resiliency of the cyber and communications infrastructure of the United States.

1   *Be it enacted by the Senate and House of Representa-*

2 *tives of the United States of America in Congress assembled,*

3 **SECTION 1. SHORT TITLE.**

4   This Act may be cited as the "Protecting Cyberspace

5 as a National Asset Act of 2010".

6 **SEC. 2. TABLE OF CONTENTS.**

7   The table of contents for this Act is as follows:

HEN10553   S.L.C.

2

TITLE I—OFFICE OF CYBERSPACE POLICY

TITLE II—NATIONAL CENTER FOR CYBERSECURITY AND COMMUNICATIONS

TITLE III—FEDERAL INFORMATION SECURITY MANAGEMENT

TITLE IV—RECRUITMENT AND PROFESSIONAL DEVELOPMENT

TITLE V—OTHER PROVISIONS

• • •

10 **"SEC. 249. NATIONAL CYBER EMERGENCIES.**

11   "(a) DECLARATION.—

12   "(1) IN GENERAL.—The President may issue a

13   declaration of a national cyber emergency to covered

14   critical infrastructure. Any declaration under this

15   section shall specify the covered critical infrastruc-

16   ture subject to the national cyber emergency.

17   "(2) NOTIFICATION.—Upon issuing a declara-

18   tion under paragraph (1), the President shall, con-

19   sistent with the protection of intelligence sources

20   and methods, notify the owners and operators of the

21   specified covered critical infrastructure of the nature

22   of the national cyber emergency.

23   "(3) AUTHORITIES.—If the President issues a

24   declaration under paragraph (1), the Director

25   shall—

• • •

77

1   "(A) immediately direct the owners and

2   operators of covered critical infrastructure sub-

3   ject to the declaration under paragraph (1) to

4   implement response plans required under sec-

5   tion 248(b)(2)(C);

6   "(B) develop and coordinate emergency

7   measures or actions necessary to preserve the

7   measures or actions necessary to preserve the

8   reliable operation, and mitigate or remediate

9   the consequences of the potential disruption, of

10   covered critical infrastructure;

11   "(C) ensure that emergency measures or

12   actions directed under this section represent the

13   least disruptive means feasible to the operations

14   of the covered critical infrastructure;

15   "(D) subject to subsection (f), direct ac-

16   tions by other Federal agencies to respond to

17   the national cyber emergency;

18   "(E) coordinate with officials of State and

19   local governments, international partners of the

20   United States, and private owners and opera-

21   tors of covered critical infrastructure specified

22   in the declaration to respond to the national

23   cyber emergency;

• • •

1   "(1) IN GENERAL.—Any emergency measure or

2   action developed under this section shall cease to

3   have effect not later than 30 days after the date on

4   which the President issued the declaration of a na-

5   tional cyber emergency, unless—

6   "(A) the Director affirms in writing that

7   the emergency measure or action remains nec-

8   essary to address the identified national cyber

9   emergency; and

10   "(B) the President issues a written order

11   or directive reaffirming the national cyber

12   emergency, the continuing nature of the na-

13   tional cyber emergency, or the need to continue

14   the adoption of the emergency measure or ac-

15   tion.

16   "(2) EXTENSIONS.—An emergency measure or

17   action extended in accordance with paragraph (1)

18   may—

19   "(A) remain in effect for not more than 30

20   days after the date on which the emergency

21   measure or action was to cease to have effect;

22   and

23   "(B) be extended for additional 30-day pe-

24   riods, if the requirements of paragraph (1) and

25   subsection (d) are met.

MORE CYBERSECURITY

Homeland Security's Cybersecurity Agreement with the Pentagon

Then last October, Homeland Security (DHS) and the Defense Department reached an agreement "regarding cybersecurity" whereby they're planning to synchronize their efforts. "We are building a new framework between our Departments to enhance operational coordination and joint program planning," DHS Secretary Janet Napolitano and DoD Secretary Robert Gates said in a joint statement. And in December, the United Nations was asked to consider global standards for policing the Internet, specifically in reaction to things like WikiLeaks. Now the Commerce Department is looking to create an Internet ID, under the label of National Strategy for Trusted Identities in Cyberspace

Maybe this is all somehow to the good, but it makes me a bit queasy. Honestly I see Homeland Security as our United States Gestapo, our federal police. It's this simple, people: Government can't allow anything to exist that it does not control. One time as governor I asked my staff to think about something on their lunch break: "Come back and tell me one thing in your life that the government doesn't regulate or control." Well, they couldn't come up with anything. One person said, "Sleep." You know how I responded? Not true—there's a warning label on your mattress. Even what you lay down on has some stamp of government control.

MEMORANDUM OF AGREEMENT

BETWEEN

THE DEPARTMENT OF HOMELAND SECURITY

AND

THE DEPARTMENT OF DEFENSE

REGARDING CYBERSECURITY

1. PARTIES. The parties to this Agreement are the Department of Homeland Security (DHS) and the Department of Defense (DoD).

2. AUTHORITY. This Agreement is authorized under the provisions of the Homeland Security Act (2002); the Economy Act; U.S. Code Title 10; Executive Order 12333; National Security Directive 42; Homeland Security Presidential Directive-5; Homeland Security Presidential Directive-7; and National Security Presidential Directive-54/Homeland Security Presidential Directive-23.

3. PURPOSE. The purpose of the Agreement is to set forth terms by which DHS and DoD will provide personnel, equipment, and facilities in order to increase interdepartmental collaboration in strategic planning for the Nation's cybersecurity, mutual support for cybersecurity capabilities development, and synchronization of current operational cybersecurity mission activities. Implementing this Agreement will focus national cybersecurity efforts, increasing the overall capacity and capability of both DHS's homeland security and DoD's national security missions, while providing integral protection for privacy, civil rights, and civil liberties.

4. SCOPE. DoD and DHS agree to collaborate to improve the synchronization and mutual support of their respective efforts in support of U.S. cybersecurity. Departmental relationships identified in this Agreement are intended to improve the efficiency and effectiveness of requirements formulation, and requests for products, services, technical assistance, coordination, and performance assessment for cybersecurity missions executed across a variety of DoD and DHS elements. They do not alter existing DoD and DHS authorities, command relationships, or privacy, civil liberties, and other oversight relationships. In establishing a framework to provide mutually beneficial logistical and operational support, this Agreement is not intended to replicate or aggregate unnecessarily the diverse line organizations across technology development, operations, and customer support that collectively execute cybersecurity missions.

PART FOUR

9/11

43

A NEW PEARL HARBOR

A Think Tank's Anticipation of 9/11

In case you've never heard of the Project for a New American Century (PNAC), it was a D.C. think tank that existed for less than ten years (1997–2006) but had probably more influence on American lives than any similar organization before or since. The founders were two neo-cons, William Kristol and Robert Kagan, and from the get-go they were pushing for "regime change" in Iraq. They argued in an open letter to President Clinton that Saddam Hussein was out to stockpile Weapons of Mass Destruction and that an invasion of Iraq would be justified by his defiance of the UN's "containment" policy.

Then, in September 2000, a few months before George W. Bush became president, the PNAC published a ninety-page report called *Rebuilding America's Defenses: Strategies and Resources for a New Century*. It makes for instructive reading, given what's happened since 9/11 in Afghanistan and Iraq. I've excerpted four pages, and I'd ask you to pay particular attention to a statement made on the last one, which says: "...the process of transformation, even if it brings revolutionary change, is likely to be a long one, absent some catastrophic and catalyzing event—like a new Pearl Harbor." Anybody think September 11th might just have been that?

The PNAC report seems like a complete game plan for the next decade, because for the most part it was followed. It should have been mandatory reading before the 2000 election, so we could all have known what they really stood for—because this was certainly not the agenda Bush ran on to become president.

Rebuilding America's Defense Strategy: Forces and Resources for a New Country

KEY FINDINGS

This report proceeds from the belief that America should seek to preserve and extend its position of global leadership by maintaining the preeminence of U.S. military forces. Today, the United States has an unprecedented strategic opportunity. It faces no immediate great-power challenge; it is blessed with wealthy, powerful and democratic allies in every part of the world; it is in the midst of the longest economic expansion in its history; and its political and economic principles are almost universally embraced. At no time in history has the international security order been as conducive to American interests and ideals.

The challenge for the coming century is to preserve and enhance this "American peace."

Yet unless the United States maintains sufficient military strength, this opportunity will be lost. And in fact, over the past decade, the failure to establish a security strategy responsive to new realities and to provide adequate resources for the full range of missions needed to exercise U.S. global leadership has placed the American peace at growing risk. This report attempts to define those requirements. In particular, we need to:

ESTABLISH FOUR CORE MISSIONS for U.S. military forces:
- defend the American homeland;
- fight and decisively win multiple, simultaneous major theater wars;
- perform the "constabulary" duties associated with shaping the security environment in critical regions;
- transform U.S. forces to exploit the "revolution in military affairs;"

To carry out these core missions, we need to provide sufficient force and budgetary allocations. In particular, the United States must:

MAINTAIN NUCLEAR STRATEGIC SUPERIORITY, basing the U.S. nuclear deterrent upon a global, nuclear net assessment that weighs the full range of current and emerging threats, not merely the U.S.-Russia balance.

RESTORE THE PERSONNEL STRENGTH of today's force to roughly the levels anticipated in the "Base Force" outlined by the Bush Administration, an increase in active-duty strength from 1.4 million to 1.6 million.

REPOSITION U.S. FORCES to respond to 21st century strategic realities by shifting permanently-based forces to Southeast Europe and Southeast Asia, and by changing naval deployment patterns to reflect growing U.S. strategic concerns in East Asia.

MODERNIZE CURRENT U.S. FORCES SELECTIVELY, proceeding with the F-22 program while increasing purchases of lift, electronic support and other aircraft; expanding submarine and surface combatant fleets; purchasing Comanche helicopters and medium-weight ground vehicles for the Army, and the V-22 Osprey "tilt-rotor" aircraft for the Marine Corps.

CANCEL "ROADBLOCK" PROGRAMS such as the Joint Strike Fighter, CVX aircraft carrier, and Crusader howitzer system that would absorb exorbitant amounts of Pentagon funding while providing limited improvements to current capabilities. Savings from these canceled programs should be used to spur the process of military transformation.

DEVELOP AND DEPLOY GLOBAL MISSILE DEFENSES to defend the American homeland and American allies, and to provide a secure basis for U.S. power projection around the world.

CONTROL THE NEW "INTERNATIONAL COMMONS" OF SPACE AND "CYBERSPACE," and pave the way for the creation of a new military service – U.S. Space Forces – with the mission of space control.

EXPLOIT THE "REVOLUTION IN MILITARY AFFAIRS" to insure the long-term superiority of U.S. conventional forces. Establish a two-stage transformation process which
- maximizes the value of current weapons systems through the application of advanced technologies, and,
- produces more profound improvements in military capabilities, encourages competition between single services and joint-service experimentation efforts.

INCREASE DEFENSE SPENDING gradually to a minimum level of 3.5 to 3.8 percent of gross domestic product, adding $15 billion to $20 billion to total defense spending annually.

Fulfilling these requirements is essential if America is to retain its militarily dominant status for the coming decades. Conversely, the failure to meet any of these needs must result in some form of strategic retreat. At current levels of defense spending, the only option is to try ineffectually to "manage" increasingly large risks: paying for today's needs by shortchanging tomorrow's; withdrawing from constabulary missions to retain strength for large-scale wars; "choosing" between presence in Europe or presence in Asia; and so on. These are bad choices. They are also false economies. The "savings" from withdrawing from the Balkans, for example, will not free up anywhere near the magnitude of funds needed for military modernization or transformation. But these are false economies in other, more profound ways as well. The true cost of not meeting our defense requirements will be a lessened capacity for American global leadership and, ultimately, the loss of a global security order that is uniquely friendly to American principles and prosperity.

V
CREATING TOMORROW'S DOMINANT FORCE

• • •

Further, the process of transformation, even if it brings revolutionary change, is likely to be a long one, absent some catastrophic and catalyzing event – like a new Pearl Harbor. Domestic politics and industrial policy will shape the pace and content of transformation as much as the requirements of current missions. A decision to suspend or terminate aircraft carrier production, as recommended by this report and as justified by the clear direction of military technology, will cause great upheaval. Likewise, systems entering production today – the F-22 fighter, for example – will be in service inventories for decades to come. Wise management of this process will consist in large measure of figuring out the right moments to halt production of current-paradigm weapons and shift to radically new designs. The expense associated with some programs can make them roadblocks to the larger process of transformation – the Joint Strike Fighter program, at a total of approximately $200 billion, seems an unwise investment. Thus, this report advocates a two-stage process of change – transition and transformation – over the coming decades.

In general, to maintain American military preeminence that is consistent with the requirements of a strategy of American global leadership, tomorrow's U.S. armed forces must meet three new missions:

• **Global missile defenses. A network against limited strikes, capable of protecting the United States, its allies and forward-deployed forces, must be constructed. This must be a layered system of land, sea, air and space-based components.**

• **Control of space and cyberspace. Much as control of the high seas – and the protection of international commerce – defined global powers in the past, so will control of the new**

"international commons" be a key to world power in the future. An America incapable of protecting its interests or that of its allies in space or the "infosphere" will find it difficult to exert global political leadership.

• **Pursuing a two-stage strategy for of transforming conventional forces. In exploiting the "revolution in military affairs," the Pentagon must be driven by the enduring missions for U.S. forces. This process will have two stages: transition, featuring a mix of current and new systems; and true transformation, featuring new systems, organizations and operational concepts. This process must take a competitive approach, with services and joint-service operations competing for new roles and missions. Any successful process of transformation must be linked to the services, which are the institutions within the Defense Department with the ability and the responsibility for linking budgets and resources to specific missions.**

9/11 WARNING I

FBI Knowledge of Terrorists Training at Flight Schools

Two months before the events of September 11th, 2001, an FBI agent in Phoenix named Kenneth Williams sent a memo to the bureau brass in D.C. and New York. The agent was warning about an unusually high number of Muslims being trained at American flight schools, perhaps part of "a coordinated effort" by Osama bin Laden. His memo was ignored at the higher levels.

(Rev. 08-28-2000)

FEDERAL BUREAU OF INVESTIGATION

Precedence: ROUTINE   **Date:** 07/10/2001

To: Counterterrorism   **Attn:** RFU
                                         SSA David Frasca
                                         IRS Elizabeth Harvey Matson
                                         UBL Unit
                                         SSA Rodney Middelton
                                         IRS Jennifer Maitner
                                         IRS Mark Connor
                                         IRS Fred Stremmel
             New York   I-46
                                         SSA Jack Cloonan
                                         SA Michael S. Butsch

From: Phoenix
         Squad16
         Contact: SA Kenneth J. Williams

Approved By: Kurtz William A

Drafted By: Williams Kenneth J

Case ID #: _____ (Pending)

Title: ███ ZAKARIA MUSTAPHA SOUBRA;
          IT-OTHER (ISLAMIC ARMY OF THE CAUCASUS)

Synopsis: ███ UBL and AL-MUHAJIROUN supporters attending civil
aviation universities/colleges in the State of Arizona.

███ **Full Field Investigation Instituted:** 04/17/2000 (NONUSPER)

Details: ███ The purpose of this communication is to advise the
Bureau and New York of the possibility of a coordinated effort by
USAMA BIN LADEN (UBL) to send students to the United States to attend
civil aviation universities and colleges. Phoenix has observed an
inordinate number of individuals of investigative interest who are
attending or who have attended civil aviation universities and
colleges in the State of Arizona. The inordinate number of these
individuals attending these type of schools and fatwas issued by AL-

M-HQI-88000177
1 OF 8

Declassified by: UC, CTU 1, NSLB,
OSC, FBI
M: 02/3/06

To: **Counterterrorism** From: Phoenix
Re: ████████████████, 07/10/2001

MUHJIROUN spiritual leader SHEIKH OMAR BAKRI MOHAMMED FOSTOK, an
ardent supporter of UBL, gives reason to believe that a coordinated
effort is underway to establish a cadre of individuals who will one
day be working in the civil aviation community around the world.
These individuals will be in a position in the future to conduct
terror activity against civil aviation targets.

██ Phoenix believes that the FBI should accumulate a
listing of civil aviation universities/colleges around the country.
FBI field offices with these types of schools in their area should
establish appropriate liaison. FBIHQ should discuss this matter with
other elements of the U.S. intelligence community and task the
community for any information that supports Phoenix's suspicions.
FBIHQ should consider seeking the necessary authority to obtain visa
information from the USDOS on individuals obtaining visas to attend
these types of schools and notify the appropriate FBI field office
when these individuals are scheduled to arrive in their area of
responsibility.

██ Phoenix has drawn the above conclusion from several
Phoenix investigations to include captioned investigation and the
following investigations: ████████████████████████, a Saudi
Arabian national and two Algerian Islamic extremists ███████████
████████ and ████████████████.

██ Investigation of ZAKARIA MUSTAPHA SOUBRA was initiated
as the result of information provided by ████████ a source who has
provided reliable information in the past. The source reported during
April 2000 that SOUBRA was a supporter of UBL and the ████████████
████ AL-MUHJIROUN. SOUBRA arrived in Arizona from London, England
on 08/27/1999 on an F-1 student visa to attend EMBRY RIDDLE
UNIVERSITY (ERU), Prescott, Arizona. ERU only teaches courses related
to the field of aviation. SOUBRA is an Aeronautical Engineering
student at ERU and has been taking courses in "international
security" relating to aviation. SOUBRA, within weeks of his arrival
at Prescott, Arizona, ████████████████████████████████████,
supporting UBL, at Mosques located throughout Arizona. SOUBRA has
also organized anti United States and Israeli demonstrations in the
area of ARIZONA STATE UNIVERSITY (ASU), Tempe, Arizona. He has also
established and organized an Islamic student association on the ERU
campus organizing the Muslim student population on the ERU campus.

██ Phoenix has identified several associates of SOUBRA at
ERU who arrived at the university around the same time that he did.
These individuals are Sunni Muslims who have the same radical
fundamentalists views as SOUBRA. They come from Kenya, Pakistan,

9/11 WARNING II

"Bin Laden Determined to Strike in U.S.," Bush Was Told

A little more than a month before 9/11, the Bush White House received an intelligence digest from the CIA with a two-page section titled "Bin Laden Determined to Strike in U.S." The president headed off for a month's vacation to his ranch in Crawford, Texas, right after that.

What these warnings—and there were others—tell me is that (a) either the Bush Administration allowed 9/11 to happen; (b) took part in it happening, or (c) were the most inept administration we've ever had. These warnings were so plain and simple that, if you didn't "get" them, you'd never win on Jeff Foxworthy's show *Are You Smarter than a Fifth Grader?*

Bin Ladin Determined To Strike in US

Clandestine, foreign government, and media reports indicate Bin Ladin since 1997 has wanted to conduct terrorist attacks in the US. Bin Ladin implied in US television interviews in 1997 and 1998 that his followers would follow the example of World Trade Center bomber Ramzi Yousef and "bring the fighting to America."

After US missile strikes on his base in Afghanistan in 1998, Bin Ladin told followers he wanted to retaliate in Washington, according to a ▆▆▆▆▆▆▆▆▆ service.

An Egyptian Islamic Jihad (EIJ) operative told an ▆▆▆▆▆ service at the same time that Bin Ladin was planning to exploit the operative's access to the US to mount a terrorist strike.

The millennium plotting in Canada in 1999 may have been part of Bin Ladin's first serious attempt to implement a terrorist strike in the US. Convicted plotter Ahmed Ressam has told the FBI that he conceived the idea to attack Los Angeles International Airport himself, but that Bin Ladin lieutenant Abu Zubaydah encouraged him and helped facilitate the operation. Ressam also said that in 1998 Abu Zubaydah was planning his own US attack.

Ressam says Bin Ladin was aware of the Los Angeles operation.

Although Bin Ladin has not succeeded, his attacks against the US Embassies in Kenya and Tanzania in 1998 demonstrate that he prepares operations years in advance and is not deterred by setbacks. Bin Ladin associates surveilled our Embassies in Nairobi and Dar es Salaam as early as 1993, and some members of the Nairobi cell planning the bombings were arrested and deported in 1997.

Al-Qa'ida members—including some who are US citizens—have resided in or traveled to the US for years, and the group apparently maintains a support structure that could aid attacks. Two al-Qa'ida members found guilty in the conspiracy to bomb our Embassies in East Africa were US citizens, and a senior EIJ member lived in California in the mid-1990s.

A clandestine source said in 1998 that a Bin Ladin cell in New York was recruiting Muslim-American youth for attacks.

We have not been able to corroborate some of the more sensational threat reporting, such as that from a ▆▆▆▆▆▆▆▆▆ *service in 1998 saying that Bin Ladin wanted to hijack a US aircraft to gain the release of "Blind Shaykh" 'Umar 'Abd al-Rahman and other US-held extremists.*

continued

Declassified and Approved
for Release, 10 April 2004

_____ _____ _____ _____

- Nevertheless, FBI information since that time indicates patterns of
suspicious activity in this country consistent with preparations for
hijackings or other types of attacks, including recent surveillance of
federal buildings in New York.

The FBI is conducting approximately 70 full field investigations
throughout the US that it considers Bin Ladin–related. CIA and the
FBI are investigating a call to our Embassy in the UAE in May saying
that a group of Bin Ladin supporters was in the US planning attacks
with explosives.

A CHANGE OF POLICY

The Pentagon's "Stand Down Order" on 9/11

The question that's haunted me from day one is how come the world's biggest military superpower was somehow oblivious to rogue airliners in American air space for more than an hour, and our top brass seemed so befuddled in terms of dealing with hijackers apparently using these four planes as flying bombs. Why couldn't our fighter jets intercept at least *one* of them?!

Well, here's one possible explanation: Donald Rumsfeld, our Secretary of Defense, never gave the go-ahead. Why? On June 1, 2001, the Joint Chiefs of Staff issued a new Instruction—superseding one from 1997—that required approval by the Secretary of Defense for any "potentially lethal support…in the event of an aircraft piracy (hijacking)."

I sure would like to know why the question of Rumsfeld doing this never came up with the 9/11 Commission. Doesn't it seem important to have asked why that critical policy got changed only four months beforehand?

CHAIRMAN OF THE JOINT CHIEFS OF STAFF INSTRUCTION

J-3   CJCSI 3610.01A
DISTRIBUTION: A, B, C, J, S   1 June 2001

AIRCRAFT PIRACY (HIJACKING) AND DESTRUCTION OF DERELICT AIRBORNE OBJECTS

References: See Enclosure D.

1. Purpose. This instruction provides guidance to the Deputy Director for Operations (DDO), National Military Command Center (NMCC), and operational commanders in the event of an aircraft piracy (hijacking) or request for destruction of derelict airborne objects.

2. Cancellation. CJCSI 3610.01, 31 July 1997.

3. Applicability. This instruction applies to the Joint Staff, Services, unified commands, and the US Element, North American Aerospace Defense Command (USELEMNORAD).

4. Policy.

   a. Aircraft Piracy (Hijacking) of Civil and Military Aircraft. Pursuant to references a and b, the Administrator, Federal Aviation Administration (FAA), has exclusive responsibility to direct law enforcement activity related to actual or attempted aircraft piracy (hijacking) in the "special aircraft jurisdiction" of the United States. When requested by the Administrator, Department of Defense will provide assistance to these law enforcement efforts. Pursuant to reference c, the NMCC is the focal point within Department of Defense for providing assistance. In the event of a hijacking, the NMCC will be notified by the most expeditious means by the FAA. The NMCC will, with the exception of immediate responses as authorized by reference d, forward requests for DOD assistance to the Secretary of Defense for approval. DOD assistance to the FAA will be provided in accordance with reference d. Additional guidance is provided in Enclosure A.

b. Aircraft Piracy (Hijacking) Preventive Measures for Military and Military Contract Aircraft. Reference c outlines general policy and authority of military commanders to protect and secure property under their command. References f and g provide policy and guidance for commanders on dealing with terrorism, and information for reducing vulnerability of DOD personnel, their family members, facilities, and materiel to acts of terrorism. Additional guidance is provided in Enclosure B.

(1) A concerted effort will be made to prevent piracy (hijacking) of military or military contract aircraft by initiating security measures designed to minimize vulnerabilities and by stopping potential hijackers before they board the aircraft.

(2) If preventive measures fail, any attempt to hijack a military aircraft will, if practicable, be resisted.

(3) Assistance to hijacked aircraft will be rendered, as requested, by the aircraft commander, and as approved by the authority exercising operational control of the counter hijacking effort.

c. Destruction of Derelict Airborne Objects. Derelict airborne objects (for example, unmanned free balloons, moored balloons or kites, unmanned non-nuclear rockets or missiles, unmanned aerial vehicles (UAV) or remotely operated vehicles (ROV)) are a potential threat to public safety. Military personnel may, upon request, be required to track and destroy such objects. The NMCC is the focal point for any requests for DOD assistance in tracking and destroying derelict airborne objects. With the exception of immediate responses as authorized by reference d, the NMCC will forward all requests for such assistance to the Secretary of Defense for approval. Enclosure D provides additional guidance.

5. Definitions. Terms used in this instruction are in the Glossary.

6. Responsibilities. The DDO, NMCC, is designated as the DOD coordinating authority between the FAA and operational commanders. As such, the DDO will forward all requests or proposals for DOD military assistance to the Secretary of Defense for approval, with the exception of immediate responses as defined by reference d. The Services, unified commands, and USELEMNORAD are responsible for compliance with this instruction and any other directives, laws, or international agreements involving aircraft piracy (hijacking) or derelict airborne object incidents. Records and logs for aircraft piracy

CJCSI 3610.01A
1 June 2001

(hijacking) and destruction of derelict airborne object situations will be maintained for a minimum of 90 days to permit later reconstruction of the sequence of events. Records and logs requiring longer retention by other directives will be retained accordingly.

7. Summary of Changes

    a. Unmanned vehicles (UAV, ROV) added to the description of possible derelict airborne objects.

    b. Statutory Authority for Responding to Aircraft Piracy enclosure removed and added to reference list.

    c. In various places throughout the document, "USELEMNORAD" was replaced with "NORAD."

    d. FAA Order 7610.4J, 3 November 1998, "Special Military Operations," was added as a reference.

8. Releasability. This instruction is approved for public release; distribution is unlimited. DOD components (to include the combatant commands), other Federal agencies, and the public may obtain copies of this instruction through the Internet from the CJCS Directives Home Page--http://www.dtic.mil/doctrine. Copies are also available through the Government Printing Office on the Joint Electronic Library CD-ROM.

9. Effective Date. This instruction is effective upon receipt.

S. A. FRY
Vice Admiral, U.S. Navy
Director, Joint Staff

Enclosures:
  A--Instructions for Use in Piracy (Hijacking) of Civil Aircraft and Military
     Aircraft
  B--Instructions for Aircraft Piracy (Hijacking) Preventive Measures for
     Military and Military Contract Aircraft
  C--Instructions for Destruction of Derelict Airborne Objects
  D--References

JESSE VENTURA

b. <u>Support</u>. When notified that military assistance is needed in conjunction with an aircraft piracy (hijacking) emergency, the DDO, NMCC, will:

(1) Determine whether or not the assistance needed is reasonably available from police or commercial sources. If not, the DDO, NMCC, will notify the appropriate unified command or NORAD to determine if suitable assets are available and will forward the request to the Secretary of Defense for approval in accordance with DODD 3025.15, paragraph D.7 (reference d).

(2) If suitable assets from a unified command or NORAD are not reasonably available, the DDO, NMCC, will coordinate with the appropriate Military Service operations center to provide military assistance.

c. <u>Military Escort Aircraft</u>

(1) When notified that military escort aircraft are needed in conjunction with an aircraft piracy (hijacking) emergency, the DDO, NMCC, will notify the appropriate unified command or USELEMNORAD to determine if suitable aircraft are available and forward the request to the Secretary of Defense for approval in accordance with DODD 3025.15, paragraph D.7 (reference d).

(2) Pursuant to reference j, the escort service will be requested by the FAA hijack coordinator by direct contact with the NMCC. Normally, NORAD escort aircraft will take the required action. However, for the purpose of these procedures, the term "escort aircraft" applies to any military aircraft assigned to the escort mission. When the military can provide escort aircraft, the NMCC will advise the FAA hijack coordinator of the identification and location of the squadron tasked to provide escort aircraft. NMCC will then authorize direct coordination between FAA and the designated military unit. When a NORAD resource is tasked, FAA will coordinate through the appropriate Air Defense Sector/Regional Air Operations Center.

CONTROLLED DEMOLITION

The "Free Fall" of Building 7

The third skyscraper that got reduced to rubble on 9/11 was the 47-story World Trade Center Building 7, which went down late that afternoon. According to the government, the reason was fires caused by the collapse of the Twin Towers. What I wondered about from the front was, how come fires had never before destroyed a steel skyscraper?

The document you're about to read sure makes it look to me like Building 7 was brought down by demolition charges from within. This comes from the final report of the National Institute of Standards and Technology, NIST, which looked into the 6.5-second plunge (a few tenths of a second longer than it's said Oswald fired those three shots at JFK).

Here's the rub: Building 7 came down so fast that it was at virtually the same rate as a free-falling object. Members of the 9/11 Truth Movement have been pointing this out for years. But that didn't jive with the official story, because free fall can only take place when an object has no structural components below it. And the only way that could happen to a building would be to remove the lower structural components with an external force like explosives. Otherwise, you'd be defying Newton's laws of physics.

So, not surprisingly, when the NIST Draft for Public Comment report came out in August of 2008, they claimed that the time it took for the

17 upper floors to crumble (the only floors visible on the videos they were using) "was approximately 40 percent longer than the computed free fall time and was consistent with physical principles." There had been "a sequence of structural failures," the NIST technical expert said.

I guess they weren't counting on a high school physics teacher named David Chandler asking a question at the briefing. The teacher said this "40 percent longer" business contradicted an Internet-available video that clearly showed "for about two and a half seconds...the acceleration of the building is indistinguishable from free fall."

NIST apparently took the teacher seriously. In their final report, published in November 2008, amazingly enough they admitted free fall. After dividing the descent of Building 7 into three stages, NIST called the second phase "a freefall descent over approximately eight stories at gravitational acceleration for approximately 2.25s[econds]."

A miracle apparently took place on 9/11. Like schoolteacher Chandler said, "Free fall can only be achieved if there is zero resistance to the motion." Interestingly, the final NIST report no longer said anything about its analysis being "consistent with physical principles." Of course, they didn't admit anything about a professional demolition job either. But that's the only way this could have happened. Building 7 didn't come down because heat from fires caused the steel to weaken and collapse. It was assisted to the ground by some type of explosive device that could remove all resistance.

Pay close attention to the portions I've highlighted from the NIST report. Why the mainstream TV and press can get a report like this, and it isn't leading the news cycle and on every front page the next morning, shows you just how controlled the corporate media are.

Also check out David Ray Griffin's book, *The Mysterious Collapse of World Trade Center 7*, and the website for Architects & Engineers for 9/11 Truth. Here are excerpts from the "NIST Final Report: NIST NCSTAR 1-9: Structural Fire Response and Probable Collapse Sequence of World Trade Center Building 7."

- The observed descent time of the upper 18 stories of the north face of WTC 7 (the floors clearly visible in the video evidence) was 40 percent greater than the computed free fall time. A more detailed analysis of the descent of the north face found three stages: (1) a slow descent with acceleration less than that of gravity that corresponded to the buckling of the exterior columns at the lower floors, (2) <u>a freefall descent over approximately eight stories at gravitational acceleration for approximately 2.25 s,</u> and (3) a decreasing acceleration as the north face encountered resistance from the structure below.

- The south and west exterior columns buckled first, followed by the north and east face columns.

- All exterior columns buckled between approximately Floors 7 and 14.

- Once column support was lost in the lower floors, the remaining exterior structure above began to fall vertically as a single unit.

- WTC 7 was prone to classic progressive collapse in the absence of fire-induced damage and debris impact damage when a section of Column 79 between Floors 11 and 13 was removed. The collapse sequence demonstrated a vertical and horizontal progression of failure upon the removal of the Column 79 section, followed by downward movement at the roofline due to buckling of exterior columns, which led to the collapse of the entire building.

12.7   REFERENCES

Cantor 1985. Irwin G. Cantor P.C., Structural Engineers. 1985. Structural Design Drawings, 7 World Trade Center.

GSA. 2003. U.S. General Services Administration, Progressive Collapse Analysis and Design Guidelines for Federal Office Buildings and Major Modernization Projects, June.

Livermore 2007. LS-DYNA Keyword User's Manual, Livermore Software Technology Corporation, Version 971, May.

Sadek, F., El-Tawil, S., Lew, H.S. 2008. Robustness of Composite Floor Systems with Shear Connections: Modeling, Simulation, and Evaluation, J. Struct. Eng., ASCE, Vol 134, No. 11, pg 1717-1725.

UFC. 2005. Unified Facilities Criteria, Design of Buildings to Resist Progressive Collapse, U.S. Department of Defense UFC 4-023-03, 25 January.

3.6   TIMING OF COLLAPSE INITIATION AND PROGRESSION

The timing of global collapse of WTC 7, as indicated by downward motion of the north exterior face, was investigated using a video of the collapse taken from the vantage point of West Street near Harrison Street (Camera No. 3, Figure 5-183 of NIST NCSTAR 1-9). An initial analysis compared the observed time it took for the roofline to fall approximately 18 stories to the free fall time under the force of gravity. A more detailed analysis examined the vertical displacement, velocity, and acceleration through different stages of the collapse process. (NIST NCSTAR 1-9, Chapter 12)

The time that the roofline took to fall 18 stories or 73.8 m (242 ft) was approximately 5.4 s. The theoretical time for free fall (i.e., at gravitational acceleration) was computed from

$$t = \sqrt{\frac{2h}{g}}$$

where t = time, s; h = distance, m (ft); and g = gravitational acceleration, 9.81 m/s^2 (32.2 ft/s^2). This time was approximately 3.9 s. Thus, the average time for the upper 18 stories to collapse, based on video evidence, was approximately 40 percent longer than the computed free fall time.

A more detailed examination of the same video led to a better understanding of the vertical motion of the building in the first several seconds of descent. NIST tracked the downward displacement of a point near the center of the roofline, fitting the data using a smooth function.[3] (The time at which motion of the roofline was first perceived was taken as time zero.) The fitted displacement function was then differentiated to estimate the downward velocity as a function of time, shown as a solid curve in Figure 3-15. Velocity data points (solid circles) were also determined from the displacement data using a central difference approximation.[4] The slope of the velocity curve is approximately constant between about 1.75 s and 4.0 s, and a good straight line fit to the points in this range (open-circles in Figure 3-15) allowed estimation of a constant downward acceleration during this time interval. This acceleration was 32.2 ft/s^2 (9.81 m/s^2), equivalent to the acceleration of gravity g.

For discussion purposes, three stages were defined, as denoted in Figure 3-15:

- In Stage 1, the descent was slow and the acceleration was less than that of gravity. This stage corresponds to the initial buckling of the exterior columns in the lower stories of the north face. By 1.75 s, the north face had descended approximately 2.2 m (7 ft).

- In Stage 2, the north face descended at gravitational acceleration, as the buckled columns provided negligible support to the upper portion of the north face. This free fall drop continued for approximately 8 stories or 32.0 m (105 ft), the distance traveled between times $t = 1.75$ s and $t = 4.0$ s.

- In Stage 3, the acceleration decreased somewhat as the upper portion of the north face encountered increased resistance from the collapsed structure and the debris pile below. Between 4.0 s and 5.4 s, the north face corner fell an additional 39.6 m (130 ft).

As noted above, the collapse time was approximately 40 percent longer than that of free fall for the first 18 stories of descent. The detailed analysis shows that this increase in time is due primarily to Stage 1. The three stages of collapse progression described above are consistent with the results of the global collapse analyses discussed in Chapter 12 of NIST NCSTAR 1-9.

---

[3] A function of the form $z(t) = A\{1 - \exp[-(t/\lambda)^k]\}$ was assumed, which satisfies the initial conditions of zero displacement, zero velocity, and zero acceleration. The constants A, λ, and k were determined using least squares fitting.

[4] The central difference approximation is given by $v_{i+\frac{1}{2}} \approx (z_i - z_{i+1})/(t_i - t_{i+1})$, where z_i and z_{i+1} denote the displacement at time t_i and t_{i+1}, respectively.

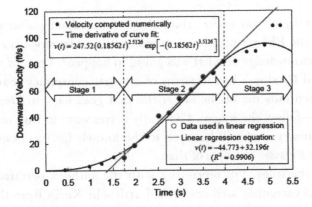

Figure 3–15. Downward velocity of north face roofline as WTC 7 began to collapse.

3.7   REFERENCES

Cantor 1985. Irwin G. Cantor P.C., Structural Engineers, Structural Drawings, 7 World Trade Center.

Flack and Kurtz 1988. Flack and Kurtz Mechanical Engineers, Mechanical and Electrical Drawings for Salomon Brothers 7 World Trade Center Headquarters.

Roth 1985. Emery Roth & Sons P.C., Architects, Architectural Drawings, 7 World Trade Center.

Syska & Hennessy 1985. Syska & Hennessy Engineers, Mechanical, Electrical, and Plumbing Drawings, 7 World Trade Center.

FOLLOW THE MONEY

Evidence for Insider Stock Trading Before 9/11

How many of you realize that, almost immediately after the events of 9/11, the FBI set up a team to look into insider stock trading that indicated foreknowledge of what was going to happen? That, of course, could have opened Pandora's box in terms of a bigger conspiracy than just al Qaeda. This reminds me of the old cliché that goes back to Deep Throat in Watergate—follow the money. Generally if you want to find out who knew what, the money trail will lead you to the knowledge you desire. And 9/11 seems to be a classic example of that.

To set the stage, I'm reprinting with the author's permission a mind-blowing and extremely well-researched article by Kevin Ryan that appeared in the *Foreign Policy Journal* on November 18, 2010. It's called "Evidence for Informed Trading on the Attacks of September 11."

Evidence for Informed Trading on the Attacks of September 11

by Kevin Ryan

November 18, 2010

Just after September 11th 2001, many governments began investigations into possible insider trading related to the terrorist attacks of that day. Such investigations were initiated by the governments of Belgium, Cyprus, France, Germany, Italy, Japan, Luxembourg, Monte Carlo, the Netherlands, Switzerland, the United States, and others. Although the investigators were clearly concerned about insider trading, and considerable evidence did exist, none of the investigations resulted in a single indictment. That's because the people identified as having been involved in the suspicious trades were seen as unlikely to have been associated with those alleged to have committed the 9/11 crimes.

This is an example of the circular logic often used by those who created the official explanations for 9/11. The reasoning goes like this: if we assume that we know who the perpetrators were (i.e. the popular version of "al Qaeda") and those who were involved in the trades did not appear to be connected to those assumed perpetrators, then insider trading did not occur.

That's basically what the 9/11 Commission told us. The Commission concluded that "exhaustive investigations" by the SEC and the FBI "uncovered no evidence that anyone with advance knowledge of the attacks profited through securities transactions." What they meant was that someone did profit through securities transactions but, based on the Commission's assumptions of guilt, those who profited were not associated with those who were guilty of conducting the attacks. In a footnote, the Commission report acknowledged "highly suspicious trading on its face," but said that this trading on United Airlines was traced back to "A single U.S.-based institutional investor with no conceivable ties to al Qaeda."[1]

With respect to insider trading, or what is more technically called informed trading, the Commission report was itself suspect for several reasons. First, the informed trades relating to 9/11 covered far more than just airline company stock. The stocks of financial and reinsurance companies, as well as other financial vehicles, were identified as being associated with suspicious trades. Huge credit card transactions, completed just before the attacks, were also involved. The Commission ultimately tried to frame all of this highly suspicious trading in terms of a series of misunderstandings. However, the possibility that so many leading financial experts were so completely wrong is doubtful at best and, if true, would constitute another unbelievable scenario in the already highly improbable sequence of events represented by the official story of 9/11.

In the last few years, new evidence has come to light on these matters. In 2006 and 2010, financial experts at a number of universities have established new evidence, through statistical analyses, that informed trades did occur with respect to the 9/11 attacks. Additionally, in 2007, the 911 Commission released a memorandum summary of the FBI investigations on which its report was based.[2] A careful review of this memorandum indicates that some of the people who were briefly investigated by the FBI, and then acquitted without due diligence, had links to al Qaeda and to US intelligence agencies. Although the elapsed time between the informed trades and these new confirmations might prevent legal action against the guilty, the facts of the matter can help lead us to the truth about 9/11.

Early signs

Within a week of the attacks, Germany's stock market regulator, BAWe, began looking into claims of suspicious trading.[3] That same week, Italy's foreign minister, Antonio Martino, made it clear that he had concerns by issuing this public statement: "I think that there are terrorist states and organisations behind speculation on the international markets."[4]

Within two weeks of the attacks, CNN reported that regulators were seeing "ever-clearer signs" that someone "manipulated financial markets ahead of the terror attack in the hope of profiting from it." Belgian Finance Minister, Didier Reynders, said that there were strong suspicions that British markets were used for transactions.[5] The CIA was reported to have asked the British regulators to investigate some of the trades.[6] Unfortunately, the British regulator, The Financial Services Authority, wrote off its investigation by simply clearing "bin Laden and his henchmen of insider trading."[7]

Conversely, German central bank president, Ernst Welteke, said his bank conducted a study that strongly indicated "terrorism insider trading" associated with 9/11. He stated that his researchers had found "almost irrefutable proof of insider trading."[8] Welteke suggested that the insider trading occurred not only in shares of companies affected by the attacks, such as airlines and insurance companies, but also in gold and oil. [9]

The extent of the 9/11-related informed trading was unprecedented. An ABC News Consultant, Jonathan Winer, said, "it's absolutely unprecedented to see cases of insider trading covering the entire world from Japan to the US to North America to Europe."[10]

By October 2001, the Chicago Board Options Exchange (CBOE) and the four other options exchanges in the US had joined forces with the FBI and the Securities and Exchange Commission (SEC) to investigate a list of 38 stocks, as well as multiple options and Treasury bonds, that were flagged in relation to potential informed trades. SEC Chairman Harvey Pitt gave testimony to the House Financial Services Committee at the time, saying, "We will do everything in our power to track those people down and bring them to justice."[11]

Mary Bender, chief regulatory officer at the CBOE, stated "We've never really had anything like this, [the option exchanges are] using the same investigative tools as we would in an insider-trading case. The point is to find people who are connected to these heinous crimes."

The people ultimately found included an unnamed customer of Deutsche Bank Alex. Brown (DBAB). This involved a trade on United Airlines (UAL) stock consisting of a 2,500-contract order that was, for some reason, split into chunks of 500 contracts each and then directed to multiple exchanges around the country simultaneously.[12] When the 9/11 Commission report pointed to a "single U.S.-based institutional investor with no conceivable ties to al Qaeda," it was referring to either DBAB or its customer in that questionable trade.

Michael Ruppert has since written about DBAB, noting that the company had previously been a financier of The Carlyle Group and also of Brown Brothers Harriman, both of which are companies closely related to the Bush family. Ruppert also noted that Alex. Brown, the company purchased by Deutsche Bank to become DBAB, was managed by A.B. (Buzzy) Krongard, who left the firm in 1998 to join the CIA as counsel to director George Tenet.[13] Krongard had been a consultant to CIA director James Woolsey in the mid 1990s and, on September 11th, he was the Executive Director of the CIA, the third highest position in the agency.

Stock and Treasury bonds traded

In 2002, investigator Kyle Hence wrote about the stocks involved in the SEC's target list. Those that had the highest examples of trade volume over the average were UAL [285 times over average], Marsh & McLennan (Marsh) [93 times over average], American Airlines (AMR) [60 times over average], and Citigroup [45 times over average].[14] Other stocks flagged included financial firms, defense-related companies, and the reinsurance firms Munich Re, Swiss Re and the AXA Group. Put options for these reinsurance firms, or bets that the stock would drop, were placed at double the normal levels in the few days before the attacks. Regulators were concerned about "large block trades" on these stocks because the three firms were liable for billions in insurance payouts due to the damage inflicted on 9/11.[15]

The four highest-volume suspect stocks — UAL, Marsh, AMR and Citigroup — were closely linked to the attacks of 9/11. The two airline companies each had two planes hijacked and destroyed. Marsh was located in the exact 8 floors out of 110 in the north tower of the WTC where Flight 11 impacted and the fires occurred. Citigroup was the parent of Travelers Insurance, which was expected to see $500 million in claims, and also Salomon Smith Barney, which occupied all but ten floors in World Trade Center (WTC) building 7. Oddly enough, Salomon Smith Barney had both Donald Rumsfeld and Dick Cheney on its advisory board until January 2001.

Marsh occupied a number of floors in the south tower as well. This is where the office of Marsh executive, L. Paul Bremer, was located. Bremer was a former managing director at Kissinger Associates and had just completed leading a national terrorism commission in 2000. The San Francisco Chronicle noted that Bremer was a source of early claims that rich Arabs were financing Osama bin Laden's terrorist network. In an article on the 9/11 informed trades, the Chronicle reported that "The former chairman of the State Department's National Commission on Terrorism, L. Paul Bremer, said he obtained classified government analyses early last year of bin Laden's finances confirming the assistance of affluent Middle Easterners."[16]

On the day of 9/11, Bremer was interviewed by NBC News and stated that he believed Osama bin Laden was responsible and that possibly Iraq and Iran were involved too, and he called for the most severe military response possible. For unknown reasons, Google removed the interview video from its servers three times, and blocked it once.[17]

The trading of Treasury bonds just before 9/11 was also flagged as being suspicious. Reporters from The Wall street Journal wrote that the "U.S. Secret Service contacted a number of bond traders regarding large purchases of five-year Treasury notes before the attacks, according to people familiar with the probe. The investigators, acting on a tip from traders, are examining whether terrorists, or people affiliated with terrorist organizations, bought five-year notes, including a single $5 billion trade."[18]

Some reports claimed that the 9/11 informed trades were such that millions of dollars were made, and some of that went unclaimed. [19] Others suggested that the trades resulted in the winning of billions of dollars in profits. One such suggestion was made by the former German Minister of Technology, Andreas von Buelow, who said that the value of the informed trades was on the order of $15 billion.[20]

The FBI Investigations

In May 2007, a 9/11 Commission document that summarized the FBI investigations into potential 9/11-related informed trading was declassified. [21] This document was redacted to remove the names of two FBI agents from the New York office, and to remove the names of select suspects in the informed trading investigations. The names of other FBI agents and suspects were left in. Regardless, some information can be gleaned from the document to help reveal the trades and traders investigated.

On September 21, 2001, the SEC referred two specific transactions to the FBI for criminal investigation as potential informed trades. One of those trades was a September 6, 2001 purchase of 56,000 shares of a company called Stratesec, which in the few years before 9/11 was a security contractor for several of the facilities that were compromised on 9/11. These facilities included the WTC buildings, Dulles airport, where American Airlines Flight 77 took off, and also United Airlines, which owned two of the other three ill-fated planes.

The affected 56,000 shares of Stratesec stock were purchased by a director of the company, Wirt D. Walker III, and his wife Sally Walker. This is clear from the memorandum generated to record the FBI summary of the trades investigated.[22] The Stratesec stock that the Walkers purchased doubled in value in the one trading day between September 11th and when the stock market reopened on September 17th. The

Commission memorandum suggests that the trade generated a profit of $50,000 for the Walkers. Unfortunately, the FBI did not interview either of the Walkers and they were both cleared of any wrongdoing because they were said to have "no ties to terrorism or other negative information." [23]

However, Wirt Walker was connected to people who had connections to al Qaeda. For example, Stratesec director James Abrahamson was the business partner of Mansoor Ijaz, who claimed on several occasions to be able to contact Osama bin Laden.[24] Additionally, Walker hired a number of Stratesec employees away from a subsidiary of The Carlyle Group called BDM International, which ran secret (black) projects for government agencies. The Carlyle Group was partly financed by members of the bin Laden family.[25] Mr. Walker ran a number of suspicious companies that went bankrupt, including Stratesec, some of which were underwritten by a company run by a first cousin of former CIA director (and President) George H.W. Bush. Additionally, Walker was the child of a CIA employee and his first job was at an investment firm run by former US intelligence guru, James "Russ" Forgan, where he worked with another former CIA director, William Casey.[26] Of course, Osama bin Laden had links to the CIA as well.[27]

Another trade investigated by the FBI, on request from the SEC, focused on Amir Ibrahim Elgindy, an Egyptian-born, San Diego stock advisor who on the day before 9/11 had allegedly attempted to liquidate $300,000 in assets through his broker at Salomon Smith Barney. During the attempted liquidation, Elgindy was said to have "predicted that the Dow Jones industrial average, which at the time stood at about 9,600, would soon crash to below 3,000."[28]

The 9/11 Commission memorandum suggests that the FBI never interviewed Mr. Elgindy either, and had planned to exonerate him because there was "no evidence he was seeking to establish a position whereby he would profit from the terrorist attacks." Apparently, the prediction of a precipitous drop in the stock market, centered on the events of 9/11, was not sufficient cause for the FBI to interview the suspect.

In late May 2002, Elgindy was arrested along with four others, including an FBI agent and a former FBI agent, and charged with conspiracy to manipulate stock prices and extort money from companies. The FBI agents, Jeffrey A Royer and Lynn Wingate, were said to have "used their access to F.B.I. databases to monitor the progress of the criminal investigation against Mr. Elgindy."[29] A federal prosecutor later accused Elgindy, who also went by several aliases, of having prior knowledge of the 9/11 attacks. Although the judge in that case did not agree with the prosecutor on the 9/11 informed trading accusation, Mr. Elgindy was eventually convicted, in 2005, of multiple crimes including racketeering, securities fraud, and making false statements.

The Boston office of the FBI investigated stock trades related to two companies. The first was Viisage Technologies, a facial recognition company that stood to benefit from an increase in terrorism legislation. The Viisage purchase, made by a former employee of the Saudi American Bank, "revealed no connection with 9/11." However, the Saudi American Bank was named in a lawsuit brought by the 9/11 victims' families due to the bank having — "financed development projects in Sudan benefiting bin Laden in the early 1990s."[30]

The second company investigated by the Boston FBI office was Wellington Management, a company that allegedly held a large account for Osama bin Laden. The FBI found that Wellington Management maintained an account for "members of the bin Laden family" but dropped the investigation because it could not link this to "Osama, al Qaeda, or terrorism."[31]

Although the connections to al Qaeda in three of these cases (Walker, the Viisage trader, and Wellington Management) can be seen as circumstantial, the amount of such evidence is considerable. The quality of the FBI investigations, considering the suspects were not even interviewed, was therefore much less than "exhaustive", as the 9/11 Commission characterized it.

The summary of FBI investigations released by the 9/11 Commission also described how the Commission questioned the FBI about damaged computer hard drives that might have been recovered from the WTC. This questioning was the result of "press reports [contending] that large volumes of suspicious transactions flowed through the computers housed in the WTC on the morning of 9/11 as part of some illicit but ill-defined effort to profit from the attacks."[32] The Commission came to the conclusion that no such activity occurred because "the assembled agents expressed no knowledge of the reported hard-drive recovery effort" and "everything at the WTC was pulverized to near powder, making it extremely unlikely that any hard-drives survived."

The truth, however, is that many such hard-drives were recovered from the WTC and were sent to specialist companies to be cleaned and have data recovered. A German company named Convar did a good deal of the recovery work.

In December 2001, Reuters reported that "Convar has recovered information from 32 computers that support assumptions of dirty doomsday dealings." Richard Wagner, a data retrieval expert at Convar, testified that "There is a suspicion that some people had advance knowledge of the approximate time of the plane crashes in order to move out amounts exceeding $100 million. They thought that the records of their transactions could not be traced after the main frames were destroyed." Director of Convar, Peter Henschel, said that it was "not only the volume, but the size of the transactions [that] was far higher than usual for a day like that."[33]

By late December 2001, Convar had completed processing 39 out of 81 drives, and expected to receive 20 more WTC hard drives the next month. Obviously, the 911 Commission memorandum drafted in August 2003 was not particularly reliable considering it reported that the FBI and the 911 Commission had no knowledge of any of this.

Statistical confirmations

Considering that the FBI and 9/11 Commission overlooked the suspicious connections of informed trading suspects like Wirt Walker, and also claimed in 2003 to have no knowledge of hard drive recoveries publicly reported in 2001, we must assume that they did a poor job of investigating. Today, however, we know that several peer-reviewed academic papers have reported solid evidence that informed trades did occur. That is, the conclusions reached by the official investigations have now been shown, through scientific analysis, to be quite wrong.

In 2006, a professor of Finance from the University of Illinois named Allen Poteshman published an analysis of the airline stock option trades preceding the attacks. This study came to the conclusion that an indicator of long put volume was "unusually high which is consistent with informed investors having traded in the option market in advance of the attacks."[34] Long puts are bets that a stock or option will fall in price.

The unusually high volume of long puts, purchased on UAL and AMR stock before these stocks declined dramatically due to the 9/11 attacks, are evidence that the traders knew that the stocks would decline. Using statistical techniques to evaluate conditional and unconditional distributions of historical stock option activity, Professor Poteshman showed that the data indicate that informed trading did occur.

In January 2010, a team of financial experts from Switzerland published evidence for at least thirteen informed trades in which the investors appeared to have had foreknowledge of the attacks. This study focused again on a limited number of companies but, of those, the informed trades centered on five airline companies and four financial companies. The airline companies were American Airlines, United Airlines and Boeing. Three of the financial companies involved were located in the WTC towers and the fourth was Citigroup, which stood to lose doubly as the parent of both Travelers Insurance and the WTC 7 tenant, Salomon Smith Barney.[35]

More recently, in April 2010, an international team of experts examined trading activities of options on the Standard & Poors 500 index, as well as a volatility index of the CBOE called VIX. These researchers showed that there was a significant abnormal increase in trading volume in the option market just before the 9/11 attacks, and they demonstrated that this was in contrast to the absence of abnormal trading volume over periods long before the attacks. The study also showed that the relevant abnormal increase in trading volume was not simply due to a declining market.[36] Their findings were "consistent with insiders anticipating the 9-11 attacks."

Conclusion

In the early days just after 9/11, financial regulators around the world gave testimony to unprecedented evidence for informed trading related to the terrorist attacks of that day. One central bank president (Welteke) said there was irrefutable proof of such trading. This evidence led US regulators to vow, in Congressional testimony, to bring those responsible to justice. Those vows were not fulfilled, as the people in charge of the investigations let the suspects off the hook by conducting weak inquiries and concluding that informed trading could not have occurred if it was not done directly by Osama bin Laden or al Qaeda.

The "exhaustive investigations" conducted by the FBI, on which the 9/11 Commission report was based, were clearly bogus. The FBI did not interview the suspects and did not appear to compare notes with the 9/11 Commission to help make a determination if any of the people being investigated might have had ties to al Qaeda. The Commission's memorandum summary suggests that the FBI simply made decisions on its own regarding the possible connections of the suspects and the alleged terrorist organizations. Those unilateral decisions were not appropriate, as at least three of the suspected informed trades (those of Walker, the Viisage trader, and Wellington Management) involved reasonably suspicious links to Osama bin Laden or his family. Another suspect (Elgindy) was a soon-to-be convicted criminal who had direct links to FBI employees who were later arrested for securities-related crimes.

The FBI also claimed in August 2003 that it had no knowledge of hard drives recovered from the WTC, which were publicly reported in 2001. According to the people who retrieved the associated data, the hard drives gave evidence for "dirty doomsday dealings."

The evidence for informed trading on 9/11 includes many financial vehicles, from stock options to Treasury bonds to credit card transactions made at the WTC just before it was destroyed. Today we know that financial experts from around the world have provided strong evidence, through established and reliable statistical techniques, that the early expert suspicions were correct, and that 9/11 informed trading did occur.

People knew in advance about the crimes of 9/11, and they profited from that knowledge. Those people are among us today, and our families and communities are at risk of future terrorist attacks and further criminal profiteering if we do not respond to the evidence. It is time for an independent, international investigation into the informed trades and the traders who benefited from the terrorist acts of September 11th.

Notes

[1] National Commission on the Terrorist Attacks Upon the United States, *The 9/11 Commission Report*, July 2004, p 172, and Chapter 5, footnote 130, http://govinfo.library.unt.edu/911/report/911Report.pdf

[2] 9/11 Commission memorandum entitled *"FBI Briefing on Trading"*, prepared by Doug Greenburg, 18 August 2003, http://media.nara.gov/9-11/MFR/t-0148-911MFR-00269.pdf

[3] Dave Carpenter, *Exchange examines odd jump: Before attack: Many put options of hijacked planes' parent companies purchased*, The Associated Press, 18 September 2001, http://911research.wtc7.net/cache/sept11/cjonline_oddjump.html

[4] BBC News, *Bin Laden 'share gains' probe*, 18 September 2001, http://news.bbc.co.uk/2/hi/business/1548118.stm

[5] Tom Bogdanowicz and Brooks Jackson, *Probes into 'suspicious' trading*, CNN, 24 September 2001, http://web.archive.org/web/20011114023845/http://fyi.cnn.com/2001/WORLD/europe/09/24/gen.europe.sh ortselling/

[6] James Doran, *Insider Trading Apparently Based on Foreknowledge of 9/11 Attacks*, The London Times, 18 September 2001, http://911research.wtc7.net/cache/sept11/londontimes_insidertrading.html

[7] David Brancaccio, Marketplace Public Radio: News Archives, 17 October 2001, http://marketplace.publicradio.org/shows/2001/10/17_mpp.html

[8] Paul Thompson and The Center for Cooperative Research, *Terror Timeline: Year by Year, Day by Day, Minute by Minute: A Comprehensive Chronicle of the Road to 9/11 – and America's Response*, Harper Collins, 2004. Also found at History Commons, *Complete 9/11 Timeline, Insider Trading and Other Foreknowledge* http://www.historycommons.org/timeline.jsp?timeline=complete_911_timeline&before_9/11=insidertradin g

[9] Associated Press, *EU Searches for Suspicious Trading*, 22 September 2001, http://www.foxnews.com/story/0,2933,34910,00.html

[10] World News Tonight, 20 September 2001

[11] Erin E. Arvedlund, *Follow The Money: Terrorist Conspirators Could Have Profited More From Fall Of Entire Market Than Single Stocks*, Barron's (Dow Jones and Company), 6 October 2001

[12] Ibid

[13] Michael C. Ruppert, *Crossing the Rubicon: the decline of the American empire at the end of the age of oil*, New Society Publishers, 2004

[14] Kyle F. Hence, *Massive pre-attack 'insider trading' offer authorities hottest trail to accomplices*, Centre for Research on Globalisation (CRG), 21 April 2002, http://globalresearch.ca/articles/HEN204B.html

[15] Grant Ringshaw, *Profits of doom*, The London Telegraph, 23 September 2001, http://911research.wtc7.net/cache/sept11/telegraph_profitsofdoom.html

[16] Christian Berthelsen and Scott Winokur, *Suspicious profits sit uncollected: Airline investors seem to be lying low*, San Francisco Chronicle, 29 September 2001, http://www.sfgate.com/cgi-bin/article.cgi?file=%2Fchronicle%2Farchive%2F2001%2F09%2F29%2FMN186128.DTL#ixzz14XPGwh 6e

[17] Lewis Paul Bremer III on Washington, DC, NBC4 TV, 11 September 2001, Vehmgericht http://vehme.blogspot.com/2007/08/lewis-paul-bremer-iii-on-washington-dc.html

[18] Charles Gasparino and Gregory Zuckerman, *Treasury Bonds Enter Purview of U.S. Inquiry Into Attack Gains*, The Wall Street Journal, 2 October 2001, http://s3.amazonaws.com/911timeline/2001/wallstreetjournal100201.html

[19] Christian Berthelsen and Scott Winokur

[20] Tagesspiegel, *Former German Cabinet Minister Attacks Official Brainwashing On September 11 Issue Points at "Mad Dog" Zbig and Huntington*, 13 January 2002, http://www.ratical.org/ratville/CAH/VonBuelow.html

[21] 9/11 Commission memorandum

[22] The 9/11 Commission memorandum that summarized the FBI investigations refers to the traders involved in the Stratesec purchase. From the references in the document, we can make out that the two people had the same last name and were related. This fits the description of Wirt and Sally Walker, who are known to be stock holders in Stratesec. Additionally, one (Wirt) was a director at the company, a director at a publicly traded company in Oklahoma (Aviation General), and chairman of an investment firm in Washington, DC (Kuwam Corp).

[23] 9/11 Commission memorandum

[24] Sourcewatch, *Mansoor Ijaz/Sudan*, http://www.sourcewatch.org/index.php?title=Mansoor_Ijaz/Sudan

[25] History Commons, *Complete 911 Timeline, Bin Laden Family*, http://www.historycommons.org/timeline.jsp?financing_of_al-qaeda:_a_more_detailed_look=binladenFamily&timeline=complete_911_timeline

[26] Kevin R. Ryan, *The History of Wirt Dexter Walker: Russell & Co, the CIA and 9/11*, 911blogger.com, 3 September 2010, http://911blogger.com/news/2010-09-03/history-wirt-dexter-walker-russell-company-cia-and-911

[27] Michael Moran, *Bin Laden comes home to roost : His CIA ties are only the beginning of a woeful story*, MSNBC, 24 August 1998, http://www.msnbc.msn.com/id/3340101

[28] Alex Berenson, *U.S. Suggests, Without Proof, Stock Adviser Knew of 9/11*, The New York Times, 25 May 2002, http://query.nytimes.com/gst/fullpage.html?res=9E06E4DB143BF936A15756C0A9649C8B63

[29] Alex Berenson, *Five, Including F.B.I. Agents, Are Named In a Conspiracy*, The New York Times, 23 May 2002

[30] History Commons, *Complete 911 Timeline, Saudi American Bank*, http://www.historycommons.org/entity.jsp?entity=saudi_american_bank

[31] 9/11 Commission memorandum

[32] 9/11 Commission memorandum

[33] Erik Kirschbaum, *German Firm Probes Final World Trade Center Deals*, Reuters, 16 December 2001, http://911research.wtc7.net/cache/sept11/reuters_wtc_drives.html

[34] Allen M. Poteshman, *Unusual Option Market Activity and the Terrorist Attacks of September 11, 2001, The Journal of Business*, 2006, vol. 79, no. 4, http://www.journals.uchicago.edu/doi/abs/10.1086/503645

[35] Marc Chesney, et al, *Detecting Informed Trading Activities in the Options Markets*, Social Sciences Research Network, 13 January 2010, http://papers.ssrn.com/sol3/papers.cfm?abstract_id=1522157

[36] Wing-Keung Wong, et al, *Was there Abnormal Trading in the S&P 500 Index Options Prior to the September 11 Attacks?*, Social Sciences Research Network, April 2010, http://papers.ssrn.com/sol3/papers.cfm?abstract_id=1588523

49

TURNING A BLIND EYE

The FBI's "Briefing on Trading" for the 9/11 Commission

Now read the twelve-page memorandum titled "FBI Briefing on Trading" that was prepared in 2003 and declassified four years later by the 9/11 Commission. As you'll see, the FBI went out of its way to say—more than once in the document—that no evidence existed to support such a nasty theory. Even when there were some "suspicious accounts the SEC turned over," these were dismissed because their investigation "revealed no ties to terrorism." You'll even see a reference to the AIG Insurance Company in here. This document fascinated me both for what it says (certain leads that might yet be tracked down by an investigative journalist) and what it doesn't say.

Memorandum   /5/

Event: FBI Briefing on Trading

Type of Event: Informal Briefing

Date: 8/15/03

Date memo prepared: 8/18/03

Special Access Issues: None

Prepared by: Doug Greenburg

Team Number: 4

Location: 9-11 Commission

Participants – FBI: Dennis Lormel, Section Chief, TFOS; Janice K. Penegor, Deputy Chief, TFOS; SA Bill Mackey, TFOS; SSA Greg A. Ruppert, TFOS (Boston FO during 9/11 investigation); SA ▮▮▮▮▮▮▮▮ NY FO, SA ▮▮▮▮▮▮▮▮ NY FO, SSA Richard Kelly, FBIHQ, CTD, ASAC Robert Blecksmith, WFO TDY to Director's Office, HQ.

Participants-Commission: D. Greenburg, J. Roth.

This informal briefing addressed the FBI's investigation of potentially illicit

securities trading in advance of the September 11 attacks. The briefing lasted

approximately 1 ½ hours. This memorandum provides a summary of what we consider

the most important points covered in the briefing, but is not a verbatim or comprehensive

account. The memorandum is organized by subject and does not necessarily follow the

order of the briefing.

Introduction

D. Lormel began the briefing by stating that the allegations of trading with

foreknowledge of 9/11 surfaced very early after 9/11, and the FBI set up a team to look

into the issue. He identified SA Bill Mackey as the team leader of the FBI's team. In addition, he said that the FBI reached out to the SEC very early on, and began

cooperating with the official heading the SEC's inquiry, Director of Market Surveillance,

Joe Cella. Lormel said he also raised the trading issue with the inter-agency Policy

Coordinating Committee (PCC). As a result, the CIA was involved in looking for

intelligence on any illicit trading. Lormel said the FBI raised the trading issue a number

of times during its many meetings with various foreign law enforcement officials about

the investigation of the 9/11 plot. In summary, Lormel said a thorough investigation was

conducted, and there exists no evidence that any person traded any security with

foreknowledge of the 9/11 terrorist attacks.

FBIHQ Investigation

Lormel turned the briefing over to Mackey to describe the investigation. Mackey

also provided a written chronology, which we received later that day, and which is Bates-

stamped, Request 5-13, 156-175.[1] [Copy attached]. Mackey explained he has worked

for the FBI since 1968 and been an agent since 1976. He said he has considerable

experience in white collar crime investigations. On 9/11, he was an instructor at

Quantico, but soon afterwards came to FBIHQ to work on the investigation. Lormel

tapped him to head the trading investigation team, formally known as the U.S. Foreign

and Financial Markets Team, which officially formed on September 17. In this role,

Mackey had two Deputies: and   [2] The purpose of the team

was to determine if anyone had profited or sought to profit by trading securities in

advance of 9/11.

---

[1] The documents Bates-stamped Request 5-13, 1-155 actually concern other subjects and bear no relation to the trading issue. The documents we received on August 15, 2003 that do concern the trading issue were Bates-stamped Request 5-13, 155-302.

[2] Mackey's chronology, dated 8/14/03 and apparently created for the Commission, provides more details on the composition and operation of his team.

Unclassified
Commission Sensitive

Mackey said his team decided almost immediately it needed to involve the industry experts, so it reached out to the SEC, CFTC, and the National Association of Securities Dealers (NASD), a Self-Regulated Organization, which regulated securities broker-dealers. The FBI decided to let these agencies take the lead and refer to it any suspicious transactions requiring further investigation. Mackey said the FBI received total cooperation. He said the level of cooperation from every agency and at every level far exceeded anything he had ever experienced in his career.

Mackey said his team began by meeting with the SEC and collectively determining how terrorists might have tried to profit from the attacks. As a result of this process, the FBI and SEC collectively came up with a list of industries, stocks, and various other securities that an investor with knowledge of the attacks might have used to try to profit from them.

Mackey said the FBI asked the SEC to make contact with its counterparts all over the world concerning the investigation, which the SEC did. Lormel added that in his meetings with various international law enforcement and intelligence officials he raised the trading issue as well.

He also asked the CIA

According to Lormel, the end result of this investigation was that the FBI was never informed of any indication of any real evidence of illicit trading overseas.

Mackey said the SEC agreed to lead the investigation and refer anything suspicious to the FBI. He generally described a series of meetings his team had with

3

Unclassified
Commission Sensitive

senior SEC personnel and others and the progress of the investigation. The chronology

is set out in some detail the document he provided and will not be repeated in full here.

The bottom line was that the investigation did not produce any evidence of any trading by

any person with advance knowledge of 9/11.

Mackey said that his team met with the SEC on September 21, 2001. At that

meeting, Joe Cella of the SEC briefed the FBI on the progress of the SEC's investigation.

[Mackey's report provides a detailed summary of Cella's briefing.] Among other things,

Cella said that the SEC was investigating all relevant options trading for the period

August 24-September 11, 2001. (Mackey said he did not know how the SEC chose the

August 24 starting date, but one of the other agents present speculated it may have

marked the first trading day after the expiration of the August options). Also at the

September 21 briefing, Cella said the SEC's preliminary inquiry identified 29 trading

accounts which profited from stock or option trading before 9/11. These profitable

positions had been established at various times, ranging from as late as September 10,

2001 to as early as February 8, 2000. The SEC told the FBI that some of these 29

accounts were either hedge funds or proprietary accounts that had been in existence for

years. As of September 21, 2001, the SEC and/or the relevant securities exchanges were

still investigating other of the 29 accounts. At the September 21 meeting, the SEC

referred two suspicious accounts to the FBI for investigation.

Mackey described these two suspicious accounts the SEC turned over to his team

for investigation on September 21. First, from September 6, 2001 through September

10, 2001, 56,000 shares of a company called "Stratesec" were purchased by

and   . The SEC informed the FBI that Stratesec

4

9/11 Personal Privacy

provides airport security systems. Subseqent FBI investigation revealed that its stock

increased from $0.75 per share on 9/11 to $1.49 when the market reopened on 9/17. As

of October 12, the [   ] had not sold the stock they purchased, leaving them with an

unrealized profit of over $50,000. The FBI's investigation revealed that [   ]

is a Director of [   ] as well as a director of [   ] which is a public

company in Oklahoma, and Chairman of the [   ] an investment firm based in

Washington D.C. The FBI investigation revealed no ties to terrorism or other negative

information concerning either of the [   ] so it concluded there was no reason to

pursue the investigation. The FBI did not interview the [   ]

The second suspicious transaction identified by the SEC was a 2000 share short

sale in UAL stock by [   ] of Palm Beach, Floridan on September 6, 2001.

[   ] also took short positions in British Telecom and Quest Communications.

Mackey said subsequent FBI investigation revealed that [   ] had multiple U.S.

residences and accounts at various brokerages dating back to 1996. He said the FBI

developed no suspicious information about [   ] and no information linking him to

terrorism. As a result, it determined no further investigation of [   ] was warranted.

It did not interview [   ]

Mackey described another meeting with the SEC on September 25, 2001, a full

summary of which is included in his chronology. Among other things, the SEC reported

that it has not found any unusual activity in its continuing investigations of options

trading, but that it would continue to investigate and report any suspicious trading to the

FBI. Also at this meeting, the SEC and FBI representatives discussed press reports

quoting German Central Banker, Ernst Welteke as stating that there was strong evidence of massive illicit trading prior to the attacks. At the meeting, the SEC representatives

said they had not received any such information from their German counterparts and

noted that the Bundesbank had retracted many of Welteke's remarks through a September

24, 2001 press release.

Mackey said that in mid-October 2001 he attended a high-level meeting with

German law enforcement officials and the FBI. Joe Cella of the SEC also attended. At

this meeting, Joe Cella made a presentation concerning the SEC's investigation. No

evidence of any suspicious trading in Germany was presented at the meeting. Mackey

said that

Mackey said that on September 27, 2001 he received a report from the Chicago

F.O. on an interview with a market maker at the Chicago Board of Options Trading, who

had handled several large put orders for UAL stock just prior to 9/11. This market maker

insisted that, regardless of what the regulators were saying, those put trades were

suspicious. Mackey advised Chicago to send a lead to New York with the names of the

trader or traders so they could be interviewed to ascertain the reason for their well-timed

trades. [The New York investigation is discussed below].

Amir Ibrahim Elgindy

In early October, Mackey's team met with AUSA Ken Breen, E.D.N.Y,

concerning an investigation of Amir Ibrahim Elgindy. They learned from Breen that on

September 10 Elgindy, a professional trader and known short-seller, told his broker he

wanted to liquidate $300,000 in stock in the accounts of his children because he believed

the market was headed down to 3,000 [a presumed reference to the Dow Index, which

Unclassified
Commission Sensitive

was then around 9,600]. The liquidation did not occur because Elgindy did not fax the
necessary written confirmation to his broker until after the markets closed on September
10. [More details on the meeting with Breen concerning Elgindy are available in
Mackey's chronology].

AUSA Breen handled the investigation of Elgindy. On May 17, 2002, Elgindy
was indicted in the E.D.N.Y., along with 4 other people, including Jeff Royer, an alleged
corrupt FBI agent, on racketeering charges. Among other things, Elgindy allegedly used
confidential information Royer provided him concerning investigations of publicly-traded
companies to extort those companies or short their stock. Mackey said he does not know
whether Elgindy had any advance information about September 11. He said he spoke
recently about the subject with AUSA Breen, and Breen said Elgindy's knowledge
remains a question mark. Breen reportedly told Mackey that Elgindy is "very quirky,"
had made some negotiations to suspect charities, and purportedly made anti-american
remarks. Lormel and others at the briefing said that the FBI has not found any links
between Elgindny and Al-Qaeda or terrorism. Moreover, one of the agents present
pointed out that Elgindy was merely trying to liquidate some accounts; there is no
evidence he was seeking to establish a position whereby he would profit from the terrorist
attacks.

Mackey said that a superseding indictment was issued in Elgindy's case on June
13, 2003, and a trial date has been set for January 12, 2004. He said he does not know if
the FBI ever interviewed Elgindy.[3]

---

[3] [Press reports state that at a May 2002 pre-trial detention hearing, AUSA Breen stated, "Perhaps Mr.
Elgindy had pre-knowledge of the September 11 attacks. Instead of trying to report it, he tried to profit
from it." Hettena, Seth, "Judge Disregards Prosecutor's Suggestion Accused Swindler Knew Sept. 11
Attacks Were Coming," AP, May 25, 2002. A magistrate judge chose to ignore these remarks. *Id.* Later

7

Unclassified
Commission Sensitive

Commodities and Treasury Securities

Mackey said the CFTC took the lead in investigating potential suspicious trading in commodities and U.S. Treasury securities. He said the CFTC informed the FBI that any relevant trading could be explained, and there were no suspicious trades warranting further investigation. Among other things, the CFTC said it reported investigating a tip from Secret Service concerning potential unusual trading in 5-year Treasury notes during late August or early September. Upon investigation, the CFTC determined this trading to be unremarkable and not warranting further investigation. The FBI did not independently verify any of the CFTC's investigative findings.

Summary and Conclusion of Mackey's Role

On October 9, Mackey prepared a summary of his team's trading investigation to date. It is reproduced in full in the chronology he provided. On October 20, 2003, he returned to his assignment at Quantico. His chronology states that his team was folded into an expanded International Financial Team, under team leader SSA Pat Ford and that information developed as a result of the Team's trading investigation was assigned to SSA James McNally, one of Mackey's Deputies.

New York Investigation

Agents ▮▮▮▮▮▮▮▮ and ▮▮▮▮▮▮▮▮ from the New York F.O. briefed us on their work in the trading investigation. ▮▮▮▮▮▮ took the lead during the briefing. He explained that he and ▮▮▮▮▮▮ who had relevant experience, were tasked to run down the leads provided by the SEC concerning potentially suspicious trading prior to

---

press reports notes that Elgindy was ultimately released to home detention, and that prosecutors "quickly dropped" the allegation he had advance knowledge of 9/11. Calbreath, Dean, "Stock Trader Elgindy out of Jail, Will be Under House Arrest," Copley News Service, September 11, 2002. Elgindy resides in San Diego. *Id.*]

September 11. He said the SEC provided a "boiled down" spreadsheet of trades in airline

or insurance stocks requiring further inquiry. These trades included both option and

stock and were primarily made by hedge funds or other institutional investors.

[   ] and [   ] ran down all these leads, conducting 25-30 interviews of traders.

Upon investigation, none of the trades proved suspicious.

As an example, [   ] described a trader who took substantial position in put

options in AIG Insurance Co., just before 9/11. Viewed in isolation, this trade looked

suspicious. Upon investigation, however, the FBI determined the trade had been made by

a fund manager to hedge a long position of 4.2 million shares in the AIG common stock.

Because the fund had a very low tax basis in the stock, selling it would create massive tax

consequences. Thus, the fund manager chose to hedge his position through a put option

purchase. After 9/11, the fund profited substantially from its investment in puts. At the

same time, however, the fund suffered a substantial loss on the common stock.

[   ] said most of the interviews he and [   ] did were in New York,

although a few were outside of New York and conducted telephonically. To the

knowledge of everyone present, [   ] and [   ] were the only agents following

these leads from the SEC by interviewing traders, although Mackey suggested the SEC

may have contacted other field offices directly. They said they were not asked to

investigate any off-shore accounts. Upon investigation, all of the trades checked out,

and they developed no evidence of any trading linked to 9/11. Moreover, they asked the

fund managers or other traders about the identity of their clients and whether the clients

provided suggested trades. In all cases, they satisfied themselves that the trading was

legitimate.

Unclassified
Commission Sensitive

Copies of documents relating to the New York F.O. investigation, including a

summary, 302s, and other documents, were provided, Bates-stamped, Request 5-13, 176-

273.

Boston Investigation

SSA Greg Ruppert, an attorney with securities fraud experience, briefed us on the

involvement of the Boston office in the trading investigation. He said his office was

responsible for two primary leads.

First, they received a tip about a suspicious purchase of 5,000 shares on

September 10, 2001, in Viisage Technologies, a facial recognition technology company

in Western Massachusetts that arguably stood to benefit from 9/11. The purchaser,

[   ] was of Lebanese descent and had at one time worked at the Saudi

America Bank/Citibank in London. Working through the London Legat, the FBI

arranged for the London police to interview [   ] He explained that he bought the

stock on a tip by his broker, which Ruppert believed the FBI corroborated (although he

could not recall how it corroborated this information). Moreover [   ] was

completely cooperative with the investigation, and investigation revealed him to have a

net worth in the range of $10 million. In sum, the investigation revealed no connection

with 9/11.

The other lead Boston followed concerned a tip that an investment company

called Wellington Management allegedly held an account on behalf of Usama bin Ladin,

with a value of $100 million. Upon investigation, which involved the SEC and an

AUSA, as well as the FBI, it was determined that Wellington held an account on behalf of other members of the bin Ladin family, who invested through an offshore company.[4]

The investigation revealed that the bin Ladin initial investment was $6 million and that

the account's value never exceeded $8 million. There is no evidence the account was

linked to Usama, Al-Qaeda, or terrorism.

Documents related to the Boston investigation were provided at Request No. 5-

13, 274-302.

Hard-Drive Restoration

We asked about persistent press reports that a certain damaged hard-drives had

been recovered from the WTC site and sent to Germany, where a company was working

to restore them. These press reports contend that large volumes of suspicious

transactions flowed through computers housed in the WTC on the morning of 9/11 as part

of some illicit but ill-defined effort to profit from the attacks. The assembled agents

expressed no knowledge of the reported hard-drive recovery effort or the alleged scheme.

Moreover, one of the New York agents pointed out, from personal experience, that

everything at the WTC was pulverized to near power, making it extremely unlikely that

any hard-drives survived to the extent they data be recovered.

Foreign Wrap-up

In response to our questioning, Lormel said he was confident that no foreign

agency found any evidence of 9/11-related trading overseas. He said the FBI received

good cooperation from almost every relevant agency, and none of them presented any

evidence of any illicit trading. He did note, the Swiss were somewhat recalcitrant to

share information, in keeping with their historical practice. As to Germany, he said the

---

[4] [Documents provided by the FBI reveal the actual investor was Globe Administration, Ltd., which manages corporate money for the Saudi Bin Laden Group. *See* Req 5-13, 300-302, FD-302 re interview of Wellington Management International, LLP employee M. Coll.]

Unclassified
Commission Sensitive

FBI had considerable contacts and a good spirit of cooperation with their German

counterparts, and the Germans never presented any evidence of illicit trading. Neither

Lormel nor anyone else present could offer an explanation for the early remarks of the

German Central Banker, except to state that the evidence did not bear out his comments.

Conclusion

The agents present stated that at present there is no open investigation related to

the trading issue and that no case was ever referred for prosecution. As far as the FBI is

concerned, there was no evidence ever found of any trading with advance knowledge of

the 9/11 attacks. [   ] stated that trading in advance of an attack would be a

very stupid strategy because of the paper-intensive nature of any securities trade. In his

view, a clear paper trail would exist with respect to any trade, making it a very risky

strategy for any terrorist to attempt.

9/11 Classified
Information

9/11 Law Enforcement Privacy

12
Unclassified
Commission Sensitive

PART FIVE

THE "WAR ON TERROR"

SUBVERTING THE CONSTITUTION

The Justice Department's Secret Plan

Six weeks after 9/11, Bush's Justice Department wrote up a long memo with the subject line: "Authority for Use of Military Force to Combat Terrorist Activities Within the United States." As you'll see from the excerpts, the whole concept basically shreds our Bill of Rights. In short, "legal and constitutional rules regulating law enforcement activity are not applicable." The military could even "attack civilian targets, such as apartment buildings, offices, or ships where suspected terrorists were thought to be." And later, "First Amendment speech and press rights may also be subordinated to the overriding need to wage war successfully."

Where does it say that, if you call something "terrorism," the Constitution and the Bill of Rights can be made null and void? All they've got to do is say the word and they can put you under surveillance without a warrant. To me, this smacks of an attack on the foundations of democracy that plays right into the *hands* of terrorists. It also sets a precedent for the kinds of tactics we went on to see at Abu Ghraib, Guantanamo, and elsewhere.

U.S. Department of Justice

Office of Legal Counsel

Office of the Deputy Assistant Attorney General   *Washington, D.C. 20530*

October 23, 2001

MEMORANDUM FOR ALBERTO R. GONZALES
  COUNSEL TO THE PRESIDENT

WILLIAM J. HAYNES, II
  GENERAL COUNSEL
  DEPARTMENT OF DEFENSE

FROM: John C. Yoo
            Deputy Assistant Attorney General

            Robert J. Delahunty
            Special Counsel

RE: *Authority for Use of Military Force To Combat Terrorist Activities*
        Within the United States

       You have asked for our Office's views on the authority for the use of military force to prevent or deter terrorist activity inside the United States. Specifically, you have asked whether the Posse Comitatus Act, 18 U.S.C. § 1385 (1994), limits the ability of the President to engage the military domestically, and what constitutional standards apply to its use. We conclude that the President has ample constitutional and statutory authority to deploy the military against international or foreign terrorists operating within the United States. We further believe that the use of such military force generally is consistent with constitutional standards, and that it need not follow the exact procedures that govern law enforcement operations.

       Our analysis falls into five parts. First, we review the President's constitutional powers to respond to terrorist threats in the wake of the September 11, 2001 attacks on the World Trade Center and the Pentagon. We consider the constitutional text, structure and history, and interpretation by the executive branch, the courts and Congress. These authorities demonstrate that the President has ample authority to deploy military force against terrorist threats within the United States.

       Second, we assess the legal consequences of S.J. Res. 23, Pub. L. No. 107-40, 115 Stat. 224 (2001), which authorized the President to use force to respond to the incidents of September 11. Enactment of this legislation recognizes that the President may deploy military force domestically and to prevent and deter similar terrorist attacks.

       Third, we examine the Posse Comitatus Act, 18 U.S.C. § 1385, and show that it only applies to the domestic use of the Armed Forces for *law enforcement* purposes, rather than for the performance of military functions. The Posse Comitatus Act itself contains an exception that allows the use of the military when constitutionally or statutorily authorized, which has occurred in the present circumstances.

Fourth, we turn to the question whether the Fourth Amendment would apply to the use of the military domestically against foreign terrorists. Although the situation is novel (at least in the nation's recent experience), we think that the better view is that the Fourth Amendment would *not* apply in these circumstances. Thus, for example, we do not think that a military commander carrying out a raid on a terrorist cell would be required to demonstrate probable cause or to obtain a warrant.

Fifth, we examine the consequences of assuming that the Fourth Amendment applies to domestic military operations against terrorists. Even if such were the case, we believe that the courts would not generally require a warrant, at least when the action was authorized by the President or other high executive branch official. The Government's compelling interest in protecting the nation from attack and in prosecuting the war effort would outweigh the relevant privacy interests, making the search or seizure reasonable.

I.

. . .

This, then, is armed conflict between a nation-state and an elusive, clandestine group or network of groups striking unpredictably at civilian and military targets both inside and outside

---

[2] *See generally* Sean D. Murphy, *Contemporary Practice of the United States Relating to International Law*, 93 Am. J. Int'l L. 161 (1999); Ruth Wedgwood, *Responding to Terrorism: The Strikes Against Bin Laden*, 24 Yale J. Int'l L. 559 (1999).

[3] On September 12, 2001, the North Atlantic Council of the North Atlantic Treaty Organization ("NATO") agreed that the September 11 attack was directed from abroad against the United States, and decided that it would be regarded as an action covered by article 5 of the 1949 NATO Treaty, which states that an armed attack against one or more of the Allies in Europe or North America shall be considered an attack against them all. Press Release, NATO, Statement by the North Atlantic Council, *available at* http://www.nato.int/docu/update/2001/1001/e1002a.htm. Article 5 of the NATO Treaty provides that if an armed attack against a NATO member occurs, each of them will assist the Party attacked "by taking forthwith, individually or in concert with the other Parties, such action as it deems necessary, including the use of armed force." North Atlantic Treaty, Apr. 4, 1949, art. 5, 63 Stat. 2241, 2244, 34 U.N.T.S. 243, 246.

[4] It is true, however, that a condition of "war" has been found to exist for various legal purposes in armed conflicts between the United States and entities that lacked essential attributes of statehood, such as Indian bands, *see Montoya v. United States*, 180 U.S. 261, 265, 267 (1901) and insurrections threatening Western legations, *see Hamilton v. McClaughry*, 136 F. 445, 449 (C.C.D. Kan. 1905) (Boxer Rebellion).

the United States. Because the scale of the violence involved in this conflict removes it from the sphere of operations designed to enforce the criminal laws, legal and constitutional rules regulating law enforcement activity are not applicable, or at least not mechanically so. As a result, the uses of force contemplated in this conflict are unlike those that have occurred in America's other recent wars. Such uses might include, for example, targeting and destroying a hijacked civil aircraft in circumstances indicating that hijackers intended to crash the aircraft into a populated area; deploying troops and military equipment to monitor and control the flow of traffic into a city; attacking civilian targets, such as apartment buildings, offices, or ships where suspected terrorists were thought to be; and employing electronic surveillance methods more powerful and sophisticated than those available to law enforcement agencies. These military operations, taken as they may be on United States soil, and involving as they might American citizens, raise novel and difficult questions of constitutional law.

• • •

Conclusion. The text and history of the Constitution, supported by the interpretations of past administrations, the courts, and Congress, show that the President has the independent, non-statutory power to take military actions, domestic as well as foreign, if he determines such actions to be necessary to respond to the terrorist attacks upon the United States on September 11, 2001 and before.

• • •

. Lower courts, however, have held that due to the President's constitutional superiority in foreign affairs, and the unsuitability of foreign affairs questions for judicial resolution, he could engage in warrantless searches of foreign powers or their agents for national security purposes. *See, e.g., United States v. Truong Dinh Hung*, 629 F.2d 908, 913, 915 (4th Cir. 1980) *United States v. Butenko*, 494 F.2d 593 (en banc), *cert. denied*, 419 U.S. 881(1974); *United States v. Brown*, 484 F.2d 418 (1973), *cert. denied*, 415 U.S. 960 (1974).

Enacted in 1978, FISA created a special procedure by which the Government may obtain warrants for foreign intelligence work on the basis of judicial review of an application for such a warrant that had been approved by the Attorney General. In support of such an application, the Government is required to certify, among other things, that "the purpose" of the proposed search or surveillance is "to obtain foreign intelligence information," 50 U.S.C. § 1804(a)(7)(B). In reviewing the application, therefore, the FISA courts have been required to consider whether "the government is primarily attempting to form the basis for a criminal prosecution," *Truong Dinh Hung*, 629 F.2d at 915, or is indeed acting for the purpose of obtaining foreign intelligence. Distinguishing between "law enforcement" and "foreign intelligence" seems, if anything, more difficult than distinguishing between "law enforcement" and "military" functions. Yet the FISA courts seem to have found little difficulty in applying the statute's "purpose" test.[24] This, we believe, reflects the care and circumspection with which the executive branch itself reviews and prepares FISA applications, and the courts' justified confidence in the executive branch's self-monitoring. Likewise here, we believe that the courts will defer to the executive branch's representations that the deployment of the Armed Forces furthers military purposes, if the executive institutes and follows careful controls.

We believe that the Department of Defense could take steps to make clear that a deployment of troops is for a military, rather than a law enforcement, purpose. The object of such steps would be to emphasize that a specific military operation is intended to counter a terrorist attack, thus furthering a national security purpose, rather than to apprehend suspects or to secure evidence for a criminal prosecution. Any criteria or procedures for distinguishing domestic counter-terrorist military operations from operations involving the Armed Forces that have primarily a law enforcement character would, of course, have to be framed, interpreted and applied in a manner that would not inhibit military effectiveness. Furthermore, domestic uses of the Armed Forces for military purposes in counter-terrorist actions may also promote the goals of the anti-terrorism portions of the U.S. criminal code. It also bears emphasizing again that it rests within the President's discretion to determine when certain circumstances – such as the probability that a terrorist attack will succeed, the number of lives at risk, the available window of opportunity to stop the terrorists, and the other exigencies of the moment – justify using the military to intervene.

• • •

In our view, however well suited the warrant and probable cause requirements may be as applied to criminal investigations or to other law enforcement activities, they are unsuited to the demands of wartime and the military necessity to successfully prosecute a war against an enemy. In the circumstances created by the September 11 attacks, the Constitution provides the Government with expanded powers to prosecute the war effort. The Supreme Court has held that when hostilities prevail, the Government "may summarily requisition property immediately needed for the prosecution of the war. . . . As a measure of public protection the property of alien enemies may be seized, and property believed to be owned by enemies taken without prior determination of its true ownership. . . . Even the personal liberty of the citizen may be temporarily restrained as a measure of public safety." *Yakus v. United States*, 321 U.S. 414, 443 (1944) (citations omitted). "[I]n times of war or insurrection, when society's interest is at its peak, the Government may detain individuals whom the Government believes to be dangerous." *United States v. Salerno*, 481 U.S. 739, 748 (1987); *see also id.* at 768 (Stevens, J., dissenting) ("[I]t is indeed difficult to accept the proposition that the Government is without power to detain a person when it is a virtual certainty that he or she would otherwise kill a group of innocent people in the immediate future."). Thus, in *Moyer v. Peabody*, 212 U.S. 78 (1909), the Court rejected a due process claim by an individual jailed for two and a half months without probable cause by the State Governor in time of insurrection. As Justice Holmes wrote, "[w]hen it comes to a decision by the head of the state upon a matter involving its life, the ordinary rights of individuals must yield to what he deems the necessities of the moment." *Id.* at 85. Thus, the Supreme Court has recognized that the Government's compelling interests in wartime justify restrictions on the scope of individual liberty.

First Amendment speech and press rights may also be subordinated to the overriding need to wage war successfully. "'When a nation is at war many things that might be said in time of peace are such a hindrance to its effort that their utterance will not be endured so long as men fight and that no Court could regard them as protected by any constitutional right.' . . . No one would question but that a government might prevent actual obstruction to its recruiting service or the publication of the sailing dates of transports or the number and location of troops." *Near v. Minnesota ex rel. Olson*, 283 U.S. 697, 716 (1931) (citation omitted); *cf. Snepp v. United States*, 444 U.S. 507, 509 n.3 (1980) (recognizing that "[t]he Government has a compelling interest in protecting both the secrecy of information important to our national security and the appearance of confidentiality so essential to the effective operation of our foreign intelligence service"). Accordingly, our analysis must be informed by the principle that "while the constitutional structure and controls of our Government are our guides equally in war and in peace, they must be read with the realistic purposes of the entire instrument fully in mind." *Lichter*, 334 U.S. at 782; *see also United States v. Verdugo-Urquidez*, 494 U.S. 259, 277 (1990) (Kennedy, J., concurring) ("[W]e must interpret constitutional protections in light of the undoubted power of the United States to take actions to assert its legitimate power and authority abroad."); *McCall v. McDowell*, 15 F. Cas. 1235, 1243 (C.C.D. Cal. 1867) (No. 8,673) (The Constitution is "a practical scheme of government, having all necessary power to maintain its existence and authority during peace and war, rebellion or invasion").

The current campaign against terrorism may require even broader exercises of federal power domestically. Terrorists operate within the continental United States itself, and escape detection by concealing themselves within the domestic society and economy. While, no doubt, these terrorists pose a direct military threat to the national security, their methods of infiltration and their surprise attacks on civilian and governmental facilities make it difficult to identify any front line. Unfortunately, the terrorist attacks of September 11 have created a situation in which the battlefield has occurred, and may occur, at dispersed locations and intervals within the American homeland itself. As a result, efforts to fight terrorism may require not only the usual wartime regulations of domestic affairs, but also military actions that have normally occurred abroad.

B.

In light of the well-settled understanding that constitutional constraints must give way in some respects to the exigencies of war, we think that the better view is that the Fourth Amendment does *not* apply to domestic military operations designed to deter and prevent further terrorist attacks. First, it is clear that the Fourth Amendment has never been applied to military operations overseas. In *Verdugo-Urquidez*, the Supreme Court reversed the court of appeals' holding that the Fourth Amendment applied extraterritorially to a law enforcement operation. The Court pointed out the untenable consequences of such a holding for our Government's *military* operations abroad:

> The rule adopted by the Court of Appeals would apply not only to law enforcement operations abroad, but also to other foreign policy operations which might result in "searches or seizures." The United States frequently employs Armed Forces outside this country – over 200 times in our history – for the protection of American citizens or national security. . . . Application of the Fourth Amendment to those circumstances could significantly disrupt the ability of the political branches to respond to foreign situations involving our national interest. Were respondent to prevail, aliens with no attachment to this country might well bring actions for damages to remedy claimed violations of the Fourth Amendment in foreign countries or in international waters. . . . [T]he Court of Appeals' global view of [the Fourth Amendment's] applicability would plunge [the political branches] into a sea of uncertainty as to what might be reasonable in the way of searches and seizures conducted abroad.

494 U.S. at 273-74 (citations omitted). Here, the Court demonstrated its practical concern that the Fourth Amendment not be interpreted and applied to military and foreign policy operations abroad. If things were otherwise, both political leaders and military commanders would be severely constrained if they were required to assess the "reasonableness" of any military operation beforehand, and the effectiveness of our forces would be drastically impaired. To apply the Fourth Amendment to overseas military operations would represent an extreme over-judicialization of warfare that would interfere with military effectiveness and the President's constitutional duty to prosecute a war successfully.

• • •

Id. at 245-47 (citation omitted); *cf. Katz v. United States.* 389 U.S. 347, 364 (1967) (White, J., concurring) ("We should not require the warrant procedure and the magistrate's judgment if the President of the United States or his chief legal officer, the Attorney General, has considered the requirements of national security and authorized electronic surveillance as reasonable.").

State and federal court decisions reviewing the deployment of military force domestically by State Governors to quell civil disorder and to protect the public from violent attack have repeatedly noted that the constitutional protections of the Bill of Rights do not apply to military operations in the same way that they apply to peacetime law enforcement activities. Thus, the courts have explained that "[w]ar has exigencies that cannot readily be enumerated or described, which may render it necessary for a commanding officer to subject loyal citizens, or persons who though believed to be disloyal have not acted overtly against the government, to deprivations that would under ordinary circumstances be illegal." *Commonwealth ex rel. Wadsworth v. Shortall,* 55 A. 952, 955 (Pa. 1903) (holding that in time of domestic disorder the shooting by a sentry of an approaching man who would not halt was not illegal). "[W]hatever force is requisite for the defense of the community or of individuals is also lawful. The principle runs through civil life, and has a twofold application in war – externally against the enemy, and internally as a justification for acts that are necessary for the common defense, however subversive they may be of rights which in the ordinary course of events are inviolable." *Hatfield,* 81 S.E. at 537 (internal quotations omitted) (upholding the Governor's seizure of a newspaper printing press during a time of domestic insurrection).[35]

C.

Our view that the Fourth Amendment does not apply to domestic military operations receives support from federal court cases involving the destruction of property. In a line of cases arising from several wars, the federal courts have upheld the authority of the Government, acting under the imperative military necessity, to destroy property even when it belongs to United States citizens and even when the action occurs on American soil. Such destruction of property might constitute a seizure under the Fourth Amendment. Moreover, the courts have held, even if such seizures might otherwise constitute "takings" under the Fifth Amendment, the exigent circumstances in which they occurred absolve the Government from liability. The cases articulate a general rule that "the government cannot be charged for injuries to, or destruction of, private property caused by military operations of armies in the field." *United States v. Pacific*

---

[35] *See also Powers Mercantile Co.,* 7 F. Supp. at 868 (upholding the seizure of a factory to prevent a violent attack by a mob and noting that "[u]nder military rule, constitutional rights of individuals must give way to the necessities of the situation; and the deprivation of such rights, made necessary in order to restore the community to order under the law, cannot be made the basis for injunction or redress"); *Swope,* 28 P.2d at 7 (upholding the seizure and detention of a suspected fomenter of domestic insurrection by the "military arm of the government," noting that "there is no limit [to the executive's power to safeguard public order] but the necessities and exigency of the situation" and that "in this respect *there is no difference between a public war and domestic insurrection*") (emphasis added) (quotations and citation omitted); *In re Moyer,* 85 P. 190, 193 (Colo. 1904) ("The arrest and detention of an insurrectionist, either actually engaged in acts of violence or in aiding and abetting other to commit such acts, violates none of his constitutional rights."); *In re Boyle,* 57 P. 706, 707 (Idaho 1899) (upholding the seizure and detention of a suspected rebel during time of domestic disorder).

R.R. Co., 120 U.S. 227, 239 (1887).[36]   Although these decisions arise under the Fifth Amendment rather than the Fourth, we think that they illuminate the Government's ability to "search" and "seize" even innocent United States persons and their property for reasons of overriding military necessity. For if wartime necessity justifies the Government's decision to destroy property, it certainly must also permit the Government to temporarily search and seize it.

In *United States v. Caltex, Inc. (Philippines)*, 344 U.S. 149 (1952), plaintiffs had owned oil facilities in the Philippine Islands (then a United States territory) at the time of the Japanese attack on Pearl Harbor. In the face of a rapidly deteriorating military situation in the western Pacific, United States military authorities ordered the destruction of those facilities. On December 31, 1941, while Japanese troops were entering Manila, Army personnel demolished the facilities. "All unused petroleum products were destroyed, and the facilities rendered useless to the enemy. The enemy was deprived of a valuable logistic weapon." *Id.* at 151. Although the Government voluntarily paid compensation for certain losses after the war, it refused to pay for the destruction of the terminal facilities. Quoting its earlier decision in *Pacific R.R. Co.*, 120 U.S. at 234, the Court denied compensation under the Fifth Amendment:

> The destruction or injury of private property in battle, or in the bombardment of cities and towns, and in many other ways in the war, had to be borne by the sufferers alone, as one of its consequences. Whatever would embarrass or impede the advance of the enemy, as the breaking up of roads, or the burning of bridges, or would cripple and defeat him, as destroying his means of subsistence, were lawfully ordered by the commanding general. Indeed, it was his imperative duty to direct their destruction. The necessities of the war called for and justified this. The safety of the state in such cases overrides all considerations of private loss.

Caltex, 344 U.S. at 153-54. The Court further observed that the "principles expressed" in *Pacific R.R. Co.* were

> neither novel nor startling, for the common law had long recognized that in times of imminent peril – such as when fire threatened a whole community – the sovereign could, with immunity, destroy the property of a few that the property of many and the lives of many more could be saved.

Id. at 154. The Court summed up its conclusion:

> The short of the matter is that this property, due to the fortunes of war, had become a potential weapon of great significance to the invader. It was destroyed, not appropriated for subsequent use. It was destroyed that the United States might better and sooner destroy the enemy.

---

[36] *See also Heflebower v. United States*, 21 Ct. Cl. 228, 237-38 (1886) ("[T]here is a distinction to be drawn between property used for Government purposes and property destroyed for the public safety. . . . [I]f the taking, using, or occupying was in the nature of destruction for the general welfare or incident to the inevitable ravages of war, such as the march of troops, the conflict of armies, the destruction of supplies, and whether brought about by casualty or authority, and whether on hostile or national territory, the loss, in the absence of positive legislation, must be borne by him on whom it falls, and no obligation to pay can be imputed to the Government.").

The terse language of the Fifth Amendment is no comprehensive promise that the United States will make whole all who suffer from every ravage and burden of war. This Court has long recognized that in wartime many losses must be attributed solely to the fortunes of war, and not to the sovereign.

Id. at 155-56.[37] Likewise, in *Juragua Iron Co. v. United States*, 212 U.S. 297 (1909), the court held that the United States owed no compensation to a United States corporation for the destruction of its property in a province of Cuba during the Spanish-American War. In that case, United States troops were endangered by the prevalence of yellow fever, and the military commander found it necessary to destroy all facilities, including the plaintiff's, which might contain fever germs.[38] Further, even after a Cuban city had capitulated and was under the control of United States forces during the Spanish-American War, the area was still considered "enemy's country," and property belonging to its residents, even if they were United States nationals, was held liable to uncompensated seizure, confiscation or destruction for military needs. *See Herrera v. United States*, 222 U.S. 558, 569 (1912).

Conclusion

We conclude that the President has both constitutional and statutory authority to use the armed forces in military operations, against terrorists, within the United States. We believe that these operations generally would not be subject to the constraints of the Fourth Amendment, so long as the armed forces are undertaking a military function. Even if the Fourth Amendment were to apply, however, we believe that most military operations would satisfy the Constitution's reasonableness requirement and continue to be lawful.

NO MORE RULE OF LAW

President Bush's Justification for Torture

A few months after September 11, President Bush sent out a "mass memo" that lays out why the al Qaeda and Taliban detainees were "unlawful combatants" and so the Geneva Convention calling for humane treatment of POWs did not apply to them. Well, if they're not covered by an international agreement, shouldn't they be covered by the laws of the United States and our Constitution and Bill of Rights? My point being, this situation has to fall under *somebody's* law. How they can come up with this limbo, in-between, "make up your own rules" idea is beyond belief. But I guess that's why you have lawyers, because every lawyer reads the law differently.

JUN. 17. 2004 2:27PM   LEGAL   NO. 499   P. 2

UNCLASSIFIED

THE WHITE HOUSE
WASHINGTON

February 7, 2002

MEMORANDUM FOR THE VICE PRESIDENT
               THE SECRETARY OF STATE
               THE SECRETARY OF DEFENSE
               THE ATTORNEY GENERAL
               CHIEF OF STAFF TO THE PRESIDENT
               DIRECTOR OF CENTRAL INTELLIGENCE
               ASSISTANT TO THE PRESIDENT FOR NATIONAL
                    SECURITY AFFAIRS
               CHAIRMAN OF THE JOINT CHIEFS OF STAFF

SUBJECT: Humane Treatment of al Qaeda and Taliban Detainees

1. Our recent extensive discussions regarding the status
    of al Qaeda and Taliban detainees confirm that the appli-
    cation of the Geneva Convention Relative to the Treatment
    of Prisoners of War of August 12, 1949 (Geneva) to the
    conflict with al Qaeda and the Taliban involves complex
    legal questions. By its terms, Geneva applies to conflicts
    involving "High Contracting Parties," which can only be
    states. Moreover, it assumes the existence of "regular"
    armed forces fighting on behalf of states. However, the
    war against terrorism ushers in a new paradigm, one in
    which groups with broad, international reach commit horrific
    acts against innocent civilians, sometimes with the direct
    support of states. Our Nation recognizes that this new
    paradigm -- ushered in not by us, but by terrorists --
    requires new thinking in the law of war, but thinking that
    should nevertheless be consistent with the principles of
    Geneva.

2. Pursuant to my authority as Commander in Chief and Chief
    Executive of the United States, and relying on the opinion
    of the Department of Justice dated January 22, 2002, and on
    the legal opinion rendered by the Attorney General in his
    letter of February 1, 2002, I hereby determine as follows:

    a. I accept the legal conclusion of the Department of
        Justice and determine that none of the provisions
        of Geneva apply to our conflict with al Qaeda in
        Afghanistan or elsewhere throughout the world because,
        among other reasons, al Qaeda is not a High Contracting
        Party to Geneva.

    b. I accept the legal conclusion of the Attorney General
        and the Department of Justice that I have the authority
        under the Constitution to suspend Geneva as between
        the United States and Afghanistan, but I decline to

                        NSC DECLASSIFICATION REVIEW [E.O. 12958 as amended]
                        DECLASSIFIED IN FULL ON 6/17/2004
Reason: 1.5 (d)   by R.Soubers
Declassify on: 02/07/12

UNCLASSIFIED

JUN. 17. 2004 2:27PM   LEGAL

NO. 499   r.

UNCLASSIFIED

2

exercise that authority at this time. Accordingly, I
determine that the provisions of Geneva will apply to
our present conflict with the Taliban. I reserve the
right to exercise this authority in this or future
conflicts.

c.   I also accept the legal conclusion of the Department of
Justice and determine that common Article 3 of Geneva
does not apply to either al Qaeda or Taliban detainees,
because, among other reasons, the relevant conflicts
are international in scope and common Article 3 applies
only to "armed conflict not of an international
character."

d.   Based on the facts supplied by the Department of
Defense and the recommendation of the Department of
Justice, I determine that the Taliban detainees are
unlawful combatants and, therefore, do not qualify as
prisoners of war under Article 4 of Geneva. I note
that, because Geneva does not apply to our conflict
with al Qaeda, al Qaeda detainees also do not qualify
as prisoners of war.

3.   Of course, our values as a Nation, values that we share with
many nations in the world, call for us to treat detainees
humanely, including those who are not legally entitled to
such treatment. Our Nation has been and will continue to
be a strong supporter of Geneva and its principles. As
a matter of policy, the United States Armed Forces shall
continue to treat detainees humanely and, to the extent
appropriate and consistent with military necessity, in
a manner consistent with the principles of Geneva.

4.   The United States will hold states, organizations, and
individuals who gain control of United States personnel
responsible for treating such personnel humanely and
consistent with applicable law.

5.   I hereby reaffirm the order previously issued by the
Secretary of Defense to the United States Armed Forces
requiring that the detainees be treated humanely and,
to the extent appropriate and consistent with military
necessity, in a manner consistent with the principles
of Geneva.

6.   I hereby direct the Secretary of State to communicate my
determinations in an appropriate manner to our allies, and
other countries and international organizations cooperating
in the war against terrorism of global reach.

UNCLASSIFIED

NO FREEDOM OF THE PRESS

The Military's Astounding "Media Ground Rules" for Guantanamo

Talk about infringement on the freedom of the press! When I came across these Media Ground Rules that had to be signed off on before anyone can gain access to where the detainees are being held at Guantanamo, I was shocked. By the time you memorized all these rules-and-regulations, you'd be so uptight you squeaked. What "policy?" This is the biggest snow job I've ever seen. If the media has to follow those rules, they're not even allowed to ask a question. The Guantanamo brass could have saved all that paper by taking one big sheet and stamping in large letters: MEDIA NOT ALLOWED.

I would have loved to adopt that identical policy when I was governor of Minnesota, with what I used to call "the Minnesota jackals." Let me put those rules up right outside the governor's reception room where the media comes in, all those pages as to what you have to abide by. How would that have gone over?

So forget about providing the public any insight into what's *really* going on behind the gates of our Naval Station. Which, as you'll see in the documents that follow, was enough to raise the hair on the back of anyone's head. (Presuming the head was still intact.)

A. Scope and Purpose of the Ground Rules

1. This policy establishes procedures with respect to media visits to Naval Station Guantanamo Bay, Cuba, (GTMO) and the media coverage of military commission proceedings. The Defense Department will facilitate media access to the maximum extent possible, in an effort to encourage open reporting and promote transparency, consistent with the Military Commissions Act and accompanying rules and regulations, and the need to protect operational and national security, and comply with international treaty obligations.

2. The ground rules are established to protect operational security and to ensure the security of personnel, as well as the integrity of military commission proceedings. They are also designed to provide guidance to News Media Representatives (NMR) concerning what information will be deemed to be "protected information" for purposes of these ground rules.

3. NMRs must agree to abide by the following rules as a condition of access to GTMO and military commission proceedings. Failure to comply with these ground rules could result in permanent expulsion of the NMR and/or removal of the parent news organization from further access to GTMO or to military commissions. Permanent removal of a news organization may occur where there have been repeated violations by various NMRs affiliated with the organization, or there are other strong indications that the organization does not intend to abide by the ground rules.

4. The receipt of this document does not guarantee media travel or access to GTMO operations and activities. Permitted presence on GTMO does not imply unlimited access to personnel or facilities.

5. The Office of the Assistant Secretary of Defense for Public Affairs OASD (PA) is responsible for the development and implementation of media ground rules at Guantanamo Bay. Any questions regarding their implementation should be directed to OASD (PA). These ground rules will be reviewed periodically and updated as appropriate. Any recommendations for changes should be submitted to OASD (PA).

6. Nothing in these ground rules affects criminal liability under any other provision of law.

B. Release Authority

Consistent with the media ground rules that are outlined here, the Department of Defense is the sole release authority for all military information contained in all media (e.g., audio visual, photography, graphics, sketches, etc.) gathered or produced within the Joint Task Force Guantanamo area of operation.

C. Protected Information

1. Protected Information necessarily includes classified information. Protected Information also includes (i) information the disclosure of which could reasonably be expected to cause damage to the national security, including intelligence or law enforcement sources, methods, or activities, or jeopardize the physical safety of individuals, and (ii) information subject to a properly-issued protective order by an official authorized to issue such orders by law or regulation.

2. NMRs shall not publish, release, publicly discuss, or share information gathered at GTMO, or in transit to or from GTMO on transportation provided by DoD (or other U.S. government entities), that is Protected Information for purposes of these ground rules.

3. A NMR will not be considered in violation of these ground rules for re-publishing what otherwise would be considered Protected Information, where that information was legitimately obtained in the course of newsgathering independent of any receipt of information while at GTMO, or while transiting to or from GTMO on transportation provided by DoD (or other U.S. government entities).

4. While at GTMO, and in transit to and from GTMO, NMRs may be exposed to aspects of detention and base operations the disclosure of which must be avoided for reasons of national security, force protection and compliance with international treaty obligations. These operations are part of the base operations that the general public is not invited or permitted to view. As a result, JTF-GTMO has designated aspects of these operations whose disclosure is not permitted, and NMRs at GTMO will be required, as a condition of their visits, to safeguard this information, which will be deemed Operational Protected Information. Operational Protected Information, as determined by JTF-GTMO, is identified in these ground rules.

D. General Photography and Video Limitations

1. At no time during a media visit is communication (verbal, written or other) with a detainee allowed. Attempting to communicate with a detainee and photographing or taking video of a detainee's attempts to communicate with members of the media are prohibited. If detainees become agitated at the presence of media, the media may be asked to leave for the safety and security of the detainees, NMR and the guard force.

2. Photographs or video shall **not** be taken of the following:

a. Frontal facial views, profiles, ¾ views, or any view revealing a detainee's identity.

b. Identifiable JTF-GTMO personnel, without their consent.

c. Deliberate views of security protocols including security cameras, metal detectors, locks, keys, gates, reinforced doors or other security measures.

   d.   The JTF-GTMO coastline between the Windmill Beach entry gate, east to
        Kittery Beach; this restriction includes views of Camp Iguana and the security
        gate from Windmill Beach and views of the tactical observation post from
        Kittery Beach.

   e.   Panoramic views (an unobstructed or complete view of an area) of JTF-GTMO
        camp facilities and Office of Military Commissions (OMC) facilities that reveal
        access roads, facilities layout, security borders or locations of security
        checkpoints.

   f.   Views of Checkpoint Roosevelt and Checkpoint Houston or observation post
        "New York".

   g.   Deliberate views of fuel, water, electrical power or ammunition processing or
        storage facilities from within their enclosed boundaries including close-up views
        of valves, electrical power panels, fuel or water distribution pipes or fittings.

   h.   Deliberate views of antennas, RADAR or communications facilities or
        equipment from within their marked boundaries.

   i.   Bunker facilities on either side of AV-34/Courtroom One.

   j.   Military Convoys arriving or departing OMC facilities or JTF-GTMO
        operational area.

E. Operational Security Review

   1. NMRs will submit all still and video imagery taken at JTF-GTMO to a security
review. Media members are responsible to ensure video imagery can be played to
television or played back on camera. To this end, media members are responsible for
providing compatible video format playback device for material review.

   2. An operational security review (OPSEC) of visual recordings will be conducted
daily, as required, or at a minimum prior to departure from JTF-GTMO. All images and
video are required to be screened prior to upload into any laptop and prior to release.

   3. During the OPSEC review, imagery that is determined to be in violation of these
ground rules will be deleted or cropped to achieve compliance. For photographs, the
NMR may request two (2) images per person per day be cropped to meet security
requirements. Cropping is defined as cutting off the parts of a digital photograph deemed
to be in violation. Blurring, smudging, fading, superimposing a black line or spot over
certain parts of a photograph, or any other digital manipulation is not a substitution for
cropping.

   4. Photos selected for cropping will be moved from NMR's photo storage media
(e.g., SD card) and saved onto a government computer. The original photo will be deleted
from the NMR storage media and stored on the government computer until the final

---

disposition of the photograph has been decided. The photos will then be cropped by a JTF-GTMO PA representative on the government computer, renamed and saved back to the government computer. The newly created file will then be transferred back to the NMR storage device. There is no appeal of JTF-GTMO's proposed cropping; if the NMR disagrees with the proposed cropping, the cropped image will be deleted and the original photo may be appealed to the JTF-GTMO CDR (or his or her designated military representative other than the JTF-GTMO PAO).

5. For videos, the NMR must bring his or her editing equipment to GTMO. The NMR will edit his or her video to meet security requirements in the presence of a JTF-GTMO PA representative. The editing process should take no longer then 10 minutes per day per NMR video. Disputed sections of video must be edited and stored while the JTF-GTMO PA decision is being appealed. For NMR who do not have such video editing capability, approval or deletion are the only options.

6. If the NMR disagrees with the judgment of the JTF-GTMO PAO that the photograph or video image is in violation of these ground rules, the NMR may request that a copy of the image (in compatible format) be forwarded for appeal to the JTF-GTMO CDR (or his or her designated military representative other than the JTF-GTMO PAO) who will have no more than 24 hours to review the photograph and render a final decision as to whether the photograph will be approved for publication. If the JTF-GTMO CDR (or his or her designated military representative other than the JTF-GTMO PAO) concurs with the judgment of the JTF-GTMO PAO then the image will be deleted.

F. Additional Rules and Procedures Specific to Military Commissions

1. The Defense Department will facilitate media access to military commissions to the maximum extent possible, in an effort to encourage open reporting and promote transparency, consistent with the Military Commissions Act and accompanying rules and regulations, and the need to protect operational and national security, and comply with international treaty obligations. In order to facilitate maximum access consistent with security requirements, the following Media Ground Rules have been established.

2. OASD (PA) is the sole approval authority for visits by media personnel in conjunction with military commission proceedings. OASD (PA) will coordinate media, briefings, interviews, and communications support in connection with commission proceedings.

3. In each military commission proceeding, the military judge will specify in advance what information is considered Protected Information for purposes of that proceeding. Such information, in the absence of an inadvertent disclosure, shall not be released to the media. Protected Information necessarily includes classified information. Protected Information, for purposes of commission proceedings, also includes (i) information the disclosure of which could reasonably be expected to cause damage to the national security, including intelligence or law enforcement sources, methods, or activities, or jeopardize the physical safety of individuals, and (ii) information subject to

a properly-issued protective order by an official authorized to issue such orders by law or regulation.

4. If Protected Information is inadvertently disclosed during a session, NMRs are urged to respect any temporary media embargo issued by the military judge until any disputes about the status of the information are resolved.

5. While at GTMO to attend military commission proceedings, and in transit to and from GTMO for that purpose, NMRs may be exposed to aspects of detention and base operations the disclosure of which must be avoided for reasons of national security, force protection and compliance with international treaty obligations. These operations are not an inherent part of the public proceedings that occur in the military commissions, but rather are part of the base operations that the general public is not invited or permitted to view. As a result, JTF-GTMO has designated aspects of these operations whose disclosure is not permitted, and NMRs at GTMO will be required, as a condition of their visits, to safeguard this information, which will be deemed Operational Protected Information.

• • •

3. <u>Open Sessions</u>. This will be the standard posture for most commission sessions and allows for maximum openness. The military judge will normally allow Open Proceedings when no Protected Information is being discussed and there is a low risk of inadvertent disclosure of Protected Information. During Open Sessions, no fewer than 11 media representatives will be allowed in the courtroom. Media will be appropriately debriefed if Protected Information is inadvertently disclosed during a courtroom session and will be urged not to use the information. The remaining media representatives will be allowed to view sessions via CCTV in the viewing area of the GTMO MOC.

4. <u>Open Sessions With Delay</u>. In some cases, the military judge may determine that there is a significant risk of Protected Information being inadvertently discussed or inadvertently disclosed. In such cases involving Courtroom One, all media will view the proceedings from the GTMO MOC, where they will receive a feed from the CCTV. The CCTV feed will have a delay to allow security officers to interrupt the feed in the event of the disclosure of Protected Information. In such cases involving Courtroom Two, where the media and public observe proceedings from behind a glass partition, there will be a delay in the transmission of the audio portion of the proceedings to allow security officers to interrupt the feed in the event of the disclosure of Protected Information. These sessions are designed to continue to permit media access when a session would otherwise be closed.

5. <u>Closed Sessions</u>. The military judge will normally order Closed Sessions, or portions of Sessions, only when Protected Information is planned to be discussed. During Closed Sessions, no CCTV feed will be provided and no media will be in the courtroom. Procedural information on the session will be provided to the media members whenever possible, though some details may be excluded. It is anticipated that this procedure will only be used when absolutely necessary, and in accordance with the provisions of the Military Commissions Act. Whenever possible, a brief summary of unclassified information will be provided at the end of a closed session.

53&54

TORTURE TECHNIQUES

The Detainees at Guantanamo

We all saw the horrendous photos and videos from Abu Ghraib prison in Iraq. Not as well known are the Department of Defense's "Counter-Resistance Strategies" for the detainees being held at our Guantanamo base in Cuba. The first document here is DOD's official request for approval of various methods under several categories. The second has Rumsfeld's signature, along with his personal handwritten note that says: "However, I stand for 8–10 hours a day. Why is standing limited to 4 hours?" He's a real stand-and-deliver guy, I guess.

I simply find this appalling that the United States of America would engage in the practice of torture. We're supposed to be the country everyone else looks up to. When you participate in this kind of behavior, forget that! When it happens to us, we'll have no reason to bitch, because if we practice torture the other side will too. The laws of humanity ought to be higher than the laws of war, don't you think?

The card they're playing, from Rumsfeld on down, is that somehow Guantanamo isn't on this earth, because it's not in the U.S. or I guess anywhere outside our base in Cuba. Is this some sort of Land of Oz? We treat Charles Manson better than we do the detainees at Guantanamo, and yet the detainees have never been convicted of anything. They never stood trial, never had their day in court. But I guess Manson's different because he's an American citizen.

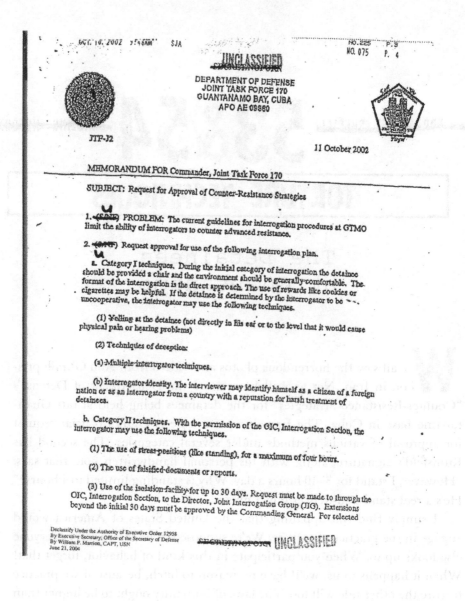

OCT. 10. 2002   9:46AM   SJA   NO. 225   P. 9
                                                                          NO. 075   P. 4

UNCLASSIFIED

DEPARTMENT OF DEFENSE
JOINT TASK FORCE 170
GUANTANAMO BAY, CUBA
APO AE 09860

JTF-J2   11 October 2002

MEMORANDUM FOR Commander, Joint Task Force 170

SUBJECT: Request for Approval of Counter-Resistance Strategies

1. (S/NF) PROBLEM: The current guidelines for interrogation procedures at GTMO limit the ability of interrogators to counter advanced resistance.

2. (S/NF) Request approval for use of the following interrogation plan.

a. Category I techniques. During the initial category of interrogation the detainee should be provided a chair and the environment should be generally comfortable. The format of the interrogation is the direct approach. The use of rewards like cookies or cigarettes may be helpful. If the detainee is determined by the interrogator to be uncooperative, the interrogator may use the following techniques.

(1) Yelling at the detainee (not directly in his ear or to the level that it would cause physical pain or hearing problems)

(2) Techniques of deception:

(a) Multiple interrogator techniques.

(b) Interrogator identity. The interviewer may identify himself as a citizen of a foreign nation or as an interrogator from a country with a reputation for harsh treatment of detainees.

b. Category II techniques. With the permission of the OIC, Interrogation Section, the interrogator may use the following techniques.

(1) The use of stress positions (like standing), for a maximum of four hours.

(2) The use of falsified documents or reports.

(3) Use of the isolation facility for up to 30 days. Request must be made to through the OIC, Interrogation Section, to the Director, Joint Interrogation Group (JIG). Extensions beyond the initial 30 days must be approved by the Commanding General. For selected

SECRET//NOFORN   UNCLASSIFIED

SECRET/NOFORN

JTF 170-J2
SUBJECT: Request for Approval of Counter-Resistance Strategies

detainees, the OIC, Interrogation Section, will approve all contacts with the detainee, to include medical visits of a non-emergent nature.

(4) Interrogating the detainee in an environment other than the standard interrogation booth.

(5) Deprivation of light and auditory stimuli.

(6) The detainee may also have a hood placed over his head during transportation and questioning. The hood should not restrict breathing in any way and the detainee should be under direct observation when hooded.

(7) The use of 20-hour interrogations.

(8) Removal of all comfort items (including religious items).

(9) Switching the detainee from hot rations to MREs.

(10) Removal of clothing.

(11) Forced grooming (shaving of facial hair etc..)

(12) Using detainees individual phobias (such as fear of dogs) to induce stress.

c. Category III techniques. Techniques in this category may be used only by submitting a request through the Director, JIG, for approval by the Commanding General with appropriate legal review and information to Commander, USSOUTHCOM. These techniques are required for a very small percentage of the most uncooperative detainees (less than 3%). The following techniques and other aversive techniques, such as those used in U.S. military interrogation resistance training or by other U.S. government agencies, may be utilized in a carefully coordinated manner to help interrogate exceptionally resistant detainees. Any or these techniques that require more than light grabbing, poking, or pushing, will be administered only by individuals specifically trained in their safe application.

(1) The use of scenarios designed to convince the detainee that death or severely painful consequences are imminent for him and/or his family.

(2) Exposure to cold weather or water (with appropriate medical monitoring).

(3) Use of a wet towel and dripping water to induce the misperception of suffocation.

SECRET/NOFORN   UNCLASSIFIED
2

UNCLASSIFIED

GENERAL COUNSEL OF THE DEPARTMENT OF DEFENSE
1600 DEFENSE PENTAGON
WASHINGTON, D. C. 20301-1800

2002 DEC -2 AM 11: 03

OFFICE OF THE
SECRETARY OF DEFENSE

ACTION MEMO

November 27, 2002 (1:00 PM)

DEPSEC_____

GENERAL COUNSEL

FOR: SECRETARY OF DEFENSE

FROM: William J. Haynes II, General Counsel

SUBJECT: Counter-Resistance Techniques

- The Commander of USSOUTHCOM has forwarded a request by the Commander of Joint Task Force 170 (now JTF GTMO) for approval of counter-resistance techniques to aid in the interrogation of detainees at Guantanamo Bay (Tab A).

- The request contains three categories of counter-resistance techniques, with the first category the least aggressive and the third category the most aggressive (Tab B).

- I have discussed this with the Deputy, Doug Feith and General Myers. I believe that all join in my recommendation that, as a matter of policy, you authorize the Commander of USSOUTHCOM to employ, in his discretion, only Categories I and II and the fourth technique listed in Category III ("Use of mild, non-injurious physical contact such as grabbing, poking in the chest with the finger, and light pushing").

- While all Category III techniques may be legally available, we believe that, as a matter of policy, a blanket approval of Category III techniques is not warranted at this time. Our Armed Forces are trained to a standard of interrogation that reflects a tradition of restraint.

RECOMMENDATION: That SECDEF approve the USSOUTHCOM Commander's use of those counter-resistance techniques listed in Categories I and II and the fourth technique listed in Category III during the interrogation of detainees at Guantanamo Bay.

SECDEF DECISION:

Approved _____ Disapproved _____ Other _____

Attachments
As stated

cc: CJCS, USD(P)

However, I stand for 8-10 hours a day. Why is standing limited to 4 hours?

D.R. DEC 0 2 2002

Page 1 of 2
X040300-02

UNCLASSIFIED

DRUG ABUSE

A Medical Experiment on the Detainees

I f you thought government experiments in behavior control ended in the 1970s, guess again. It's recently come out that the Pentagon forced all the detainees at Guantanamo prison to take high doses of a drug called mefloquine. Supposedly it's used to combat malaria, but that didn't seem to make any difference. Our military brass knew that mefloquine had severe side effects, like suicidal thoughts, hallucinations, and anxiety.

To me, this shows the continuing influence of those "experts" we brought here from Germany after World War Two. Here you have doctors stating that you need to know the complete background of the patient before using this substance—and they're injecting these people with this drug as soon as they're checked in!

The first document here, from 2002, shows that "standard inprocessing orders for detainees" included 1,250 mg of mefloquine, five times higher than the dose given to people as a preventative. And it's being given not for its intended purpose, but to study its intended side effects! I'm speechless. What ever happened to the physician's oath to "do no harm"?

In 2010, Seton Hall University School of Law's Center for Policy & Research released a study about all this, and I'm including the Executive Summary.

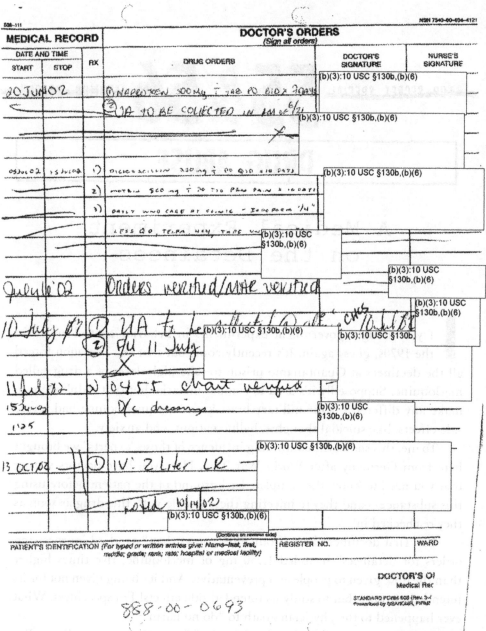

HEALTH RECORD	CHRONOLOGICAL RECORD OF MEDICAL CARE

DATE	SYMPTOMS, DIAGNOSIS, TREATMENT, TREATING ORGANIZATION (Sign each page)

JTF –160, Medical Department, Guantanamo Bay, Cuba 09593

6/18/02

STANDARD INPROCESSING ORDERS FOR DETAINEES:

1. Mefloquine 750 mg PO now, 500 mg PO in 12 hours

2. Albendazole 400mg PO once

3. Chest X-ray: PA

4. LABS:

	Hep A IgM
Hep B surface antigen/antibody	G6PD
Hep C - total	Serum (draw 2 extra red tops)
HIV	Hep B core antibody
Malaria Smear and PCR	

Circle if indicated: Consults:

1. AFB Smear QAM x 3   Needs reading glasses? Y or (N)
                                                                Optometry
2. Td .5ml IM once   General Surgery

3. Tetanus IG 250 Units IM once   Orthopedic Surgery

4. PPD – read in 48 to 72 hours   Dental

5. Additional Orders:

UA in am — ordered   (b)(3):10 USC §130b,(b)   (b)(3):10 USC §130b,(b)

Zantac 150 mg po bid — ordered

(b)(3):10 USC §130b,(b)(6)

Staff Signature: (b)(3):10 USC §130h

Signature: _____

(Medical Officer or Independent Duty Corpsman)

GTMO JMG 18

Drug Abuse: An exploration of the government's use of mefloquine at Guantanamo

Seton Hall University School of Law
Center for Policy and Research

Executive Summary

Mefloquine is an antimalarial drug that has long been known to cause severe neuropsychological adverse effects such as anxiety, paranoia, hallucinations, aggression, psychotic behavior, mood changes, depression, memory impairment, convulsions, loss of coordination (ataxia), suicidal ideation, and possibly suicide, particularly in patients with a history of mental illness. A prescribing physician must exercise caution and informed judgment when weighing the risks and potential benefits of prescribing the drug. To administer this drug with its severe potential side effects without a malaria diagnosis and without taking a patient's mental health history is not medically justified. Yet as a matter of official policy, the standard operating procedure implemented by the United States military at Guantanamo Bay was to administer high doses of mefloquine to detainees whether or not any use of the drug was medically appropriate and without consideration of the detainees' mental health.

It is clear that the military employed a medically inappropriate treatment regime at Guantanamo Bay (GTMO). It is less clear why, although the available evidence supports several possible conclusions. In view of the continued and unexplained refusal of the government to release full medical records for all detainees, it is not possible to determine whether this conduct was gross malpractice or deliberate misuse of the drug. In either case, it does not appear plausible from the available evidence that mefloquine was given to treat malaria. This suggests a darker possibility: that the military gave detainees the drug specifically to bring about the adverse side effects, either as part of enhanced interrogation techniques, experimentation in behavioral modification, or torture for some other purpose. While this Report does not reach a conclusion about the actual motives for this course of conduct, it does explore the legal rules that would apply were it determined that mefloquine was administered not to treat malaria but rather to exploit the neuropsychiatric effects of the drug.

Findings:

This Report demonstrates that the U.S. military routinely administered doses of mefloquine to detainees upon their arrival at GTMO without medical justification:

- 1250 mg of mefloquine was given to all detainees as a standard measure during inprocessing.
- Mefloquine is used for treatment of malaria only in mild to moderate cases of infection with the p. vivax or p. falciparum parasite.
- At GTMO, mefloquine was given to detainees before testing them for malaria, without regard for whether the detainee actually had malaria at all, let alone whether he carried one of the parasites treatable by mefloquine.

- The standard of care rejects administering mefloquine to persons with a history of mental illness or a family history of mental illness, due to a greatly increased risk of severe adverse side effects for such persons.
- At GTMO, mefloquine was given to detainees without regard to prior mental health history or family mental health history.

This Report further demonstrates that the U.S. military knew, and any competent medical professional would have known, of the severe side effects caused by mefloquine:

- Mefloquine was first developed by the United States military.
- Mefloquine is a quinolone, a drug family the CIA experimented with under a project called MKULTRA that studied psychotropic drugs for behavioral modification for use as a weapon and interrogation tool.
- As of 2002, Roche USA, the manufacturer of mefloquine under the brand name Lariam, warned of its contraindications and at least some of its severe side effects on the drug's package insert.
- Beginning at least as early as 1990, multiple peer-reviewed medical studies documented the severe adverse effects associated with mefloquine.

While it is impossible to make definitive conclusions as to the purposes for this policy without additional information, particularly detainee medical records, the available evidence may support one of several possible conclusions:

- Gross medical malpractice: If government intended this mefloquine regime for malaria treatment and control, it was done in a manner that jeopardized the health and perhaps the lives of the detainees and that violated basic standards of medical care.

- Mefloquine was given in order to bring about the adverse effects for one of three reasons. Any of these would likely satisfy the legal definition of torture as articulated by the Department of Justice in 2002.

    o As part of a program of enhanced interrogation, the psychotropic effects of mefloquine may have been intended as an aid to breaking a detainee's resistance. This would be the psychological equivalent of waterboarding.
    o As part of an experimental study to gather data on the side effects of mefloquine.
    o As a punitive measure.

Methodology

This Report documents the administration of mefloquine to detainees and establishes that the U.S. military's administration was a violation of normal standards of medical care. The Center for Policy and Research at Seton Hall School of Law typically issues reports based on government documents. In this case, however, that has proved impossible because the government has continually refused to release detainee's medical records to the detainees or their attorneys. The only medical record available is that of ISN 693.

Additionally, two pages of the inprocessing form for ISN 760 are available and were analyzed. In order to supplement these sources, the Center's Research Fellows analyzed other publicly-available documents. These include contemporaneous statements by government authorities regarding malaria treatment practices at GTMO, Standard Operating Procedures, and published, peer reviewed medical studies.

***

I. Mefloquine was not given to detainees in a manner consistent with malaria treatment. Mefloquine is an antimalarial drug that can be used for prophylaxis or for treatment with different dosages and administration for each. The dosage administered and the timing of each dose of mefloquine to detainees suggests that the military may have used it for treatment purposes without first ascertaining whether the detainee actually had malaria. It is highly likely that the military was treating uninfected individuals with high doses of a dangerous drug.

The prophylactic dosage of mefloquine, 250 mg, is much smaller than the treatment dose given to GTMO detainees, 1250 mg, and is administered once per week as opposed to the single dose1 used for treatment purposes.2 Severe adverse side effects do occur during prophylactic use, but adverse effects during use for treatment are far more common and more severe, probably due to the larger dosage. Use of mefloquine, even when used to treat a confirmed case of the disease, is contraindicated3 when the patient has a history of certain disorders.4

Detainees were given 1250 mg of mefloquine during inprocessing at GTMO; 750 mg as an initial dose and 500 mg 12 hours later.5 There is no indication that the routine administration of mefloquine to arriving detainees considered each detainee's medical history.6 Administering the drug at the higher treatment dose without previously determining the need for any treatment was a dramatic departure from the accepted standard of medical care.7 Doctors have widely prescribed mefloquine, commercially sold as Lariam by manufacturer Roche USA, throughout the United States and elsewhere as a prophylactic against malaria infection.
10 Mefloquine can cross the blood-brain barrier,11 and has a relatively long half-life at 15 to 33 days until elimination.12 This means that the drug can enter brain tissue and remains in the body for a long period of time. As Dr. G. Richard Olds, an internationally recognized tropical disease specialist and Founding Dean of the University of California at Riverside School of Medicine, told the Center, "Mefloquine is fat soluble and as a result it does build up in the body and has a very long half-life. This is important since a massive dose of this drug is not easily corrected and the 'side effects' of the drug could last for weeks or months." Dr. Olds's view is well supported by the medical literature reviewed by the Center for this Report.

A. Side Effects Can Be Severe
Mefloquine, at any dose, is known to cause adverse neuropsychiatric effects such as anxiety, paranoia, hallucinations, aggression, psychotic behavior, mood changes, depression, memory impairment, convulsions, loss of coordination (ataxia), suicidal ideation, and possibly suicide.14 As many as 25% of persons who have taken mefloquine reported such severe side effects.15 These neuropsychiatric side effects are more prevalent

and more severe in patients with a history of certain disorders and conditions or when taken in combination with certain medications, requiring careful prescribing that is dependent on a thorough and complete review of each patient's medical history.16

* * *

II. Mefloquine Was Given to Detainees Without Regard for Necessity or Contraindications

Upon a detainee's arrival at GTMO, military personnel administered 1250 mg of mefloquine to each detainee as part of standard in-processing orders, according to GTMO Medical Standard Operating Procedures (SOPs).48 This is corroborated in practice by government medical records for two detainees.49 Very few medical records have ever been released for GTMO detainees, and those the government has released are heavily redacted and may be incomplete.50 Based on the documents that are available, however, it is clear that detainees have been given a high dose of this powerful anti-malarial drug that potentially causes severe neuropsychological side effects. Since the dosage far exceeds the recommended dose for prophylactic purposes, the only medical justification would be particularized reason to believe the detainees were suffering from malaria. Further, while at least some detainees were tested for malaria, the mefloquine was seemingly administered in advance of and without regard to the results of the test. In any event, there does not appear to have been any individualized assessment of medical and psychological history prior to mefloquine administration for the purpose of avoiding administration to detainees with contraindications to mefloquine, which would render the administration of the drug inappropriate even if malaria infection were confirmed.

* * *

B. The Standard In-processing Orders Form
Mefloquine was given to each detainee as a matter of standard procedure without waiting for the results of any test for malaria. This is further made clear by an examination of the "Standard In-processing Orders" form, presumably applied uniformly for all detainees.64 The form includes administration of mefloquine at the 1250 mg dosage, split into two distributions: "750 mg PO [taken orally] now, 500 mg PO in 12 hours."65

The form is structured as a checklist, with numbered items circled as they were completed. The first item on the list is "1. Mefloquine," followed by the dosage.66 On both ISN 693's form and ISN 760's form, number "1." is circled, indicating the mefloquine dose was administered.67

* * *

C. No Malaria In Cuba
According to the Centers for Disease Control and Prevention, there is no malaria in Cuba.90 "Malaria is not a threat in Guantanamo Bay," according to an official memorandum on the "Department of Defense Operational Use of Mefloquine."91 U.S. military personnel and contractors are not prescribed any anti-malarial medication for assignment to GTMO.92

57&58&59

ENHANCED INTERROGATION

The Paper Trail on the CIA's Destruction of 92 Torture Videos

On April 15, 2010, a FOIA lawsuit filed by the ACLU managed to pry out of the CIA a series of documents related to the destruction of ninety-two videos of "enhanced interrogation" of al Qaeda detainees, in particular Abu Zabaydah, who'd been transferred to a "black prison" in Thailand in 2002. He ended up being waterboarded eighty-three times in a month, deprived of sleep for days on end, subjected to extreme cold while being held naked in his cell, and forced to listen to near-deafening levels of music.

What you're about to read is an inside look at how and why the CIA decided that these videos had to be wiped out—even though the many redactions made by the Agency make you wonder what else is being covered up. The first memo is from October 2002, when the CIA began discussing the sensitivity of these "interrogation sessions." The next document describes the destruction of the ninety-two video tapes that took place on November 9, 2005.

The next day, two emails were sent to CIA Executive Director Dusty Foggo by someone who's never been identified. (Foggo later got convicted of bribery in the scandal involving California Congressman Duke Cunningham). The emails show, among other things, that the CIA interrogator was the very one who wanted the tapes destroyed.

All this is pretty self-explanatory. Clearly they could never allow the American people to see what they're doing to these detainees so you destroy the evidence. But what looms even larger is that there *was* evidence, and of such a nature that required it to be destroyed. That tells you how bad it must have been.

The destruction of the tapes was approved by Jose Rodriguez Jr., who headed up Clandestine Services for the CIA. In November 2010, federal prosecutor John Durham announced he was not going to charge Rodriguez for authorizing the videotapes' disappearance. Rodriguez' attorney called his client "an American hero, a true patriot who only wanted to protect his people and his country."

You be the judge.

SECRET

ROUTE COMMENTS:

PAGE 001
TOT: 251945Z OCT 02

SECRET

STAFF
TO: IMMEDIATE [REDACTED] INFO [REDACTED] DIRECTOR.

FROM: DDO INFO [REDACTED]

SLUGS:
SUBJECT: EYES ONLY - DISPOSITION OF VIDEOTAPES

REF: A.
      B.

TEXT:

    1. ACTION REQUIRED: PLEASE REVIEW BELOW GUIDANCE.

    2. THIS CABLE HAS BEEN COORDINATED WITH [REDACTED]
[REDACTED] ON 05 SEPTEMBER 2002, HQS ELEMENTS DISCUSSED
THE DISPOSITION OF THE VIDEOTAPES DOCUMENTING INTERROGATION
SESSIONS WITH ((ABU ZUBAYDAH)) THAT ARE CURRENTLY BEING STORED AT
[REDACTED] WITH PARTICULAR CONSIDERATION TO THE MATTERS DESCRIBED IN
REF A PARAS 2 AND 3 AND REF B PARA 4. AS REFLECTED IN REFS, THE
PARTICIPANTS OF THIS MEETING CONCLUDED THAT THE CONTINUED
RETENTION OF THESE TAPES, WHICH IS NOT/NOT REQUIRED BY LAW,
REPRESENTS A SERIOUS SECURITY RISK FOR [REDACTED] OFFICERS
RECORDED ON THEM, AND FOR ALL [REDACTED] OFFICERS PRESENT AND
PARTICIPATING IN [REDACTED] OPERATIONS; THEY ALSO RECOGNIZED THE
ADDITIONAL CONCERNS DESCRIBED IN REFS, SUCH AS THE DANGER TO ALL
AMERICANS SHOULD THE TAPES BE COMPROMISED. IN THIS POSSIBLE
CIRCUMSTANCE, THERE ALSO EXISTS A CLEAR DANGER THAT THE OFFICERS
PICTURED ON THE TAPES COULD BE SUBJECT TO RETRIBUTION FROM
AL-QA'IDA ELEMENTS. ACCORDINGLY, THE PARTICIPANTS DETERMINED THAT
THE BEST ALTERNATIVE TO ELIMINATE THOSE SECURITY AND ADDITIONAL
RISKS IS TO DESTROY THESE TAPES [REDACTED] THE BEST MECHANISM
FOR DESTROYING THE TAPES FOLLOWS:

    A. DEPLOYMENT OF [REDACTED] A

SECRET

(12/28/07) TCG:00392

0A053-392-7

~~SECRET~~

███████████████ WILL BE DEPLOYED ██████████ AT THE EARLIEST
OPPORTUNITY TO BE PRESENT AND ASSIST IN DESTROYING THE TAPES
COMPLETELY:

    B. POLICY ON USAGE OF TAPES: STARTING IMMEDIATELY, IT IS
NOW HQS POLICY THAT ██████ RECORD ONE DAY'S WORTH OF SESSIONS ON
ONE VIDEOTAPE FOR OPERATIONAL CONSIDERATIONS, UTILIZE THE TAPE
WITHIN THAT SAME DAY FOR PURPOSES OF REVIEW AND NOTE TAKING, AND
RECORD THE NEXT DAY'S SESSIONS ON THE SAME TAPE. THUS, IN EFFECT,
THE SINGLE TAPE IN USE ██████ WILL CONTAIN ONLY ONE DAY'S
WORTH OF INTERROGATION SESSIONS. (A SPECIFIC EXCEPTION TO THIS
TIMETABLE MAY BE MADE WHERE REQUIRED IN THE CASE OF A PARTICULAR
DAY'S SESSION.)

    3. HQS IS CONFIDENT THAT ██████ UNDERSTANDS THE REASONING
BEHIND ABOVE POLICY FOR THE VIDEOTAPES. THIS WILL ENSURE THE
PROTECTION AND SAFETY OF ██ OFFICERS AT ██████████ HQS WILL ADVISE
DETAILS OF THE DEPLOYMENT OF THE ██████████ SEPARATELY.
THANK YOU AND BEST REGARDS.

    4. ████████████████████████████████████

END OF MESSAGE   ~~SECRET~~

~~SECRET~~

(12/28/07) TCG:00393

TOP SECRET/ ████ /SI//ORCON/NOFORN//MR

Document: ████████████ 09 NOV 2005
Subject: EYES ONLY FOR ██████ - DESTRUCTION OF ██████ VIDEO TAPES

ACTION: ██████████████████████████████████
EYESONLY, ██████████████████████████████████
██
████████████████████

TO: PRIORITY DIRECTOR.

FOR: ██████████████████████
████████████████████████

SUBJECT: EYES ONLY FOR ██████ - DESTRUCTION OF ██████ VIDEO TAPES

REF: A ████████████████████████████
B, ████████████████████████

TEXT:

██
██

1. ACTION REQUIRED: FYI

2. PER REF A, ALL 92 ██████ VIDEO TAPES WERE DESTROYED ON 09
NOVEMBER. DESTRUCTION ACTIVITY WAS INITIATED AT 0910HRS AND
COMPLETED AT 1230HRS.

3. FILE: ██████████

██
████████████████████

CABLETYPE: ██████████████████

END OF MESSAGE ██████████

Document: ████████████ 08 NOV 2005
Subject: EYES ONLY FOR ██████ - DDO APPROVAL TO DESTROY ██████ VIDEO
TAPES

TOP SECRET/ ████ /SI//ORCON/NOFORN//MR

2007-8808-IG001867

000611

SECRET//MR

Attachment classified as above. Classification of transmittal document (when separated from attachment): SECRET

11/10/2005 05:48 PM   To: Dusty Foggo
                               cc:
                               Subject: short backgrounder

Dusty - at both the DO update and right after the G-7 the issue of the Abu Zubaydah tapes were discussed. You may recall these concern the tapes which were made during his interrogations at ███ and being held by the ███ of that country. It was recommended to previous DO management that the tapes be destroyed. This was after the IG had reviewed them and deemed that transcripts were an accurate reflection of what happened and they were no longer needed from their perspective ███ ███ For whatever reason it seems, previous DO asked (nfi) someone (nfi) downtown and as a result got cold feet and did not order them destroyed Current ███ not wanting - smartly - to continue to be custodian of these things was advised to send in a cable asking for guidance. He did so. Guidance just sent - cleared by IG, DDO and ███ - told him to destroy. He did so. Rizzo found out today this had occurred as was upset - apparently because he had not been consulted - not sure if there was another reason. He raised at DO update but was 'calmed' (only slightly) when told ███ had approved. Jose raised with Porter and myself and ███ after G-7 and explained that he (Jose) felt it was extremely important to destroy the tapes and that if there was any heat he would take it (PG laughed and said that actually, it would be he, PG, who would take the heat.) PG, however, agreed with the decision. As Jose said, the heat from destoying is nothing compared to what it would be if the tapes ever got into public domain - he said that out of context, they would make us look terrible; it would be 'devastating' to us. All in the room agreed but noted that we needed to find out Rizzds concern and whether it was substantive or just being 'left out.' Jose was going to pursue this. Believe this is end of it, but in case it comes up, you need the background. ███

SECRET//MR

11/10/2005 07:25 PM   To: Dusty Foggo
                               cc:
                               Subject: short backgrounder - part 2

Dusty - ok - on the Zabaydah tapes - - I am no longer feeling comfortable. While I understand Jose's 'decision' (and believe the tapes were bad news) I was just told by Rizzo that ███ DID NOT concur on the cable - it was never discussed with him (this is perhaps worse news, in that we may have 'improperly' destroyed something). In fact, it is unclear now whether the IG did as well. Cable was apparently drafted by ███ and released by Jose; they are only two names on it, so I am told by Rizzo. Either ███ lied to Jose about 'clearing' with ███ and IG (my bet) or Jose misstated the facts. (It is not without relevance that ███ figured prominently in the tapes, as ███ was in charge of ███ at the time and clearly would want the tapes destroyed.) Rizzo is clearly upset, because he was on the hook to notify Harriet Miers of the status of the tapes because it was she who had asked to be advised before any action was taken Apparently, Rizzo called Harriet this afternoon and she was livid, which he said was actually unusual for her. Rizzo does not think this is likely to just go away. Rizzo has advised ███ of this latest 'wrinkle.' Sounds like we will regroup on Monday.

AN ORDERED BEHEADING

Decapitation of a Detainee by U.S. Forces in Iraq

And you think these officially sanctioned policies didn't rub off on our troops on the ground in Iraq? I wish I could say that was the case. When WikiLeaks released some 400,000 documents about the ongoing war in Iraq, they contained some pretty grim disclosures, including this one about American forces decapitating an Iraqi on order of their higher-ups. You can only go by what the document says as to whether this really happened or not, but it's definitely disturbing to read and think about.

___ DETAILED DESCRIPTION OF EVENT: ON 25MAY09, MAJOR ___ (SWAT CDR) AND COL (___) TOLD -___ LEADERSHIP THAT THEY WERE GOING TO DELIVER TWO DETAINEES TO ___ IN THE NORTH BECAUSE THERE WAS MORE INCRIMINATING EVIDENCE ON THE TWO DETAINEES IN ___ THAN IN HADITHAH. WHILE ___ NORTH, MAJ ___ HIS CONVOY TO PULL OVER AND TRANSFER THE TWO DETAINEES TO HIS UNCLE AND FOUR BROTHERS. ACCORDING TO COL , ___ IP FOUND ONE OF THE DETAINEES DECAPITATED AND THE OTHER WAS RELEASED BY MAJ ' ___ MEMBERS. MAJ ___ ˊCURRENTLY IN IP CUSTODY.

OVER A YEAR AGO MAJ ___ RELIEVED AS HADITHAH SWAT CDR DUE TO HIS ALLEGED INVOLVEMENT IN THE RAPING OF A FEMALE LOCAL NATIONAL. THE BEHEADED DETAINEE IS REPORTED TO BE THE BROTHER OF THE RAPED FEMALE WHO ALLEGEDLY KILLED MAJ ' ___ IN RETALIATION FOR THE RAPING OF HIS ___.

HN/MMA

EMBASSY CABLES

The State Department's Take on Drug Money Leaving Afghanistan

The WikiLeaks cache of State Department cables contains quite a few about our war in Afghanistan, but none more revealing than what our diplomats really know about the country's president, Hamid Karzai. One secret cable talks about how he'd released 150 of the 629 detainees that the coalition had transferred to Afghan custody since 2007—and pardoned five border police who were caught with 273 pounds of heroin in their vehicle and already been sentenced to prison. Karzai's brother is portrayed as a corrupt drug baron.

It's time we faced facts: fighting the Taliban over there is at the same time propping up the biggest drug-based regime in the world. The cable I'm reprinting here is all about how the money gets smuggled out of Afghanistan to countries like Dubai. And be sure to catch point number 6, about how our Drug Enforcement folks got a bit suspicious of the Afghan vice president entering the country with $52 million early in 2009.

Monday, 19 October 2009, 13:58
S E C R E T SECTION 01 OF 02 KABUL 003364
SIPDIS
DEPT PASS TO S/SRAP, S/CT, EEB, and SCA/A
EO 12958 DECL: 10/19/2019
TAGS EINV,EFIN, KTFN, PGOV, AF
SUBJECT: <u>AFGHANISTAN</u>: CAPITAL FLIGHT AND ITS IMPACT ON FUTURE
STABILITY
REF: A. KABUL 2791 B. KABUL 3326
Classified By: CDDEA Ambassador E. Anthony Wayne for reasons 1.4 (b) and (d).

Summary

1. The US ambassador describes the flight od capital out of the country, including one incident in which the then vice-president flew into Dubai with $52m in cash. According to confidential reports, more than $190 million left Kabul airport for Dubai during July, August, and September 2009. Actual amounts could be much larger. Key passages highlighted in yellow.

2. <u>Read related article</u>

1.(S) SUMMARY: Afghanistan's is a cash-based economy, relying on historic trade linkages with neighboring and regional partners. Given Afghanistan's strategic location, ongoing conflict, and deep involvement in illicit trade (e.g., narcotics), as well as some neighboring country currency exchange policies, vast amounts of cash come and go from the country on a weekly, monthly, and annual basis. Before the August 20 election, $600 million in banking system withdrawals were reported; however, in recent months, some $200 million has flowed back into the country. In terms of total money leaving the country, analysts are uncertain whether it is generated within Afghanistan or is moving through Afghanistan from other countries such as <u>Pakistan</u> (Pakistan's strict currency controls makes smuggling through Kabul International Airport (KIA) an attractive option). Experts also do not know the ratio of licit and illicit monies leaving the country. Given Afghanistan's general political uncertainty, lack of credible and safe investment opportunities, and unsettled election, it appears that individuals moved more money than normal out of the Afghan banking sector and country as a hedge before the elections. While some of the money appears to be returning, Mission -- with support from Washington agencies and other posts in the region -- will work to closely monitor the cash movements, both as a sign of public confidence in GIRoA and for possible illicit financial activities. End summary.

Recent Trends

----

2. (S) *While reports vary widely, records obtained from Kabul International Airport (KIA) support suspicions large amounts of physical cash transit from Kabul to Dubai on a weekly, monthly, and annual basis. According to confidential reports, more than $190 million left Kabul for Dubai through KIA during July, August, and September. Actual amounts, however, could be much larger.* An official claiming first-hand knowledge recently told the Treasury Attache some

$75 million transited through KIA bound for Dubai in one day during the month of July. The primary currencies identified at the airport for these three months include (in declining order): Saudi riyals, Euros, U.S. dollars, and UAE dirhams. Some Pakistani rupees and British pounds were also declared, but in much smaller amounts. Comparatively, in 2008, approximately $600 million was declared at KIA and another 100 million Euros and 80 million British pounds were declared bound for Dubai, according to available reports compiled by the Central Bank's Financial Intelligence Unit. According to our sources, established couriers primarily use Pamir Airlines, which is owned by Kabul Bank and influential Afghans such as Mahmood Karzai and Mohammad Fahim who is President Hamid Karzai's current vice-presidential running mate.

One Factor: Election Unease

----

3. (S) In an October 7 meeting, Afghan Central Bank Governor Abdul Qadeer Fitrat stressed there are no indications of significant capital flight. He pointed to a stable exchange rate and increasing assets in the formal financial system as supporting his perspective. Fitrat also mentioned that the formal banking system is well capitalized and the regulatory capital ratio of all banking institutions is above the minimum threshold (12 percent of risk-weighted assets.) Nevertheless, Fitrat did note the Central Bank was aware roughly $600 million had left Afghanistan's banking system before the elections, due, he said, tainty as to the outcome of the election and the prospects for the new government. Fitrat could not say what percentage of this money actually left the country. (Note: Nor are there statistics showing how much was withdrawn or transferred through the more informal hawala network. End note.) As of October 7, more than $200 million has returned to the banking sector according to Fitrat. The Central Bank Governor restated this figure in an October 13 meeting between Fitrat and the Coordinating Director for Development and Economic Affairs (ref B).

4. (C) Separately, and in the same timeframe as the meeting with Fitrat, CEOs from several leading banks approached the Treasury Attache with concerns over significant cash withdrawals and wire transfers to other accounts in Dubai and Europe. In separate meetings October 12, several bankers reported deposits are growing and appeared positive about future prospects. However, the various bankers noted widespread uncertainty about the ongoing election process and overall security situation will likely continue to spook Afghanistan's existing and potential investors, and as a result, undermine growth. One experienced banker flatly said no legitimate business person would keep significant sums of money in Afghanistan right now given the overwhelming risks of doing so.

KABUL 00003364 002 OF 002

Illicit Versus Licit

----

5. (C) Taking capital out of Afghanistan (physically through cash or value or by using wire transfer) is not illegal, as long as it is declared. For example, formal financial flows (e.g., wire

transfers) over $10,000 are recorded by banks and submitted to the Central Bank's Financial Intelligence Unit for analysis. All 17 licensed banks submit these reports on a monthly basis. Similarly, cash couriers transiting KIA or crossing the land border must declare carried cash if it exceeds $20,000. This regulation is better enforced at KIA than along Afghanistan's porous borders, which further complicates full-understanding of this already complex problem-set.

6. (S) While it is impossible to know for sure at this point, our sense is the money leaving Afghanistan is likely a combination of illicit and licit proceeds. Drug traffickers, corrupt officials, and to a large extent licit business owners do not benefit from keeping millions of dollars in Afghanistan and instead are motivated (due to risk and return-on-investment) to move value into accounts and investments outside of Afghanistan. *For example, the United Arab Emirates government revealed, as part of an ongoing Drug Enforcement Administration/Afghan Threat Finance Cell investigation, that it had stopped Afghan Vice-President Ahmad Zia Masood entering the country with $52 million earlier this year -- a significant amount he was ultimately allowed to keep without revealing the money's origin or destination. Moreover, Sher Khan Farnood, the Chairman of Kabul Bank, reportedly owns 39 properties on the Palm Jumeirah in Dubai and has other financial interests spread widely beyond Afghanistan.* (Note: Many other notable private individuals and public officials maintain assets (primarily property) outside Afghanistan, suggesting these individuals are extracting as much wealth as possible while conditions permit. End note.)

Comment

----

7. (S) The sense among Mission elements is that significant volumes of cash leave Afghanistan through wire transfers, the hawala network and physically through the airport. We do not know, however, whether this money is generated within Afghanistan or brought in from other countries such as Pakistan for transfer (Pakistan strictly enforces currency controls, making smuggling through KIA an attractive option.) We also do not know the ratio of licit and illicit monies leaving the country (with the former more likely to return at some point.) Given Afghanistan's general political uncertainty, lack of credible and safe investment opportunities, and unsettled election, we are inclined to believe several individuals moved more money than normal out of the Afghan banking sector and country as a measure of protection before the elections. We will continue to monitor and engage on the issue here. However, input from Washington agencies as well as from other missions in the region will be key in developing a clearer understanding of the composition, size, and directions of these cash flows. End comment.

EIKENBERRY

"AFGHANISTAN'S OPIUM ECONOMY"

A World Bank Report on Drugs

The World Bank issued a report in 2006 on "Afghanistan's Opium Economy." I'm just including the chapter summaries, but you can read the whole thing on the World Bank website, including "Prices and Market Interactions in the Opium Economy."

Isn't it interesting that we're fighting a "war on drugs," yet over there we have no problem with this? Certainly those drugs are going to get here eventually, again just follow the money. But obviously the Afghans involved can buy protection and continue doing their business.

Chapter 1
Introduction and Overview: The sheer size and illicit nature of the opium economy mean that it infiltrates and seriously affects Afghanistan's economy, state, society, and politics. The opium economy is a massive source of corruption and gravely undermines the credibility of the government and its local representatives. While the chapters in this report cover diverse topics and use different research methods, their findings are broadly consistent and they have many common themes. This introductory chapter focuses on methodology, main themes, chapter summaries, and conclusions and recommendations.

Chapter 2
Macroeconomic Impact of the Drug Economy and Counter-Narcotics Efforts: The opium economy is equivalent to more than one-third of Afghanistan's licit economy. Iit is the country's largest source of export earnings, and it comprises a major source of income and employment in rural areas. However, because a large share of drug proceeds leave or never enter the country, and some of the rest are used for imports, the impact of the opium economy is less than its size would suggest. Correspondingly, the harmful macroeconomic effects of successful measures against drugs may be somewhat limited and manageable, although monitoring is needed. The critical adverse development impact of counter-narcotics actions is on poor farmers and rural wage laborers.

Chapter 3
Responding to the Challenge of Diversity in Opium Poppy Cultivation: This chapter argues that diversity in rural household characteristics, assets, and access to markets means a diverse pattern of dependency on the opium economy, and of decision-making about whether to cultivate opium poppy under varying local circumstances. There is also diversity in households' responses to shocks like elimination of opium poppy cultivation in their locality, and to which degree they are able move into alternative livelihoods, or remain dependent on opium. Households with the least assets and limited access to local resources (land, irrigation water) and market opportunities tend to be the most dependent on opium. All of this diversity calls for a commensurate response on the part of the counter-narcotics strategy – working with the diversity that exists rather than ignoring it, and making use of the knowledge that has been gained about rural households and opium cultivation in different localities.

Chapter 4
Opium Trading Systems in Helmand and Ghor Provinces: This chapter looks into the next level up – opium traders and patterns of opiumtrade – based on fieldwork in Helmand, the dominant center of opium production and trade in the south, and Ghor, a much more recent and marginal producer toward the west. Geographical and climatic differences, continuity of different trading systems from the past, and drug-related economic interactions between the two provinces, have shaped the very different size and evolution of the opium trade. There is a case for anticipatory action in Ghor to restrict the spread of opium cultivation in that province. A persistent theme is the engagement of key provincial and district authorities in the opium economy, and both interdiction and eradication measures may have inadvertently contributed to key drug industry actors and their sponsors gaining tighter control over distribution and trade.

Chapter 5
Prices and Market Interactions in the Opium Economy: This chapter analyzes prices of opium and opiates to assess price trends, market structure, and the degree of market integration. Opium prices in Afghanistan have fluctuated sharply in recent years and have been volatile, reflecting supply side factors (weather, cultivation bans) mediated somewhat by inventory adjustments. Spatial price patterns indicate that opium markets are flexible and mobile; actions against the opium economy can have an impact on local markets, but they tend to encourage a shift of production and trade to other areas. Based on econometric tests, opium markets have become less integrated in recent years, probably due to the differing strength and effectiveness of counter-narcotics actions in different areas. Helmand and Kandahar in the south appears to be functioning as a "central market" for opium in Afghanistan.

Chapter 6
The Nexus of Drug Trafficking and Hawala in Afghanistan: This chapter explores the very important but murky nexus between the drug industry and the informal financial transfer system (hawala). The hawala system facilitates the transfer of drug-related funds in Afghanistan, while at the same time serving as a vehicle for licit commercial transactions, aid flows, and remittances. In the settlement process hawala dealers are heavily reliant on formal banking channels in regional countries around Afghanistan. The

positive role of the hawala system must be recognized, and through partnership and incentives it can progressively be brought into compliance with existing registration and taxation provisions. The international community also needs to be more diligent in its use of the hawala system to prevent its funds from becoming intermingled with illicit transfers. But imposing stringent anti-money laundering standards too quickly on the re-emerging formal financial sector risks alienating the Afghan people from using banks. Anti-money laundering provisions need to be more strictly enforced for nearby countries' banks which support the hawala trade.

Chapter 7

Drug Trafficking and the Development of Organized Crime in Post-Taliban Afghanistan: This chapter looks at the drug industry in Afghanistan from an organized crime perspective, focusing on its consolidation, changing internal structure, and linkages with different levels of government. In an environment of criminalization of narcotics, increasing albeit uneven law enforcement and eradication campaigns, and ongoing efforts to rebuild state institutions, the drug industry in Afghanistan is becoming increasingly consolidated. The chapter argues that at the top level, around 25-30 key traffickers, the majority of them in southern Afghanistan, control major transactions and transfers, working closely with sponsors in top government and political positions. The chapter concludes that there are no easy solutions to the drug industry as an increasingly organized set of criminal activities. New analytical frameworks and thinking will be needed, countering organized crime will require a careful balancing act, and improvements in specialized law enforcement agencies alone will not be sufficient. Broader state-building and governance improvements will be key.

RETHINKING THE "WAR ON TERROR"

The Rand Report
on Terrorism

The Rand Corporation has been around forever, it seems, doing policy analysis for the government on all kinds of things. I mean, the government is always basing policies on what the Rand people say. Well, in 2008, Rand came out with a major study titled "How Terrorist Groups End," looking at data on all such between 1968 and 2006.

Their findings apparently weren't too heartening to our policy-makers, if they bothered to read the study. The whole war on terror notion needs to be rethought, according to Rand, because in simple terms "countering al Qa'ida has focused far too much on the use of military force."

If the government follows Rand on other matters, why not give them due consideration on this? Supposedly this is their job and they're the experts. I mean, realistically, the "war on terror" is the equivalent of trying to exterminate the Hells Angels. You don't need the military to do it!

Here's the two-page summary of the study, including how you can order the whole thing.

I hope after digesting all this—if you can stomach it, pardon the pun you'll agree with me that it's time to end these "phony wars on terror" and get down to the serious business of rebuilding our own democracy from the ground up. Let me close with a quote from Theodore Roosevelt, from his Progressive Party presidential platform in 1912:

"Behind the ostensible government sits enthroned an invisible government owing no allegiance and acknowledging no responsibility to the people. To destroy this invisible government, to befoul this unholy alliance between corrupt business and corrupt politics is the first task of statesmanship."

Research Brief

How Terrorist Groups End
Implications for Countering al Qa'ida

RAND RESEARCH AREAS
THE ARTS
CHILD POLICY
CIVIL JUSTICE
EDUCATION
ENERGY AND ENVIRONMENT
HEALTH AND HEALTH CARE
INTERNATIONAL AFFAIRS
NATIONAL SECURITY
POPULATION AND AGING
PUBLIC SAFETY
SCIENCE AND TECHNOLOGY
SUBSTANCE ABUSE
TERRORISM AND
HOMELAND SECURITY
TRANSPORTATION AND
INFRASTRUCTURE
WORKFORCE AND WORKPLACE

This product is part of the
RAND Corporation research
brief series. RAND research
briefs present policy-oriented
summaries of published,
peer-reviewed documents.

Headquarters Campus
1776 Main Street
P.O. Box 2138
Santa Monica, California
90407-2138
TEL 310.393.0411
FAX 310.393.4818

© RAND 2008

www.rand.org

The United States cannot conduct an effective counterterrorism campaign against al Qa'ida or other terrorist groups without understanding how such groups end. While it is clear that U.S. policymakers will need to turn to a range of policy instruments to conduct such campaigns—including careful police and intelligence work, military force, political negotiations, and economic sanctions—what is less clear is how they should prioritize U.S. efforts.

A recent RAND research effort sheds light on this issue by investigating how terrorist groups have ended in the past. By analyzing a comprehensive roster of terrorist groups that existed worldwide between 1968 and 2006, the authors found that most groups ended because of operations carried out by local police or intelligence agencies or because they negotiated a settlement with their governments. Military force was rarely the primary reason a terrorist group ended, and few groups within this time frame achieved victory.

These findings suggest that the U.S. approach to countering al Qa'ida has focused far too much on the use of military force. Instead, policing and intelligence should be the backbone of U.S. efforts.

First Systematic Examination of the End of Terrorist Groups
This was the first systematic look at how terrorist groups end. The authors compiled and analyzed a data set of all terrorist groups between 1968 and 2006, drawn from a terrorism-incident database that RAND and the Memorial Institute for the Prevention of Terrorism jointly oversee. The authors used that data to identify the primary reason for the end of groups and to statistically analyze how economic conditions, regime type, size, ideology, and group goals affected their survival. They then conducted comparative case

Abstract

How do terrorist groups end? The evidence since 1968 indicates that terrorist groups rarely cease to exist as a result of winning or losing a military campaign. Rather, most groups end because of operations carried out by local police or intelligence agencies or because they join the political process. This suggests that the United States should pursue a counterterrorism strategy against al Qa'ida that emphasizes policing and intelligence gathering rather than a "war on terrorism" approach that relies heavily on military force.

studies of specific terrorist groups to understand how they ended.

Of the 648 groups that were active at some point between 1968 and 2006, a total of 268 ended during that period. Another 136 groups splintered, and 244 remained active. As depicted in the figure on the next page, the authors found that most ended for one of two reasons: They were penetrated and eliminated by local police and intelligence agencies (40 percent), or they reached a peaceful political accommodation with their government (43 percent). Most terrorist groups that ended because of politics sought narrow policy goals. The narrower the goals, the more likely the group was to achieve them through political accommodation—and thus the more likely the government and terrorists were to reach a negotiated settlement.

In 10 percent of cases, terrorist groups ended because they achieved victory. Military force led to the end of terrorist groups in 7 percent of cases. The authors found that militaries tended to be most effective when used against terrorist groups engaged in insurgencies in which

How 268 Terrorist Groups Worldwide Ended, 1968–2006

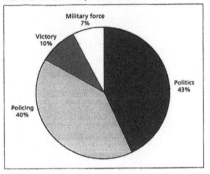

the groups were large, well armed, and well organized. But against most terrorist groups, military force was usually too blunt an instrument.

The analysis also found that

- religiously motivated terrorist groups took longer to eliminate than other groups but rarely achieved their objectives; no religiously motivated group achieved victory during the period studied.
- size significantly determined a group's fate. Groups exceeding 10,000 members were victorious more than 25 percent of the time, while victory was rare for groups below 1,000 members.
- terrorist groups from upper-income countries are much more likely to be left-wing or nationalist and much less likely to be motivated by religion.

Police-Oriented Counterterrorism Rather Than a "War on Terrorism"

What does this mean for counterterrorism efforts against al Qa'ida? After September 11, 2001, U.S. strategy against al Qa'ida concentrated on the use of military force. Although

the United States has employed nonmilitary instruments—cutting off terrorist financing or providing foreign assistance, for example—U.S. policymakers continue to refer to the strategy as a "war on terrorism."

But military force has not undermined al Qa'ida. As of 2008, al Qa'ida has remained a strong and competent organization. Its goal is intact: to establish a pan-Islamic caliphate in the Middle East by uniting Muslims to fight infidels and overthrow West-friendly regimes. It continues to employ terrorism and has been involved in more terrorist attacks around the world in the years since September 11, 2001, than in prior years, though engaging in no successful attacks of a comparable magnitude to the attacks on New York and Washington.

Al Qa'ida's resilience should trigger a fundamental rethinking of U.S. strategy. Its goal of a pan-Islamic caliphate leaves little room for a negotiated political settlement with governments in the Middle East. A more effective U.S. approach would involve a two-front strategy:

- Make policing and intelligence the backbone of U.S. efforts. Al Qa'ida consists of a network of individuals who need to be tracked and arrested. This requires careful involvement of the Central Intelligence Agency and Federal Bureau of Investigation, as well as their cooperation with foreign police and intelligence agencies.
- Minimize the use of U.S. military force. In most operations against al Qa'ida, local military forces frequently have more legitimacy to operate and a better understanding of the operating environment than U.S. forces have. This means a light U.S. military footprint or none at all.

Key to this strategy is replacing the war-on-terrorism orientation with the kind of counterterrorism approach that is employed by most governments facing significant terrorist threats today. Calling the efforts a war on terrorism raises public expectations—both in the United States and elsewhere—that there is a battlefield solution. It also tends to legitimize the terrorists' view that they are conducting a jihad (holy war) against the United States and elevates them to the status of holy warriors. Terrorists should be perceived as criminals, not holy warriors. ∎

EPILOGUE

RESOURCES FOR CURIOUS READERS

If you're interested in following the document trail in the future, there are plenty of places to look, including those listed below. I found these links especially useful in putting together this book. It's time we used the "information age" to our advantage, in reclaiming our democracy from the secret-keepers.

*WIKILEAKS: By the time this book is published, who knows where you'll find Julian Assange's team? Right now, you can look at www .mirror.wikileaks.info. They have a list of the growing number of "mirror sites" that plan to publish the State Department cables and other documents. WikiLeaks is a nonprofit organization that launched their website in 2006 and, within their first year of existence, had a database of over 1.2 million documents. They publish submissions of private, secret, and classified documents obtained from anonymous sources and news leaks.

*CRYPTOME: Their website has been around since 1996, hosted in the U.S.A. "Cryptome welcomes documents for publication that are prohibited by governments worldwide, in particular material on freedom of expression, privacy, cryptology, dual-use technologies, national security, intelligence, and secret governance—open, secret and classified documents—but not limited to those." They've hosted more than 54,000 files, including suppressed photos of American soldiers killed in Iraq, purported agents for Britain's MI6, and much more. They have two DVDs loaded with hard-to-find documents leaked by whistleblowers both government and private, available for a $25 donation. Check out http://cryptome.org for some fascinating browsing.

*NATIONAL SECURITY ARCHIVE: This is an independent research institute and library, located on the George Washington University campus. They are an amazing repository of government records listed by topic, historical and contemporary, from the Cuban Missile Crisis to the war in Afghanistan and more. They get their documents by a variety of ways, including the Freedom of Information Act, Mandatory Declassification Review, collections of presidential papers, congressional records, and court testimony. The Archive was behind the groundbreaking legal effort to preserve millions of pages of White House email records from the Reagan, Bush, and Clinton administrations. Check out www.nsarchive.org to find the vast amount of material that they've gathered.

*GOVERNMENT ATTIC: This website posts electronic copies of hundreds of interesting federal government documents obtained under the Freedom of Information Act. They recently revamped their document menu to consist of four distinct parts: Department of Defense; Department of Justice; Executive Branch Departments, the White House and Legislative Agencies; Independent Federal Agencies, Govt. Corporations and State/Misc. Records. Go to: www.governmentattic.org.

*PUBLIC INTELLIGENCE: Administrator Michael Haynes tells us: "This is an international collaborative research initiative working to facilitate equal access to information by enabling anyone to anonymously submit documents or information for online publication. In less than two years of operation, the site has published thousands of restricted documents related to issues of national security, the war in Afghanistan, banking and international finance, as well as government and corporate surveillance. The site maintains one of the largest collections of documents produced by U.S. fusion centers available to the public." Go to: http://publicintelligence.net.

*THE MARY FERRELL FOUNDATION: This nonprofit is your best source for documents about the assassinations of the 1960s, the Watergate scandal, and the post-Watergate investigations into intelligence abuses. The digital archive contains over 1.2 million pages of documents, government reports, books, essays, and multimedia. Go to: www.maryferrell.org.

*OPEN THE GOVERNMENT: It's a coalition composed of journalists, consumer and "good government" groups, library groups, environmentalists, labor and others coming together to make the federal government a more open place. They're non-partisan and include progressives, libertarians and conservatives. Go to: www.OpenTheGovernment.org.

*OPENLEAKS: This is a new website scheduled to be up-and-running in 2011. Its founders have been closely linked to WikiLeaks in the past, but have since parted ways and are describing themselves as more of a technological service provider to media organizations than as a central hub for leaks. Go to: www.openleaks.org.

*DOCUMENTCLOUD: Program Director Amanda Hickman tells us: "DocumentCloud (http://www.documentcloud.org) is a catalog of primary source documents and a free and open-source tool that reporters use to annotate, analyze, organize, and publish documents they're reporting on. DocumentCloud's catalog, assembled by reporters, archivists, and researchers, includes everything from FBI files to sample ballots, Coast Guard logs to legistation, and court filings. The project is designed to help reporters publish more of their primary source documents online, and to make those documents accessible to the general public in an indexed catalog."

*CIA: The Central Intelligence Agency has a digital database called CREST that consists entirely of declassified documents. A finding aid is located at: www.foia.cia.gov/search_archive.asp.

*OPEN SECRETS: This is your prime resource for tracking money in American politics and how it affects elections and public policy. It's part of the Center for Responsive Politics. Go to: www.opensecrets.org.

*THE FEDERATION OF AMERICAN SCIENTISTS (www.fas.org) offers a rich archive of resources on national security policy. The Federation's *Secrecy News* blog (www.fas.org/blog/secrecy) produces original reporting on U.S. government secret policy and provides direct access to valuable official records that have been withheld, withdrawn or are otherwise hard to find.

*THE NATIONAL ARCHIVES (www.archives.gov) is the repository for millions of government documents, and their Archive-It FOIA Collection lists sites that deal with FOIA requests at: www.archives.gov/ogis /foia-records.html.

Now get this—there are 407 million pages of classified documents waiting to be opened to the public at the National Archives. Mostly these consist of a backlog of historical records more than twenty-five years old and it's a slow-moving process. But they do have a National Declassification Center that was created by President Obama's Executive Order at the end of 2009. For example, the CIA still has around 50,000 pages of classified records related to the Kennedy assassination. What could the CIA still be protecting after almost fifty years?

Of course, you can always file Freedom of Information Act requests yourself, and this is an important tool of democracy. There's a report called "Rummaging in the Government's Attic: Lessons Learned from 1,000 FOIA Requests" from 2010, available at: www.governmentattic.org/3docs /Rummaging_2010.pdf.

And just in case you're wondering what the feds might have on you, check out www.GetMyFBIfile.com.

NOTES

NOTES

NOTES

NOTES

NOTES

NOTES

NOTES

NOTES

NOTES

NOTES

NOTES

NOTES